LINCOLN'S SECRET SPY

Lincoln's Secret Spy

*The Civil War Case That Changed
the Future of Espionage*

Jane Singer and John Stewart

Guilford, Connecticut

An imprint of Rowman & Littlefield

Distributed by NATIONAL BOOK NETWORK

British Library Cataloguing in Publication Information Available

Library of Congress Cataloging-in-Publication Data Available

ISBN 978-1-4930-0810-0 (hardcover)
ISBN 978-1-4930-1738-6 (e-book)

♾™ The paper used in this publication meets the minimum requirements of American National Standard for Information Sciences—Permanence of Paper for Printed Library Materials, ANSI/NISO Z39.48-1992.

For James Martin Singer
For Gayle Winston

Contents

INTRODUCTION

If this were played upon a stage I could condemn it as an improbable fiction.

—TWELFTH NIGHT: ACT THREE, SCENE FOUR,
BY WILLIAM SHAKESPEARE

WILLIAM ALVIN LLOYD. HERE WAS A MAN, A COMET, STREAKING THROUGH decades with impudence and impunity. A simmering broth of lust, indefatigable energy, greed, and larceny, he was magical, priapic, musical, inventive, a survivor and a scoundrel. From a jangled, jarring Kentucky boyhood where he learned a tailor's trade, he then ran from that trade, covering his dye-stained hands with white gloves, and, on occasion, his face with the burnt cork of the minstrels, his minstrels. For a time Lloyd owned the tambos, the bones, the banjos, and the men that played them. He was a publisher, a blackmailer, seeking scandal, a moth to a fire. And in the war, his time in the war was at first a salvation that brought him a little wealth then stripped him bare, disarmed and desiccated him. Then accused, nearly hanged as a Union spy by the men who ruled Dixieland, the land he'd loved.

At the end of the war, no longer a comet but a mere spit of light, he crawled away from the rubble of that land to emerge—twisted, numb— to reconfigure, to proclaim that he was Abraham Lincoln's personal secret agent throughout the Civil War. Was William Alvin Lloyd truly Lincoln's own, or a cunning imposter? And his lawyer, Enoch Totten, who for years doggedly pursued Lloyd's claim until it became the basis of an important Supreme Court precedent—one that to this day affects the legal rights of clandestine operatives and assets—was he the architect of a great fraud?

Authors Jane Singer and John Stewart have both written books about the Civil War and are devoted students of spy craft, priding themselves on prying secrets from the jaws of a murky trade that rarely succumbs to hard research. Tracking the oft mentioned but never researched William

Alvin Lloyd through private collections, genealogical sites, old newspaper article databases, the National Archives, the Library of Congress, the New York Public Library, and numerous historical societies was revelatory. Finally after scouring unpublished primary source documents, witness testimonies, and court transcripts, the true story of his claim and of a life writ large emerged. But in spite of our inescapable conclusions we were, and still are, riveted by the tireless moxie of the man. And though he might howl to learn that two twenty-first-century authors have shone a hard light on his long-hidden secrets, he could not help but applaud his top billing. William Alvin Lloyd is onstage again. But this time he is truly the star of his own show.

1

I Was the President's Spy

WASHINGTON CITY

THROUGH AN OLD STEREOSCOPE VIEWER, CAUGHT IN A PHOTOGRAPHER'S explosion of black powder and flashes of light, see a man. Though featureless, note that he is on his last leg—one is shriveled—barely allowing him to stand so he must lean on makeshift crutches, crude wooden rods that steady him. He fades, blurring as he inches painfully along. He will stumble, right himself, and at times like this, slip from view.

But there are facts—not unwarranted colorizations—accompanying William Alvin Lloyd. Know he has endured harsh imprisonment and bears the scars of a near-fatal shooting. Know he has hobbled out of the ravaged Confederacy—torn sinew and aching bones—to the depot at Danville, Virginia. There he boarded a shuddering night train that took him to Richmond, then by rail and steamer to City Point, Virginia, and finally into the nation's capital.

But as sorry a sight as he is, unlike the masses of maimed and scarred Union veterans flooding the city, William Alvin Lloyd is no ordinary soldier. He is a man on a mission. He has secreted a packet of documents on his person. And he is armed.

If all goes according to plan, Lloyd will make his way to the War Department and seek an audience with Lieutenant General Ulysses S. Grant, who is headquartered there. But he will not kill the enemy chieftain whose mighty armies defeated Lee's forces. Rather he has come to wound the Yankee government and make it bleed. Money. A great deal of it. The documents he clutches, he hopes, will prove that he has been

President Abraham Lincoln's secret agent in the Confederacy. His timing is perfect. There could be no firm handshake from the president Lloyd said employed him. The dead don't shake hands.

While there is no record of Lloyd's meeting with Grant at his War Department office, it is fact that his documents were received and examined by someone on the busy general's staff. So we must envision Lloyd entering a nearly empty building and leaving the papers with a clerk, perhaps an indifferent drudge who tosses them on a pile and rushes off to the parade, the Grand Review of Union Armies, an "immense and imposing display" of men and weaponry.[1] Much of the city is festooned with flowers. Victory banners proclaim, "All Honor to the Brave and Gallant Defenders of Our Country! The Union Forever!"[2]

It is May 24, 1865, three weeks after the assassination of President Lincoln. The moist, heavy air of the preceding days—sorrowful days of endless mourning for the President—has lightened, dried, and cooled. Black cloths that draped the Capitol like giant widow's weeds have been removed. Flags, once at half-mast, now flutter in ruffles of summer wind. President Andrew Johnson has ordered this day and the next to be one long celebration, a welcome respite for the denizens of the city who crowd rooftops, peer excitedly from windows, and pack the streets. Hearty *huzzahs* echo through alleyways, over the fetid canals, and up Pennsylvania Avenue. Banners, foodstuffs, horse dung, and spent cartridges litter the cobblestones as do the drunks, whores, and beggars who've flooded the city since the first of the regiments came by train and horseback to march as one for the last time before returning to civilian life.

"I saw the day the return of the heroes," Walt Whitman wrote after watching the parade from somewhere in the crowd. "I saw the interminable corps, I saw the processions of armies, worn, swart, handsome, strong. . . . No holiday soldiers—youthful, yet veterans . . ."[3]

Gaze at a sea of bonnets, straw hats, and top hats, and below them, know that if William Alvin Lloyd does cheer with the masses that have gathered to watch a quarter of a million Union victors, he will do it for show. And does he see in the reviewing stand, just opposite the White House—seated in the canopied wooden bleachers along with President Andrew Johnson and his cabinet—Lieutenant General Grant, smoke from his ever-present cigar clouding his face as his victorious troops parade before him?

Schools have been let out and masses of children stream by waving flags and singing. Amid blizzards of confetti from rooftops, Grant remembered, "the national flag flying from almost every house and store . . . the doorsteps and sidewalks crowded with colored people and poor whites who did not succeed in securing better quarters," and the loud strains of the "Battle Hymn of the Republic" amid the cannon salutes. The great pageant will last over six hours.[4]

And as for Lloyd, with the first stage of his mission completed and though he has been bested by a Yankee circus, a two-day circus at that, it must be time for him to join his accomplices at a designated meeting place, for he has not come alone to the city where war was declared and war was ended alone. There is Virginia, his very young wife—one of several. She has endured him and remained with him through much of the war. And there is Thomas H. S. Boyd, his clerk, his princely underling, a hair-trigger ruffian with an ever-ready bowie knife concealed in his coat. And little Clarence Lloyd—small and frail at five, and Ellen Robinson "Nellie" Dooley, a sturdy English country girl, the nanny who cares for him.

Together they'd assembled the particulars of Lloyd's claim. The documents he left in Grant's office said that back on July 13, 1861, he made a verbal agreement with President Lincoln to be his personal spy in the Confederacy: Two hundred dollars a month for his services, as yet unpaid. A vast sum, but for a man who would say he risked his life at every turn, he would claim, justified. There were other papers that proved he'd done time in Confederate prisons. And there was a pass from the President, a slim, worn, much folded piece of cardboard—nearly ruined—not unlike the man who'd secreted it for four years:

Please allow the bearer, William A. Lloyd to pass our lines south and return on special business. A. Lincoln, July 13, 1861.[5]

"Special business," the pass said. Lloyd's "special business" was prosaic. He was collecting desperately needed revenue for his *Southern Steamboat and Railroad Guide* throughout the Confederacy. But for Lloyd, at this time, in Washington City, his true sentiments, his anti-Lincoln writings, if known, might well bring a mob down upon him. Anyone who spoke ill of the martyred president faced arrest, imprisonment, or street justice. Amid wild jubilation over the end of the war, Lincoln's assassination was a grim counterpoint. And the trial of John Wilkes Booth's accomplices before a military tribunal, covered word for word in the papers. Surely Lewis Payne, David Herold, and George Atzerodt would hang. Less certain was the fate of Dr. Samuel Mudd, the country physician who'd set Booth's broken leg. As for Booth's childhood friends Michael O'Laughlen and Samuel Arnold, both in on the plot to kidnap the president, and Edman Spangler, the curtain raiser at Ford's Theatre allegedly following Booth's orders, prison sentences were called for. And the fate of Mary Surratt, the God-fearing widow who kept "the nest that hatched the egg," providing succor and a safe house to the conspirators, was as yet undecided. But by July 7, she would hang.[6]

It was of comfort to some that Booth met his end in a burning barn on April 26 and that his accomplices were incarcerated, but "Beware the people weeping," Herman Melville wrote in the aftermath of the crime, "when they bare the iron hand."[7] And there surely were the iron hands of Lincoln's avengers—the grief-stricken war secretary, Edwin M. Stanton, and his frosty, unforgiving judge advocate general, Joseph Holt—both of whom were busy calling for the heads of all Confederate higher-ups. Jefferson Davis, the former occupant of the Confederate White House in Richmond, was imprisoned, awaiting a trial for treason. It was not enough. "The stain of innocent blood must be removed from the land," Stanton vowed, beset by fits of uncontrollable sobbing.[8]

Likely no sobs emanated from the sparse rooms in a tumbledown boardinghouse where Lloyd's impoverished band would have stayed, waiting for news about his claim. Three days passed. Endless days. Finally, on May 27, there was movement. Grant had forwarded Lloyd's documents to Secretary Stanton. Whether Grant had perused them himself is not clear. But someone on his staff surely had.

"The papers of Mr. W. Alvin Loyd [*sic*]," Grant wrote, "have been examined and respectfully forwarded to the War Secretary, and satisfactorily proved that he has been in southern prisons over two years. Also that he has a pass from President Lincoln on special business. Mr. Lloyd desires payment for services in accordance with a verbal agreement with Mr. Lincoln."[9]

The fatigued and disconsolate war secretary passed the materials on to an organ within the War Department—the Bureau of Military Justice—to Major Addison A. Hosmer, a Harvard law graduate who'd served with distinction during the war. Now he was the judge advocate in the absence of Joseph Holt who was busy day and night as the chief prosecutor at the trial of Booth's coconspirators. Holt was "officially the nation's chief arbiter and executor of military law" and rarely in his office. Hosmer explained his interception, saying, "The Secretary was greatly indisposed." In fact, Stanton's indispositions abounded in the long, difficult weeks after the president's murder. Still bereft over the great loss of a man he loved, Stanton was inconsolable, profoundly depressed, and thought at times to be delusional.[10]

Major Hosmer surveyed the muddle of papers before him. He was troubled by the informal presentation of Lloyd's clandestine work for President Lincoln and the outrageous sum he was demanding for those services. On May 30, Hosmer wrote to Stanton:

War Department, Bureau of Military Justice, Washington, DC,

To the Secretary of War. The primary and main object of Mr Lloyd is to obtain the payment to him of a large sum of money claimed as compensation for alleged secret service in the South under agreement said to have been made by the late President in July 1861. The amount demanded is $9600, being at the rate of $200 per month for about four years, which, if justly due, should be paid; but the presentation of the account is so informal and unsupported by affidavits or reference to any proof, either in possession of the claimant or the Government, that it will be impracticable for this Bureau in the present situation of the inclosed [sic] papers, to reach any satisfactory conclusion without performing simultaneously the somewhat incompatible duties of an attorney for the claimant and the judge passing upon the merits. For these reasons it is recommended that the papers

be returned to Mr Lloyd in order that he may, by consulting suit-
able advisers and availing himself of the assistance of an attorney,
prepare and submit his demand properly in form and substance.
(signed) A.A. Hosmer, Major & Judge Adv. in the absence of the Judge
Adv. General.[11]

Somehow Lloyd learned of Hosmer's response, took the advice, and perhaps after scanning newspaper ads, saw this: "Enoch Totten attorney and counselor at law, Washington, DC (PO box 492) will procure back pay, pensions and patents, settle officers' accounts, and collect all claims against the government."[12]

No time to spare. Too much money at stake, riches to be made, time, time was of the essence. Just two days later, inside Totten's office at 5th and E Streets, picture a scene: Totten, Ohio born, ten years Lloyd's junior, fumbles to grasp a pen with his one good hand. His other hand was useless. For good reason: A lieutenant in the Fifth Wisconsin Infantry, Totten led a charge against Rebel earthworks at the Battle of the Wilderness in 1864. One minute there was a hand wielding a saber. Next minute no saber, and not much of a hand. Not much of a left foot either. For his valor, they honored him and promoted him. Colonel Totten, he was now: new in town and hungry for clients.

There seemed to be as many attorneys in Washington as there were war claimants. Admittedly, some of the claims were somewhat trivial—a Yankee soldier had ripped the siding off a farmer's barn and used it for firewood. Another man's well was polluted by rotting mules. Who would pay? Then there were the six young field slaves, worth about two thousand dollars each, who had escaped from the overseer. How was the offended party going to survive without compensation? And the burning of a plantation by General Sherman's marauding bummers; railroad tracks torn up or commandeered by the enemy; or the use of private homes as field headquarters, soldiers trampling precious carpets with their boots or guzzling stocks of rare brandy, defiant southern women being insulted, or worse.

Lloyd wouldn't give a damn about other people's claims. He told Totten the particulars of his: Back on July 13, 1861, he'd sat with Lincoln in the White House and verbally agreed to a most secret espionage contract guaranteeing him two hundred dollars a month for this perilous service. Lloyd was to gather enemy intelligence by infiltrating Rebel fortifications, reporting troop movements, and sending back dispatches to the president via a network of trusted couriers as often as he could. That was the story—how he suffered in Confederate prisons and nearly died in the service of Abraham Lincoln.

Totten smelled money. This was no ordinary claim. Grant's office had already been taken in by it, and no one in the War Department had come flat out and said they disbelieved it. It just might work. But Totten knew quite a lot had to change if it was to go anywhere. For a start, the contract with Lincoln could no longer be verbal. That was no good at all. Verbal? That was amorphous, words, whispers in some darkened hallway. Foolish. It had to be a written contract. Lost, Totten decided, of course, during the war. That was the first thing. Totten was the architect now and together with Lloyd created the wording of the nonexistent contract, supposedly written and signed by Abraham Lincoln. It would never be seen, but it must have a shape. It must sound credible, it must impress, it must buttress Lloyd's claim.

The bearer, Mr. Wm. A. Lloyd, is authorized to proceed south and learn the number of troops stationed in the different points and cities in the insurgent states, procure plans of the fortifications and forts, and gain all other information that might be beneficial to the Government of the United States, and report the facts to me, for which service Mr. Lloyd shall be paid two hundred dollars per month. Abraham Lincoln, July 13, 1861

Time, no time. Totten said they would immediately have to go before a notary and swear to the existence of this contract under oath. Totten would procure the notary and coach the witnesses. They first had to memorize the wording and be prepared to repeat it as fact. Verbatim. Each one of them. Lloyd assured Totten that his wife, clerk, and nanny would stick with his story. Fine, but, wait, who was this man Lloyd, this wreck, this stranger, this—imposter, or huckster, or—who was he? What was his life story, his war story? Totten must hear it to the smallest jot of a detail, all of it; everything about Lloyd—everything—so there would be no surprises. Begin, then. Begin.

Through the stereoscope, somewhere in the distance through filaments of light, see the wavering form of a small boy. Droplets of water puddle on smudged glass. See a wide river. It is too far away as yet to know it is the Ohio. But it will come into view. It will. He will.

2

My Old Kentucky Home

HIS MEMORIES OF THOSE EARLY YEARS—IF MEMORY SERVED AT ALL and had not been tempered or tampered with as was his wont—would be redolent of peril and uncertainty, of his family's harrowing migration from Virginia into hostile Indian lands with uneasy stops along the Ohio frontier and into the wilds of Kentucky. But with no clear path to follow through the woodlands, trails, and mountains of his family's westward journey, this much is known: William Alvin Lloyd known familiarly and forever as "Alvin," was born on July 4, 1822, somewhere in Kentucky. His father, Thomas G. Lloyd, Alvin's mother whose name is lost to history, his beloved younger brother James Talford, and Thomas G.'s brother William comprised the peripatetic little family.

Like so many emigrants swarming out of Winchester, Virginia, the Lloyds would have traveled by wagon through what is now West Virginia into the state of Ohio and down the Ohio River on a keelboat into Kentucky. Or, if they had reason to go by way of Indiana, at Jeffersonville just across the river from Louisville they could have bought passage on one of the ferries loaded with hogs, iron, and horses—wheezy tubs that pitched and groaned toward Louisville. Travelers of adequate means wouldn't be seen dead in the fetid lower decks of a ferry, but they would certainly be seen alive taking a much more comfortable passage on a side-wheel paddle steamer that rumbled through the newly built Portland Canal, skirting the treacherous Ohio Falls.

Others coming from much farther south slogged along a well-trod and difficult wagon and stage route: the Wilderness Road. Originally a buffalo trail forged by Daniel Boone, the road traversed the rugged, rutted Cumberland Gap that was slashed through the mountains into Kentucky.

Whatever their route, and though their footprints are faint, it seems that Alvin's father was unable to make a living in tiny burgs along the way that needed peddlers, not skilled cloth-cutters. So on they went like thousands before them to Louisville, where it was hoped that well-crafted woolens and leathers—not bearskins or deer hides—would clothe a more civilized lot.

For all new arrivals, the first sights and smells—multitudes of river birds, wide-winged herons, cormorants, and gulls swooping and seesawing overhead; the hum and thrum of the steamers' engines as they nosed in numbers into their berths; the musky tang of dried tobacco; billows of whiskey fumes; calliope strains drifting over the churning water—dazzled and dizzied. The raucous muddle of old Indian fighters, merchants, gamblers, slave dealers, slave catchers, wary free and enslaved blacks, fools, and dreamers was not just another stopping place for the Lloyds. This was Louisville in 1830. This was journey's end. This would be home.

For the next fourteen years, Alvin's life there formed him, taught him a trade, spawned his errant ways, and stoked his wanderlust. And through the years of his growing the boy and the city came to resemble each other: brash, inventive, musical, explosive, and corrupt. Later he remembered what he chose to remember of those years and forgot or confabulated the rest.

Glimpse the child-Lloyd, perhaps, an eight-year-old roaming unchecked along the dirt roads, alleyways, and cobbled streets of his new home. Know that the place was besieged by typhoid, cholera, and yellow fever epidemics borne out of the miasmic and stagnant ponds and the stew of animal carcasses and human waste in the water. But boys like Alvin on their rambles would not have worried over such things, transfixed, as was the pioneer chronicler and historian Caleb Atwater, by "the roaring of the guns belonging to the numerous steamboats in the harbor, the cracking of the coachman's whip . . . the sound of the stage driver's horn saluting the ear."[13]

A daring and curious boy would follow the mule skinners and peddlers and dodge the stages careening down Market Street, the "center of commerce through the heart of Louisville."[14]

And if running along that river, heading east toward the Bourbon Stock Yards and into Butchertown, the stench of the slaughter pens, tanneries, soap makers, and distilleries would hold a grim fascination. There were the newly arrived German immigrants' breweries and saloons—rough and brawling places teeming with thirsty customers clamoring for the local "whiskies, apple brandies and hard ciders." And there were the prostitutes—accounting for "the great and unusual increase of tippling houses and houses of ill fame," servicing the gamblers from the riverboats and the men from upper Main Street out on a pleasure crawl.[15]

It was a forbidden place for a boy hungering for things forbidden. Then. Always. Farther up Main were the proud palatial new homes, far from his family's reach. They were "[t]wo and three lofty stories in height, standing upon solid stone foundations, exceeded any thing [sic] of its kind in the United States," Atwater rhapsodized and exaggerated.[16]

See a tailor's drudge like Alvin after a long day in his father's shop, walking along Market Street, north of 5th, past the Louisville City Theatre, the only one in town. Perhaps he stops, drawn to the music pouring through an open door, the gabble of voices, the smells of cheap cigars and the stink of full spittoons. If he slips through a side entrance, stepping on peanut shells, slipping on gobs of chewed tobacco—because there is no one to tell him, go home, child, go to sleep—he creeps down into the theater pit. For seventy-five cents a ticket, and for two back-to-back shows lasting at least three hours, an audience of seven hundred packs the place. *A Day After the Wedding*, a "favorite farce," is just ending. Actors Parson, Raymond, and Howard are bowing to mild applause. Soon, a mournful fiddle summons the cast back onstage. The "home-bred piece . . . a melo-drama" called the *Kentucky Rifle*, a "prairie narrative," a bathetic tale of survival in the wilderness, began. A "comic Negro song," the playbill promised, would lighten things up when Thomas Dartmouth Rice would perform in blackface as the slave Sambo.[17]

After characters Father Silversight, Thomas Buckthorn, and Farmer Felltree fight Indians and all manner of ailments, with an-off key trumpet blast, Sambo the slave shuffles onstage in a dilapidated coat, a pair of patched, tattered shoes, and a "dense black wig of matted moss," topped by a tattered straw hat.[18]

The audience hoots and throws peanuts until Sambo sticks his fingers in his ears, shushing them, grinning and rolling his eyes. "Listen all you gals and boys, I'se jist from Tuckyhoe. I'm goin' to sing a little song, my name's Jim Crow." Rubbery limbed, his knees knocking together to the rhythm of the tambourines and bones, Rice sings, "Weel about and turn about and do jis so . . ." And as he turns, he flaps his arms, "eb'ry time I weel about I jump Jim Crow." Then came a crook-backed tap dance, topped by an exaggerated bow, his hat hanging, and his wig askew. And the finish: "Weel about and turn about and jump Jim Crow."[19] The audience applauds wildly.

Jim Crow was a star. Thomas D. Rice was a star. Many had seen the actor striding about the town and now couldn't believe the transformation. Unlike the caricature that made a mediocre performer famous, Rice was in fact a handsome young man, "about twenty-five years of age," his grandson Edward Le Roy Rice wrote, "of a commanding height—six feet full, the heels of his boots not included in the reckoning—and dressed in scrupulous keeping with the fashion of the time." Sweeping through the doors of the Galt House Hotel in a tight-waisted black frock coat, gleaming leather boots, and form-fitting trousers, Rice created his caricature of a happy slave, attributing "[h]is casual hearing of a song trolled by a negro stage-driver, lolling lazily on the box of his vehicle," as the origin of "a school of music destined to excel in popularity all others."[20]

As the fractious issue of slavery began to dominate national discourse, the world of burnt cork and banjos portrayed a patronizing, comedic, stereotypical version of a brainless, slothful slave like Sambo/Jim Crow, or the wily Zip Coon, the creation of minstrel and songwriter George Washington Dixon. Zip Coon, the "Larned skoler," able to sing a "possum up a tree," and jump over "dubble trubble," schemed his way though a love triangle in Dixon's "Coal Black Rose," one of the first songs published in Louisville in 1830. By 1837, Louisville book and music stores were advertising "New Negro Song books," with ditties like "Coal Black Rose" and "Jump Jim Crow" to feed the growing appetites of the burgeoning industry.[21]

Because African Americans were not able to perform on stage before the Civil War, white entertainers "blacked up," much to the delight of audiences in the North and South. They loved these stereotypes, and no doubt these entertainments reinforced the idea that there could never be racial equality. And they promulgated the notion that all blacks—free and enslaved—would be better off under the lash of the master or tucked under the benevolent wing of the white man. Though at first the Jim Crow character made Rice the darling of audiences throughout the country, the name, the moniker, the stereotype he became would haunt for generations; the laws bearing that name would punish emancipated blacks after the Civil War and well into the twentieth century.

Years pass, and Alvin is fourteen. He has a sister and second brother now, Nancy, born in 1832, and baby Marcus, in 1834. In time—and it was not time yet, for then the boy and the city were still young, without a moment of shame as the ways of shame were unfamiliar to him and with music whirling in his head, sounding from rinky-dink saloons, concert halls and showboats—with a lifelong pattern of uncommon daring and no fear of consequence, he would find a way to be more than a tailor's apprentice. It was a hard slog that would last as did most apprenticeships until he was twenty-one, when he could proclaim himself a full-blown tradesman.

Where might he or any hardworking boy find distraction and peace? There was always the Ohio River: turgid or glassy, bold blue, gray, or black late at night. The engine booms, hisses, and gabble of voices from the side-wheel wooden-hulled, flat-bottomed steam packets; the fine wood, etched glass, and tall smokestacks like heron's necks were things of great beauty to Alvin. Later he would come to know every intimate detail of their design and chart to the second their comings and goings, a fixation that would remain with him personally and professionally for the rest of his life.

One day he might flee downriver on a craft like the *Daniel Boone*, "a fine, low pressure steam boat" bound for New Orleans loaded with rich brown sugar, fine china, and sundries, advertised as wanting "freight or passengers with fine accommodations" in an ad boasting it was able to make the one-thousand-mile journey to New Orleans in just under twenty days.[22]

And of the embarking passengers: frontiersmen, gamblers, settlers, and ladies—some painted, some dour, some girlish, many bejeweled. As he grew older, he eschewed the whores, but the women—the ones he took for proper ladies—were like gilded, come-alive statues perhaps to touch, or own, for a time at least. That some stayed and others glided away on the next boat didn't matter. There would always be more coming by water, decorating the seedy wharves like bunches of bluebells.

Of course there were the ever-present hoards of enslaved humanity dragged through the city streets in coffles. They were exhibited, shackled in wooden pens along the Ohio, to be "sold down the river" to New Orleans slave auctions and from there to large plantations farther south. But because the Kentucky slave trade was the largest in the United States before the Civil War, the sights and sounds of this suffering were familiar to all, visitors, buyers, and town denizens alike. And so were the slave catchers, poring over the runaway slave ads, lurking along the waterfront, skirting the edges of the tobacco farms, seizing both free and enslaved blacks for a quick sale or a bounty.

Through all the time of his growing and beyond, Alvin would see this degradation, this misery, this snatching of souls, and not find any of it out of the ordinary. For it was *his* ordinary. His world. The riverboats. The songs, dances, the tears and lamentations of people sold like cattle: the caged people and the beautiful women from the riverboats. Always the women.

Before that, a time of which he would remember nothing, he would learn of a peripatetic lineage, a vague beginning. "My parents were from Winchester, Virginia," was all he would say much later when he was in a Confederate prison during the war.[23]

Though records are scant, there is a letter written from Mount Washington, Bullitt County, Kentucky, on October 18, 1838, by one Joseph Lloyd, to his nephew James McCracken Lloyd, in response to the latter's request for genealogical data. "My father, John Lloyd, was born in the City of London in the year 1704 Old Christmas Day."[24]

That's the old Christmas Day, before they changed the calendar. The writer goes on to say old John's father was from Wales, hence the double L in the name, Lloyd. When he was fourteen, John was apprenticed to a boot- and shoemaker. On February 6, 1727, John Lloyd, of the parish of St. Botolph's, Aldgate, stole several items from his former master, Samuel Peters. On February 22 he was tried at the Old Bailey. "The Prosecutor depos'd [*sic*]," the records state, "That the Prisoner had lodged at his House, and upon making Enquiry for the Loss of his Things, he heard the Prisoner was stopt [*sic*] with the Ring, which he pretended he found in the Entry, but it not being believ'd that he could find the working Tools too, a gold ring (worth 9 shillings) along with several shoemakers tools (knives, pinchers, awls, etc) . . . the Jury found him guilty."[25]

John Lloyd was sentenced to transportation (deportation) to America. Forty-five days later, he arrived in Baltimore on the *Rappahannock*, a fully rigged ship, captained by Charles Whale. In 1742, after his indenture to an unknown master was completed, he married Prudence Emery in Orange County, Virginia. John Lloyd's grandson was William Lloyd, who, as it turned out, would also be William Alvin Lloyd's grandfather. This William Lloyd, via two wives, would keep producing and keep producing until he was seventy years old, thirteen children in all. The second of these children was Thomas G. Lloyd, Alvin's father, born in 1792.

Thomas G., the tailor—termed a renovator, a scourer (scraping and finishing the leathers to fine, workable condition), and dyer—was one of eight tailors in Louisville. Picture him in everyday wear, for he would have to impress, as would his son Alvin growing up in the father's business. T. G. would have worn a long linen shirt. He would have slept in the same shirt. His "pants had a front flap that attached to the waistband. The cravat (tie) was like a scarf wrapped around the collar and tied in front . . . and stockings held up with garters." Over this ensemble, he'd wear a waistcoat. He would be clean-shaven, with longish hair, topped by a "wide brimmed or tall hat made of fur, silk or straw" when he went outside.[26]

T. G.'s brother William was a grocer—a white shirt and apron would have done for him—one of twenty-eight like merchants in a town that had "three print offices, six taverns, two carriage makers, six saddlers, six bake houses . . . twenty-two doctors and twelve lawyers."[27]

Brother William didn't stay in Louisville long, likely driven away by the competition, but Thomas would remain there for the rest of his life, a life filled with abysmal, whiskey-sodden lows, the highs of a well-turned tailoring business, a shaky vow never to drink again, and eventual redemption as a temperance street lecturer well after it would have saved his family's humiliation. Old Joseph Lloyd's Bullitt letter of 1838 says simply, "Thomas lives in Louisville."[28]

Another new arrival in town was Joseph Holt, a young lawyer who hung up his shingle on the north side of Jefferson, between 5th and 6th Streets. In 1865, Alvin Lloyd would monumentally dupe Holt. So lawyer and future predator inhabited the same place and may or may not have known each other, though much later, Holt would marry the first cousin of Thomas G. Lloyd's second wife. Much marrying and mixing among successful businessmen's families would naturally occur in Louisville, a place that hadn't borne the veneer of civility for very long at all.

In the late 1700s it was a tiny, protected encampment, a huddle of buildings by the Ohio of no more than a thousand people. "Without a store, or a tailor within a hundred miles, no blacksmith or saddlers," assorted home-sewn bearskin and "hunting shirts of linsey linen and dresses of the same" garbed the men and women of the town. Along the banks and in the outlying forests old Indian fighters—constantly warring with braves of the Shawnee and the Delaware tribes—guarded and manned the forts. They were game hunters—the buckskin-clad frontiersmen—and their families. Survivalists they were, rough foragers all. What they couldn't hunt or make was brought by "the keelboats and barges . . ." carrying "lead, flour, pork, and other articles."[29]

These keelboats returned laden with sugar, coffee, and dry goods, "suited for the markets of Genevieve and St. Louis on the upper Mississippi," or branched off and ascended the Ohio to the south side of the foot of the falls at Louisville, where the rapids precipitously dropped twenty-four feet for two miles along sandbars and limestone ledges.[30] People traveling the Ohio River naturally paused at the falls, or foundered on the sandbars, hence it became the natural stopping place for the founding of a town on the south side of the tumbling waters.

But by 1811, when the first steamships were sighted on the river—hulking behemoths, engines blasting, studded with lanterns like so many fireflies, nosing into the wharves—change came, fast. Until February 13, 1828, Louisville had been a town. Now it was officially a chartered city fattened by settlers from the boats and the sales of slaves.

Though in August 1829 the first Louisville public schools opened—segregated according to gender and forbidden to anyone of color—there is no record of Alvin Lloyd's formal education. But as evidenced by a kind of literary sensibility and publishing acumen later in life, the boy was by no means illiterate or unread. For excitement, and if the boy could find a quiet hearth, or venture into the public library on Jefferson Street atop the first courthouse, he might inhale the works of Byron or the adventures of Sir Walter Scott's *Ivanhoe*, rather than the ponderous tomes of natural science and botany. And for the boy, there were literally sounds of music from the showboats, concert halls, and street corners. A music library managed by piano maker William C. Peters and Sons published songs like "Jump Jim Crow" and soothed souls longing for a dose of Mozart with their Stephen Foster minstrel tunes.

Yes, there was music abounding, but what of Alvin's beliefs, and whom to believe in? There he was, living in a city that was waging a war on itself and was becoming a microcosm of the great rift that was to tear the United States apart years later. Fire-eaters, bloody shirt wavers, crooked politicians, many identifying with the workingman's Democratic party and just as many excoriating the Whigs (eventual Republicans) for their seemingly elitist stances and their vow to create a national bank. They argued, speechified, and tried to run the unwieldy, fractious city.

And as Alvin Lloyd would eventually have an editorial voice himself, the war between newspaper editors—Jacksonian Democrat Shadrach Penn Jr., the established and opinionated editor of the *Louisville Public Advertiser*, vs. the Whig-turned-Republican George D. Prentice of the *Louisville Journal*—was vicious and impossible to ignore. Prentice was brought to Louisville in 1830 to write native Kentucky son and Whig party founder Henry Clay's biography. The *Journal* was founded to support Clay's run for the presidency. But when Penn's editorial dominance was threatened and his readership began to drift away, his vitriol increased. By 1841, and on his last editorial legs, Penn was fiercely attacking Prentice, saying he had "come out a full abolitionist of slavery." Penn said, "It is worse than folly—it is treachery to the South."[31]

That Lloyd-the-man became a full-blown southern rights advocate and anti-abolitionist, echoing the Southern Democratic party's stance and never varying his beliefs, is fact. Eventually, and in print, Alvin damned Lincoln for his abolitionist ways and his vow to end slavery. And though Alvin's brother J. T. boasted that he had known the statesman Clay, Alvin would have damned him too. Clay, the "Great Compromiser" and Whig party founder, was applauded and excoriated for his refusal to let slavery expand and overtake the free states. And so throughout the time of Lloyd's coming of age in Louisville, the rights of the southern states and their adherence to the institution of slavery would be argued again and again, eventually exploding into the Civil War.

There were natural cataclysms as well: Fires and floods, but none as horrific as the Great Flood of Louisville that began on February 10, 1832, and lasted until the twenty-first of that month. "This was an unparalleled flood in the Ohio . . . having risen to the extraordinary height of 51 feet above low-water mark. . . . Nearly all the frame buildings near the river were either floated off or turned over and destroyed."[32]

After the great deluge and when things had normalized, the city resumed its rapid growth. With expansion came a corresponding need for religious institutions. There was the old Baptist Church, and there were the Reformed Baptist, and the New Baptist, as well as the Methodist Episcopal and the Methodist Protestant, and, due to the number of free blacks in Louisville, enough to hire themselves out and worship, there were the African Church and the Baptist Church. On May 27, 1832, the first Unitarian Church would be dedicated in Louisville, on the corner of 5th and Walnut. That same year Alvin's father and Uncle William appear in the Louisville City Directory as tailor and grocer.[33]

There are no sightings of the Lloyd family for the next five years, but in 1837, it seems Alvin's mother passed away of unknown causes. If alcohol had been his father's frequent pleasure, with the death of his wife he became an uncontrollable drunk, neglecting the three youngest children, abandoning them in the city streets. And what could fourteen-year-old Alvin do to rescue the lot of them from alcoholic rages, starvation, or worse? It is not known how he managed, but according to early census records that recorded only the name of the heads of household and the ages of the resident children, it appears he did remain with his father as a caretaker. That Alvin surely survived by his wits is evident but it is not known if he manned the tailor shop on his own or tried to find his abandoned siblings, James, Nancy, and Marcus, at that time no better off than the stray dogs and cats hunting for scraps along the wharves.

A kindly, charitable sort, a woman known only as Mrs. Gray, found the Lloyd children begging in the streets. Nancy Lloyd (no age given), James Lloyd (aged seven), and Marcus Lloyd (aged four) were all admitted to the Protestant Episcopal Orphan Asylum as intakes Nos. 33, 34, and 35, respectively, all children of Thomas Lloyd. Marcus died there. James T. was pulled from the orphanage, bound out to James E. W. Blanks, a Louisville carpenter. Nancy survived.[34]

Their true salvation was prosaic.

It seems that a Mrs. John Roberts, a widow whose wealthy husband had died when cholera swept through Bardstown, came with her three sons to Louisville and opened up a hotel, the Marion House on Jefferson, between 3rd and 4th. The 1838–39 Louisville Directory lists Thomas G. Lloyd & Co, tailors, Jefferson, between 3rd and 4th. This is the address of the Marion House. So it looks as though the widow Roberts boarded the inebriate tailor even though his surviving daughter was still in the asylum. Alvin, and one would hope he was included in this rescue, would have the company of one of the widow's sons, Sam Roberts, a budding actor, later a famous minstrel known as Johnny Booker.

On July 11, 1838, In Louisville, Thomas G. Lloyd married the widow Roberts. Saved and finally sober, after his new wife vouched for him, his surviving children were returned.

From an errand-boy apprenticeship in his father's shop, learning to stitch, pattern, dye, and fit the clothes made of fine wools and linens, Alvin grew older, serving gents, tradesmen, and their apprentices. Perhaps he strode about the city as a well-dressed businessman, with a silk top hat, a long greatcoat trimmed with beaver fur in winter, straw hat and light nankeen trousers in summer; appearing as much a dandy as he could stitch and fashion on his own time, until at last he turned twenty-one. His apprenticeship over, he was truly a tailor.

Three years later. Alvin went hunting. For a mate and found one. A respectable one. A pregnant one, it seemed. Elizabeth Ann (Lizzie)

Dailey was just his age, from a policeman's family, the oldest of four sisters. Alvin and Lizzie eloped to the town of Henderson, to the west of Louisville just up the river. They married on June 27, 1844. Might they have stayed in Henderson, a town grown fat on tobacco profits where rich farmers and their slaves abounded? No, back they came to Louisville. Alvin was now a proper tailor with his own shop on 4th Street between Jefferson and Green. Their daughter Belle was born in 1845. Soon Alvin's wife was pregnant again. Charles W. Lloyd was born in 1847.

Like many in the city who patronized the blacked-up entertainers' shows, who welcomed the minstrel troupes who steamed up and down the Ohio, stopping frequently in Louisville, surely Alvin Lloyd would see them stepping from the steamers onto the dock, toting their trunks full of burnt cork, banjos, bones, and tambourines, surrounded by townsmen and women, eager for a night of music and ribaldry, a night away from the ordinary. Soon Alvin's life as a husband and father would change with the currents, with the changing, coursing currents of the river.

It was August 26, 1846, at the Apollo Rooms and there was a minstrel show in progress. In the dim light of the low-slung, smoky venue was a group of men in blackface giving a concert, "eliciting the greatest applause from all classes," the *Louisville Daily Democrat* of August 21, 1846, crowed. No Jim Crow shabby rags here. Dressed as spanking fine gents they were: starched white shirts, black twirl-ties, jeweled cuff links, and shiny patent leather low boots. The fact that Rainer's Sable Melodists were in concert that night is worth mentioning and they are most likely the group Alvin saw.

That year, the Melodists had done a lot of touring: Nashville, Cincinnati, and Boston. Louisville was a one-night appearance, "fresh from the fashionable watering places throughout the country" raved the *Louisville Journal*. Finding the troupe "superior to anything we ever heard from the sable gentry," the *Journal* reserved the most worshipful praise for the banjo player, going "so far in his solos . . . that it was incredible . . . that the instrument was a banjo."[35]

That night, the music, the strange, sweet-sour perfume of malt and tobacco ... intoxicating. Soon, Alvin was gone, taking the first tentative step away from the tedium and toxins of the Louisville tailoring and scouring business.

He never left any writings behind to indicate what it was that propelled him out into that brand-new milieu, the world of minstrels. Was it a single event, the Sable Melodists or another similar troupe coming to town? Had he had enough of his life as it was shaping up? Could he foresee the long, dreary life ahead of him, a future like his father's, a fate like his father's? And so it seemed when the banjos, tambos, and bones summoned Alvin Lloyd, who as a boy had sprouted to manhood along the river, he was at last *on* the river. Leaving home. Leaving everything.

3

Oh, to Be a Minstrel!

Gone is the tailor's smock, stained from scouring hides. White gloves cover his hands. Alvin Lloyd has vaulted into his consuming adventure, into the world of black and white minstrels populated by energetic and talented performers and curious, aberrant beings, a milieu that lent itself to—at times, encouraged—a disregard for law and order. It was a lusty, brawling circus life, always on the move from town to town, carefree bachelors or married men with no wives in attendance, temptations running riot at every whistle-stop town they played in and even more so in the big cities. It was a demi-monde, where lived the fakirs and the fakers, the traveling freaks, the hypnotists, sham doctors and hair-restorers, fortune-tellers, and peddlers of the elixir of life.

"'Col.' Alvin Lloyd was first brought to the notice of the show world by being connected with a troupe called the Sable Harmonists, in 1847." So says *Burnt Cork and Tambourines,* a seminal book on the history of black and white minstrelsy in the United States. So recorded T. Allston Brown in his "Early History of Negro Minstrelsy," a series that ran in the *New York Clipper* newspaper in 1912–13, and which itself—the chapter on Lloyd, anyway—is a rehashing of an August 1, 1891 *Clipper* article on the history of the New York Theatre, also written by Colonel Brown: "Mr. Lloyd had been a manager of a minstrelsy band known as 'The Sable Harmonists' in 1847."[36]

T. Allston Brown, who was as much a colonel as Alvin Lloyd was, wrote the classic, authoritative, but not always unerringly accurate *History of the American Stage* (1872) and *History of the New York Stage* (1903). In 1863 he became editor of the *New York Clipper.* As early as 1858 he had begun collecting data on theatrical performers in the United States, many of whom he knew personally.[37]

Alvin joined the Sables in late 1846 as their advance man, their factotum. The Sable Harmonists, a band of nine minstrels, had started off in St. Louis in 1844 under the direction of well-known British singer William G. Plumer, late of the Opera Troupe. The other eight original Harmonists were Huntley the accordionist; James B. Farrell; Joe Murphy; singer, composer, and pianist Nelson Kneass; J. Tichenor; William Roark; Tom F. Archer; and a man named Cramer.[38]

In 1845 the Sables did a lot of touring—Nashville, Louisville, Cincinnati, Boston—and 1846 grew even busier the more well-known they became; so well-known, indeed, that other troupes started taking their name. Within a short space of time, this particular group was forced to identify itself in the Eastern press as the Southern Sable Harmonists, or the Western & Southern Sable Harmonists, just so confusion could be avoided. It is not known exactly when and where Alvin joined the Sables. It was probably Louisville in the fall of 1846, but it might have been in Nashville, where they played on October 21 and 22, or in Jackson, Mississippi, on December 10. He was part of the troupe when they opened at the American Theatre in New Orleans on December 19, 1846.[39]

It appears that Alvin was with the Sable Harmonists at this time, but how was it determined that he was an advance man? In 1849 he would become a minstrel director with the very same troupe, the Sable Harmonists, but that was still two years away. However, he would have received his training somewhere, and that training certainly wasn't as a manager; otherwise his name would have appeared in the press in 1846 and 1847. And he wasn't a performer at that time. Even though in much later years, when he was touring his famous Lloyd's Minstrels, he would occasionally assume a role or two on stage, a performing role was just not feasible for Alvin Lloyd in 1846–47, or he would have garnered press notices. That leaves the role of advance man: A promo man. A hype specialist. First of the troupe into a new town, setting up the venue, dropping in on the editor of the local paper to persuade him to do some sort of editorial mention in exchange for buying ads for the Sables, and even, sometimes, paying for those ads. Drumming up interest before the players arrived. It was a job tailor-made for W. Alvin Lloyd, a lifelong salesman, to the con born.

Back in 1846 advance men got no mention at all in the ads of touring minstrel groups. By the 1860s, that would change. W. Alvin Lloyd would be one of the first minstrel chiefs to give prominent billing to his advance men, and that was probably because he harbored a soft spot for advance men, knowing what it was like to work very hard and get no recognition.

There is another reason of record that proves he was with the Sable Harmonists at this stage of his life, and that is the "List of Letters."

The Harmonists played the last night of their New Orleans run on Christmas Eve, 1846. The following morning their name, "Harmonists Sable," appeared in the *Times-Picayune* newspaper, in the "List of Letters." Another name that appeared in that very same list was "Wm A. Lloyd."[40]

In census records for the United States in the period 1845 to 1869, there are many William Lloyds, not to mention the ubiquitous abolitionist William Lloyd Garrison. When one sees the name William Lloyd in a newspaper, the chances of it being Alvin are remote. However, when the name William Alvin Lloyd appears, or W. Alvin Lloyd, there is no doubt that this is the man, and Alvin Lloyd was in the papers a lot. It's the Alvin part that gives it away. In that gray area between William Lloyd and Alvin Lloyd come the variants: "W. A. Lloyd" and "Wm A. Lloyd." When you see "Wm A. Lloyd" in New Orleans in late 1846, with a letter waiting for him, it's got to be Alvin, without question.

Back in those days, most houses didn't even have a street number, but that was changing, a change demanded by the rapid and sudden urbanization throughout the country, especially in the west, and the correspondingly huge increase in mail traffic. If you were in, for example, Louisville, Kentucky, and you sent a letter to "Wm A Lloyd, Poydras Street, New Orleans, Louisiana," you could be sure it would get there, especially if you put a stamp on the envelope. However, if you didn't know exactly whereabouts Mr. Lloyd would be staying in New Orleans, you'd simply address it "Wm A. Lloyd, New Orleans," and it would wind up in the *poste restante* section of the post office there. And it would wait in a box until Wm A. Lloyd came to pick it up. There was no charge for this service, not at that point in the process anyway. If Mr. Lloyd failed to pick up his mail the post office would advertise it for a month in the local daily newspaper with the largest circulation—"List of Letters." If, at that point, Mr. Lloyd saw the ad and came to collect his mail, he would be obliged to show some sort of identification and would incur a small charge. If he didn't come, the letter would eventually find its way to the dead letter office in Washington, DC. Even then, Mr. Lloyd could still get his letter if he wanted it badly enough, but, of course, the charge would be a lot higher.

Most of the time, letters advertised in this way suffered the fate of the dead letter box, and that's because the addressee had moved on, hadn't yet arrived in town, or had simply failed to pick up his letter for one reason or another. Just because the Sable Harmonists were in New Orleans in the week before Christmas doesn't mean that their advance man was. He was almost certainly away in another town, setting up the next appearance. That's why he didn't pick up his letter.

That next town they played was most likely St. Louis. That's where the troupe is of record again in early 1847, and then it was on to Louisville, and from there, to Nashville for a two-night stand at the Odd Fellows Hall on February 16 and 17, 1847. Then it was on to play the Melodeon in Cincinnati for a good run into April.[41]

One night a young man in the Melodeon audience became so entranced by the show that when he went home, he wrote a song for Tichenor, the lead singer, and presented it to him the following day. He read the opening line, "I came from Alabama wid my banjo on my knee," and hummed it. Tichenor especially liked it when he got to the chorus, "Oh, Susanna." He decided to use it in his act the following night. At least that's the way the story has been circulated in some quarters. Some say it was first presented by a quintet in Andrews' Eagle Ice Cream Saloon in Pittsburgh on September 11, 1847.[42] Stephen Foster would go on to write a few songs for the Sable Harmonists, including "Old Uncle Ned" for William Roark and "Louisiana Belle" for Joe Murphy. They would be collected together in the *Sable Harmonists' Songbook* of 1848.

In April 1847 the Sables opened in New Orleans again, this time for a very long run, and by September were back at the Melodeon in Cincinnati. Then it was up to Cleveland to play the Empire Hall. Their last night there was September 25, 1847, and then they reorganized. Part of the shuffle was Alvin Lloyd who, for whatever reason, left the minstrel business and, it is assumed, went back to tailoring in Louisville, just in time to get his information into the upcoming 1848 City Directory. [43]

The 1848 Louisville City Directory lists several Lloyds, including "Tos. G. Lloyd, renovator, cnr 5th, between Main and Market; home the Marion House." It also lists his wife, Mrs. Elizabeth Lloyd, at the Marion House, between 3rd and 4th. That's all to be expected. What *is* unique in the history of Louisville city directories are the two entries James T. Lloyd, "at Geo. W. Noble's," and "Wm A. Lloyd, renovator, at 4th, between Jefferson and Green." Alvin's younger brother, J. T., was working for George Noble, the Louisville printer and bookseller, learning his trade: One of Noble's young advertising promoters. [44]

Alvin had now set up shop on his own account, independent of his father. It is curious that a young man of his temperament, an exciting year on the road under his belt, was now forced to fall back on his old trade of tailoring, facing the drudgery of the average working tradesman. This couldn't last.

And his father, the alcoholic tailor, now a reformed evangelist and presumed teetotaler, was writing to the press, convinced that a snake-oil remedy saved his life. On January 31, 1848, T. G. Lloyd of Louisville wrote an open letter extolling the Keely cure:

> "This will certify that I have for eight years been laboring under a most afflicting neuralgic affection. It was with difficulty at times that all the exertions of an attentive family could keep life in me. Many nights I have been in spasms, from want of circulation of the blood, with my flesh very cold. Many of the most eminent physicians have attended me, and have exhausted their skill in vain in endeavors to restore me. It affords me pleasure to say that, to the exertions of Mr. Keely, I am indebted for complete restoration, the misery in my head and spine having entirely disappeared—in short, I feel like a new man."

This was Isaac I. Keely, the Indianapolis magnetizer (hypnotist) who enjoyed a vogue back then—"No cure, no pay"—just as Leslie Keeley, another charlatan with a similar name would do in the 1890s. As the long-suffering patient was raised to his feet by the extraordinary "Doctor" I. I. Keely, and then, prompted in a suitably commanding way to walk away unaided, there always happened to be a clutch of "close relatives" at hand to weep uncontrollably at the patient's good fortune. No affliction was too great for Dr. Keely—the blind, deaf, lame, the hopeless.[45]

That Alvin only appears in one Louisville city directory in 1848 suggests that he left Louisville for good in that year. The same goes for his brother. However, Alvin's absence from the city directory does not necessarily mean he was not tailoring there for a short time. But like a windwalker, Alvin Lloyd soars into double incarnations: tailor and minstrel. The Sable Harmonists kept touring and in September 1849, the troupe arrived in St. Louis, a city then of forty-five thousand people and still reeling from its great fire.

Every city has its great fire. St. Louis had one on the night of May 17, 1849. It started on the steamboat *White Cloud*, lying at the head of the levee, and before it could be brought under control the following morning, it had swept through the hemp and tobacco lying on the wharves, taken six hundred buildings and twenty-five river steamers, and engulfed fifteen square blocks of the city's downtown district. By the time the Sable Harmonists hit town, the most massive and determined efforts were in progress to eliminate all traces of the catastrophe.[46]

This from the *Daily Missouri Republican* of Sept. 18, 1849: "Sable Harmonists. A company of sable harmonists are giving a series of concerts in the saloon of the Planter's House. They come highly recommended by the cities in which they have performed." The following day, the same paper wrote: "Sable Harmonists. The entertainments, generally of this talented company, at the Planter's House Saloon, attracted a large and fashionable audience. The manner in which the pieces are executed is sufficient evidence that they are musicians of the highest order."

The Planter's House, fronting on Fourth Street, immediately north of the Court House, was then only eight years old, but already one of the famous hostelries of the West. On the night of September 20, 1849, while the Harmonists were playing the saloon there, William A. Lloyd entered into a partnership with James Oliphant to run the troupe. They performed there again the next night, the twenty-first, and again on the twenty-third. That day, William A. Lloyd, director, took out a lengthy ad in the *Daily Missouri Republican*.[47]

The troupe got to New Orleans on October 18, 1849: "They have arrived. Lloyd's great troupe of Sable Harmonists. . . . This fine band of minstrels . . . bring with them a brilliant reputation from the North and West, and we anticipate a rich treat."[48]

On Sunday night, October 21, they opened at the Concert Room on Perdido Street. At that precise point in time, the lineup was Mr. Wm N. Chambers, Mr. William Roark, Mr. A. Weston, Mr. J. Milton Foans, and the violinist Mr. William Whitney.[49]

They played at the Concert Room again on the twenty-second, and on the Tuesday, Alvin and J. T. arrived in town on the steamer *Portland* from St. Louis. That night, the Harmonists played their third night on Perdido.[50]

The next day, the twenty-fourth, at a meeting of the troupe, Mr. Roark was called to the chair, and "Mr Jas T. Lloyd," Alvin's brother, then only nineteen, was appointed secretary. That night, still in New Orleans, the Harmonists played the St. Louis Hotel Ballroom. They played at the ballroom on the twenty-sixth, and, although their contract there had specified six nights, the twenty-seventh was their last before moving over to the Commercial Exchange Hall on St. Charles Street for the night of the twenty-eighth, which was a benefit for Alvin Lloyd.[51] The following night, Monday, they again played the Exchange with a wide variety of new songs, choruses, refrains, and duets. Admission was fifty cents, and front seats were available for ladies.[52]

On November 2, 1849, Lloyd and Oliphant dissolved their partnership. Mr. Roark took over the management, and the troupe was joined by G. G. Temple. The Harmonists continued on at the Exchange, without Mr. Lloyd, of course, until December. Alvin had been a minstrel chief for precisely forty-two days.[53]

Another side of Alvin Lloyd—dodgy, daring, and often dangerous—was blossoming. The *Clipper* article of 1913, the one reproduced in the book *Burnt Cork and Tambourines*, reports that Lloyd was said to have run away from the Sable Harmonists while in the west, leaving them without paying any salaries, nor their board bills: "Several of them, having no money, were arrested and locked up, where they were compelled to work out their indebtedness." But T. Allston Brown is confusing this event with one that would happen in 1867, with the second and final incarnation of the troupe known as Lloyd's Minstrels. In 1849, Alvin's association with the Sable Harmonists seems to have been a simple dissolution at the end of that year, and there certainly seems to have been no undue trauma in the parting of ways.[54]

There is no mention of Alvin from November 2, 1849, when he leaves the Harmonists, to January 1, 1851, when he suddenly arrives in New Orleans as the director of the Empire Minstrels. As he is wont to do, he slips from view completely in 1850 and there is no record of him in the 1850 census. Nor are found his wife and children, or his in-laws, the Daileys.

Alvin's brother, J. T. Lloyd, also left the Sable Harmonists at the end of 1849 when Alvin left. In fact J. T. left the world of minstrelsy forever. It wasn't for him. He drifted back to St. Louis, where he got a job as a steamboat agent, living on Tom Sprout's steamboat. That summer of 1850 he took a room in Joseph R. de Prefontaine's house on the south side of Myrtle, near 7th.[55] Prefontaine was at that time editor of the *St. Louis Union*, and he had a daughter, Mary Ann, just a year younger than J. T. Within a few months the youngsters had married, and J. T. had gone to work for his new father-in-law as a riverboat reporter. There would be a child, the marriage wouldn't last, and Prefontaine, his daughter, and the child would all go to San Francisco in 1852. From there Mary Ann would divorce J. T. in 1855.[56]

On December 19 and 20, 1850, the Empire Minstrels played Spengler's Saloon in Jackson, Mississippi, and the day after Christmas they opened, with nine players, at the Institute Hall in Natchez. It is assumed that Alvin was their manager by then.[57]

Richard H. Sliter was the none-too-savory star of the group. Alvin, like all the others—Christy, Kneass—claimed to present wholesome family fare. It was not, in fact, true. Beneath the haze of sanctimony lay bunches of very talented ruffians.[58]

Sliter had organized the Empires in Buffalo back in 1848, and they'd been a raging success ever since. Money flowed in, but it didn't always flow out where and when it should. In addition to being a famous minstrel group, Richard Sliter's outfit was a small, all-cash business, like all of them were. How that ingress and egress were handled came down to the ethics of the manager. Until Alvin took over, the Empires were in the exclusive and tyrannical hands of star dancer Dick Sliter.[59]

By the end of 1850, Sliter was under pressure from some of his men—the sly, droll Cool White, and G. G. Jones, the bones man—to relinquish either his managerial role or his turn in the limelight. He decided to acquire a professional to direct the group. That professional was W. Alvin Lloyd.[60]

On New Year's Day, 1851, when Alvin Lloyd arrived in New Orleans, billed as the manager of the Empire Minstrels, the troupe was still in Natchez, about to give their final performance. They would join their manager in the Crescent City on January 4, arriving on the steamer *Brilliant*. On the sixth they opened at the Commercial Exchange Hall.[61] On January 13, there was a benefit performance for Alvin Lloyd, and then, money in hand, he quit the Empire Minstrels, leaving town for destination unknown.

Eight months later Lloyd unmistakably comes into frame. This ad was placed in the *Natchez Courier* on September 5, 1851: "At the Institute Hall. Lloyd's Sable Harmonists, will give two of their unique and fashionable Ethiopian Soirees, at above, commencing on this evening, Friday, Sept. 5, 1851. Cards of admission 50 cents. Doors open at 7 o'clock. Concert to commence at 7½ precisely. Lloyd, director."

For the rather shadowy period in Alvin's life between the dissolution of this last minstrel group in September 1851 and his re-emergence as a newsworthy figure in the middle of 1854, T. Allston Brown offers this mention: "For 'reason' he served a long sentence in a Kentucky penitentiary, but escaped, was caught (having his chains on at the time) and was returned to his quarters; but his health became so bad that he was discharged."[62]

Colonel Brown, reworking this piece in 1913, says: "For committing some crime he was shortly thereafter arrested and served out nearly his time in the penitentiary in Kentucky, when he escaped, but was pursued by the jailer and overtaken, having his chains on at the time. He was severely beaten by his captor, and once more safely caged, but his health becoming so bad that, fearing that he would die, he was set at liberty."[63]

Both *Clipper* articles agree that this prison term was between his time as a minstrel and his Cincinnati experience, placing it in the period 1851–54. Even though Alvin certainly spent time in a Confederate jail in Savannah in 1861–62, it is possible that Brown's report was confused with Alvin's Civil War durance. Lloyd-the-prisoner, his time as a prisoner, is fact. But though he does not appear in the records of the Kentucky State Penitentiary, at least in those that are extant and legible, and many are not, he may well have been there, wrongly indexed or listed on a page that cannot be read. Alvin Lloyd was, in fact, imprisoned for bigamy several years later. So a good look at the Kentucky State Penitentiary is not unwarranted.

The prison had been going since the late 1700s, always a drear and harsh place. In the early 1850s, life as an inmate there was hell. There was even a move afoot in 1851 and 1852, whether it was seriously intended or not, to mark or condemn for life the inmates so that they would be instantly recognizable if they escaped—to literally brand them.[64]

If Alvin was truly in the Kentucky State Penitentiary, and if he can be spotted crouching over a waste bucket, or gnawing on an offal bone, then what was his crime? It could be any one of several things ranging from bilking to assault and battery, or even killing a man. But the most likely is bigamy. Alvin was a confirmed and chronic bigamist, a cruel crime by any standards.

In pursuit of fresh victims, a bigamist almost always left his string of wives, one after another. Consider the plight of nineteenth-century women. Those were the days when a woman would have a very difficult time making it on her own, unless she came from money. And if she was left with a child, or children, and had no income source, no one to take her in and provide for her, the situation was often perilous.

Every state had a bigamy minimum and maximum if convicted, and the offender served his time in the state penitentiary. Kentucky's 1852 revised statute made it a three- to nine-year sentence. That was about the norm throughout the country. Sometimes there was a heavy fine as well; in other states you would be at hard labor, whereas in Kentucky, as in many other states, offenses such as sodomy or bestiality were punishable by much less time.

However, there were loopholes, ways you could get off a bigamy charge, especially if you'd done it more than once. One, and the most commonly used, was that there was a statute of limitations of three years on bigamy. So, unless you were caught within three years, you'd not be punished—at least in theory. Another argument was this: A man left his first wife and married another. However, the second marriage was not legal; therefore he couldn't be accused of marrying twice. If it was that simple, then why did any bigamists go to jail? The answer is because a jury was involved, and jurors judged bigamists harshly. There was always at least one bigamist in the Kentucky State Penitentiary at any given time, and, occasionally, such as on November 1, 1851, when there were 166 inmates in all, there were two bigamists inside. These two remain name-less statistics, but it's not such a stretch to suppose that one of them may have been named William Alvin Lloyd.

Another possibility to account for this period of Alvin's life is offered by Alvin himself. In a letter he wrote to Robert E. Lee on February 25, 1862, while languishing in jail in Savannah, he says, "Myself and Brother . . . were connected with Major J. P. Heiss, publishing the *Delta* in 1852 & 1853."[65]

And that may be, that Alvin was with the *Delta*, at least for part of those two years. In New Orleans, there were two *Deltas*. There was the *Delta* and there was the *True Delta*. Only the first was the true *Delta* and that is the paper Alvin claimed to have been associated with.[66]

However, the truth about Alvin's lost years may be much more mun-dane, although with Alvin mundaneness is most other people's exciting. Unknown to T. Allston Brown, and certainly never talked about by Alvin, was the historical truth. After the September 1851 minstrel episode in Natchez, Mississippi, Alvin went back home, to Louisville, to a family that may or may not have shunned him.

On January 30, 1852, his first Louisville ad appeared, and it was, of course, on the bold side, a proud entry in the *Daily Democrat*: "Notice to the Ladies. White Crape Shawls cleaned in a beautiful style at Lloyd's Renovating Establishment. Second street, near Main." The *Daily*

Democrat even gave him a blurb in their January 31 edition: "Good news for the ladies. Mr. Wm A. Lloyd, at his establishment on main street, near Second, is prepared to cleanse white crape shawls and other silkes in beautiful style." [Lloyd's spelling.]

So, here he was a tailor again, a trade he could always fall back on. When that ad ran out, he took a new one, a much bigger one. "We call the attention of our readers to the advertisement of William Lloyd, in another column. His dyeing, renovating, and repairing establishment is on Second street, near Main, where he is at all times prepared to renovate in a style to appear as when new."[67]

An early glimpse of the kind of scathing verbiage Lloyd would use to blackmail, impugn, and agitate time and time again is seen in this ad:

"The Place." Lloyd's Dyeing, Renovating and Repairing Establishment is on Second Street, near Main. The only place of the kind in the city where ladies and gentlemen, having their wearing apparel out of order, can have them renovated in a style and finish to appear as when new. White Crape Shawls cleaned; Silk Dresses cleaned; Piano covers cleaned; carpets cleaned, and Window Curtains cleaned. Look out for humbugs, as they are numerous. They will spoil your goods if you trust them with them. I have work brought to me every week from these pretenders to be done over. "Have a quick eye to see; they have deceived others and may do thee."

Here, it seems, Alvin is referring to a competitor, but appealing to a reading audience, a jumbled audience of the high-minded, the literate and near-literate.

The one who got some person to write an advertisement for him, in which he tries to appear before the citizens as a "timid Master Modas,"[68] . . .

. . . and says he does not expect to make a decided hit; I would inform the Modus that he hasn't the common sense to make any kind of a hit, except a "Baker" hit. Again the youth says he employs the best of an agent. That of paying the printer is all gas from a small meter.

And again he says he does not expect to get perfect in the "black art." If he refers to Niggerology, I would inform him that he tried that once to his sorrow; a reference to a small affair a year ago would suffice upon that subject. Again; "Gaseous"; will the Modus give the definition himself? Any person or persons calling at my establishment can have the names of those, even within a week back, who have had their goods nearly ruined by the humbug. And again, Modus says, if persons will call and look at his work, he will "gain applause." Well, if a certain young lady on Jefferson street was to call Modus would get applause over the—head, or be off to Ohio for six months.

Lloyd clearly has an unknown agenda here.
And here is Lloyd's pitch:

But to business: Lloyd's Establishment is "the place," if you want your work done in good order and with dispatch. Bring or send it, and it will be attended to. Look for the shop. Keep away from the "sign shops"; you will save trouble by it, as I am sick and tired of doing botched work over, which is brought from impostors. A word to the wise. Lloyd of Lloyds, Second street, near Main.

Like his first one, this ad ran for a month. We don't know whether he paid or not because there seem to be no extant issues of the *Democrat* after March 4, 1852, at least not for several months, until July, and then Alvin vanished again.

On January 19, 1853, an ad appeared for the first time in the St. Louis paper the *Missouri Daily Republican*. It had been placed by Lloyd's Dying, Scouring & Repairing Establishment [*sic*], located at "The Place," on Third Street, St. Louis: "Gentlemen may rest assured that whatever repairing or renovating done to their clothing will be done in a style unequalled in the city. The process of renovating is done entirely on chemical principles. Gentlemen may depend that no soap will be used in cleaning their garments, as soap injures the cloth, attracts dust, and in a few days leaves their clothes worse than though they had not been treated." The dyeing department was entirely under the supervision of Mr. Lloyd. He explains that he is fully conversant with chemistry and has invented a chemical mixture that refreshes the cloth and gives an additional luster. This ad ran until July 13, 1853. Then, in a blast of scourer's acrid dust, Alvin Lloyd disappeared.

4

W. Alvin Lloyd, Publisher

TIME FLITS BY, AND ALVIN LLOYD HAS BEEN ABSENT FOR SEVERAL months. But like an errant rabbit out of a very tall hat, he will soon emerge on the Mississippi River aboard the swift-running steamboat, the *Persia*. As for the particulars of this voyage, the sights along the way, the ship has some distance to travel on the Ohio before Lloyd strides aboard.

The steamer left Pittsburgh on November 4, 1853, cruised the 485 miles downriver to Cincinnati, and arrived four days later.

On November 9, 1853, the *Persia* pulled out of the port of Cincinnati to begin her long trip to Louisiana. The *Persia* always covered those 1,548 miles in eight to ten days. This trip would take ten. Much to everyone's relief, the Ohio was now on a rise at Pittsburgh, which meant that vessels could get out, and there was a lot of traffic, steamers like the *Persia* and fleets of coal boats flocking downriver, which was good news for Cincinnati and cities farther down, such as Louisville, where coal had been scarce.[69]

The ups and downs of the Ohio were deadly serious issues to all the towns west of Pittsburgh, a matter of life and death. The coal would come in from the Pennsylvania fields and be shipped out of Pittsburgh by coaler to all the principal ports not only along the Ohio but also up and down the Mississippi, to St. Louis, Memphis, Vicksburg, and New Orleans. When the river level sank it made river transportation impossible. And when the Ohio froze over, same thing. In short, the famous navigable Ohio River was not so navigable after all.[70]

This hadn't been such a problem in the old days, when pretty much everything west of Pittsburgh was frontier. There was little civilization there then, and frontiersmen were hardy, or at least expected to be. But now, by 1853, there were millions of citified, urbanized riverine settlers who had no idea how to look after themselves except by the expenditure of a hard-earned dollar. Progress hadn't caught up with change yet out there on the Ohio, and, with the massive influx of immigrants, the river was daily posing a greater and greater threat to the survival of millions. Something had to be done to ensure a more reliable delivery system. So along with Alvin Lloyd's beloved steamboats, the glistening river marvels of his childhood, was the railroad. These tracks, and the smoke-belching engines that rumbled along them, thrilled Alvin, transported him, obsessed and finally ruined him.

On November 10, the *Persia* docked at Louisville, 139 miles down the Ohio from Cincinnati.[71]

The very evening the *Persia* arrived in Louisville, a large meeting was taking place there to contemplate the possibility of running a direct rail line to Memphis. It was the beginning of a massive and vital project that would see its fruition just as the Civil War was breaking out eight years later. The line would become a vital leitmotif running through the story of W. Alvin Lloyd. The coming of the trains into the south heralded the most difficult, thrilling, and dangerous days Alvin Lloyd was yet to see.

The steamer *Persia* now had 1,409 miles to go. She pressed on down the Ohio, with the state of Kentucky always, always on the left and, to the north, the state of Indiana merging into Illinois at the Wabash. She finally passed Paducah and reached Cairo, where the Ohio meets the Mississippi. There, on the Mississippi, she turned south and headed toward Memphis.[72]

The *Persia* pulled into the landing at Memphis on November 16. A small group of passengers boarded, recorded as William Alvin Lloyd and his family and another unknown person traveling with them. Had he been attending to his family, or was this a passing interlude, a tease?[73]

The *Persia*, like all other better-class riverboats, had not only outstanding accommodations available to those who could pay for them, but also food of almost unparalleled luxury. Perhaps Lloyd's family were on a lower deck, eating plain fare and dreaming of the wondrous feasting that was going on in the first-class dining room. A typical dinner meal on such steamers included, among much else, sheep's head, knuckle of veal, fricasseed veal, pig's head, calves' feet, smothered heart with port wine sauce, rich desserts, claret, and sauternes. Other wines and liquors could be had at the bar.[74]

On the *Persia* went, to Vicksburg and down into New Orleans, where the Lloyd party arrived on November 19, 1853, and checked into the City Hotel that day. On November 21, 1853, "W.R. Lloyd [*sic*], G.B. Nagle and lady, Ky." checked into the St. Louis Hotel in New Orleans. (Often the newspapers confused or misprinted initials.) It would soon be known that Lloyd left the City Hotel without paying his bill and moved on to the St. Charles, where again he vanished without anteing up the requisite money. There is every reason to believe that he would do the same at the St. Louis. But the paper does not mention family. So who is the lady? Did she belong to Nagle, or to Lloyd? And Kentucky? Well, of course, William Alvin Lloyd was from Kentucky. But when he checked in to the City Hotel on the nineteenth, he announced or signed that he was from New York.[75]

The lady remains a mystery, as do the *Persia* passengers listed as "family" accompanying Alvin. Had he left Lizzie, Belle, and Charles somewhere, if they were ever with him at all? These are the moments—in newspapers—recorded arrivals and departures, when William A. Lloyd is a flicker, a passerby. These are glimpses that capture a moment, a riddle of a moment, and do not always allow for more.

Whatever else Alvin was doing in that come-alive, roaring city, on November 22, 1853, three nights after arriving in New Orleans, and a couple of hours after Captain Hutchinson took the *Persia* upriver at five o'clock on its return trip to Pittsburgh, Alvin went on a spree: a crime spree that was repeatedly noted in the papers: "William A. Lloyd was arrested on St. Charles Street, on the charge of obtaining money under false pretenses."[76]

The *Times-Picayune* of November 23, 1853 says: "Recorder Vaught's Court. William A. Lloyd was last night arrested in St. Charles Street on the charge of having obtained money under false pretenses." The same paper, same edition, also says, but of a different crime: "False pretenses. W.A. Lloyd was yesterday charged by the clerk of the steamboat *Persia* with having swindled the owners of that boat out of $35 in passage money by some story about some trunks. The examination will take place on the 25th inst." The *Daily Crescent* reported: "False pretenses. The clerk of the steamboat *Persia*, Mr. Guthrie, made a deposition in this court [Recorder Winter's Court, First District] charging him with having obtained passage on said boat from Memphis to this city for himself, family and another person by means of false pretenses. The case will be examined today."

For other less larcenous-minded visitors, there was a time to be grateful, and days of peculiar amusements. December 22 was Thanksgiving Day in the state of Louisiana, the date having been appointed by Governor Hebert the previous month. At the Southern Museum, on Charles Street, you could slip a quarter to the man at the door and go in to see the world's largest woman, Madame Graham, weighing in at 706 pounds with a five-and-a-half-foot waist. Or you could go to Dan "Daddy" Rice's, and see the man of Jim Crow legend himself. For those into boxing or shooting, one could always jog along to Roper's Sparring Rooms, next to Travis's Pistol Gallery, over the shades on Perdido Street, or, if you feared your fate and wished to know it, you could pay a visit to Madame Alwin, the German fortune-teller just in from New York and now at 123 Julia Street, upstairs on the second floor, second door down from Camp Street.[77]

On January 8, 1854, with a bit of confusion about the first initial of his name, but seeing that Alvin was working his cons with astonishing regularity, the *New Orleans Times-Picayune* noted: "Swindling. J.A. Lloyd was, this morning, arraigned on the charge of having swindled the proprietors of the St. Charles and City Hotels, by false pretenses. The arrest was made by J.L. Page. The examination will take place on the 11th inst."

A few days later . . . "Recorder Winter's Court. Swindling. J.A. Lloyd was yesterday examined on the charge of having, by false representation, swindled H.M.O. Key out of $9.60 at the St Charles by pretending that he wished to pay for telegraphic despatches which he never received . . . The accused was sent before the Recorder's court."[78]

The *Daily Crescent*, still in error over Alvin's initials: "A respectable looking individual named F.A. Lloyd was yesterday sent before the First District Court charged with having borrowed a small sum of money from the clerk of the City Hotel by means of false representations."[79]

By January 14, 1854, the papers rattled off Alvin's crimes. The *New Orleans Times-Picayune* says this: "Recorder Winter's Court. Swindling. W.A. Lloyd, whose name nearly every day graces the police books, was last night again arrested for obtaining $4 in money by false pretenses from Jesse R. Irwin of Irwin & Co, of 40 Camp Street, under the pretense that he was a clerk of Ward, Jonas & Co, and wished the money to pay a freight bill."

And again: "False pretences. An affidavit was made against Wm A. Lloyd charging him with having come to the store of Irwin & Forno, No. 40 Camp street, and obtained four dollars, stating that he was a clerk in the store of Ward & Jonas, and wanted the money to pay a freight bill. Deponent charges that Lloyd was not at the time a clerk of Ward & Jonas, and that the money was obtained with a fraudulent intention. Accused was required to give bail for his appearance before the Criminal Court."[80]

It is probable that he posted bail and when a man like Alvin for whom court appearances were often daily doings moved upriver, it was no surprise. In those years, it was ridiculously simple to steam away. From everything. That was to change.

By May 1854, Alvin and his little brother J. T. were in Cincinnati, starting a new enterprise. They had decided to go into the publishing business together. The brothers took a post office box at the central post office in downtown Cincinnati and an office in the building of the *Daily Cincinnati Commercial*, on the northwest corner of 3rd and Sycamore. To make it all look better, much more of a national concern, J. T. traveled to St. Louis, where he took a space in the *Herald* building. [81]

Like their competitors the Cincinnati *Enquirer*, the *Times*, and the *Gazette*, the *Commercial* had rapid steam-power presses on-site that never stopped running. Not only did they print their own paper on a daily basis, but they also did job printing for anyone who was prepared to pay— journals, books, pamphlets, circulars, labels, checks, and cards, anything printable. In addition to all that, they rented office space in their building to entrepreneurs such as the Lloyd Brothers.[82]

By mid-year 1854 Alvin and J. T. had formed a publishing company, with Charles C. Rhodes. The safest name for this new corporation was James T. Lloyd & Co., so that was what it was called. This little enterprise would last until February 11, 1857, by which time J. T. Lloyd's new wife Ella had been enlisted as a front woman, so as to avoid the Lloyd brothers' notoriety, and Lambert A. Wilmer as the resident intellectual, a writer who would go on to write a paean to J. T. praising his honesty and fine character, was part of the organization. But by the time the company folded, it had gained a reputation as one of the principal pirates of the Philadelphia publishing world.[83]

On June 7, 1854, the *New York Daily Tribune* advertised *Tallis's Pocket Map of the City of New York*, which showed the numbers at the corners of each street, together with a railroad and steamboat guide, and a business directory of the principal merchants in the city, with other valuable information for citizens and strangers. The Lloyd Brothers thought this was a good idea, and so their first venture as James T. Lloyd & Co., Publishers, was to commence work on their *Great New York Business Chart for the Western States*.[84]

In a way, this chart was a forerunner to today's yellow pages, and the brothers proposed to the most reliable business houses in New York City that they could advertise in this mammoth chart, which would be going all over the West—everywhere, to all merchants and tradesmen. The issue date of this chart would be August 20, 1854. "The long connection of the undersigned with the press, and general acquaintance with the Western people, we flatter ourselves . . ." etc. "All letters directed to us at the St. Nicholas Hotel, or at the Post Office, will meet with prompt . . ." etc. The St. Nicholas was in St. Louis, and the Post Office in question was the one in Cincinnati. The ad was signed "Jas T. Lloyd, *St Louis Herald*" and "William A. Lloyd, *Cincinnati Commercial*."[85]

It would cost advertisers twenty dollars for ten lines or less, and display ads would be charged accordingly. A bunch of agents sallied forth to sell this product on a commission-only basis, hoping that they would, in due course, actually receive their hard-earned cash. If they had only known the truth about the Lloyds they would never have embarked on such a fruitless exercise. And of course, J. T. was never associated with the *St. Louis Herald*. The yellow-pages-like project didn't work out, and the chart was never published. There were no refunds forthcoming to all those disappointed New Yorkers.[86]

On October 30, "Wm A. Loyd was charged with taking and receiving from the US Post Office in Cincinnati a letter directed to James Sparks McCormick, and of destroying said letter." Alvin was required to post bail of one thousand dollars to answer this charge.[87]

By late May 1855, J. T. was advertising his company's new steamboat directory, which was to come out in October: *Lloyd's Steamboat Directory, and Disasters on the Western Waters*. It was, at this moment, "in the course of preparation," but it would be, J. T. assured his readers, "one of the most interesting books ever published." He then informs us: "The author has, for six years, been gathering together all the facts and items in regard to the numerous steamboat disasters on the Western and Southern waters, and now intends publishing them in book form." Washington & Co. of Cincinnati would issue it. By remitting only one dollar to J. T. Lloyd & Co., you would receive in the mail a copy of the above work. This ad ran for weeks—months—in many of the nation's papers. Of course, such advertising would have cost a fortune, but J. T. presented himself very well, as did his brother Alvin, and the monies collected were never a problem, not for the Lloyds. It was only bad news for the publishers who got cheated by the brothers.[88]

Beginning in June 1855 the Lloyds sent out advance sheets of the publication, which contained humorous or interesting nuggets, the sort of things newspaper editors frequently like to use as filler. That was also free advertising for the upcoming and always imminent directory. Their ads were always taken out for a month's run. At the end of the month the paper had a choice. If it was big enough, such as the *Evening Star*, it could drop the ads immediately once it became evident they had been swindled by the Lloyd brothers. Smaller, more provincial papers could do that too, and some did, but there were others who were more desperate for the promised revenue of such a big, long-running ad, and so they kept it running a lot longer than they should have in the hopes that some money might eventually come their way. It rarely did. Besides, for the Lloyds, there were always new papers to con, all over the place, big and small. And the Lloyd brothers sometimes paid, if they felt a particular paper needed placating.

Alvin revived the idea of the business chart, but now included the southern states as well as the western ones, and switched his targeted victims from New York to Philadelphia, a city in which he was now beginning to spend more and more time. In August 1855 this directory, as he now called it, came out, and attracted press, not so much for itself as for Alvin's attacks on anyone he felt like attacking. This was a method of operation he would use when he came to publish his famous steamboat and railroad guide a few years later.[89]

Aside from this new blackmail enterprise of his, Alvin was also the chief salesman of the *Steamboat Disasters* book, crisscrossing the country, selling ads, visiting newspaper editors, and hyping like P. T. Barnum. Successfully. Late in 1855 he was in Charleston, South Carolina, staying at the Charleston Hotel. This from the December 17, 1855, edition of that city's prominent newspaper, the *Courier*: "We had the pleasure yesterday of receiving a visit from W.A. Lloyd, Esq., one of the editors of 'Lloyd's great Steamboat Work,' which is to contain . . ." etc. The *Courier* continued: "The first edition is to exceed one hundred and forty thousand copies, as there are said to be at this time one hundred and twenty thousand copies ordered. Mr. Lloyd is pursuing his inquiries here, and informs us that the work will be positively ready by the first of January."

The book itself contains a history of the first application of steam as a motive power, lives of John Fitch and Robert Fulton, a history of early steamboat navigation on western waters, sixty very good maps, lists of steamboats and disasters, a history of all the railroads in the country, photos galore, sketches of cities plagiarized from Lippincott's 1854 *Gazetteer*, a hundred fine engravings. It also served as a guidebook for the traveling public. It was published in Cincinnati by James T. Lloyd & Co., and in Chicago by D. B. Cooke & Co., and stereotyped by J. A. Tiernan, the superintendent of Jesper Harding & Sons, of Philadelphia, the printers of the book. The long section on the steamboat disasters is clearly J. T.'s work, and is a signal contribution to nineteenth-century, fact-based research. It was, in fact, a singular achievement. But like all such accomplishments, the brothers and, later, Alvin on his own, would find a way to compulsively sabotage everything.

Meanwhile, J. T. Lloyd made the *Cincinnati Sun* into a spicy independent gossip sheet, a "thumb paper," a vicious anti-immigrant Know-Nothing Party rag, solidly behind Fillmore for president in the race of

1856—that is, until July, when he deserted a sinking ship and transferred his allegiance to John C. Fremont, whose stand against slavery was bold and decisive.

However, one of this paper's principal designs was to obtain money from businessmen by using the old trick of blackmail. Those who paid were left alone; those who did not were mercilessly attacked and often ruined in the hate columns. Here were the Lloyd brothers: fiercely devoted to each other, fiercely energetic, talented, bright, ambitious, and larcenous.[90]

For the most part, the *Cincinnati Sun* became so offensive that, toward the end of the year, J. T. was forced to leave town and moved to Philadelphia, where he took an office in the *Inquirer* building at 57 South Third Street and continued work on his *Steamboat Directory*.

Likewise, Alvin was run out of Cincinnati in 1856 for publishing a scurrilous article about M. D. Potter, the owner of the *Daily Commercial*. He hightailed it down to New Orleans, and from late December began to publish a cheap fifty-cent edition of what he was now calling *W. Alvin Lloyd's Steamboat and Railroad Directory and Disasters on the Southern and Western Waters*. "Fifty advertisements will be taken. 10,000 copies have already been sold." This was done from an office in the *Times-Picayune* building. That didn't last long, and in January 1857 he moved over to the offices of the *Crescent*.[91]

It was Alvin's success with the cheap edition of the *Steamboat Directory* that led him to consider making it a monthly publication. He settled on the title *W. Alvin Lloyd's Southern Steamboat and Railroad Guide*, and the first edition came out in April 1858.

In spite of the birth of the guide and the pride apparent in such a splendid birth, Alvin exploded. In the press. In an attempted murder.

On the evening of Wednesday, February 24, 1858, "W. Alwyn Lloyd [*sic*]" shot J. C. Mackey in front of the City Hotel in New Orleans. Lloyd had owed money to Mr. Constance and said he'd pay; Mackey was Constance's thug; earlier, Mackey had gone to see Lloyd to collect; Lloyd had said nasty things about Mackey's relationship with Constance; naturally Mackey took offense, and went for his cane; Alvin's hand went to his breast pocket, but the gun never emerged; instead, he called Mackey a "damned puppy." (A strong insult at that time.) Then, a little later, on the twenty-fourth, came the shooting. Apparently, Alvin shot at Mackey's head, but missed, the bullet passing through Mackey's hat. On the twenty-sixth there was a warrant out for Alvin's arrest, and the following day he was arraigned in Recorder Stite's court for the attempted murder.[92]

And of Alvin's brother? On May 31, 1858, J. T. was arrested in Philadelphia for swindling. It was fast becoming too hot in the City of Brotherly Love for Alvin's bilking brother. On June 4 he was bound over for trial. Down in New Orleans, on June 11, 1858, Alvin jumped $750 bail over the issue of the shooting of Mr. Mackey and set out for Mobile, where he continued, with remarkable impunity, to put out his railroad guide. But he now had other things on his mind, aside from publishing.[93]

While still married to Lizzie and with his family—the family he visited when it moved him to visit—not anywhere in sight, Alvin headed to Chicago and the eastern cities. Somewhere along the way he had become a serious collector. Of women. On November 12, 1858, in Bridgeport, Connecticut, fifty-eight miles east-northeast of New York City, Alvin married Virginia Van Rensselaer Higgins, of Brooklyn. She was thirteen. Toward the end of January 1859 she became pregnant. She was still thirteen.[94]

Virginia was a Norfolk, Virginia, girl originally, born in 1845 to Eugene Jeremiah Higgins and his wife Juliet Hutchings. Whatever Alvin Lloyd was, or wasn't—mesmerist, outlaw, scofflaw, libertine, liar—Virginia and her brother Eugene would remain in Alvin's life to the end of his days. Especially Virginia: the child bride Virginia, the lover and mother, the betrayed wife, the accomplice-wife, and finally, the caretaker.

But several months after he married Virginia, Alvin went after the wife of a Louisville photographer, George T. Shaw. Shaw did all the things a "photographist" would normally do at a Louisville gallery—daguerreotypes, ambrotypes, family groups, and children's pictures. Mr. Shaw's wife of eighteen, Angeline, ten years his junior, was "possessed of considerable charms."[95]

The *Louisville Daily Democrat* of July 16, 1859, reported that "On Friday night, July 8, the wife of Geo. T. Shaw, a highly estimable photographist on Main Street, deserted her home, and in company with a fellow named Wm A. Lloyd, formerly somewhat known in the community, and now, we believe, a resident of Philadelphia, fled."

"Hitherto highly regarded," the press called her. The truant wife barely made it into the next county before the police apprehended her at Shelbyville and brought her back. Alvin was nowhere to be seen. Back with her husband, temporarily, with Annie's promise never to leave again, on the following Monday she met Alvin at Hobbs Depot and took the train to Lexington, where they stayed at a hotel. G. T. Shaw found out where they were, and again sent a man to have them arrested. It seems he was now fully reconciled to the fact that his wife had left him. What upset him was that she had taken some of his property. By the time the police arrived at the hotel, Alvin and Annie had fled in a carriage, leaving their baggage behind. Mr. Shaw then dashed over to Lexington, and, with the aid of the chief of police, formed a posse. However, they were too late by two hours. Their prey had taken the train for Paris, Kentucky, and then up to Maysville, on the river, "where it is supposed they intend taking a boat for the East." Lloyd may well have married her, or promised her he would. Mr. Shaw, the "unconsoled photographist arrived back in Louisville on the 14th."[96]

The September 16th, 1859, issue of *Penny Press* of Cincinnati reported that "Bill Lloyd, the notorious libertine, who ran away with Mrs. Shaw of Louisville, is now in jail at Chicago, Illinois. After enjoying the honeymoon, he left her, saying that she was a rather expensive piece of crinoline to suit the state of his exchequer."

The same *Penny Press* article reports the words of the *Louisville Democrat*: "He took with him . . . a diamond breastpin belonging to Mrs. Shaw, a gift from her husband. Incensed at this, she pursued him to Chicago and had him arrested. He is now in jail awaiting the appearance of the husband to prosecute the case. While it is very proper that Lloyd and Mrs. Shaw should pay the penalty of the law, it is to be hoped that the husband will give himself no further concern about them, than to see that justice be done, and that is what the fugitives most fear."

Mrs. Shaw would eventually return to her husband by whom she would have a daughter. G. T. Shaw died serving the Union during the

Civil War, and in 1871 Annie married again, to the recently divorced Dr. John Pirtle. She died of blood poisoning at the age of thirty-nine.[97]

As for Alvin, on September 30, 1859, at the Barnum's Hotel, in Baltimore, the town in which he had set up his new base, his wife—or rather, one of his wives—Virginia gave birth to a son. His name was Clarence Alvin Lloyd, and he would lead a most adventurous life, at least as a child.[98]

Then it was back to New York, this time to the Metropolitan Hotel. W. Alvin Lloyd was now devolving out of Baltimore, and acquiring printing works on Centre Street, Manhattan.[99]

As Alvin's life as a bigamist, con man, and publisher is in full flower, the country begins to fracture, on the edge of a great cataclysm. Alvin will take sides, dissolve, reshape, and reappear in an old identity made new again. And he will gather acolytes and accomplices. In time and together, they will find a way to bring off the biggest crime of his career.

5

Acolytes and Accomplices

ALVIN LLOYD SWOOPED INTO NEW YORK, LANDING IN THE HEART OF THE publishing world at Centre Street. Back in 1856, the block was part of a new monolith that had sprung up between Leonard and Worth Streets, and been given the address 81, 83, and 85 Centre Street. It had been erected especially to house printing establishments and those of the other mechanical arts, and named the Caxton Building for Englishman William Caxton, who around 1483 was the "first to set up his own printing press in London and the first to print a book in English," most notably Chaucer's *Canterbury Tales*.[100] Longtime printer Richard C. Valentine was the first occupant of the Caxton Building on the third floor of No. 83, in command of one of the most complete stereotype foundries in the country. The stereotype was a singular kind of printing plate "developed in the late 18th century and widely used in letterpress, newspaper and other high-speed press runs." They were made by "locking all the type columns, illustration plates, and advertising plates of a complete newspaper page into paper mache." When dried, the "mat is used as a mold to cast the stereotype from hot metal."[101]

It was at this venerable building that W. Alvin Lloyd, the publisher, rented space. During this time, with the first two members of the future Lloyd Gang in place—Alvin and Virginia—in October 1859, Alvin met Thomas Hewlings Stockton Boyd, his aggressive, and not always dutiful, acolyte for the first time. Alvin was looking for an homme d'affaires—a ready assistant in the grand old style—and he got one who would play a most significant role in his life.[102]

T.H.S. Boyd, or "Alphabetical" Boyd as he'd come to be nicknamed for the tumble of the first initials of his name, was born in Montgomery

County, Maryland, in September 1837, and named for famous Methodist preacher Thomas Hewlings Stockton, because Alphabetical's own father was Reuben Tyler Boyd, the not-quite-so-famous Methodist preacher. When Alphabetical was three, the family was posted to Cincinnati, then Clinton County, Ohio, just north of the city, and that's where Alphabetical's younger brothers Charlie, who would play a role in the Lloyd drama, and Reuben were born in 1844 and 1847 respectively. After a few more moves, the family moved to Clarksburg, Maryland, in 1859, and there they stayed.[103]

As for Virginia, it seemed that Alvin wanted her and Clarence out of the city. An ad was placed in the *New York Herald* on November 24, 1859. "Country board wanted—for a lady, child, and nurse, for the winter—the comforts of a home desired, and if they cannot be had none need apply. The husband of the lady will be at home a portion of the time. Address Thos Boyd, Metropolitan Hotel." The nurse may have been Nellie Dooley, but that is not a certainty. Miss Dooley's later testimony tells us that the Lloyds employed her on December 10, 1859.[104]

Ellen Robinson ("Nellie") Dooley would also be a major part of the Lloyds' life for several years. An English girl, from Cheshire, she had come to Fall River, Massachusetts, at the age of ten. At twenty she made the fateful decision to become Clarence Lloyd's nursemaid.[105]

The Lloyds, as well as much of the country, would find themselves on a new stage, in a new drama with no certain ending. Throughout the latter part of 1859, with abolitionist John Brown's execution on December 2 of that year, anti-slavery proponents warred physically and verbally with state's-righters as politicians took sides and bloody-shirt rhetoric reached a fever pitch. But as much of the ordinary lives of ordinary people went on as usual—in marked contrast to or ignorant of the trials to come—all through 1860, Lloyd was determined to make good on his great publishing venture. Lloyd and Boyd were constantly back and forth between New York and Philadelphia, as well as traveling the country soliciting ads and collecting monies owed: New York State, Ohio, Indiana, Illinois, Kentucky, Tennessee, Mississippi, and Louisiana.

Lloyd returned to New York and Alphabetical carried on in the South, attending to his master's business while the future Confederate states were fomenting secession after the election of Abraham Lincoln on November 6, 1860. Even as Lincoln lamented the possibility of outright war he urged his countrymen to think of the South not as "enemies, but as friends," to look to the "better angels of our nature."[106]

No matter the upheavals, life and the adventures of life played on at the grand Metropolitan Hotel with Lloyd the publisher, bon vivant and profligate guest, center stage. The hotel was a wonder, with its stunningly beautiful five brownstone-cased stories occupying an entire city block of 366 feet fronting Broadway, and 210 feet on Prince Street, with its steam-heated rooms for more than six hundred guests who, once they were settled in, could thoroughly admire their good fortune in the largest plate-glass mirrors in the country, and brag about it down the speaking tubes that were a forerunner to the telephone. Hot and cold running water in every room, bathrooms on every floor, Wilton carpets everywhere, rosewood furniture upholstered in rich brocatelle, fine dining in the restaurant, elevators, room service whenever you wanted it. You never had to leave—if you could afford it. For ten dollars a night, you'd be well served.[107]

Lloyd sought advertisers like the hotel's owner, Warren Leland, who, like his brothers, was an abolitionist but also a wily, opportunistic businessman. Leland immediately saw the possibilities of W. Alvin Lloyd's urging that he advertise the Metropolitan in the guide. Half a million people in Dixie would see his portrait and his biography, read about a great New York hotelier, one who would be sure to look after his good southern friends when they came up to conduct business or sport. The hundreds of plantation owners, commission merchants, and cotton brokers from Georgia and the Carolinas, from Virginia and Louisiana—men fully committed to the institution of slavery, yes—they would be made to feel very much at home in Warren Leland's Metropolitan Hotel. And what's more, these southern gentlemen could board their slaves in special and very good quarters, right in the hotel itself. And Alvin Lloyd's *Southern Steamboat and Railroad Guide* would surely attract brand-new business.

The *Memphis Appeal*, on April 27, 1860, reviewed that month's edition of the *Steamboat Guide*, calling it "invaluable to all Southern travelers.

The only correct guide published for the Southern country. . . . The guide is in universal use throughout the entire South with a monthly circulation of over seven thousand."

And here was a distinction, a mission statement from Alvin, as he used "we" to quell fears of a "Yankee" influence and identify himself as a true southerner. "We observe that the publisher allows no advertiser in the *Guide* but those whose interests are directly identified with the South, and those who sell exclusively to the Southern and South-western states. . . . We must say that it is got up very tastefully. . . . It is published in New York, but for many years in New Orleans."[108]

The June 1860 number of *Lloyd's Southern Steamboat and Railroad Guide* came out at the end of May. The table of contents included biographies of railroad executives, "Views of New Orleans, Tours of the South, Rules for railroad travelers, Arrivals and departures of steamboats and ocean vessels, Correct timetables of all the Southern railroads." It included every railroad station between New Orleans and New York, with historical facts connected with each station, railroad advertisements, a list of first-class hotels, the fashionable watering places and summer resorts throughout the United States, and advertisements for the wholesales houses that sold to the South.

The July issue included articles on "The Great Staple of the South"; the Mississippi & Central Railroad; biographies of Fernando Wood (during the war a Confederate sympathizer and separatist) and Memphis Railroad executive Sam Tate; an editorial on G. W. Bradley, general agent of the Mississippi Railroad; portraits of Lynchburg, Virginia, merchant John Robin McDaniel and Metropolitan Hotel owner Warren Leland; and W. Alvin Lloyd's Time Indicator.

The August 1860 number came out in late July with much of the same included.

Alvin and Alphabetical had by now bilked as many customers as they could and they had no credibility left as they were accruing large bills. So Alvin took out an ad disavowing Boyd. By doing this Alvin was legally able to absolve himself and the company of any debt. Of course Boyd was never cut loose by his employer and the two men must have had a great laugh over the ad Lloyd placed in the *Memphis Appeal* of September 11,

1860: "Caution. The public are respectfully informed that Thos. H.S. Boyd is no longer authorized to transact business for 'W. Alvin Lloyd's Southern Steamboat and Railroad Guide.'" Signed, "W. Alvin Lloyd." This wouldn't be the last time the pair would use this legal tactic to escape debt.

As an early and unwanted Christmas present, Alvin came in for a fierce shellacking in the *Louisville* press. "The *New York World* gives Mr. W. Alvin Lloyd, publisher of the *Southern Steamboat and Railway Guide*, some notoriety by particularizing his attempts at black mail. W. Alvin Lloyd once lived in this city, but we are not aware that it lost much by his change of residence."[109]

Alvin had left his mark in Louisville. More than his mark, he had left a stain, and now he was doing something similar in New York by besmirching and exposing northern merchants who traded with the south. Lloyd frequently excoriated abolitionists, calling them "Black Republicans," a slur used by pro-slavery defenders against the radical, anti-slavery, pro-abolitionist wing of the Republican Party.

Lloyd fought back against his attackers, among them the *New York World*. "W. Alvin Lloyd, who publishes a Southern blackmail sheet in New York called the 'Southern Steamboat and Railroad Guide'—and denounces Northern merchants to Southern customers for their political opinions—has sued the proprietors of the *New York World* for libel, the *World* having excoriated the said Lloyd in a terrible manner for his rascally tendencies."[110]

In spite of the trail of excoriations swirling, hovering, descending, Alvin, like his younger brother, was in perpetual motion. His *Steamboat Guide* was coming out each and every month from 83 Centre Street, full of inflammatory secessionist sentiment and rants against Abraham Lincoln. Alvin ran an ad in the *New York Herald* that related stories of his blackmailing attempts on advertisers in New York City by threatening to expose them for being Southern sympathizers. "Every name will soon be known," he threatened. Then he referred to the ruinous state of the country brought on by the election of Abraham Lincoln and advised Southern merchants not to sell to Northern businessmen—traitors to the Southern cause. "Avoid Black Republican Houses. . . . If you are not with us, you are against us. . . . We are a Southerner by birth, education, and in heart.

No money can buy our principles. . . . We mean what we say. W. Alvin Lloyd."[111]

On December 20, 1860, South Carolina seceded from the Union. Over the course of the next seven months, ten more states would follow suit: Mississippi, Florida, Alabama, Georgia, Louisiana, Texas, Virginia, Arkansas, North Carolina, and finally, Tennessee. But as 1861 emerged, Alvin was promoting his *Guide to the South*, defending his decision not to publish the actual names of the businessmen but reassuring his readers that he will "guide them to sympathetic merchants in New York so as to avoid Black Republican Houses." He promised a blacklist of names and establishments soon.[112]

Alvin was in Memphis in January of 1861. There exists a free railroad pass he got from Bentley D. Hasell, the chief engineer and general superintendent of the Memphis & Ohio Railroad, that 130-mile stretch of track to Paris, Tennessee, that comprised the southernmost of three parts of the soon-to-be-opened line from Memphis to Louisville.

About the same time, George G. Hull, superintendent of the very important Atlanta & West Point Railroad (a five-foot gauge road running the eighty-seven miles between those two Georgia towns), gave Alvin a complimentary ticket. Same thing with the Muscogee Railroad; the Macon & Western Railroad (this road ran 104 miles from Macon to Atlanta in six hours); the Alabama & Florida Railroad (running 45 miles from Pensacola to the Alabama state line, and then another 116 miles from the line to Montgomery); the Nashville & Chattanooga Railroad (this road ran 150 miles between the two towns); and the South-Western Railroad (a valid line until January 1862).[113]

On February 4, 1861, the Confederacy came into being, with Montgomery, Alabama, as its capital. On the eighteenth, Jefferson Davis became president. As for Alvin, the ever-changing Alvin—as would be seen just a few months later when he came under heavy fire in New York City for his secessionist ravings—left the world of publishing and remarkably, swiftly, did an identity backflip and went back on the road.

The first news blast in the *New York Herald* of February 19 and 20, 1861, said: "The Great Congress of Artists. Floyd's Minstrels. Fifteen performers. Cool White Stage manager." They got his name wrong—an omen, perhaps—but the message was loud and clear. This was Alvin assembling the elite of minstrelsy. August Asche was leader of Lloyd's Double Brass Band, who would give a free concert on the balcony before each performance of their upcoming grand tour of the United States. Billy Birch and Charley Fox—the "rival comedians"—were two of the stars of the troupe. Other members included celebrated French tenor Gustave Bidaux and, of course, Cool White. Tenor Dave Wambold, the famous ballad singer from Elizabethtown, New Jersey, was twenty-five then, and had come over from Dan Bryant's Minstrels; Nick Oehl was a German magician living in New York, and Charley Blass was another German, also living in New York. Fifteen top performers altogether: Minstrel royalty, blacking up for hungry audiences.[114]

On Monday, February 25, Lloyd's Minstrels began their tour at the Concert Hall, in Newark, New Jersey, with a three-night performance. After a few more New Jersey towns, they opened at Philadelphia's Musical Fund Hall, on March 4, for a week's stint. "Look out for the Lloyds," screamed the *Cleveland Daily Herald*. After Newark the troupe played New Brunswick on February 28 and March 1, 1861, and on the second were at Trenton. It wasn't a warning when a Cleveland paper wrote, "Look out for the Lloyds." It's just that they were expecting Lloyd's Minstrels soon, and in their edition of March 4, 1861, the *Herald* took it upon themselves to alert their readers to the fact that the troupe was opening that very night in Philadelphia.[115]

April 1 saw the debut of Lloyd's Minstrels at Niblo's Saloon, one of the big New York venues. "Enthusiastic reception. Glorious success," trumpeted the *Herald*, singling out for praise several acts, including the scenes from *Smiggy McGlural* and *Dixie's Land*. The curtain rose at 8:00 p.m. For twenty-five cents, a night of entertainment was yours. The same paper of April 8 said that Lloyds were "sustaining the reputation of the African Opera famously."

Imagine Alvin strutting, doffing his black silk top hat, his boots polished to a high luster as he and his troupe attended the funeral of minstrel Jerry Bryant. The *New York Clipper* reported, "Mr Lloyd, proprietor of Lloyd's Minstrels, walked in the (funeral) procession with his company."[116]

The company remained at Niblo's, with continued success and raves in the papers.

Part One of the performance would begin with the Overture by Lloyd's Minstrels. Then they went into the operatic overture "Ho, Boys, Let's March Away." Then came Billy Birch's act, "The Soap Fat Man," then Gustave Bidaux singing "Vive L'America," followed by Charley Fox's sketch, "Willie's Gone for a Soldier," and many more. Part One wrapped up with "The Star-Spangled Banner," performed by Mr. Percey, Dave Wambold, Gustave Bidaux, H. Wilks, J. Eastmead, and Little Arthur, the musical prodigy. All very patriotic, and it would be, given the times.

Part Two featured clog dancing, ballads, and comedy sketches, with Billy Birch and Cool White doing scenes from *Macbeth* and *Othello*: Minstrels performing Shakespeare. The entire troupe appeared onstage for the finale.

April 1861 was a good month for W. Alvin Lloyd, but certainly not for the country. On April 12 the Civil War began when Confederate General P.G.T. Beauregard's forces bombarded Fort Sumter, a Federal installation. On April 29, 1861, Jefferson Davis was promising in an address to his Congress that the Confederate cause was "just and holy."

As men from both sides were mustering and marching, Alvin Lloyd's minstrel troupe was imploding. Colonel Lloyd, as he called himself, was proving to be not as magnanimous toward his company as his newspaper ads would have one believe. In fact, they hated him, or, more specifically, his overbearing and insolent manner. This side of Alvin—always ready and willing to show itself—manifested itself most alarmingly when the minstrels demanded their salaries. Alvin's drive to bilk always included his own personnel. They all sat around a table. Alvin put the money on the table, put his revolver next to it, and dared them to go for it. Dave Wambold threatened to kick his head in, and then quit, on May 6. On May 18, Dave set sail for Europe.[117]

This from the *New York Herald* of May 20, 1861: "Lloyd's Minstrels— complimentary benefit of W. Alvin Lloyd to-night." However, by now business was falling off drastically. That's because the public had found out about Alvin's other life—not his bigamous life, which would have been bad enough, but his *Steamboat Guide*, and the secessionist rants he was putting in it. Not a good time for that, and the crowds stayed away in droves. Salary for those members who stayed on—or, rather, the concept of salary—was reduced in order to cut expenses. The troupe was fracturing. The reasons for the collapse of Lloyd's Minstrels are basically twofold—crowds falling off and Lloyd's mismanagement. Yes, audience numbers were diminishing, and that was partly for the reason T. Allston Brown gives—that the public did not like a secessionist.

"Business was very bad with the party in May, 1861, which was attributed to fact of the manager [Lloyd] being the proprietor of a Southern publication," wrote T. Allston Brown.[118]

However, many New Yorkers were of mixed loyalties, so it's a little more complicated than that. General economics in the city, and the inevitable law of diminishing theater returns, also played their part. As for the mismanagement, Alvin was so difficult and dangerous that none of the other entertainers would deal with him anymore.[119]

To add to Alvin's woes, it may well be that the *Steamboat Guide's* publication was suppressed by New York City aldermen about this time. The April edition certainly came out, but what about May and June? The September 18, 1861, edition of the *Richmond Whig* would run an item about Alvin Lloyd when he was down in that city during the war. It says that the guide was "suppressed by the Despotism there prevailing [meaning New York], on account of the freedom with which it denounced the abolitionist. The editor is now in this city, and we hope he will resume the publication of this valuable work in a land of liberty." No official corroboration has been found of this alleged suppression and it is possible Alvin told the paper what to write.

"Lloyd's Minstrels will close Niblo's Saloon for repairs, on Saturday night, June 8th, and re-open with a new company on or about the 15th of August," said an ad in the *Herald* of June 5, 1861. "Artists of acknowledged talent desirous of negotiating for engagements with Lloyd's Minstrels for the ensuing fall and winter season, can address to W. Alvin Lloyd, Niblo's Saloon, New York. Lloyd's Minstrels will not travel this summer. W. Alvin Lloyd."

Yes, closing night was going to be the eighth, a benefit night for August Asche, the musical director, but, as Asche had quit, like pretty much everyone else, the last night turned out to be June 6, as an ad in the following day's *Herald* tells us: "Lloyd's Minstrels. Niblo's Saloon. Thursday evening. June 6, 1861. Most positively the last night of Lloyd's Minstrels." And it was, the troupe disbanding officially later that night.

However, what is clear from the June 5 ad is that Alvin had every intention of reopening with Lloyd's Minstrels at Niblo's in August. He wouldn't have gone to the time, trouble, and (in theory) expense of advertising for talent if he hadn't been serious. Not even Alvin would have done that. That he didn't open again in August was because something, someone, got in the way and within a few short weeks, he raced south—straight toward the promise of profit—straight into the war.

6

Escape from New York

HERE IS NEW YORK CITY ON JULY 4, 1861. AMID LOUD REVELS, "THE firing of guns," pistols, cannons and rockets "chasing each other though the skies," the city salutes the eighty-fifth birthday of the United States with patriotic displays: concerts, illuminations, pyrotechnic "tableaux formed by burning blue, green and yellow lights."[120] Though celebrations light up the night streets, on some corners, in some alleyways, there is blood-borne anger: man-on-man anger, mob-on-citizen anger as the combustible mix of Northern and Southern sentiments explodes. New and old Yankees fired to a fever by the Fourth vs. fixed and defiant Rebels.

Somewhere late in this roiling night, at 11:32 p.m., William Alvin Lloyd was—or so he claimed—cornered by "a mob of twenty one scoundrels . . . a committee of Black Republicans." He said the mob "ordered me to leave the state of New York and join my Rebel friends in the South within twenty-eight minutes or take the Oath of Allegiance to the Lincoln government." Writing to General Robert E. Lee and Confederate Adjutant General Samuel Cooper from a hellish durance in a Savannah prison, telling them the band of fanatics blamed "my writing and publishing articles against the abolitionists and sustaining my own country the truth [sic], branded me a base rebel." Ordered to take the Oath, or else, "I refused," he wrote. "I left the city in the time allowed me." Claiming he was given twenty-eight minutes to get out of town—imagine one of the mob looking at his watch as it ticked away toward midnight— Lloyd added, "I was not allowed time to go to my office at 83 Centre Street . . . and of course I have lost everything—my office, type, plates, maps—and all."[121]

And as T.H.S. Boyd later swore that the mob threatened to hang Lloyd, it was die, or flee into the night when "[y]oung America was jubilant with firecrackers, pinwheels, torpedoes and Roman candles," the air thick with black powder and sulfur. Fireworks falling on wooden buildings—the ready tinderboxes studding the city streets—sparked thirty-eight blazes throughout the day and evening. There were structures burning on East Broadway, Bleecker, Washington, Grand, Cedar, Broome, Horatio, Greene, and others that brought the sturdy dray horses lumbering to their rescue, dragging brass-belted wagons manned by brawny, ham-fisted Irish firemen to flood the flames.[122]

The city swirls and smokes around Lloyd. And if he is spotted near his Centre Street office as he moves or runs or hunkers down among the sodden revelers who have stumbled along Bowery into the Five Points, he will not stay. Strewn about the rotting warrens, saloons, and whorehouses was the embattled turf of the street gangs: Dead Rabbits, the Forty Thieves, the Roach Guards, and Swamp Angels, their shivs, long knives, snub-nosed revolvers, and brickbats at the ready. This killing field—a thug's war within a national war—unimaginably bloody and endless, was no place for Alvin Lloyd, a gentleman to all outward appearances. Like so many who'd come by foolish design or accident, he'd be robbed of his money and his weapon, stripped of his hand-tailored clothing, and beaten. Or killed.

So he must be afoot elsewhere as midnight passes and his Yankee Doodle birthday is over. Even if he'd celebrated July 4 as had many in the South as a right, a true American paean to the founding fathers who would have been outraged at the disemboweling of the country they'd birthed, Lloyd would not have joined the party. But he did, of course, in print and in person, damn the public, the prying press, and the Yankee authorities that he claimed had recently suppressed his beloved guide. He would defend his stance thusly: His writings were meant for his Southern readers, for all those who wished to voyage through Dixie.

Has he slipped past to catch a last omnibus at the terminus just near the City Hall? The car would have been full, crammed with sots and red-eyed whores. He'd left scum like that in the Louisville gutters, where the memory of mornings when he'd likely found his father passed out and urine-stained would have pained him. Or revolted him. Lloyd would not linger in such a conveyance. He wends his way through the last of the celebrations, the remains of the "annual jubilee."[123]

American flags flutter from rooftops; cannons salute the heralded De Kalb Regiment commanded by Colonel Von Giles, among the last remaining out of the seat of war, and the men of the Rhode Island Battery waiting for the enemy in their entrenchments just across from Virginia— all reminders of a young war Alvin Lloyd was too old to fight and too fired up not to. There were many New York denizens silent in darkened houses, with no Union flags or illuminations in their night—the secret and not-so-secret Rebels like Lloyd all over the city, some far more prominent than he was: the spies sending intelligence to Confederate troops massing across the Potomac, the wealthy merchants fed and fattened by the cotton trade. But had a mob gone after Mayor Fernando Wood that night, their demands would have been met with the mayor's toughs and hard-eyed silence. For Wood ran the city and encouraged sedition. The Copperhead Democrat, in the guise of a peace advocate who wanted to fly a new, independent New York City flag, seceded from the Union. Dependent on and nourished by the fortunes made by cotton trade with the South, along with the arms traffickers who'd flocked to New York to get rich supplying the Confederacy, the insurgent rebels themselves were not the enemy as many in New York City were sympathetic to their cause. Rather the chaos of war and the blockade of southern ports by the Union authorities made the cotton trade and arms dealing very difficult. So it was the very war itself, not the south that was the enemy. And the signs of that war and the traders and traffickers' imminent ruin were everywhere. And hadn't Lloyd publicly declared himself a true Confederate? Was it such a surprise that some people in the fractious city had had quite enough? Or was his violent mob encounter only partly true?

At some point, he would have reached his destination: the Metropolitan Hotel, his lair, his trysting spot where according to 1860 census records, he'd been living with a woman who passed as his wife, a Mrs. W. A. Lloyd, age twenty-five, born in New York. She was certainly not seventeen-year-old Virginia, as the ages and places of birth of these women differed greatly.[124]

Unless he'd secreted yet another wife, which was possible, perhaps *this* Mrs. Lloyd was the daughter of a wealthy New York merchant hiding from her family. If Lloyd committed the crime of bigamy with her, as was his wont, he would not think of it as a crime. He would rationalize his compulsion; call it saving women from starvation of the spirit, from dullness of heart, from ordinary men, from an ordinary life.

But in the end, for Alvin Lloyd, far more than the protection of his women preoccupied him. Failure stalked him, the stink of failure. Lloyd's Minstrels was over, dead as a doorstop. Closed up. At Niblo's Saloon, where his troupe had many a glorious night of minstrel magic, and where his ingrate star, Cool White, had gotten wild applause for his Othello and Macbeth, and Percey, and Fox too, he'd damn them, damn all their hides for abandoning the great William Alvin Lloyd. Where would they go? They would never do better than Lloyd's Minstrels. Top of the bill. Without William Alvin Lloyd they'd be booed and damned, pissed on. Without him. But the troupe's demise was *all* about him.

Remembering Colonel T. Allston Brown, journalist and editor of the *Yankee Clipper* when he wrote "Business was very bad with the party in May, 1861, which was attributed to fact of the manager [Lloyd] being the proprietor of a Southern publication," it was high time Lloyd left New York. He was broke and desperate, though he'd been in similar fixes in the past when he'd crisscrossed the South, selling ads for his guide, pandering to railroad executives and bankers over champagne and lobster, promising them space in his glorious guide, cheating and being cheated as the ads didn't appear, or his customers didn't pay. So with promises, penny notes, and profits, empty pockets or on a good day payments in gold, he'd hopped a train or boarded a steamboat. He'd been forced to leave towns before—police, irate businessmen, and husbands hot on his heels. But he'd usually outrun them and moved on.[125]

Now he needed a new plan. One sure thing: He must have some kind of revenue. Somewhere. One option would have been to go back down south to collect the monies advertisers owed him for his guides. But the South was the Confederacy now, and he couldn't sally forth as before, on and off trains, climbing aboard a riverboat, hearing the calliope over the chug and slap of paddle wheels and smelling brandy fumes and the perfumes of ready women. He'd need a pass to travel south through the lines and go deep into the Confederacy: the defiant new country. Passes, or passports as they were sometimes called—printed or handwritten documents with the name of the person and the purpose of his trip—were certainly issued this early in the war. But there were restrictions. On July 1, 1861, a "Military Regulation, concerning Passports" was issued " . . . by permission of the chief executive . . . that no passport, by whomever signed or countersigned will entitle any person to pass the lines of the United States army, unless the same be also countersigned by himself or the commander of a military geographical department."[126]

In spite of the mob, and with his usual defiance, Alvin Lloyd would not flee in utter haste. It appears that he lingered at least six days in the city, or spent part of that time with Virginia and Clarence in Westchester County. After that, he wrote Confederate President Jefferson Davis that he left for the Confederacy, not just to support the cause, but because he'd been "written against so much in the *New York Tribune, Times* and *World.*"[127]

He would get his affairs in order, his clothing, his day diary, his roster of those owed and owing. Picture him with a new girl in tow, dressed for the leaving: He in a wide-brimmed hat placed just so, a tan linen topcoat, a jeweled stickpin—an emerald gleaming atop a long gold shaft, stuck smartly at just the right angle in the collar of a light, white woven cotton dress shirt, perhaps the last of his fine clothing and accessories. Was the girl a new Mrs. Lloyd, or an imposter-wife garbed, perhaps, in a silken, wide-skirted day dress with a lightweight cape and hood to hide her face, as she, too, was on the run?

Lloyd would go to Washington City, straight to the White House, attempt to see the President himself, and hope he was far too busy to have caught wind of his published excoriations of Lincoln and all he stood for. It had to be Lincoln. Alvin would not seek out some minor official to scrawl on a card, with a nod or an officious sneer to send him on his way. No, he'd see the rail-splitter himself. Nothing less than a pass from the president would satisfy Alvin Lloyd. In fact, Abraham Lincoln issued numerous passes, many as favors, and some as necessary for various parties to cross the lines. Alvin would enter the executive mansion like a spit-polished Kentucky gentleman, leave and go south, go home where he would serve the Confederacy *his* way and serve it well.

⌐⌐

The New York and Hudson River Railroad depot loomed, a solid brick sentinel at 30th Street and Ninth Avenue. The sweeping roof, the separate waiting rooms for gents and ladies, the gabble and shouts of the meat-pie vendors, the tearful good-byes, the wives, mothers, and children embracing their crisp, ready soldiers as they sent them off to war. Onboard, the black locomotive shuddered and heaved as the furnaces were fired and the engine rumbled to life. Inside, the car was a mix of mahogany and burled maple leather-studded wood paneling. Cigar smoke and the smell of sweat choked the air, even with the windows wide open. It was hard to converse on a train at the best of times, what with the crush of passengers and the grinding of the wheels on rough tracks. And as for sleeping, the constant huzzahs of the soldiers rendered that luxury impossible. For any traveler, it was an arduous, twelve-hour trip to Washington City that involved three separate trains. The first leg was on the Philadelphia & Wilmington Railroad into Philadelphia, where they would transfer to the Baltimore & Ohio just as the newly elected Abraham Lincoln had done on his whistle-stop route through towns from Springfield, Illinois, on February 11, 1861, amid fears of an assassination plot.

Detective Allan Pinkerton's field operatives, who'd gleaned pieces of this plot hatched by fanatical Baltimore secessionists to prevent the president's inauguration, were alarmed. Pinkerton, who'd been hired to monitor railroad security of bomb and assassination threats along Lincoln's route through Baltimore, was warned that "on his [Lincoln's] arrival at Baltimore, during the rush and crush of the crowd . . . by knife or pistol, the assassination was to be effected."[128]

On the night of February 22, 1861, though the president-elect did not want to take drastic security measures, Pinkerton ordered the telegraph lines to Baltimore cut so the conspirators would not be able to communicate. When Lincoln left Harrisburg, Pennsylvania, on a special train, he was reluctantly in the company of Pinkerton detective Kate Warne. Draped in a long shawl with a "scotch cap" hiding his face, the president, as Warne's "invalid brother," slipped through the darkness. At the West Philadelphia Depot, because a special ordinance did not allow rail passage through downtown Baltimore, any traveler, including the president, had to take a horse-drawn carriage between President Street and Camden Street stations to the Washington-bound train. On February 23, in Baltimore, with Lincoln nowhere to be seen, as he had already passed safely and had arrived in Washington City, a greatly relieved Pinkerton sent a partially coded message to Samuel Felton, the Philadelphia, Wilmington and Baltimore Railroad president who'd employed the detective: "Plums delivered nuts safely."[129]

As for Lloyd, in the absence of furious mobs or angry fathers, on or about July 11, 1861, the train carrying him and his young lady pulled into Washington City. All arriving passengers would go into the long, low-slung brick-and-stucco brownstone at the corner of New Jersey Avenue and C Street, the B & O Railroad depot. Around them swarmed state militia men from New York, New Hampshire, Connecticut, Rhode Island, Maine, and Massachusetts, answering the president's call for three months, just three months. The hive of volunteers as young as sixteen and as old as fifty were gathered by state, trying out smart salutes and hefting bags over their shoulders. They would gladly muster into regular army regiments as Abe Lincoln had deemed it necessary and ordered it so.

Washington City—overcrowded, swampy, pestiferous, and disease-ridden—was irrevocably altered by war. "No one can imagine the deplorable condition of this city," wrote Edwin Stanton to General John Adams Dix on June 11, 1861.[130]

New York City diarist George Templeton Strong, returning home from a visit to Washington, was repelled. "Of all detestable places, Washington is the first . . . heat, bad quarters, bad fare, bad smells. Mosquitoes, and a plague of flies . . ."[131]

With the threat of a Rebel invasion from Confederate forces massing on the Virginia side of the Potomac River, there were warnings that there would surely be a collision in the coming days. "God grant our first battle not be a national defeat," Strong wrote.[132]

To the White House, then, for W. A. Lloyd, a man on a mission. The most common route would mean hailing a carriage at D Street, across New Jersey Avenue, continuing along D to Pennsylvania Avenue, past Willard's Hotel at 15th Street, making a sharp left at the Treasury Department Building, arriving at the left side of the semicircular drive that fronted the mansion. As there is no record of the girl accompanying Lloyd to see the president in any of the later testimonies that report the visit, in all probability she would have been deposited at a boardinghouse or hotel along the route. But we will soon find out just who this hapless young woman was.

"The White House and its surroundings . . . had much the appearance of a Southern plantation—straggling and easygoing," wrote Lincoln bodyguard William Crook.[133]

And within this sprawl of outhouses, stables, and goats nibbling at the grass just outside the president's window, Lloyd would have to approach the grand porticos, walk through the entry vestibule, past a group of soldiers, perspiring, half-awake in the July heat, and, as did most visitors, negotiate his way up a flight of stairs through people from all walks of life—office seekers, favored friends, and mothers pleading for a deferment for their sons. Secretary of State William Seward described the crowds clamoring for an audience with the president: The "grounds, halls, stairways, closets, are filled with applicants, who render ingress and egress difficult."[134]

"Our city teems with spies," Presidential Secretary William O. Stoddard wrote, decrying the "male and female traitors" that slipped by, noting that "the very air is full of rumors," and though danger lurked, at that time, Lincoln's private office was guarded not by an armed soldier but by his dour, officious, and very young private secretary, John Hay. John Nicolay, known as "the bulldog in the anteroom," was "sour and crusty," but his assistant John Hay was the dragon at the gate. "President Lincoln . . . is a little thinner and paler than on the day of his inauguration . . . at times weary and harassed," Stoddard reported.[135]

Although we know that Lloyd did receive a pass, either by request to Hay or in an actual meeting with the president, the procedure was often arduous and frustrating. According to California journalist and friend of Lincoln's, Noah Brooks, "the name . . . being given to the usher by the President, that functionary shows in the gratified applicant who may have been cooling his heels outside for five minutes or five days."[136]

Imagine the scenario: Perhaps after vigorous congratulations on the president's election and prayers for a speedy end to the war, Lloyd told the president what he needed and why: A pass to go south because Lloyd was a publisher and well acquainted with all the railroad executives and business owners throughout the Rebel states. He'd done trade with them, placing ads for their establishments and railroad lines all over the south. But alas, with the war, in order to collect the money Lloyd was owed, he must travel south. He must.

"With admirable patience and kindness, Lincoln hears the applicant's request . . . asked a question or two in his quiet but shrewd way . . . and takes a card on which he writes . . ." Using a steel-tipped double-nib pen he dips in gall ink, and in a large scrawl that covered the length of the card, "Please allow the bearer, Mr. William Alvin Lloyd to pass our lines south and return on special business. A. Lincoln, July 13, 1861."[137]

After leaving the White House and stopping quickly to pick up the girl, for they were surely together now, Lloyd went straight back to the depot and boarded a night train, stopping in Cincinnati, then on to Louisville. Yes, Lloyd knew once they were truly south, and after they crossed the lines, he must secrete the pass. Should it be found, it would be most incriminating. Skilled tailor that he was, it is reasonable to assume he fashioned a tiny hidden pocket to conceal the pass.

Thus ticketed, they climb aboard, hurtling into the unknown.

7

The Memphis Caper

THE OHIO RIVER WAS RISING ON THE MORNING OF JULY 15, 1861, AND there was only one steamer from Cincinnati to Louisville, and that was the *Major Anderson,* a new, wooden three-masted bark: A gleaming ship, fresh and new, as was the probable, hasty marriage of Lloyd and his newest victim. Leaving Cincinnati and the free state of Ohio where abolitionists gathered and the Underground Railroad—the tunnels, homes, and churches—provided the way stations to freedom for so many fleeing the slave state of Kentucky, the *Major Anderson* brought Alvin Lloyd home.[138]

The place where he'd sprouted to manhood was no longer the half-savage town, the old jumble of wild men, whiskey, and empty pockets. Their arrival was noted. "W. Alvin Lloyd, the publisher of railroad papers and periodicals . . . passed through this city . . . with his new paramour," the *Louisville Daily Journal* announced.[139] Paramour? Had he married her around July 13, somewhere between Washington City and their brief stop at Cincinnati? It is likely.

At first look, it was obvious that the town's male population was depleted. Thousands had gone away to the Union or Confederate army. Ads were running in the papers for able-bodied men to make up the numbers of this company or that brigade, the pay between eleven and twenty-three dollars per month, board and clothing included. Just go down to the recruiting office on the corner of Shelby and Market, or, if you were interested in joining the Garvin Rifles, go to Lieutenant J. M. Smith's store on Market Street.[140]

The Tiger Rifles, an artillery company of Confederates from Louisiana, were still in town, just having paraded a day or two before, with their caps bearing the prominent initials T.R. "Turn & Run," the Union men, the defamers, said.[141]

As for lodgings for the couple, good ones abounded. The beautiful and just renovated National Hotel was on the corner of Main and Fourth, in the very heart of the downtown business district of Louisville, with its ground floor and four floors of rooms, with horse-drawn streetcars plying by it at all times. One dollar and fifty cents a day.[142]

Or there was the Gulley House, on the north side of Market, between First and Brook. A dollar a night, or three dollars a week.[143]

There was good food, if you could afford it: C. C. Rueffer's St. Charles Restaurant, that week offering their famous young grouse received daily by express, fresh clams, crabs, frogs' legs, squabs, and specialty of the day— young squirrels—all washed down with Mr. Rueffer's celebrated Dayton ale and porter.[144]

And around the corner, at Sixth Street and Court Place, opposite the city courtrooms and open for business day and night, stood a saloon and restaurant owned by Annie Shaw's betrayed husband, George T. Shaw.[145]

But with a new woman on his arm, the Shaws were the least of Lloyd's concerns. Alvin's own father was somewhere around Louisville ministering to the intemperate, warning of the evils of drink—old T. G. Lloyd who'd tossed away his family before he saw sobriety, saw the light.

And Lizzie, the very first Mrs. William Alvin Lloyd, she was there too. And his daughter Belle, and the younger child, Charles W., not yet born when he'd run off to join the minstrels. If Lloyd had seen them when he'd passed through Louisville—his sometime stopping place, no longer his home—there is no record of when, or for how long. If he'd fretted over this, and if the quick stabs of guilt he might have felt pained him, for now—though they would later reappear—his Louisville family must remain a gauzy tableau, frozen in place.

And with warrants out for his bigamous offenses, the police might be tailing him, but, he would likely argue, shouldn't they have better things to do than chasing after a man who rescued women from the drudgery of rolling bandages and pie dough and gave them a great adventure?

But now Lloyd needed to keep moving. Alone. The woman, once a passing pleasure, was seemingly a distraction. He had to focus on his work. His salvation. Or maybe, and this would surely be a great fear, he'd get nothing at all. What if his chief clients, the railroad execs, had become casualties of war and couldn't pay up? Yes, they'd grown fat like Christmas geese from their travel profits, but what if the boon years were over? And the mill owners, what about them? How was business in Georgia and the Carolinas? The great mill states, if they were not faring well, then what? How would Lloyd manage?

The war was changing everything: a devil wind creeping along the banks of the Ohio River, bringing blood and ruin and sure to bring more. And though Lloyd was surely rooting for the Confederacy to smash the Yankees and end it, end it quickly, he and other like-minded partisans prayed that the South would never fall easily, submit to the bluecoat savages, the Lincoln-loving curs. Unlike some Kentuckians—a lot of them in fact—who sided with the Yankees, even as Lincoln was forcing the state to remain in the Union, Lloyd's southern sentiments grew even stronger.

He couldn't help but see the Union flag flying from the Louisville courthouse. A man of his leanings would cheer on secessionist Governor Magoffin as he refused to send militias when "the ape in the White House, the abolitionist," called for them. Magoffin had stood up to Joseph Holt, thought to be Lincoln's pawn when he was sent to his home state of Kentucky to gin up support for the Union. Holt "directly criticized Magoffin for his 'hostile and defiant refusal to send troops to the Union's aid.'" And so this Kentucky son went on the stump for the president and the Union. Lincoln, Holt declared, "has the courage to look traitors in the face."[146]

Had Lloyd been there to hear Holt, he might have slung a bottle at his head. How could slave-holding Kentucky be divided, or worse, at the start of the war, neutral? Kentuckians, many Rebel sympathizers felt, were lily-livered. And now that Union soldiers were flowing into the city, how long would it be before the trains Lloyd rode like a sultan were commandeered by Yankee troops?

Now imagine him moving through the streets past the old familiar sights: the paddle steamers, the showboats painted up like gaudy women, the riverboat pilots with their slick beaver-fur hats and sun-blistered faces; the cardsharps with snub-nosed derringers concealed among the ruffles of their shirts; the farmers in stained denim coveralls hawking their prize pigs and coxcomb roosters. And the slaves, always the slaves, grunting, sweating, hefting barrels of whiskey. Familiar, so familiar to a man who'd grown up there, tired of life there, and left there.

For one night, to please her, then leave her, Lloyd and his lady checked into the Galt House, an elegant three-story sprawl of a building, and the best hotel in town, where some years before the touring literary legend Charles Dickens was inspired to gush that he'd been "lodged as though we had been in Paris." [147] Perfect for honeymooners or lovers.

But with the dawn, on Tuesday, July 16, Lloyd quickly abandoned the lady. As he left for the depot, was he hearing the calliope strains of "My Old Kentucky Home" drifting over the Ohio? Did the old tunes, the memories, choke him, haunt him still? And if they'd wed—with no historical record to support another marriage at this time—he left her behind amid the rubble of his past.

He boarded the Louisville Express to Memphis. Behind him, there was war news: "Federal Forces Routed," the *Daily Democrat* trumpeted on July 16, 1861. Confederate General Benjamin McCullough's twelve thousand men had engaged the Union troops in blue at Springfield, Missouri, killed nine hundred of them, and forced the unconditional surrender of the rest.

Lloyd is traveling now. Beneath frequent and copious showers, the eighteen-hour-and-twenty-minute trip was a trial but faster than taking the riverboat down from Louisville, the 643 miles of the Ohio, then the Mississippi. Sixty hours of rising Big Muddy, whatever river one traveled. But Lloyd's livelihood depended on his arrival farther south, so he made haste.

What Lloyd didn't know, as the train pulled into Memphis late that night, was that the woman he'd abandoned in Louisville had gone to the police, to prominent city detective Dick Moore, and told him of her plight. She'd been deserted. She was ruined. She was alone. Moore asked the girl where Lloyd had gone. Memphis, she said. Lloyd was known to Moore. He had a file on Lloyd.

"Dick Moore has been watching his maneuvers for some time past," the *Daily Courier* of July 17 noted. Indeed, Moore had. He wired ahead to Memphis.

"Arrived at Memphis, July 17th (midnight)," Alvin wrote. It was actually the sixteenth, as will be seen.[148] Thus begins Lloyd's journal entries, part of a summary of his activities in the Confederacy. He did in fact keep a record of his travels, and we can journey with him and read real-time news reports of his adventures, crimes, and misadventures. However, any and all mentions of spying for Lincoln were only added after June of 1865 when, together with his lawyer Enoch Totten, a new summary peppered with spying episodes was created expressly to buttress Lloyd's claim that he had been Lincoln's secret agent and deserved compensation for that service. This summary forms one of the groups of documents pertaining to Lloyd in the National Archives and known as Enclosure 13. As well, there are of record some loose diary pages, some of which met with timely loss, others altered and selected by Lloyd and his lawyer to further "prove" his claim.

Here was Lloyd in Memphis. It had been seven months since he had last pulled the Memphis shift, but as in Louisville, things had changed here in that short time. The Confederate flag flew from rooftops, unfurled and defiant. He was in another country now. Unfamiliar, but very welcome.

Lloyd's arrival in Memphis did not go unnoticed. For once, there was a real Dixie welcome: "Among the arrivals at the Gayoso House . . . was our friend, Mr. Alvin Lloyd, publisher of the *Southern Railroad Guide*," the *Memphis Daily Appeal* reported. "Mr. Lloyd comes directly from New York, from which city he was compelled to leave in consequence of his strong Southern sympathies. We extend to him a cordial welcome to the more congenial society of the South."[149] It is probable that Lloyd told a member of the press—some of whom commonly met the trains and went to the hotels to interview and record the new arrivals in town—the story of how he was "compelled to leave" New York City.

The following morning, waking up in a room at the Gayoso, a guest would feel flush at discovering the gas-lit chandeliers, marble floors, and indoor plumbing. It was raining steadily, the wind was howling, and distinguished guests such as J. E. Davis, the Confederate president's brother, and General Nugent, of New Orleans, at that very moment were checking into Lloyd's hotel.[150]

Lloyd's only pressing business that day was with Ralph C. Brinkley, one of the directors of the Memphis & Charleston Railroad and president of the Memphis & Little Rock Railroad, a little road leading thirty-eight miles out from Hopefield, Tennessee, to Madison, Arkansas. It was a visit well worthwhile—$125 dollars in gold. The rest of that Wednesday was spent planning his next stops.[151]

Finally it was a chance meeting with Joe Davis that inspired Lloyd to spend the morning of the very cloudy and sultry Thursday penning a letter to Joe Davis's brother: "Hon. Jefferson Davis. I hope you will pardon me, an entire stranger, for addressing you, but my love for my country's safe deliverance must be my excuse." In this letter he tells Davis that he had been in Grafton, Virginia, with General McClellan of the Union Army, a couple of weeks earlier and that McClellan had divulged to Lloyd his plans for taking the East Tennessee & Virginia Railroad. "I give you this information gratis," Lloyd wrote. "I think if you have not that section of Virginia fortified, it would be well to attend to it at once, and give him a warm reception." He ends the letter with: "Will be in Richmond a week or so. I would wish to have our army victorious. Your friend, W. Alvin Lloyd."[152]

That afternoon, Lloyd went out to the Memphis & Little Rock Railroad to pick up another one hundred dollars in gold. Then it was on to a meeting with a host of assembled Memphis bigwigs, including Sam Tate and W. J. Ross, president and general superintendent respectively of the Memphis & Charleston. They were all rabid secessionists like Lloyd. And it would be the last carefree night Lloyd would spend in Memphis.

The next morning, Lloyd boarded the six-thirty mail train, bound for another successful money-gathering spree. Things were looking up. A few hours later he arrived at his destination, Grand Junction. Fifty-two miles away, it was the first big station you got to when going east on the Memphis & Charleston Railroad. Then things went horribly wrong. How many times in his life had Lloyd stepped out of a train, only to have police waiting, on the lookout for him?

"You are our prisoner, and must return to Memphis with us." So said the police, at least according to the 1865 testimony of Charles T. Moore, one of the false witnesses called by Totten to depose for Lloyd.[153]

And Alvin Lloyd did return to Memphis on a train that arrived back at one o'clock that very afternoon. Police Captain Hayne Irby Klinck was waiting. And a storm of press was reporting on Lloyd's criminal doings and the real reason for his arrest: The *Louisville Courier* of July 21 and July 22, 1861, carried this:

> *Bigamy. . . . Officers Moore and Sweeney, of this city, received a special dispatch from Memphis, from Captain Klink of the police, announcing the arrest of W.A. Lloyd, who is charged with bigamy. Said Lloyd is formerly of this city and is somewhat notorious in the marrying line. His last villainy was practiced upon the daughter of a merchant in New York. He is also, we learn, under indictment in Columbus, Ohio, for a similar offense. He was arrested at Grand Junction, and taken to Memphis, where he will be held to await a requisition."*

After only four days in the city, here he was—behind bars.

"I paid Capt. Clink and the lawyer (Yerger) one hundred dollars ($100) each and was discharged. Left July 20th." Lloyd would later, much later write in his revised summary that he'd been arrested as a Yankee spy. And he charged the Federal government for his expenses. "Three hundred dollars for amount paid to rebel detectives to discharge me from prison at Memphis, Tenn., in gold. $30 expenses while in prison in Memphis, Tenn., pd in gold."[154] This marvel of a lie, charging the Federal government for money he spent to get rid of the bigamy rap was in its own way, perfect.

Lloyd was told to get out of town and never come back. And so he did, taking the five o'clock slow train to a little town just across the Mississippi line. Officers Moore and Sweeney duly arrived in Memphis to take Lloyd back to Louisville, but the notorious bigamist had fled.

The following morning, in Holly Springs, Lloyd had an interview with E. G. Barney, superintendent of the Mississippi Central Railroad. It was a most distressing meeting. Mr. Barney didn't tell Lloyd this, but he had only recently been alerted to the fact that his visitor was the brother of the notorious J. T. Lloyd who a few years before, in the blackmail rag the *Cincinnati Sun*, had printed vicious lies about not only the railroad but about Mr. Barney himself. So Barney refused to pay. No more Yankee debts being honored. What was worse, Barney started a rumor in Holly

Springs that Lloyd was a Yankee spy and an abolitionist. Lloyd, outraged at the time—and what a cruel joke that was—would later use this accusation to buttress his claim against the government when swearing he'd spied for Lincoln.

But here, in truth, being simply *accused* of spying for Lincoln, when of course he never spied for Lincoln, was not the real peril; there was more afoot, something Lloyd couldn't sweet-talk, deny, beat, shoot, pay or bribe his way out of. Soon there would be no escaping it.

8

Of Actresses and Wives

ON THE MOVE AGAIN AND WITH E. G. BARNEY'S DANGEROUS ALLEGATIONS a few hours behind him, the following evening, Lloyd hopped a train and arrived in Canton, Mississippi, amid a violent storm of thunder, lightning, and strong wind. Canton was the home of Edward D. Frost, the assistant superintendent of Barney's line, a true Confederate, a man much more to Lloyd's liking, and besides, unlike Barney, he bore no personal grudge. It was while Lloyd was with Frost the following day that the news came in of the Union defeat at Manassas, the first significant battle of the war. General Beauregard's men had routed the Union forces on a field studded with mimosa and oak trees and sent them back, in total disarray, tearing though the woods toward Washington City. There was wild celebration in Canton. It seemed possible that the Confederate forces would now invade the capital and win the war. There was jubilation, hope, and more jubilation in this small Mississippi town.

Curiously on that very day, in New York City, a woman named Harriet gave birth to a baby named Ernest P. The father's name on the birth record was William Alvin Lloyd. Lloyd may never have known of this child. Ernest P. Lloyd would die during the Civil War at the age of twenty-two months.[155]

Lloyd left Canton and boarded the New Orleans, Jackson & Great Northern train at 11:50 on the night of Tuesday, July 23, 1861, a 206-mile ride through the night. Thirteen miles down the good track, on the banks of the Pearl, the cars halted for a while at the state capital of Jackson.[156]

While the passengers slept, the train thundered down the dead center of the state past a string of lost and faceless Mississippi towns, villages really, tiny depots, and everywhere the eye could see—in daylight, anyway—the eternal bales of cotton stacked high, cotton everywhere—picked by slaves, thousands of slaves—King Cotton, waiting to be transported, just like the passengers, just like Alvin Lloyd.[157]

The train made a brief stop at the lonely Lawrence County town of Brookhaven, and then crossed into Louisiana, traveling down the narrow length of Tangipahoa Parish, around Lake Pontchartrain, to join the Great Muddy just before the town of Kenner. Twelve hours and ten minutes after leaving Canton, Alvin Lloyd stepped off the train at the railroad's depot at the foot of Calliope where it intersected with Magnolia. "Arrived in New Orleans July 24th," he wrote.[158]

The next morning, far away from the Crescent City, the president of the Confederacy opened the daily mail at his office in Richmond. One letter had possibilities. It was Lloyd's offer to spy for the Confederacy, for Jefferson Davis himself. He passed the correspondence on to his subordinates for further examination. If Davis had been limitlessly privy that day to the national press, he might have reconsidered, for notices of Lloyd's bigamous crimes were appearing in the papers. A *Memphis Appeal* article began with "Bigamy," and quoted in detail the *Louisville Courier*'s account of Lloyd's arrest for bigamy.

The *New York Herald* of that day ran the story, as did the *Tribune*, with the banner "Lloyd the Bigamist Arrested," the *Trib* adding, for those who might be in any doubt about the criminal's identity, "This Lloyd is the Secessionist who made himself notorious by his denunciation of Union men and businessmen in his 'Southern Railroad Guide,' published in this city last year."

Pretty much everyone within a hundred-mile radius of New York City saw this article one way or another on the day it came out. Including wives. The *Herald* and the *Tribune* together had such a deep penetration in New York and surrounding areas that it is difficult to imagine anyone missing a sensational story like this, especially if that someone was related to Lloyd.

As for his teenage wife, Virginia, it is probable that she had been communicating with him. The new Post Office Bill, passed by Congress on March 7, 1851, and effective as from July 1 of that year, had laid down up-to-date, and hopefully more efficient, rules for mail delivery. A post office would now hold a *poste restante* letter for a week, or the most convenient part thereof, and every week would sort out those that had not been collected from the pigeonhole under L for Lloyd. They would then advertise, once, in the newspaper that had the largest circulation in that town, once only, and then, if they hadn't been collected within three months, would then send them to the dead letter office at the main post office in the nation's capital. If you collected a letter at the post office as the result of the ad, then you paid a cent. If you got it out of the dead letter office, it now cost you six cents. The post office bill and summaries thereof appeared with great regularity in the newspapers of the day. In addition, in some papers, one would find in every issue at the top of the "List of Letters" a short explanation of the rules.

Even before the bigamy item, in fact just minutes after Alvin had left Westchester County, Virginia had seemingly dashed off two letters to the "Hon. Wm A. Lloyd, Louisville." The term "Honorable" is a mystery, perhaps a prearranged code or a joke. Alvin never got to read the letters. He'd already moved on to Memphis by the time they arrived in Louisville. The next two letters sent to the Louisville Post Office were addressed to "Wm Alvin Lloyd." Certaintly no longer "Honorable." Had Virginia read the papers? Assuming from the wording in the press that he was a captive in Louisville, she probably figured he'd send out for his mail. But he never got those last two letters either. By then he was in the Deep South. It appears that Virginia sent one more letter, but, like the others, it just languished at the post office until all the uncollected Lloyd mail finally made its way to Washington, DC.

Virginia Lloyd certainly went south, as she would later swear. But in fact, she delayed for a month for unknown reasons. She might well have wondered whether the detectives had truly taken Lloyd to Louisville, as the papers said. Whatever the actual arrangement, remarkably, out of loyalty or some overriding, intense attachment to this man, she would meet him in Clarksville, as will be seen.

Alvin, now in New Orleans, went to see Theodore S. Williams, a Damn Yankee, as a man from the north was called after he had been fourteen years or more in the south.[159]

In spite of that, Williams was a business associate. Knowing that he was going to be spending a lot of time on the New Orleans, Jackson and Great Northern, Alvin needed a free pass, valid until the end of the year, and T. S. gave him one, issued to "W. Alvin Lloyd, Esq., *Lloyd's RR Guide.*" The general superintendent wrote, "This ticket will pass but one person," and then signed "Theodore S. Williams."[160]

And as Alvin moves through time, and we follow him, here is clearly seen just how his spying episodes were concocted in the later summary presented to Federal officials. In New Orleans he wrote: "Remained 4 days. Visited the fortifications and defenses of the city forts at Algiers, where they were building two 'Rams,' Govt boats." He continued, "Had conversations with the most prominent military men." In contrast, his partial and selected diary pages, the ones that were not scrutinized by US authorities, merely said: "Arrived at New Orleans July 25th 1861. Left on Sunday July 28 1861 for Mobile." When preparing this *evidence* at his lawyer Enoch Totten's instruction, there was a clear endgame: The US authorities needed to see again and again how he was buttressing his claim.[161]

Of interest as well, in the loose diary pages—and it is a wonder that his outright lies weren't exposed—are the crossed-out words and dates, mostly to obscure his original entries but in some cases to hide his encounters with other women. Often he is remarkably incautious, but by 1865, he and his lawyer are addressing inconsistencies. For example, he had written another New Orleans arrival date, but it has been partially obliterated. What he had actually first written was the correct arrival date—the 24th. Why he changed it to the 25th is that on that day he met a girl, the eighteen-year-old daughter of a French immigrant of Buffalo, New York. Louise Browner, known as Larry, was visiting with friends in New Orleans.[162]

Alvin had pressing business in Alabama. He and Larry Browner left New Orleans together.

In the old days, they could have gone by steamer between New Orleans and Mobile—simply cut around the gulf—but only the month before all steamer service had been stopped. Short of a swift and determined horse, the only alternative was the train. One of the frustrations in those days was that you couldn't simply transit the short map distance by train, across the southern fringes of Louisiana, Mississippi, and Alabama, hugging the Gulf Coast, straight into Mobile. It had to be the hard way—back up to Jackson, Mississippi, on the line Alvin had come down on, then change to the Southern across to Meridian, and then down on the Mobile & Ohio. Even so, he and Larry Browner made good time.[163]

Again, here are discrepancies: While Alvin's diary says, "Arrived Monday morning July 29/61," the entry in the concocted summary (Enclosure 13) adds "Arrived at Mobile, July 29th, Monday morning. Remained 1 day. Visited the different forts and defenses about the city [as per his alleged contract with Lincoln] and conversed with the prominent men of the place."[164]

And of course a man on the move needs railroad passes. While he was in town, Alvin managed to secure one from J. H. Parkes, superintendent of the M & O, who that day issued a free pass to "Wm Alvin Lloyd, Publisher *RR Guide*." It was valid until the end of 1861. "Left Mobile for Montgomery, Ala., on Monday afternoon, July 29th," Alvin writes.[165]

He left Mobile by steamer, but he wasn't going south into the Gulf, of course. From Mobile you could voyage upriver on either the Tombigbee due north, or the Alabama to the northeast. The Alabama would take you to Selma, and on from there to Montgomery.

"Left for Atlanta, Ga., Saturday, August 3rd."[166]

Montgomery through Opelika to West Point on the banks of the Chattahoochee was a railroad trip of eighty-eight miles on the Montgomery & West Point Railroad, which took five hours. Of all the roads to the south and west of Charlotte, North Carolina, this one was the only standard-gauge four-foot, eight-and-one-half-inch line in a network of what were otherwise all five-foot gauges. That meant two things. One, you had to get out at West Point and change, which wasn't so serious. The other, which was hugely damaging to the Confederacy, was that they couldn't maintain a smooth run at this vital crossroads. It was a situation similar to one north of Charlotte, where the North Carolina Railroad ran on standard gauge while Virginia ran on the five-foot gauge.[167] At West Point, then, a traveler made the change to the Atlanta & West Point Railroad for the eighty-seven-mile, four-and-a-half-hour trip into Atlanta.[168]

More contradictions: "Arrived in Atlanta, August 3rd, at Chattanooga, August 3rd, at Knoxville, August 4th, Sunday." A small detail, but worthy of note. An obfuscation—another woman is in the picture.

"Arrived at Atlanta (Ga.) August 3rd. Left the same night. Arrived at Knoxville (Tenn.), August 4th, Sunday." He has omitted Chattanooga. By the time Alvin and his lawyer came to convert his diary into the summary Chattanooga has been deleted. It simply disappears. But there is a reason for this. Larry Browner.[169]

Alvin's 1865 receipts and expenses list says: "Miss Larry Browner of Buffalo N.Y. loaned her $44 to get home. Loaned Larry Browner $44 August 3rd 1861 at Chattanooga, Tenn. She was going back to Buffalo, N.Y." This date, August 3rd, has been written over July 25th, which has been crossed out.[170] While Miss Browner left Chattanooga, Alvin took the train to Knoxville.[171]

But why go to all this trouble over a diary entry? Back then Alvin was still a vigorous man, answering to no one. But in 1865 he was a cripple, old at forty-three, and he needed his wife Virginia, an odd thing for him, but still, one he would have recognized. Virginia would have been well aware of the items in Enclosure 13, as she would have studied them with Alvin and his lawyer in 1865. So there was no need for Alvin to mention Larry Browner and his interlude with her.

In a later testimony, Alphabetical Boyd claimed that Lloyd had been "drifting about in Tennessee" during the months of August and September of 1861. But drifting about was not Alvin's style, it is not the way he functioned. What he was doing, in fact, was collecting monies and putting together his *Railroad Guide*, and moving from town to town like a well-oiled clockwork mechanism. His life revolved around railroad schedules.[172]

Lloyd arrived in Knoxville. Four years later, he would write for the US government's eyes: "conversed with the RR men and others. Campbell Wallace and some others started a report that I was a spy." Wallace was president of the East Tennessee & Georgia Railroad. Alvin makes no mention of Wallace in his diary, let alone why that dignitary should spread such a rumor. These crucial entries, this strategy of Totten's to underscore the suspicion that Alvin was indeed a Union spy, is calculated, and well calculated.[173]

He left "Knoxville for Mossy Creek, the residence of Mr. Jno. Branner, President of the E Tenn & Va RR. Saw Mr. Branner sick in bed. Returned to Knoxville, August 5th." The distance between Knoxville and Mossy Creek was twenty-nine miles—on Mr. Branner's own railroad.[174]

John Roper Branner, a banker by trade, and president of the East Tennessee & Virginia since January 20, 1861, was very much a Knoxville figure, and a secessionist. Lloyd returned to Knoxville, which seems an odd thing to do, given what Campbell Wallace's rumor might have caused.

Now to ordinary business: "Left August 6th. Arrived at Lynchburg August 7th. Remained 1 day. Had a long confidential conversation with Jno. Robin McDaniel and other gentlemen." John Robin McDaniel, born in Lynchburg fifty-four years earlier, was not only one of the most successful and revered businessmen in Lynchburg, he was also the Grand Master of Masons in Virginia. Alvin continues: "Presented my bill to the president of the Va. and Tenn. RR, Robt L. Owen, for payment, which was refused until Jno. R. McDaniel, who had been president of the road, stated it was correct, and ought to be paid. The company then paid me a portion of it only. Left August 8th."

Alvin's receipts page says, "August 8th. Lynchburg, Va. Va. & Tenn. RR—$300." This was in gold.[175]

But according to his diary: "Arrived August 9th a.m. Left for Knoxville August 13th/61."[176]

And Lloyd's summary (Enclosure 13), states, "Arrived at Richmond August 9th, and remained 4 days. Visited the fortifications, etc, in the city. Called to see the President, but could not see him. Saw his nephew, Col. Joe Davis, at the door." This was Joseph Robert Davis, the son of Isaac Davis, then aged thirty-six and aide to his uncle. "No admittance to Jefferson Davis, I was informed. Genl Winder's detectives were on the watch for me, and had me under observation. During my stay in Richmond, one of the detectives came in the dining room of the Exchange Hotel, and went behind the screen near the kitchen, and took a photograph of me while I was eating dinner. Left August 13th."[177]

Because Alvin related the particulars of the entire Winder episode for obvious effect, again to underscore the growing concerns that he was a

Union operative, in fact, he must have at times looked oddly out of place. Wandering? Hanging about a railway station, a man on the move, looking for his next conquest? But whatever caught the eye of Winder's detectives it is true that General John H. Winder was suspicious of any passing stranger. This West Point man and dubious hero of the Mexican War, a recently promoted Confederate brigadier general, and even more recently, inspector general of posts, was a self-important and tyrannical man feared not only by northerners in Richmond but by his own people as well. His band of "plug uglies," fellow Maryland thugs-turned-detectives, randomly arrested and imprisoned people whose guilt or innocence, in some cases, was never proven. In fact, a few months later, Timothy Webster—a Pinkerton detective embedded in Richmond and at the time a trusted courier of John H. Winder's, a skilled spy who traveled back and forth across the lines with communications from Winder to his family—then, "reported [in person or in writing] to Pinkerton, who in turn, submitted detailed reports to General George McClellan."[178]

But Webster was exposed when two of Pinkerton's operatives, Pryce Lewis and John Scully, were sent through the lines to Richmond in search of Webster, who'd been out of touch. Scully and Lewis were recognized as Union detectives when they were visiting an ailing Webster. All were arrested, threatened with hanging. Lewis and Scully were spared execution when they outed Webster, admitting they were all indeed Pinkerton men. An enraged Winder vowed to make an example of Timothy Webster. Even as President Lincoln and Detective Pinkerton petitioned for Webster's release, he was tried and hanged on April 29, 1862.

Winder's reign of brutality continued. By the end of the Civil War, his notoriety as "Hog Winder," the man who ran Andersonville Prison along the lines of a death camp, would have gotten him hanged as a war criminal had he not died of a heart attack at Florence, South Carolina, the site of his last prison, late in the night of February 6, 1865.[179]

And here is Alvin, out of Richmond and harm's way as he continues his journey. And in the summary, Enclosure 13: "Arrived at Knoxville August 14th. Remained 2 days. Conversed with several military men and RR men." But in the diary: "Arrived August 14th." (Of course, there is no mention of conversing with military men.)

His receipts page for Thursday, August 15, has, "East T & Va. RR—$200." However, in a transcription of his receipts page, he has padded the expense and puts three hundred dollars. Either way, he seems to have picked up some much-needed money in Knoxville.[180]

Diary: "Left for Chattanooga & New Orleans, August 16th/61. Arrived at Chattanooga August 16th/61. Left for New Orleans August 17th. Arrived at Nashville August 18/61."

In contrast, in Enclosure 13, noting his spying episodes: "Left August 16th. Arrived at Chattanooga night of August 16th. Left August 17th a.m. Arrived at Nashville August 18th. Remained 1 day. Saw several prominent citizens and RR men, and conversed with them about the feelings of the people in reference to the war and dissolution, etc."

W. Alvin Lloyd usually made a splash in the papers when he arrived in the Crescent City. But not this time. Not even a mention. He was keeping a low profile. There was an actress living there, whom he had met on his last trip, just before he'd met Larry Browner.

As for spying for Lincoln, in the concocted summary Lloyd says, "Remained 10 days. Visited the forts, defenses, etc. Had a room downtown, near the Parish Prison. A colored woman kept the house."[181]

Why did this peripatetic man linger ten days in New Orleans?

Back on January 31, 1861, the *New Orleans True Delta* had run a small item: "Mobile is rejoicing in the advent of a new 'star,' Mrs. Annie L. Taylor [also known as Miss Annie Taylor], a well-known lady of that city, said to be accomplished, talented, and beautiful. She made a successful debut not long since, and is to be complimented by a benefit in which the first citizens lend a ready hand. Send her along, for the stage needs ladies of untarnished reputation, accomplishment, talent and beauty."

Naturally, with his penchant for all things theatrical, Alvin caught Annie in his sights very early into his New Orleans visit. He should have stayed away from the young actress. For him, it was just another pretty conquest. There was no way he could have known that this beautiful young woman would imperil his life.

Alvin left for Mobile on Sunday, September 16. He hadn't actually forgotten his rendezvous with Virginia up in Clarksville, but first he had to take Miss Taylor home to Mobile.

Enclosure 13: "Left Sept 1st/61."

As usual, and according to his 1865 summary, he would say he was spying there. "Arrived at Mobile Sept. 2nd, daylight. Remained 1 (one) day. Visited the new fortifications, defenses, etc. Took drawings of the same."[182]

He stayed in Mobile only long enough to spend the night, and then he was on the cars again, heading for Clarksville, Tennessee. In her November 15, 1872, deposition before the United States Court of Claims, Alvin's wife Virginia was asked this question by her counsel: "Did you follow soon after?" meaning soon after Lloyd left Washington in July 1861. She replied, "Yes, Sir."

By alarming contrast, in her July 18, 1865, deposition, Virginia deposes and swears that "on or about the 15th of September 1861 she was in the city of New York and . . . was informed that her husband was imprisoned as a spy in Memphis, Tenn., by the Rebels."[183]

Yes, Alvin was indeed imprisoned in Memphis, just as Virginia says, but it was only for one night. And it certainly wasn't for spying, as she knew well. It was for bigamy. Alvin was only imprisoned in Memphis overnight, and he was out by July 21, 1861. That was the only jail time he ever served in Memphis in his life: one night's worth. His next incarceration would not be until the end of that year. So, when Virginia says she was informed that her husband was imprisoned as a spy in Memphis, the truth is very different.

"She immediately made preparations to go to her husband." Finally, several days later, she "started for Memphis, Tenn., in the latter part of September 1861." She was not traveling alone. She had a retinue—Clarence, her son, aged not even two yet; and Nellie Dooley, the maid, who, in her June 3, 1865, deposition, would swear "that she was with Mr. and Mrs. Lloyd all the time Mrs. Lloyd was in the Southern States, except about nine months when they were in Savannah, Ga."[184]

Virginia continues "that she had in her possession when she started more than the sum of twelve hundred dollars, and that she had left when she reached him twelve hundred dollars in gold which she turned over to her husband immediately after joining him."[185]

The truth is, Virginia, Clarence, and Nellie the maid arrived in Clarksville as arranged on September 1, 1861. It was not as Virginia would claim in her deposition of June 3, 1865: "on or around the 1st of October 1861."[186]

By the time of her 1872 deposition, she had forgotten the name of the place: "At some little town in Tennessee, but I do not now recollect the name." Clarksville is—and was then—on the main rail line from Louisville to Memphis.[187] Clarksville was the county seat of Montgomery County right up on the Kentucky line. In fact it was the first town you came to in Dixie proper if you were traveling by rail from Louisville toward Memphis. Both town and county had voted unanimously to join the Confederacy. However, Clarksville wasn't as little and forgettable as Virginia made out. There were twenty thousand people living there at that time. There was virulent anti-Lincoln sentiment in the city, not to mention ridiculous humor; for example: "We have been reliably informed that Old Abe, the Kangaroo President, is the bastard son of a man by the name of Cisney."[188]

J. S. Neblett and J. A. Grant, the publishers and proprietors, printed the *Clarksville Chronicle* once a week on Fridays. The paper of October 11 had a list of letters waiting at Clarksville. One of them was for W. A. Lloyd, which indicates that he had been there.

Of course, having joined him in Clarksville, Virginia found he was no longer imprisoned. So the entire rigorous and dangerous journey made so impulsively and generously from New York to Dixie—for her, the little boy, and the maid—may well have been for nothing. Or perhaps she knew all along.

At night on the fourth of September, according to Alvin's concocted testimony, he arrived at Nashville, Tennessee, where he claimed he "was arrested in the cars as an abolitionist by a guard and a major on a telegraphic dispatch from the agent of the M & O RR at Corinth (Miss.). He is the son-in-law of the proprietor of the eatinghouse at that point. I had a lady in charge going north at the time. The guard went with me to Nashville, where my baggage was searched thoroughly, and nothing being found to detain me, we were set at liberty, but watched."[189]

In his June 3, 1865, deposition, Alvin would claim to have been "confined in prison for several weeks in Nashville and in Memphis," although he gives no dates. Of course, he cannot, as these weeks of incarceration never existed. However, on his 1865 expense claim, he itemizes both stints behind bars, the Memphis one in considerable detail. All he says for the term in Nashville is: "Sept. 1861. $75. Expenses while imprisoned in Nashville, Tenn., pd in gold."[190]

No other Nashville imprisonment is presented on his expense sheet, and if there had been another one, he would have listed it there to gain sympathy from US officials.

But now, there is evidence of yet another woman:

Diary: "Left for Clarksville Sept 5th. Arrived same evening."

Concoction: "Left Sept 5th. Took the lady, Miss Eliza J. Miller to the cars going to Louisville, Ky, at Junction. She went North to her friends." What this means is that, going north from Nashville on the Nashville to Louisville line for ten miles, they came to Edgefield Junction, from where Miss Miller continued the 173 miles farther on to Louisville, while Alvin got off and changed to the Edgefield & Kentucky Railroad—the road that connected Nashville with western Kentucky—for the short, 37-mile trip as far as Guthrie, on the Kentucky state line, and then caught the Louisville to Memphis train from Guthrie for the 19-mile ride to Clarksville. "Arrived in Clarksville, Tenn, Sept 5th, same evening."[191]

Meanwhile, in Mobile, Annie Taylor had received some wonderful news. Walter Keeble, the actor-manager, was putting together a troupe called the Southern Star Company. Annie had been picked as the leading ingénue. It was a five-week residence at the Nashville Theatre, opening night September 23, with "The Gamester," followed by an interval of music, and to conclude with the farce, "Urgent Private Affairs." And Nashville was so close to Clarksville. So she must have immediately dashed off a letter to Alvin, care of the post office in Clarksville.

Although Alvin doesn't say so in any of his 1865 evidence or depositions, he was now traveling with Virginia, Clarence, and Nellie. The quartet took the same route Alvin had taken a few days before, but in reverse—first to Guthrie on the Memphis to Louisville, then from Guthrie down to Edgefield Junction on the Edgefield & Kentucky, and finally into Nashville on the Louisville & Nashville.

On they went:

Diary: "Left Nashville for Knoxville Sept 9th. Arrived 10th."

Enclosure 13: "Left Nashville on Sept 9th. Arrived at Knoxville Sept 10th. Visited round the place, camps, etc." This rather weak entry is supposed to support Lloyd's spying claim.

Now Virginia, the maid, and child were to take the cars south, to Augusta, to stay with Virginia's friends or relations. It is not of record with whom Virginia stayed, but as she was there often, it would certainly have been a close connection. Alvin was to stay in Richmond. One thing he did while there was write a letter. It is dated September 14:

To His Excellency, Jefferson Davis. Pardon the seeming boldness, in me, a stranger, for addressing you these few lines [perhaps he had forgotten that he had written Davis on July 18, while in Memphis, or maybe he figured that letter had never reached its destination]. If you have any place or position to give a Kentuckian, either in the army or bearer of dispatches, I am willing to serve you. I have lost all my type, office, etc., in New York, where I removed to, Office of "Lloyd's Southern Steamboat & R Road Guide", from New Orleans two and a half years since. I was driven from New York for writing for the South and against abolitionism in my Guide, on the night of July 4th. I presume Your Excellency has read the accounts of the affair. [There were no accounts of the "affair" other than the single mention in the Memphis paper told by Alvin.] Hoping, Sir, I have not obtruded too much upon your patience, knowing how many similar calls you have made to you. If you should have any use for me in any way that I am competent to fill, I will call upon you or your secretary and show you who I am. Very truly your friend, W. Alvin Lloyd, Publisher, Lloyd's S St Bt & RR Guide. Richmond, Sept. 14th/61. I do not know, Your Excellency, whether this is the proper mode to make known to you my wishes or not, as I have never been an office seeker. Very truly, your friend, W. Alvin Lloyd.

There is also a Davis endorsement, meaning he would have seen the letter and passed it on:

Referred to the Postmaster Genl for his consideration, with a view to further conference. [signed] J.D. [Jefferson Davis.][192]

On Tuesday, September 17, 1861, Alvin wrote to Davis again:

To His Excellency, Jefferson Davis. I presented the enclosed (your order) to Mr. Clements yesterday morning as I could not procure an interview with Judge Reagan [John H. Reagan, the Postmaster General], and was informed that there were no vacancies in the Dept—excepting as special mail agents in Louisiana, etc., and there was no one had power excepting Your Excellency to appoint one, as there were only seven special mail agents in the Eleven States [special mail agents accompanied mail on steamers and in railroad cars. They would later be known as couriers]. I regret it indeed as I am out of means sufficient to start the publication of my Guide at present, as everything has been taken from me in New York. If your Excellency has an appointment either in the army or the Post Office Dept., I would be glad to have the position. If not, I will not further annoy Your Excellency, knowing you must be annoyed by such request daily. Wishing you speedy recovery of health and a long and prosperous life. I am your friend, W. Alvin Lloyd. Richmond, Sept. 17/61.[193]

The same day he wrote this letter to Davis, on September 17, Alvin left Richmond.

The Richmond *Whig* published a very brief article on the eighteenth, mentioning that Lloyd had been there. Alvin arrived at Norfolk the same day he left Richmond, Tuesday, September 17, 1861, and remained there two days.

The two days in Norfolk are of interest:

Diary: "Visited Crany [*sic*] Island, etc, at Norfolk."

Enclosure 13/summary: "Remained 2 days. Visited Crany [*sic*] Island, fortifications, camps, etc, etc. Met T.H.S. Boyd at Norfolk."

Alphabetical Boyd arrived in Norfolk on or around August 1, at least according to him. He says he waited in that town for sixty to ninety days before Lloyd showed up, which would have made it October or November that Alvin arrived. Yet here we have Lloyd arriving in Norfolk on September 17, within forty-eight days of Alphabetical's arrival there—not sixty or ninety. Clearly this was added in 1865.

This short visit was the only one Lloyd made to Norfolk in 1861, according to him. So, Alphabetical Boyd's memory of Norfolk in 1861 must be regarded with strong suspicion. Alphabetical tells of spending two weeks with Lloyd there, spying, of course, whereas Alvin claimed to have been there only two days. Boyd is very specific:

> *I remained in Norfolk with Lloyd about two weeks, and was engaged in visiting the different fortifications and batteries on both sides of the Elizabeth and Nansemond Rivers, and the camps and fortifications adjacent to Norfolk and Portsmouth. Drew a map of the harbor and batteries on each side, and the number of troops then under the command of General Huger [Benjamin Huger]. The map was taken charge of by Mr. Lloyd and sent to Mr. Lincoln. The map went to Mr. Lincoln by a man who was an engineer on a transport between Norfolk and Craney Island. He went in a boat to Fortress Monroe. Lloyd left Norfolk for Savannah about the latter part of November 1861.[194]*

That Lloyd was in Norfolk seems not to be a question. He had in his possession two passes to visit Norfolk. In his December 19, 1861, letter to Confederate Secretary of State Judah Benjamin, Colonel Rockwell (Alvin's captor in Savannah) would write: "He had in possession two passes from the War Department, one, I think, to visit Norfolk, and he acknowledged to me that he had been to Craney Island."[195]

Meanwhile, T.H.S. Boyd was still on Captain Nelligan's roll in the Confederate army for the months of November and December, on detached service as a clerk in the regiment's commissary department—still a private. He was mustered out on December 11, and that surely signifies that he was present. The commissary department was responsible for feeding the Army, and, of course, each regiment had its commissary department, headed by the commissary. According to Boyd's 1907 obituary, he was made his regimental commissary.[196] Most importantly, Boyd was clearly and of record a Confederate soldier.

Alvin left Norfolk on Thursday, September 19, 1861, to return to Richmond, arriving there the same day, at 8:00 p.m., and remained there five days. "Endeavored to see Jefferson Davis the first day, but without success." This was to follow up on his letters to the president of the fourteenth and the seventeenth, inquiring after a government post. Alvin writes that he "did see him on Sept. 23rd." Jefferson Davis, that is. "Had a conversation with him about giving me an office or position under his Government. He declined, etc, etc. Was accosted by a detective by the name of [he rather inconveniently leaves out the name, substituting a dash] and sounded as to where I resided, occupation, etc. He stated he was a stranger in the city, etc."[197]

Alvin left Richmond on September 25, headed for New Orleans. We know New Orleans was his destination, for General Winder tells us so in a later communication. It took Alvin quite a while to get from Richmond to New Orleans, as he had stops to make along the way. It wouldn't be until November 7 that he arrived in the Crescent City. En route, he "arrived in Knoxville Sept. 26th. Remained 4 days. Endeavored to see Brannan [sic], but could not do so with safety." Branner, judging from his 1865 letter, seems never to have been aware that Alvin was in town.[198]

By contrast, "Left Knoxville for Nashville and New Orleans, Octr 2d/61." In other words, on October 1 he was not in Clarksville, as Virginia claimed, but in Knoxville, two hundred miles away. To get from Knoxville to Nashville was not as easy as it is today. One had to take the East Tennessee & Georgia line down to Chattanooga, 120 miles, and then change to the Nashville & Chattanooga, then 150 miles up to Nashville. A long, tedious trip.[199]

At this point, Alvin's 1861 diary (i.e., the extrapolated pages) comes to an end, and from that point on, his prepared summary with added spying episodes remains.

"Arrived in Nashville Oct. 3rd/61."[200]

In Nashville, the *Daily Patriot*'s amusements column advertised the play *The Serious Family*, concluding with "Kiss in the Dark" and "The Secret." There, in a list of the performers, was "Miss Taylor."[201]

Lloyd "Remained 14 days, visiting fortifications, camps, etc, etc."

Annie Taylor was now performing acting roles as well. Prior to September 26, she was merely a star vocalist. That night she had stepped into her new costume for the benefit of the Tennessee Volunteers. Two nights later she had scored a hit with her rendition of "Trust to Luck" in the play *Rough Diamond.* The *Nashville Daily Patriot* advertised, "Admission to suit the times: Parquette and dress circle, 50 cts; Gallery, 25 cts; Colored Gallery, 25 cts; Colored boxes, 50 cts; Box office open from 10 to 12, and 2 to 4 o'clock. Commences at 7½ o'clock precisely. No extra charge for reserve seats."[202]

The following night, the fourth of October, she had a star singing turn in *The Merry Monarch* and Saturday night she was in *How to Rule a Wife* and *The Maniac Lover.* She played in Nashville again on the following Monday, Tuesday, and Wednesday, and on Thursday, October 10, the *Nashville Patriot* ran this item: "Miss Annie Taylor has only to study and become entirely accustomed to the business of the stage, to be emphatically 'The Star of the South.' She has chosen the profession from ambition alone, and with appreciation, will create a sensation unequalled since the time of Mrs. Mowatt. Alabama may well be proud of her gifted daughter."[203]

Annie Taylor's career was afire in Nashville. Alvin, who could publish from any town that had a suitable press, decided on Nashville to settle down. At least that was the thought he had as he went to visit the *Patriot's* editor, who reported: "*Lloyd's Steamboat and Railroad Guide.* This interesting and very valuable periodical, which has been published in New York for some years, will, we learn, hereafter be published here. So soon as our difficulties culminated, Mr. Lloyd removed South, and has identified himself with the cause of our glorious Confederation."[204]

However, even as the press plaudits were ringing in her ears, Annie Taylor's career came to a sudden and heavy-handed end. Alvin it seems had forbidden her to appear on the stage anymore. No proper woman of his was going to be an actress. And she went along with it, and him.[205]

Saturday, October 12, 1861, was Miss Annie Taylor's farewell performance. "The admirers of the drama in this city have come to regard Miss Taylor as a lady of great promise and universally regret her determination to abandon a sphere in which she could shine so brilliantly," mourned the *Patriot.*[206]

Alvin Lloyd and Annie Taylor left Nashville on Thursday, October 17, 1861. Virginia Lloyd, when asked in 1872 about Alvin's movements—"After he left there, then where did he go?"—replied, "He went to Savannah, Ga." She may not have known the truth.[207]

But Savannah was a couple of months away yet. Virginia fails to mention any of the towns in between Nashville and Savannah, some of which would be the venues of extraordinary events in the life of William Alvin Lloyd. But, that's because Virginia didn't accompany Lloyd on this part of his trip. Annie Taylor did.

"Arrived at Atlanta Oct. 18th. Left Oct. 18th." The following day, Saturday, saw Alvin and Annie arrive in Montgomery, where he "remained four and a half days." He picked up twenty-five dollars in gold from the Exchange Hotel in Montgomery, owned by Watt, Lanier & Co. That was for advertising money in advance for the next issue of the guide, whenever that might be.[208]

On the morning of Wednesday, October 23, 1861, Alvin Lloyd left Montgomery on the Alabama & Florida Railroad. One hundred and sixteen miles of dead straight road to the state line where Alabama meets Florida at the Escambia River, and then, still on the same train, following the course of the river down the remaining forty-five miles into Pensacola, arriving there later that same day and checking in to a hotel for a good night's sleep. That sleep was necessary, as it turned out, for the following day in Pensacola would be rather busy. "Remained 1 day. Visited the fortifications, etc. Was arrested by order of the provost marshal. Discharged. No proof against me." In addition to all this activity, he picked up twenty-five dollars in gold from the Alabama & Florida Railroad Company. This alleged arrest, is of course, not of record.[209]

That evening Alvin and Annie left Pensacola and the following morning were back in Montgomery. On Saturday, October 26, 1861, they left Montgomery, bound for Selma. "Remained 2 days. Conversed with RR men, citizens, etc." Of course, Alvin never mentions his traveling companion.[210]

The two of them left Selma on the twenty-ninth, and arrived back in Annie Taylor's hometown, Mobile, on Wednesday, October 30, 1861. And Enclosure 13 alludes to spying when he was really on a romantic getaway. "Remained three days, visiting camps, etc."[211]

They left Mobile on Sunday, November 3, 1861, heading north on the Mobile & Ohio to Meridian, Mississippi. In Alvin's coat pocket was a receipted hotel bill for the board of "Mr. W.A. Lloyd and Lady." He was still traveling with that lady, Annie. At Meridian the couple caught the Southern across the state, through Jackson, to the Mississippi River.[212]

"Arrived at Vicksburg (Miss.) Nov. 4th. Remained 2 days, visiting defenses, etc." Remembering that all of Lloyd's supposed visits to defenses and fortifications are sheer fiction, not to mention the repeated assertions that he was spying, is astounding, to say the least. On November 6 Lloyd was issued a free ticket on the Southern Railroad to "pass Mr W.A. Lloyd over Southern RR." Perhaps more important, he had also appeared earlier that morning before a Vicksburg justice of the peace and married Annie Taylor. As the Warren County, Mississippi, marriage records repeat, "William A. Lloyd and Annie S. [*sic*] Taylor, Nov. 6, 1861."[213]

"Left Vicksburg for New Orleans, Nov. 6th," Alvin writes, omitting his new wife. But Alvin didn't immediately avail himself of the free Southern Railroad ticket he had received in Vicksburg. He'd changed his mind, or had had it changed for him. Mr. and Mrs. Lloyd decided to take the southbound steamboat, and later that evening pulled into a sleepy hamlet close to where the Red River comes out into the Mississippi. Then they took a coach the few miles over into Avoyelles Parish, in Louisiana, where he again married Annie. "Nov. 6. William A. Lloyd and Mrs Annie L. Taylor," the Avoyelles Parish marriage record states.[214]

Hardly pausing to stop, certainly not for a honeymoon in rural Louisiana, they hopped another steamer and late that following bright and pleasant day came to the end of their whirlwind cruise. What better to do on a protracted honeymoon, but spy. Again and again. "Arrived at New Orleans, Nov. 7th. Remained 4 days, visiting defenses, building Rams at Algiers, etc, etc."[215]

There was a third marriage between Annie and Alvin—"Orleans Parish, La. Saturday, Nov. 9, 1861. W. Alvin Lloyd and Annie L. Widow Taylor." Although Alvin fails to mention this event, it can be seen to this day in the New Orleans marriage register index. However, this index is, at least in this case, an illusion. It does not record an actual marriage between Alvin and Annie; rather Alvin's taking out of a license to marry Annie. A big difference. If a marriage license applicant did not have a fixed abode in Orleans Parish, then he had to pay a five-hundred-dollar bond. He then had three weeks in which to get married, and to bring or send proof of that marriage to the registry. Failure to comply cost him the bond. Although there is no record of the marriage itself, it is hard to imagine Alvin forfeiting such a huge sum, so, probably, within a few days, possibly even on the same day, they married somewhere close by.[216]

On Monday, November 11, 1861, W. Alvin Lloyd left New Orleans with Annie. "Arrived at Mobile Nov. 13th. Left same evening on steamer *Jeff. Davis.*"[217]

"Arrived at Selma Nov. 15th. Thanksgiving Day. Remained 3 days" in Selma.[218]

Alvin was in Selma on November 16, for that was the Saturday Thomas H. Millington, general superintendent of the Ala. & Tenn. River Railroad Co., issued a free pass for "W. Alvin Lloyd, Esq., Pub. *Southern RR Guide*," valid until January 1, 1863. From Mr. Millington he also received fifty dollars for an ad in the planned January 1862 edition of the *Railroad Guide*.[219]

He left Selma on the eighteenth, and the following day was back in Montgomery, where he "remained nine days." On Sunday, the twenty-fourth, he collected fifty dollars in gold from the Montgomery & West Point Railroad Co., and then, on Thursday, November 28, 1861, left town, arriving in Atlanta the same day.[220]

In Atlanta, Alvin "remained six days, visiting camps, etc." His second day there he collected one hundred dollars in gold from the Atlanta & West Point Railroad Co., and the day after that fifty dollars from the Western & Atlantic Railroad Co.[221]

On Wednesday, December 4, Alvin left Atlanta bound for Macon. "Arrived same day at 7.30 p.m. Remained 1 day, conversing with RR men, etc." During his short stay there he managed to collect one hundred dollars in gold from the Macon & Western Railroad Co.[222]

"Arrived at Columbus, Ga., Dec. 6th, at 7.15 p.m." The South-Western Railroad passenger train would leave Macon at 1:30 a.m. and arrive at Columbus at 7:13 a.m. [223]

In Columbus, he "remained 4 days, visiting manufactories, camps, etc."[224]

On Tuesday, the tenth, Alvin left Columbus bound for Savannah, Georgia, where, the next day, he and Annie checked into the upstairs room at the Gibbons House Hotel. There W. Alvin Lloyd's fate awaited him at the hard hand of a Confederate colonel, a powerful Mason, puritanical and punitive, an enemy in gray.[225]

9

He Said He Would Hang Me

ON A DARKENED STAGE ALREADY SET FOR THEIR ENTRANCE, ALVIN AND Annie Taylor Lloyd arrived in Savannah, a place he thought he knew well. But in December 1861 after a mere eight months of hostilities, Savannah was struggling for life, strangled by the "anaconda of war," General Winfield Scott's "blockade of the ports of the secession states." The great snake was already cutting off cotton sales to Europe and ending the sway and profits of both rice and cotton, depriving the southern economy of war funds needed before the real carnage began. [226]

Now federal ships prowled the waters around Charleston and Savannah. And groups like the Savannah Vigilance Committee—vowing to root out "spies against and traitors to the South . . . who are residing among us"—prowled the city. "So cunningly and cautiously . . . have they [spies] carried out their plans that detection has been impossible." Police posses combed Savannah not just on the hunt for spies, but for escaped slaves. [227]

In the restive city, fearing a northern invasion and slave insurrections, masters blamed "rumors of liberation on house negroes, and the election of Lincoln." And already-cruel practices to slaves intensified. Even "free people of color" found themselves under threat. But Joe Bryan was still touting his merchandise in Market Square, without much luck: "Prime girl, 12 years old, country raised"; and "Other middle aged and old Negroes"; and "Boy, 10 years old, smart and likely." Bob Erwin's cook Susannah had escaped in August, and Bob was now offering one hundred dollars to anyone who would bring her back. If a slave fled through the low country, "Shotgun toting white men ventured into the swamps and quickly retrieved the fugitives." [228]

There were fewer establishments where visitors could dine or stay. Mr. Chick's Pavilion House had opened up as a hostelry a year before. There was the Marshall House, of course, and the recently renovated City Hotel, on Bay Street, at two dollars a day, or ten dollars a week. Mr. McAllister ran the Athens Hotel, at half the price the City charged, and got twice as many customers, of half the caliber. There was the Planter's, and underneath it was George Gemenden's Oyster & Refreshment Saloon.

And there was the Gibbons House. Alvin Lloyd chose it for himself and his newest wife. A place "now open to the traveling public. Having completed accommodation for 20 persons more, I will take a few more regular boarders. L.B. Morse, Proprietor." It was a fateful selection.[229]

Once settled with Annie in their lodgings, Alvin Lloyd got a free railroad pass from George W. Adams, general superintendent of the Central Georgia Railroad, valid until January 1, 1863. He also received two hundred dollars in gold from the same company for an ad to be placed in the upcoming January 1862 edition of the *Southern Steamboat & Railroad Guide*. All good news for Alvin, except that a tumble of circumstances, half-truths, and great misunderstandings were descending like thick sea fog all around him. There was little time left for Alvin Lloyd of old, for life as he knew it, the manic days of cheating, dashing, wooing, and conquering, was fast coming to an end.

It began with a seemingly unrelated event that occurred just up the coast, in Charleston, the night of Thursday, December 12. About ten o'clock alarms had sounded calling the citizens to quell a fire at Russell & Co.'s Sash & Blind Factory. An hour later, the flames had taken hold and were spreading throughout the city. In the subsequent extent and rapidity of its ruinous sweep, the great fire would compare with the most terrible conflagrations that ever visited the American continent.[230]

Fires. Flames in Charleston, and in Savannah, no fires but even more paranoia. The *Morning News* carried this item, as did many other southern newspapers:

Some weeks since, there was published in the New York Herald *a full list of our army, its members, officers, and location, a statement which no man in the Confederacy outside of the Departments at Richmond could have furnished. . . . Now it seems that the same paper has the name and full description of every vessel belonging to the Confederacy, privateers and all, with the commanders and the number of men on each. This list too could be furnished by the Departments at Richmond and nowhere else. Thus it is clear we have in some of the most important and confidential positions of our government, right in the very heart of it, spies in the pay of Lincoln.*[231]

The following day was Friday the thirteenth, a lucky day for Alvin. He received fifty dollars in advertising gold from Messrs. Luffburrow & Timmons, partners in the Forrest City Foundry.[232]

However, in 1865 he would claim that on the next day, December 14, he was spying for Lincoln, "visiting camps, Fort Pulaski, etc, etc." Fort Pulaski was at that time defended by the Confederates. It would fall in February to the Union.[233]

And in the same testimony came another item. And this was the truth: "I was arrested upon an affidavit of a Mrs. Elizabeth Morse, whose husband kept the hotel (Gibbons House), as a Yankee spy, and sent with a guard of 4 men and a lieutenant to Oglethorpe Barracks, Lt. Col. Rockwell commanding."[234]

Witness the circumstances of Alvin's arrest:

At this time, the Gibbons House owners, the Morses, were the next-door neighbors of Lieutenant Colonel William Spencer Rockwell, the commander of Oglethorpe Barracks. Rockwell was born in 1809 in Albany, New York. When he was a child his parents moved to Milledgeville, Georgia, where the father became a lawyer. When young W. S. Rockwell finished school, he joined them there in Dixie, marrying in 1837. He followed in his father's professional footsteps, but that wasn't enough of a challenge in this Georgia town. So in addition to his legal work, he became an Egyptologist. What's more, he rose rapidly through the Freemason ranks, becoming Grand Master of the Grand Lodge of Georgia, and, perhaps partly because of this inside track, in 1857 Rockwell was elected secretary of the Milledgeville Railroad Company. Coexisting with Rockwell in Milledgeville for years and years was the Morse family.

In the late 1850s, they all moved to Savannah, and Rockwell joined the Confederate Army.[235]

It was just as Alvin and his wives—for it seems that Virginia and Clarence joined him there—had arrived in Savannah that Rockwell's entrance on the same stage spelled doom. Alvin and his new bride Annie were staying in an upstairs room at the Gibbons House. After breakfast, Alvin claimed he made his way up to his room and found Mrs. Morse there; perhaps she was cleaning the room, perhaps there was more to it, but it seems she mentioned the terrible fire in Charleston. Lloyd provides the particulars of the event: "Arrested on Dec. 14, Saturday, 12.30 p.m., as a Yankee SPY [that last written in large letters, in dark ink, so you can't miss it], and for saying that I did not care if all Charleston burnt up. If I had my way, all could burn. Sent to jail, where I remained 12 months." Twelve months is an exaggeration. In what purports to be Alvin's original diary entry, the figure "12" has been added over another figure, which he had obliterated at the behest of his lawyer.[236]

What appears to have happened on that day was that Mrs. Morse, and very likely Mrs. Annie L. Taylor Lloyd, went to a justice of the peace and signed affidavits accusing Alvin of being a Yankee spy. Mrs. Morse claimed the fire story, and Annie, who'd abandoned her promising stage career to follow him—shamed at finding out that her new husband was a bigamist, and seeing or hearing about his wife Virginia and their small son—turned on Alvin.

The charges were deadly serious, and branded Lloyd as a traitor to the Confederacy: a hanging offense, if proven.

This was real now. Not a play, not anything Alvin could manipulate. He was trapped. In Enclosure 13, we read:

He [Rockwell] kept me in the hot sun under guard for six hours. When I asked to see him, he examined my papers and ordered me to jail, where, by his order, I was kept six months—a greater portion of the time in a dark cell, locked up day and night. He said he would hang me. I was treated worse than a felon by this Rockwell, who now enjoys every privilege of an American citizen. He was one of the 13 who called a meeting in Savannah after Genl Sherman entered the city, and agreed to remain a good loyal Union man. See his [Rockwell's] charge against me to Sec of War at Richmond.[237]

Alvin was imprisoned at Oglethorpe Barracks, in Rockwell's keep. Oglethorpe was a military complex that had been purchased by the United States Government from the City of Savannah in 1833.[238] In downtown Savannah, occupying about three-fourths of an acre, the whole complex was enclosed by a brick wall ten feet high.[239]

Lloyd would not remain at the barracks for long. There were no suitable accommodations there, Rockwell claimed, and no opportunity for him to issue rations to prisoners. But intent on keeping Alvin incarcerated, Rockwell transferred him to the Chatham County jail, in the keep of jailer Waring Russell.[240]

And of the jail, at first glance it was hard to imagine the horrors within: The exterior, which took up a whole city block near the corner of Hall and Whitaker Streets, close to Oglethorpe Barracks, was in the castellated style of Gothic architecture. Its yellow brick walls, with octagonal turrets, gave off an Old World European air, something remarked upon by many foreign visitors who at first thought it was a castle.

As for the prison wing of the building, the cells were surrounded by a narrow hall and had a ventilated passage between them only two feet wide. At the south end of the cells were four wing rooms, twelve by twenty-four feet. Three of these were intended for the detention of United States prisoners, suspected spies, free persons of color taken from vessels, and witnesses. The other wing room had two large bathing places sunk in the floor and plastered with cement. These bathing pits were commonly and often used as torture chambers and were filled with quicklime or salt.[241]

Prisoners at the jail were part of a lend-lease situation between Oglethorpe and the jail. The overnight stay of each of Rockwell's prisoners would be billed by Russell to the Confederate States Government, and duly paid.[242]

Prominent present-day Savannah historian Hugh Golson described the jail in 1861 as a "horror house."[243]

The inmates were prostitutes, drunks, and suspicious persons like Alvin Lloyd, many of whom were arrested by the night patrols, vicious thugs employed by the city. Many of these suspects would arrive in a hopelessly battered condition. Some survived the night in their new quarters. Others did not. The balance of the prisoners was formed by slaves from the outlying rice plantations who had defied their overseers in the fields. Their owners, at the cost of five dollars a head, had sent them to the jail for remedial attention, which involved the whipping room followed by a dunking in the brine pit, which loomed ever present in the middle of the prison. Apparently all inmates throughout the night could hear their screams. If true repentance followed such torture, a slave might—just might—be allowed to go back to the plantation. But it would have to be determined by the jailers and masters that the slaves were fit to return to their field labors. Otherwise they rotted and often died in the jail.[244]

By 1861 there were few prisoners who had the luxury of an individual cell. If a man was considered very dangerous, then he would be confined solitarily. As for food, the war, even at this early stage, had really taken its toll, so it comes as no surprise that, unless visitors brought in fresh fruits or otherwise unattainable foodstuffs, a prisoner was fated to insect-infested bread and watery gruel, if that. Alvin may well have been one of those prisoners.[245]

On Thursday, December 19, 1861, Colonel Rockwell notified Confederate Secretary of War Judah P. Benjamin of Alvin's arrest as a spy. "Sir. A man calling himself Mr. Alvin Lloyd was arrested and brought to this post some days since as a spy. There is evidence here to show that he has told several contradictory stories about his antecedents." A curious mention to be sure. But there is no record or further explanation of these alleged stories. "I am satisfied that he is an imposter," Rockwell wrote. "Imposter"? That is, someone posing as the famous William Alvin Lloyd. "He had in his possession two passes from the War Department [the Confederate War Department], one, I think to visit Norfolk, and he acknowledged to me that he had been to Craney Island." It was true—Lloyd had been in Craney Island, but not to spy for the Union. Rockwell suspected Lloyd was feeding enemy intelligence to northern newspapers. Rockwell continues,

From his conversation, I incline to the opinion that he may be connected in some way with the information said to be published in the

New York papers in relation to the strength and stations of the Confederate troops. I am unwilling to trust this matter to the telegraph, and General Lawton [Alexander Robert Lawton, commanding the Department of Georgia], as well as his assistant adjutant being temporarily absent, I venture to ask unofficially if anything is known of this man Lloyd in the Department. Should you desire it, I will forward such of his statements here to me and others which subject him to grave suspicion.

Rockwell's carefully chosen words do not bode well for Lloyd. Rockwell's letter goes on, asking for secrecy in the Lloyd matter—a delaying tactic, as will be seen.

If he be a spy and in communication with the enemy, it is obvious that the less publicity given to measures to insure his detection, the more certain will be the result. I have the honor to be, very respectfully, etc, Wm. S. Rockwell, Lieutenant Colonel, First Georgia Volunteer Regiment, C.S. Army, Commanding Post.[246]

Secretary Judah Benjamin endorsed the letter with, "Do you know anything of this man?" and sent it on to General John H. Winder, in Richmond. Winder returned it with, "Mr. Alvin Lloyd is on record in the police book as a suspicious person and was under observation while here at the Exchange Hotel. He left here for New Orleans. I am satisfied he ought to be viewed with great suspicion. He is supposed to be a reporter for newspapers. Jno. H. Winder."[247]

There had been no edition of *W. Alvin Lloyd's Southern Steamboat and Railroad Guide* since February 1861. As soon as he came south, that July, he was trying to get the finances together to start up again in Dixie, but had not succeeded. Toward the end of the year he was well on the way to getting a new edition out in January 1862, but was imprisoned. Somehow, by being allowed to send a letter out of the prison, Alvin managed to get word to the *Savannah Daily Morning News*. On Christmas Eve the paper ran an ad, addressed to railroad superintendents and others:

Owing to unforeseen circumstances, over which I have had no control, Lloyd's Southern St. Bt. & RR Guide cannot possibly be re-released in January, as was anticipated, but will be re-issued on or about the 16th of February. Railroad superintendents will please forward the schedules of their different roads for publication to W. Alvin Lloyd, Richmond, Va. Respectfully, W. Alvin Lloyd. Publisher Lloyd's Southern St. & RR Guide. Memphis Appeal *please copy one week, and send bill to W. Alvin Lloyd, Richmond, Va.*

The date in the ad—February 16—is very specific. It might mean that he expected to be released by then or it may be that someone else was working on the guide for him. A February release was not to be. It would be well over a year before the next guide was published. Alvin remained imprisoned, facing a trial.

On December 30, 1861, Albert Taylor Bledsoe, the chief of the Confederate Bureau of War, replied to Rockwell's December 19 query about Lloyd: "The Secretary of War directs me to say that W. Alvin Lloyd is on record in the police book of Genl Winder as a suspicious character, and was under observation while in this city. He is supposed to be a reporter for Northern newspapers, and should be regarded with great distrust."[248]

Sometime around New Year of 1862, under close guard, Alvin was given permission to go into town and get ambrotype portrait photos made so he could send them off to friends who would vouch for his actually being who he said he was—W. Alvin Lloyd—and not an imposter.[249]

On January 9, 1862, Alvin wrote a despairing letter to Jefferson Davis.

Dear Sir, I am still confined in prison and have been here now twenty-seven days. . . . It is an outrage. . . . My business is going to ruin . . . and Col. Rockwell is not acting properly with me; the woman I called my wife [i.e., Annie L. Taylor] and he are intimate; she boasts of it, Sir. She is a woman who was an actress, and because I would not allow her to go upon the stage, she is determined, she boasts, to keep me in prison. Sir, I appeal to you for justice.

Alvin goes on to describe the incident with Mrs. Morse: "This northern woman was in my room. She is from Pennsylvania . . ." His plea, his plea to his captors, his promise to take an oath if he is allowed to go out during the day into the city, "to return every night until they can prove something against me which I defy them or the southern confederacy to do . . . I will prove who I am. . . . I am a ruined man."

And he *was* a ruined man, blaming vengeful women for this ruination. It did no good.

Jefferson Davis received Alvin's letter on January 15. It came with an added endorsement signed by Custis Lee, Robert E. Lee's eldest son and aide to Jefferson Davis.[250]

On or around January 10, 1862, both E. D. Frost and John Robin McDaniel received letters and photographs (ambrotypes) from Alvin. McDaniel wrote back, same day, in Lynchburg, "I, John Robin McDaniel, hereby testify that in the ambrotype which I to-day rec'd from Savannah, Geo., and herewith returned, I recognize a likeness of Wm Alvin Lloyd, who published 'Lloyd's Steamboat and Railway Guide', in several numbers of which was published the likeness & Biography of myself, also that of Col. Sam Tate, Dr. H.F. McFarland & others. The likeness is so striking that I think I could easily have recognized him anywhere."[251]

On January 11, 1862, "Edward D. Frost, Superintendent of the Mississippi Central Rail Road," appeared before a notary public in Madison County, Miss., and swore that "he is well acquainted with one W. Alvin Lloyd," and that Lloyd "was for some time the publisher of a *Southern Rail Road & Steamboat Guide* in the city of New York." Frost goes on to say that he "has seen said Lloyd a number of times" and that he last saw said Lloyd in Canton, Mississippi, in the latter part of July, "being the day when the news of the battle of Manasseh was received. . . . Further, that the ambrotype likeness herewith transmitted, and to identify which this deponent has put his signature in his own proper handwriting on the face of the said ambrotype, is a likeness of the said W. Alvin Lloyd." Frost wraps up his deposition by saying that the last time he saw Lloyd he was "preparing to commence the publication of the *Guide* at some point in the South, and left here for the purpose of collecting material for the same."[252]

It is also known, from a later report written by General Lawton, that Alvin applied for a habeas corpus hearing [a demand to produce evidence, try him, or free him] before Levi Sheftall D'Lyon, judge of the City Court. This request was allowed, and the hearing, not a trial, took place with Alvin represented by counsel, and the government not represented.

In his 1865 claim, Alvin itemizes two expenses from the event that he charges to the US government. "Dec. 1861 – first part of 1862." The first is for seven hundred dollars, "Amt paid for legal services in application for Habeas Corpus while imprisoned in Savannah, Ga., in gold," and the second, for eight hundred dollars, as Lloyd appears to have been ailing, was "Amt paid for medical attendance, and medicines for myself and for the necessities of life, while confined in prison in Savannah, Ga. (pd in gold)."[253]

Judge D'Lyon heard Alvin's evidence, and took several days to ponder it during which it is distinctly possible that D'Lyon was pressured by General A. R. Lawton—himself an experienced lawyer and war hero—who later wrote that if Alvin were tried he would likely go free. On Sunday the nineteenth, Alvin dashed off letters to John Robin McDaniel in Lynchburg, and E. D. Frost in Holly Springs, asking if they could both see their way clear to coming to Savannah to bear witness for him. Both requests were met with very similar answers.

Judge D'Lyon finally recommitted Alvin to Chatham County Jail. This was in the few days between January 25 and early February, when a letter arrived at the jail from John Robin McDaniel, a letter written from Lynchburg on January 28 to "Mr W. Alvin Lloyd, Savannah." The letter was received, opened, read, and copied by Waring Russell, the keeper of the jail. Alvin's friend McDaniel was full of excuses. This was a severe blow to the isolated and increasingly fearful Lloyd.[254]

McDaniel wrote,

Dear Sir, Yours of the 19th inst. found me in deep, deep affliction—In one day I lost my dining room servant, George, a servant without equal for devotion to his master & mistress (I never spoke a cross word to him in my life, my interest and comfort was his, first, last and constant care and seemed to engross all his thoughts)—the loss of the slave

is nothing, but as my friend it was a heavy loss indeed. . . . Also my
nephew, who was to me as a child. My wishes at all times was laid
with him. My two best friends are gone. I send under cover to Genl
Lawton my certificate which I hope answer all you desire. I trust you
will soon be released. It is impossible for me to leave here. I did not get
Mr. Owens or the Mayor's certificate. I thought it best not to ask them.
Your friend John Robin McDaniel.[255]

It wasn't long afterwards that Alvin received the second of his answers, this one terse and dismissive, written on February 3 by E. D. Frost at Holly Springs, on railroad company stationery, and addressed to "Mr. W. Alvin Lloyd, Chatham Jail, Savannah, Georgia. Friend Lloyd, I have written Col. Rockwell as you desired. It is entirely out of the question for me to leave here now. Mr. Goodman [Walter Goodman, president of the road] has been gone for nearly a month, and I am here alone with the whole road on my hand. Yours, etc. E.D. Frost, Super."[256]

Secretary Benjamin wrote to General Lawton on February 10: "The President has handed to me the enclosed communication." Upon first inspection, one would think this "enclosed communication" is the Lloyd letter to Davis of January 9. However, General Lawton, in his detailed report of the Lloyd case to Jefferson Davis, written on March 21, 1862, refers to two letters sent by Lloyd to Davis—on February 4 and February 21. The one of February 21 is of record. The one of February 4 is not. It is assumed Lawton made a mistake—should have said January 9. However, he may be right. Maybe Alvin did write another one on February 4 but it has not been located.[257]

During his testimony in the 1872 Court of Claims Case, the bold postmortem attempt to collect the large sum of money falsely owed to the Lloyd estate, Alphabetical Boyd says he saw Alvin "in Savannah in January or February 1862." Throughout January and the first part of February, Boyd was still on detached service as a clerk with the Confederate Commissary Department, and we know that on February 20 he left camp without leave, being officially declared a deserter the following day. However, he hadn't deserted. He was with Governor Letcher, of Virginia, wangling a commission, and is therefore still on the Commissary Department's roll of March and April. If he was at his post at the Commissary Department until February 20—which he was—and then from the twentieth was with Governor Letcher, and then on March 15 was back with the Commissary Department, it doesn't leave him any time to have been with Alvin in Savannah. As with most, if not all, of Boyd's conflicting and perjured testimonies this too was an impossibility. This too was a lie.[258]

Boyd continues his fiction about his visit to the imprisoned Lloyd:

> *He was in jail at Savannah. I saw him in jail. I found out what he was in jail for from the colonel commanding the post. I can't remember his name. He told me Lloyd had been arrested as a Yankee spy, and showed me an affidavit signed by Miss Jordan, an actress who stated that she had overheard conversations between Lloyd and other parties in which Lloyd was sending information to the United States Government, in regard to the plans of fortifications surrounding Savannah.*[259]

Where Boyd got the name Miss Jordan from is unknown. It appears only once in the entire case, in Boyd's 1872 deposition. And nowhere in a detailed study of the American theater of that time is found a suitable actress named Miss Jordan, in Savannah or anywhere else. Alphabetical must simply have gotten the name wrong. He should have said Miss Taylor, if in fact the wronged Annie Taylor hadn't made the whole accusation up. And it is more than likely that she did, as Alvin was of course, never a spy. On the other hand, the affidavit Boyd mentions does sound like one of the truths, like swarms of dust motes, sparsely and rarely sprinkled throughout his and other former Lloyd associates' testimonies. Alvin says he was arrested on an affidavit from Mrs. Morse, the hotelier's wife. And he was. And Colonel Rockwell, Alvin's captor, confirms that it was Mrs. Morse—even attaches her affidavit (which has not been located). No other affidavit is mentioned by either Lloyd or Rockwell. However, it seems probable that later in the war, Alvin told Boyd of his great betrayal by Annie, the young actress he said was intimate with Rockwell.

Rockwell later wrote that he heard rumors that Lloyd was in

"communication with the Lincoln cabinet through a man named Boyd who brought him a letter from Mr Chase in his boot."[260]

Curiously, even though Rockwell alludes to the rumor of a man named Boyd being Lloyd's intermediary with the Lincoln cabinet, neither Alvin nor Rockwell ever mentions the actual Boyd visit to Savannah, and Rockwell certainly would have been more descriptive of Alphabetical if he had, indeed, met him. In addition, Rockwell, having heard rumors of Boyd and Chase and the boot, would have, if he had laid eyes on the man, had Alphabetical immediately arrested.

This rumor about Boyd being Lloyd's courier. This Chase connection. Here we have a contemporaneous reference to it, and from Rockwell. In short, Boyd's supposed courier career had entered the picture at this early date. Yet, nowhere does anyone else—Boyd, Lloyd, anyone—mention Boyd as a runner anywhere this early in time, and they would have. It could only have added to the strength of Lloyd's 1865 bogus claim. And if Lincoln's treasury secretary Salmon Chase had truly been involved, then he would have been Alvin's witness in 1865. However, he clearly wasn't, as he has never been mentioned again in this plot, before or since. Even more important, the Chase letter in the boot story would have been too good to pass up, especially for Boyd. Where did Rockwell hear this rumor about Boyd? If it had been from Alvin, then Alvin would have used it later. Surely Lloyd and Boyd must have been aware of the rumor—one way or the other—but for their own reasons chose never to revive it, especially as it is more than likely that it came from Annie Taylor, who would probably have known of, but not necessarily met, Boyd.

Again, Boyd in 1872 claimed, "Lloyd was confined solitarily in Savannah for about six weeks, on account of an intercepted dispatch." Alvin himself refers to "cruel and inhumane treatment" that he suffered while at Savannah. As for the "intercepted dispatch," it is not clear what Boyd is talking about. No one, least of all Rockwell, ever mentions such a dispatch. In fact, on the contrary, Rockwell had no real evidence at hand to hang Lloyd. And such a dispatch would most definitely have seen him executed.[261]

On February 15, 1862, Alvin wrote to General Robert E. Lee, at that time "overseeing the fortification of the cities on the southeastern coast."[262]

"I appeal to you for justice," he wrote, telling Lee of his experience with the New York mob and that he had applied to Jefferson Davis for an "appointment . . . but there were no vacancies." He tells of Mrs. Morse, calling her a "yankee woman" who was in his room when he made the remark about the Charleston fire. "I did not want her in my room," Lloyd adds. "She made an affidavit against me . . . that she believed me to be a spy. . . that sir, is all the proof they can procure against me. . . . I am as true and loyal to our Confederacy as President Davis himself. No man could fight for the south as I have without loving it." It is also quite clear from this letter that Virginia, Clarence, and a nurse had arrived in Savannah by this stage. "Governor Harris [of Tennessee] has given me permission to send one hundred and fifty dollars . . . to bring to the south a lady, child and nurse." Nellie Dooley may not be the nurse in question, as she would later claim to have been in the South with Mrs. Lloyd all the time except for the "nine months" in Savannah. But Virginia and Clarence's presence, of that there can be little doubt. And it seems that Mrs. Annie Taylor Lloyd had gone, left the man that married her three times, never to be heard of again.[263]

Two days later, on February 17, Lee sent a response to the authorities, to Henry C. Wayne, adjutant and inspector general in Milledgeville, but that letter has not been found.

That same day, the seventeenth, Alvin wrote another letter to Lee:

Genl Lee, I send you my Rail Road passes & Passports. Col. Rockwell and Genl Lawton have all my letters stating what my business was at the different places I have visited. Genl Lee, do be kind enough to investigate my case. I have been confined 65 days today. I am as true and loyal a man as there lived in our young Confederacy. Resptly, W. Alvin Lloyd. Feb. 17th/62. Genl Lawton has also the affidavits stating my loyalty [these are the McDaniel and Frost affidavits]. I received another letter this morning from John Robin McDaniel, Esq., of Lynchburg [this letter has not been located]. Respectfully, W. Alvin Lloyd.[264]

Yet again, on the seventeenth, in his determined effort to create a profile of his suspected spy, one he hoped would be convicted and hanged, Rockwell wrote to Captain W. H. Taylor, Assistant Adjutant General.

Captain, in obedience to the reference by order of Gen. Lee of certain documents accompanying a letter of W. Alvin Lloyd for a statement of the facts of the case with a view of ascertaining what steps can be taken to arrive at the guilt or innocence of Mr Lloyd. I have the honor to state that Mr Lloyd was brought to this post on the—Decr. Last, arrested upon an affidavit made by Mrs Morse, a copy of which is herewith forwarded. I was directed by General Lawton to examine him carefully, which I proceeded to do, a copy of which examination is also hereto attached. Before the examination was concluded, a number of papers taken from Lloyd's possession, were placed in my hand, and I discovered that many of his statements were inconsistent with the facts disclosed by the papers. He asserted himself to be traveling with his wife & child.

Had Rockwell actually laid eyes on this wife and child? It doesn't sound like it. The wife and child referred to here have to be Virginia and Clarence, yet we know Alvin was traveling with Mrs. Annie L. Taylor. A case could be made for Alvin traveling with Virginia and Clarence, but the woman he was in company with right then was definitely Mrs. Taylor.

The woman he called his wife he said he had married on the 9th of Nov. 1861 [this, of course, is Annie Taylor; remember the proof extant in the Orleans Parish marriage register of that date]. Among the papers was a receipted Hotel Bill for the board of Mr W.A. Lloyd and Lady [Annie] dated the 3rd Nov., and a free ticket on the Vicksburg R.Rd for Mr Lloyd & Lady [Annie] dated 6 Nov. 1861. He admitted the lady professed to in the hotel bill is the same woman he calls his wife [Annie]. There was abundant evidence in the papers submitted to me . . .

This evidence unfortunately is not seen in this document, but presumably they are some of the bigamy articles. After all of Rockwell's fevered attempts to prove that Lloyd was a spy, here was the real reason that Rockwell was so determined to make Lloyd suffer further.

. . . to establish the fact that he had for several years imposed upon the community, both North and South, women in the character of wife who had no title whatever to the appellation, if he were the person he assumed to be.

What could this abundant evidence have been that so incriminated Alvin as a bigamist? Newspaper clippings, perhaps? Marriage certificates? Letters from outraged wives and lawyers? Rockwell doesn't elaborate, and this abundant documented evidence is never referred to in the welter of correspondence between Rockwell, Lawton, Davis, Lee, et al.

But Rockwell, though demurring, must continue. He must prove his case against Lloyd.

Although I could not take cognizance of offences against good morals, yet as I had positive evidence that he had misrepresented his position and stood convicted of falsehood in one particular, his professions of loyalty weighed against his facilities for procuring information, and the fact that exact statements of the Confederate forces had reached the public through the Northern press in some unaccountable way, seemed to me not of the most trustworthy character. It was while examining this portion of the testimony, consisting in part of free tickets and passes on the Southern Rail Roads, my attention was drawn to the fact that he carefully withheld all mention of being in possession of such passes over Northern R.Rds. Those upon the Southern Rail Roads he voluntarily tendered for inspection as proof of his loyalty to the South. Perhaps he conceived the argument equally good for his loyalty to the North, though he was not aware that I was in possession of tickets of like character issued to him by Rail Road companies in the Northern, Eastern and Western states.

Alvin knew they were in his bags, knew Rockwell was searching his bags, and therefore must have known he had these tickets, which in and of themselves were not at all incriminating.

Rockwell presses on.

I took occasion, however, to ask him, while he was detailing the manner of his escape from New York, if he was not provided with free tickets on the roads over which he passed in his flight? To this he replied in the negative. I append a list of the Southern Rail Roads upon which he had free tickets, and which he produced, and also a list of the Northern R.Rds equally generous to him, which he carefully suppressed. The General will observe that a pass over the Cleveland and Erie Rail Road is herewith forwarded, which was among his papers taken from his possession, which he stated in his examination was part of his route from New York to Cincinnati. I also noticed in this connection a free pass over the Ohio & Miss RRd to the end of the year 1860, upon which road the copy of the Steam Boat & R Rd Guide, *of which he claims to be the publisher, informed me that Capt. (now Major General) Geo. B. McClellan was general superintendent. He also called my attention to several articles published in the* Steam Boat & R Rd Guide *as indications of his sympathy with the Southern cause, and which he says caused his violent expulsion from N. York. I was certainly unable to view them in that light as they were mostly directed to the abuse of the Abolitionists as a party, & calculated only to solicit Southern trade.*

And now Rockwell is intent on criticizing Alvin-as-writer.

On a comparison since of the articles with his epistolary appeals to Gen. Lawton & the Secretary of War, I am induced to believe that his only relation thereto is that of publisher and not author. I did not view them therefore as indications of his sentiment toward the South, and consider them of no greater weight than the rumors conveyed to me of his communication with the Lincoln cabinet through a man named Boyd who brought him a letter from Mr. Chase in his boot, or the statement made to me in Richmond by a person present on the occasion of his being charged by one who professed to be cognizant of the fact, with voting for Lincoln. I enclose also for the consideration of the General, a letter from the War Dept., bearing upon the character he sustained at Richmond, at the very time he was applying to the President for a situation under the Government.

Rockwell summarizes Lloyd's escape from New York as Lloyd wrote in his letter to Robert E. Lee.

He [Lloyd] left the city within the time allowed him, without pausing on the very extraordinary number of minutes allowed in this highly improbable proceeding. In his examination it is obvious to remark he failed to mention this peculiar exhibition of violence, and stated to me that his clerk informed him that they were about to hang him summarily, and in corroboration produced a printed notice to that effect, which I returned to him, and he said he fled immediately to escape the danger. The extension of time vouchsafed to him, according to his later statement, may account for his carrying with him a great number of blank checks on the Leather Manufacturers Bank, evenly & carefully cut, apparently with scissors which were found among his papers, and whose presence in the baggage of a person leaving in a hurry would argue some degree of premeditation.

That is probably true as Lloyd didn't fear the mob and was arranging to flee with the merchant's daughter. And knowing Lloyd, the "mob" may have been one or two businessmen he'd blackmailed.

Rockwell now addresses what he considers to be very bad judgment on the part of jailer Waring Russell.

When Lloyd was placed in custody, the jailer unusually allowed him to send off a large number of letters. In these he might have conveyed away all evidence of a direct character to impeach his loyalty. I cannot but believe however where suspicion is so evident, he having been arrested heretofore in Memphis and escaping for want of proof, and in Nashville (where he applied to Gov. Harris for permission to send gold North to bring home his wife and child, not a lady nurse and child as he represents to General Lee), and escaping there for want of proof. Delay and circumspection may render conviction absolutely certain, if he be a spy. If not, his detention would be none too grave a punishment for his moral delinquencies.

"Moral delinquencies." And there it was—Rockwell's real and pressing condemnation of Alvin Lloyd. He is morally delinquent. And finally, another jab at Lloyd's writing skills.

It will be seen that the letter of Lloyd strengthens me in the conclusion I have reached in my estimate of his literary abilities. I have the honor to be, Captain, very respectfully, Wm S. Rockwell, Lt Col, etc, comdng Post.[265]

Here is Rockwell, a man with a good deal of power, so far unable to find enough evidence to hang a perceived traitor, a Yankee spy, who in reality has sashayed around the south with wives and lovers on his arm. Imagine Rockwell's frustration. His impotence. His rage. His jealousy, perhaps.

If Lloyd was privy at all to the next communication, he might feel a modicum of relief. Henry C. Wayne, adjutant and inspector general at Milledgeville, replied to Lee, on February 19, 1862: "I received this morning and submitted to the Governor [Governor Joseph Emerson Brown, of Georgia] your letter of the 17th instant, relating to W. Alvin Lloyd, a suspected correspondent of the enemy. His Excellency desires me to say that he has never heard of the case before, and that he must leave him in the hands of the civil authorities in Savannah and of the Confederate officers in command there."[266]

Now an emboldened Alvin is writing to Lee on February 20, 1862: "Genl Lee, please send me by the girl my 'Guides,' passes (R.R.), passports, affidavits, which I sent you a day or so since. Respectfully, W. Alvin Lloyd. Feb. 20th, 1862. Will you be kind enough to let me know when the case was sent to Richmond for investigation and what further proof is required. Please give me an answer. Respectfully, W. Alvin Lloyd."[267]

Who is the girl Lloyd refers to? That is unknown, as she is not mentioned again. Lee must have complied with Alvin's request, because the passports and affidavits are all of record and viewable.

With no word or sign of a release forthcoming, Alvin wrote to Judah Benjamin on February 21, 1862. He begged the secretary to hasten the investigation, as he had been in prison seventy-one days now. This letter was received at the War Department on February 27, 1862. The same day, Alvin wrote to Adjutant General Samuel Cooper in Richmond.[268]

The Savannah newspaper of February 24, 1862, advertised that a letter was waiting at the post office for "Mrs. Annie Louisa Taylor." However, Annie had gone and Virginia was in the city.

Alvin sent another letter to Lee in an effort to explain that he told Rockwell about his connection to a New Orleans newspaper that may have been confusing. It seems Lloyd was desperate to prove his veracity, retell his story and equally desperate to find a reason to again communicate with Lee.

> *Genl Lee, In my memorandum to Col. Rockwell, it seems he misunderstood me to say that I was connected with the New Orleans "Delta" now. He misunderstood me. Myself and Brother (who is in Fort Lafayette, or was) [this may well be true about Fort Lafayette, but there is no corroborating evidence to that effect] were connected with Major J. P. Heiss, publishing the* Delta *in 1852 & 1853 [John P. Heiss was, indeed, publishing the* Delta *in that time period]. I mention this, Genl Lee, so that you will not think I told an untruth. I published my guide at the* Delta *office in 1857 [from an examination of the New Orleans newspapers of the time, it was the* Times-Picayune *office, or the* Crescent's *office, but it is not certain], then I moved to New York, where I have published since that time, circulating it South, and it is the only (truly) Rail Road Guide ever published. Yours truly, W. Alvin Lloyd. I was born in Kentucky. My parents were born in Winchester, Va. W.A.L. Feby. [25] 1862.[269]*

On February 25, 1862, Alvin wrote a second letter to Samuel Cooper, pushing the adjutant general to investigate his case immediately. Alvin had been in jail now two months and thirteen days. "It is indeed hard upon me," he writes. He told Cooper that his health was failing, and that he was threatened with paralysis. "I have no air. No exercise."[270] He is *in extremis.*

By March 17, 1862, Alvin Lloyd had been in jail for seventy-one days, and he knew he couldn't last much longer.

Frantic, he wrote another letter to Judah Benjamin. He was "suffering innocently . . . a new born babe," wanting "justice," etc. He let the secretary of state know that he would like to "get a little fresh air (which I stand greatly in need of)." Alvin's letter went unanswered.[271]

Which is not to say nothing happened as a result of that letter. On March 21, 1862, from Savannah, General Lawton wrote a letter to Jefferson Davis, making a report on the Lloyd case. After summing up the history of Lloyd's arrest and confinement, Lawton tells the President,

> *The question does not, at present, seem to be an enquiry into the facts to ascertain the guilt or innocence of the prisoner. If he be a traitor, the municipal courts are competent to try and determine the complicity with the enemy. I have no means of determining if a Grand Jury could be furnished with sufficient proof to put the prisoner on his trial, nor can the fact be ascertained before the session of the Superior Court, which will occur in May next. Should the proof be at hand, however, the Court on conviction could pronounce his punishment. The civil judicatory has already ruled that his capture and detention was not illegal, and there, as far as these tribunals are concerned, the matter rests at present.*

And then comes Lawton's opinion: A real blow.

> *On the other hand, if he be a spy, the civil courts possess but a doubtfull [sic] jurisdiction over the offence [sic]. The military courts, however, have ample power to try and punish. The evidence to ascertain the fact and convict of such a charge is at any time exceedingly difficult to obtain, and in the present condition of the Country, almost impossible. If he be, as is suspected, and that upon reasonable grounds, as correspondent of the Northern newspapers, it is obvious that the evidence to increase the suspicion to certainty is beyond the reach of the Government, and, if brought to trial, he must be discharged for want of proof, even in the face of grave suspicion. The circumstances surrounding his case, it would seem, though short of absolute certainty, would rather warrant the conclusion that it would be unwise to set him at liberty. It appears also that Lloyd has been arrested upon similar charges twice before, once at*

Memphis, and again at Nashville, and while in Richmond, with most unblushing impudence, applying to the President for official stations, he was actually under the surveillance of the police, and suspected of the very crime which has brought him into difficulty here.

Lawton is obviously unaware of the bigamy arrests.

I have therefore not deemed it prudent to overrule the decision which deprives him at present of his liberty. I transmit herewith Lt Col Rockwell's report to me with the accompanying papers, viz:—copy of letter from War Department; copy of Lt Col Rockwell's report to Genl Lee; schedule of free tickets upon Rail Road in Lloyd's possession; proceedings upon the Habeas Corpus; and a letter from Govr Harris of Tennessee, written at Lloyd's request. I have the honor to be, Very Respectfully, Your obdt servant, A.R. Lawton, Brig Genl comdg.[272]

The Lawton report was endorsed by G. W. Randolph, Secretary of War: "Respectfully submitted to the President in answer to his call. The War Department has taken no further action in the case." Finally, Jefferson Davis endorsed it with, "Let the prisoner be informed of the report of his case as presented within."[273]

Proof, it was always about proof. And there was none. Only suspicions and nagging doubts.

But here is the reason Alvin was detained without trial for so long: The authorities, particularly General Lawton, knew that a trial would set him free, but they also suspected him of being a spy. So, they dispensed with due process, and kept him incarcerated. But certain questions loomed:

General Lawton surely would have known Lloyd. Yet he didn't seem to. Lawton had for years before the war been president of the Savannah and Augusta Railroad. Rockwell, too, had been secretary of the Milledgeville Railroad. He had to have known Alvin. Yet it seems he didn't. Was Lloyd such a disreputable scoundrel in the guise of a glad-handing, peripatetic rover? Did his serial bigamies, his travels with so many women, disturb and disgust those who should have and would have known him such that he became to so many a pariah, a soul-deficient sinner?

Time crawls. Lloyd remains imprisoned. It is now July 4, 1862. It used to be Independence Day in Georgia as it was in Maine, as it had been all over the old United States of America, but since the war, it was just another day on the Dixie calendar. But it was still Alvin's birthday, regardless of politics. It was also the day he penned another letter to the Confederate President. From his jail cell he wrote:

To His Excellency, Jefferson Davis, Richmond. Mr. President, it has been nearly 4 months since I received a letter from Col. Davis [Joseph E. Davis] stating to me that you had written to Genl Lawton the charges, proof, etc., against me to be forwarded to you, so that my case should receive the proper attention. Since that time I have not heard one word relative to my case. I have been in jail nearly 7 months, Mr. President, and no trial, and no proof against me, and I know full well, for I have done nothing in the world against our stripling country. On the contrary, I have done all in my power for the Southern Confederacy.

He goes on:

I have my family here and they are nearly destitute. It has cost me all the means I could command to support them and myself for 7 months. . . . Lieut Col. Rockwell here has kept back the letters and affidavits in my favor he showed my wife a couple of months since—Govr. Harris' (of Tenn.) letter stating that I was a true and loyal Southern man beside 15 or 20 others from gentlemen in Louisiana, Mississippi and Virginia. Col. Rockwell told my wife that I had injured myself by writing to you, and that I had written too many letters, etc. I pray you, Mr President, to deal with me as you would be dealt by. I am poor, and am as innocent as you yourself of any disloyalty. Once more, I beg of you, Sir, to have my case investigated, for my life is wearing away in jail. Why is it that an innocent man should suffer the way I have and am suffering. I humbly beg of you to have justice done me, and let me go free to serve my country & attend to my business.

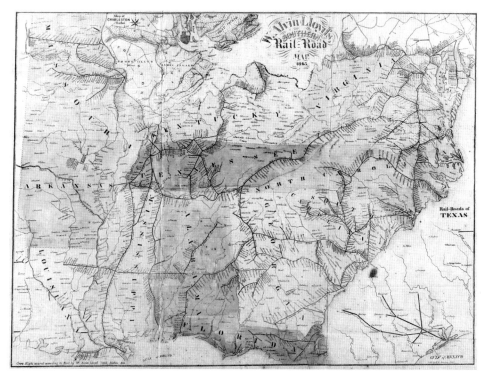

W. Alvin Lloyd's Southern Railroad Map, 1865   NATIONAL ARCHIVES, WASHINGTON DC

Lloyd's Minstrels advertisement, 1867
JACKSON CITIZEN PATRIOT, APRIL 17, 1867
(JACKSON, MI)

Enoch Totten, William Alvin Lloyd's lawyer
FROM THE GUY BUTTERFIELD COLLECTION AT THE
WAUKESHA COUNTY MUSEUM, WAUKESHA, WI

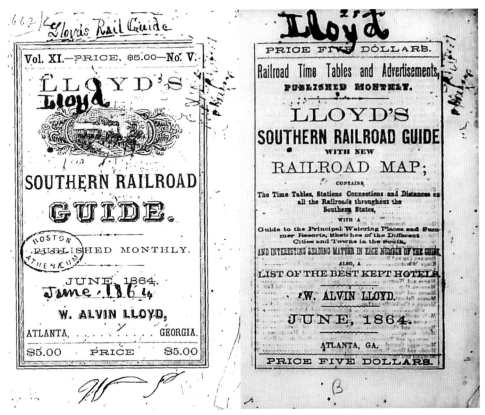

Lloyd's Southern Railroad Guide, June 1864 NATIONAL ARCHIVES, WASHINGTON, DC

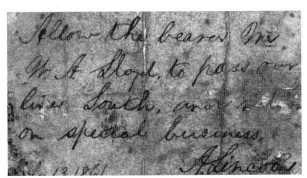

Pass to William Alvin Lloyd signed by Abraham Lincoln,
July 13, 1861. Front and back views.

OFFICE OF W. ALVIN LLOYD'S RAIL ROAD GUIDE,

Franklin Buildings, Sixth Street, near Arch, Philadelphia, Pa.

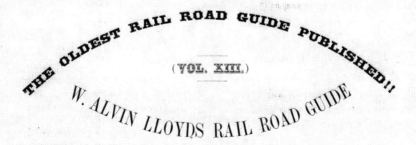

☞ CIRCULATES in the SOUTHERN STATES. ☜

WILL BE RE-ISSUED MARCH, 1866,

— I N —

PHILADELPHIA.

The fame of **W. ALVIN LLOYD'S RAIL ROAD GUIDE** is "NATIONAL," while, as a correct and succinct compendium of all matters pertaining to **RAIL ROADS AND OFFICIALS THROUGHOUT THE UNITED STATES,** it has **NO EQUAL!**

It will be the aim of the proprietor and publisher to sustain, if not enhance, the reputation of his **GUIDE;** and thus place it again in the hands of every traveler, Rail Road official and business man throughout the country.

The **GUIDE** will be circulated in all the cities and towns North and South. Copies will be found upon every train, and at Rail Road Stations and Depots.

Merchants and Business Men desirous of Extending their Business

Will find this old and reliable **GUIDE** the best medium to bring their business before the public.

W. ALVIN LLOYD,

Publisher "W. Alvin Lloyd's Rail Road Guide."

Advertisement for W. Alvin Lloyd's 1866 Railroad Guide

Colonel William Spencer Rockwell, CSA THE ATLANTA MASONIC MUSEUM AND LIBRARY ASSOCIATION

General Robert E. Lee
LIBRARY OF CONGRESS

Judge Advocate General Joseph Holt
LIBRARY OF CONGRESS

General Ulysses S. Grant at his headquarters in Cold Harbor, Virginia, 1864 LIBRARY OF CONGRESS

President
Abraham
Lincoln, 1864
LIBRARY OF
CONGRESS

Confederate States of America
President Jefferson Davis
LIBRARY OF CONGRESS

Grand Review of the Armies, Washington, DC, May 23-24, 1865
LIBRARY OF CONGRESS

W. A. Lloyd's railroad passes
LIBRARY OF CONGRESS

Thomas D. Rice as
Jim Crow, 1832
LIBRARY OF CONGRESS

President Abraham Lincoln,
1865
LIBRARY OF CONGRESS

Ulysses S. Grant memo to Secretary of War Edwin M. Stanton, May 27, 1865

NATIONAL ARCHIVES, WASHINGTON, DC

And he self-pityingly adds: "Col. Rockwell does not like me because I have written him letters that spoke the truth."

The letter was received on July 11, 1862. Jefferson Davis wrote, "Secretary of War. The papers in this case were sent to the War Office. Have they been examined? If so, what conclusion has been reached? [signed] J.D." Secretary of War George W. Randolph added, "W. Alvin Lloyd asks an investigation of this case. Chief of Bureau. Is anything known of this case, or the papers referred to by the Presdt.?"[274]

Remarkably, impossibly, according to Alphabetical Boyd, in his 1872 examination, Alvin was spying for Lincoln at the exact time he was imprisoned. An outright lie, of course, but as Boyd relates these events, lawyer Totten would hope the examiners were not privy to all of Alvin's lengthy correspondences with Confederate officials. They were not.

> He [Lloyd] Boyd says, ". . . made a trip to Richmond on parole. He remained in Macon about four months altogether. He visited Richmond from Macon. He went to Richmond and got a pass from Jefferson Davis. He went under the surveillance of a detective, and got a pass from Davis to report to General Winder. He then visited the defenses of Richmond. This was in June 1862. He got information as to strength and location of batteries and number of troops around Richmond" [to report to President Lincoln].

Of course, in June 1862 Alvin was in prison in Georgia. When the examiner questions Boyd in 1872, he answers with this:

> Question: "What did he do with this information?"

> Answer: "He made a report in writing, which he gave to me for Mr. Lincoln, which I delivered in the latter part of July, or first of August, to Mr. Lincoln in person."

In the cross-examination of his 1872 deposition, Boyd elaborates on this fiction during the month of June 1862.

Question: "You speak of information as to the number and strength of batteries and number of troops around Richmond as having been contained in the dispatches delivered by you to the President in the latter part of July or first of August 1862. Did Mr. Lloyd visit those defenses?"

Answer: "Yes, Sir."

Question: "When?"

Answer: "I think it was about June 1862."

Question: "Were you in Richmond at the time he visited these defenses, as you say?"

Answer: "Yes, Sir."

Question: "Did you accompany him in his visit?"

Answer: "Yes, Sir."

Question: "You state that when Mr. Lloyd went to Richmond in June 1862, and visited the rebel defenses, he was still under surveillance of the rebel authorities, including General Winder. How did he get access to the fortifications and defenses around Richmond, being a suspected man?"

Answer: "He went in company with myself, and was acquainted with a great many prominent officers commanding the various batteries, and visited them socially."

Boyd then goes on to say that he and Lloyd saw "General Pendleton [Confederate General William Nelson Pendleton] of the Artillery commanding defenses around Richmond. Also a Major Harding commanding Batteries 4 and 5."

Question: "Where did he see General Pendleton?"

Answer: "At his headquarters between Batteries 4 and 5."

Question: "Did you hear any of the conversation between them?"

Answer: "Yes, Sir."

Question: "Who commenced the conversation?"

Answer: "I commenced the conversation."

Question: "What was the purpose of that conversation so far as it relates to the defenses of Richmond?"

Answer: "Lloyd asked the general the number of batteries, the number of guns mounted, and how many artillerists were employed in the defenses. He took us and showed us the new barbette batteries of rifled guns commanding the Charles River road. Explained the defenses."

Question: "How did you get access to General Pendleton's Head Quarters?"

Answer: "I had an order from General Lee."

Question: "Did Lloyd have an order from General Lee?"

Answer: "No, Sir."

After Richmond, preposterously, it seems Alvin had to slip back undetected into the Chatham County Jail in Savannah, in order to write up his report of the observations he had made while in the Confederate capital.

In reality, at the beginning of July, Alvin was still confined to jail. His original diary, the selected pages torn out and presented to Union authorities in 1865, add a bit of brightness:

Friday, July 4th, 1862. In prison. I am 36 years of age to-day. My dearest Virgin- (wife) ia & Clarence came at 7½ a.m., and spent the day with me. My Virginia brought me Green corn, Tomatoes, Cucumbers, Cantalope, Water Melon, [illegible vegetable]. A splendid dinner, and we were happy. This morning a villain dared to follow Virginia, and called at the house last night.

He was not thirty-six. He had adjusted his age. He was forty. His March 1869 death certificate, the details for which were provided by his widow, Virginia, gives July 4, 1822, as his date of birth. That's obviously the date Virginia understood to be his birthday. However, she does say he was born in Louisville, and that his mother was born in Kentucky. Both facts are wrong. But July 4 is correct. The birth year—vanity, perhaps? Lloyd *was* diminished and ailing.

The house referred to is almost certainly one Virginia took in Savannah, to be close to her husband. Lloyd's surviving diary entry continues:

She gave it to him good. Poor Virginia and Clarence. Got [illegible] last night [illegible] follow her as Kincaid, the scoundrel, followed Virginia again. He will live to regret it. Savannah can boast of nothing but mean men—a lady whose husband is in prison cannot walk the streets in open day light without being insulted. Where is Southern chivalry? Where is the high-toned Southern gentleman? God will protect dear Virginia & her child. Dear Virginia & Clarence remained all night with me and did not leave until 6 p.m. Saturday, as it was raining & my sweet Virginia & Clarence left at 6 p.m. to make some purchases and to see if the scoundrel spoke to her again.

This man, Kincaid, is a mystery, if he truly existed.

There are problems with this "diary." The first is that it was not written on the day, July 4. Nor on the day following. Although the diary heading is "July 4th" Alvin is actually recording the events of the fourth and fifth, after both days have passed. So, when was it actually written?

Usually a personal diary, a private record, is a sprinkling of days, or a precise order of days, so that what might otherwise have been lost to the natural memory over the years, such as who Virginia was, can be preserved. Given the sheer number of wives Alvin had at that moment in time in different parts of the country, it is hardly surprising that he had to stop and think. He was on pretty safe ground until the end of that written line, in other words as far as "My dearest Virgin-," and then found himself struggling, and wrote "(wife)."

Another problem is that Alvin forgets to mention the rather salient fact that on that very day, July 4, he had written a letter to the President of the Confederate States of America. It seems he might have intended this diary for use as an exhibit in the claim that was destined for a very sensitive US War Department in June 1865. It would have been damning to include the fact that he had written a letter to Jefferson Davis.

Another selected diary entry says: "Wednesday, July 9th, 1862. My dearest Virginia & Clarence came to spend the day with me. They came at 7½ and left at 7.10. God bless them. Dr. King called twice."

And on July 10, 1862: "My dear Virginia & Clarence came & spent the day with me. They came at 7½ a.m. and left at 6.30. Dr. King called."

On July 11, Jefferson Davis received Alvin's July 4 letter, and still on July 11, this from Alvin's diary: "My dearest Virginia & Clarence came & spent the day with me. They came at 7½ a.m. and left at 6.38 p.m. Dr King and A.S. Hartridge, aid to Genl Mercer, called and brought an order to the Lieutenant, namely Russell, to allow me to go into the garden at any time. The order was positive, and, if he refused, Genl Mercer would arrest & put him (Russell) in irons. The order was [illegible] with Virginia, and Clarence went into the [illegible]."

In May, General Lawton had been transferred to Virginia, and General Hugh Mercer had taken his place at Savannah. Things were about to change for Alvin—for the better—notably in the form of Dr. William Nephew King, his attending physician, and conscientious intercessor for Alvin with General Mercer. Dr. King was a homeopath as well as an allopathic doctor. If it weren't for Dr. King, Alvin would have remained in the Chatham County Jail. Dr. King was the best friend Alvin ever had, except for Virginia. Her devotion to a man no longer able to provide for her or their child—a man she'd married when she was a child of thirteen, who'd been repeatedly unfaithful—is astonishing. She chose to remain, spending endless hours with her suffering, imprisoned husband and exposing her small son to a barbaric city jail and its inmates, to his father's plight. Virginia chose this life, at this difficult, torturous time.

On July 14, 1862, Dr. King wrote to Alvin. Maybe now, his durance would be less torturous. Maybe.

> *I had a conversation with General Mercer a little while ago, telling him your condition in detail. He says he thinks it best that you change your quarters. I mentioned Augusta as a pleasant point, but he said he could not send you there at the present time, as they had no military prisoners there, & it would put the Government to an unnecessary expense in keeping a Guard with a file of men, but that he would send you to Macon if you wished, tomorrow night in the quarter to 10 p.m. train, yourself, wife & child, who will be allowed to visit you daily and you are to be allowed the liberty of the prison yard. I am very sorry on account of Mrs. L that you would not go to Augusta.*

Virginia had friends or relatives in Augusta, where Confederate Powder Works, the largest gunpowder factory in the Confederacy, made the town an armed camp that contained a huge arsenal.

Dr. King continues:

> *I tried my best for you, but saw that the Gen had reason, for the refusal said nothing more about it, but should [illegible] for any prisoner sent there will [illegible] you. He says he cannot say when your trial will come off, as it will require time to collect evidence, witnesses & papers, but that he will do what he can for you, & I think you may rely upon him in your absence to assure I shall do all I can to bring about & further your cause. I handed the Gen your note this morning. I fear I will not have time to see you this afternoon, therefore I am scratching you these hasty lines. I will see you in the morning. I remain, My Dear Sir & shall ever, Very Sincerely Yours, Wm Nephew King. P.S. I send you two powders which put with ½ tumbler full of water and taken every 2 or 3 hours after eating. WNK.* [275]

It is not known what these powders were or how they might have helped Lloyd, nor what exactly was wrong with him.

And this, from Dr. King, on July 15:

Savannah. Mr W. Alvin Lloyd. My Dear Sir, I have had to go out to White Bluff, and do not think I can get back in time to make my adieu to yourself & Mrs. L, which I regret much, as I should have been glad to know your condition before starting, but I hope, however, you are much better, and that you will take a favorable turn by your change of locality & atmosphere. I shall be happy to hear from you & will do all in my power to assist you, to hasten your trial. I know the Gen will do what is right. I hope you will not think anything by my not presenting you a bill for my services, but I have none against you. Your thanks are quite compensation enough. I only wish I could have done more for you. With kind wishes for yourself and Mrs L. I remain, My Dear Sir, Very Sincerely Yours, Wm Nephew King. Excuse haste.[276]

Alphabetical Boyd, in 1872, clearly forgetting his earlier testimony when he claimed Lloyd wasn't imprisoned, said, "He remained, altogether in prison in Savannah, about nine months, when he was sent to Macon by order of a physician, about June 1862 [it was mid-July]." Boyd also says, "His health was much reduced while he was in Savannah. He suffered considerably from paralysis." It is true that when Lloyd limped into Washington City, he was greatly impaired. But the real reason for this serious debility will become apparent.

That night, July 15, 1862, Alvin, Virginia, and Clarence pulled out of Savannah Station on the Central Railroad's scheduled 9:45, for the 190-mile trip to Macon, arriving at their destination just after 6:00 the following morning. Macon would be their home for the next two months or so. But the prisoner-Alvin would not be housed in Camp Oglethorpe, the prison stockade by the railroad tracks on the banks of the Ocmulgee River, where in April of 1862 Union prisoners of war were transported, held, and often died. But not Alvin, spared because of the all-important intervention of Dr. King.

Virginia, in 1872, testified about her husband that "he was taken very ill in the prison, and he was then sent up to Macon, and ordered to be put in the prison there, but he was not put in the prison, but in the jailer's house, and while in Macon he was paroled."[277]

Lloyd says, "After remaining in close confinement for 6 months, Genl A.R. Lawton, the Brig General who had charge of the city was removed to Virginia. Genl Mercer, at the desire of my physician, Dr William Nephew King, ordered me to be removed to Macon, for the benefit of my health, which was greatly impaired by confinement, where I remained 3 months longer, when Genl Mercer discharged me (see the discharge)."[278]

In Macon, Lloyd lived in the home of his jailer: "I was treated very kindly as well as my wife and child at Macon by Col. Jack Brown whom I ever shall remember with great kindness."[279]

William Andrew Jackson Brown was thirty-two then, a Georgia lawyer and planter, married with children. He had actually been promoted to colonel only on June 21, 1862. Jackson was at Macon only a short time.

This letter, dated July 20, 1862, is Enclosure 24 in the Lloyd Papers. The envelope in which it arrived, reading, "W. Alvin Lloyd, Esq., Macon, Geo. Kindness of the Guard," is Enclosure 25.

Savannah. Mr. W. Alvin Lloyd, Macon. My Dear Sir, I am in rect. of your letter, which was left in my absence from the office, on the table, in an out of the way place, so I did not get it until the Guard called to inquire for the reply. This will account for the delay, which I sincerely regret, as it has kept you in that hell [underlined] so many more days. I called upon Gen Mercer but he was out. I handed your letter to his son, Capt. Mercer, and explained to him the treatment you had been subjected to. He seems much astonished and promised to attend to it by that evening's Guard going up. I hope by this time you are comfortable again, and feeling well. I have been done to death for the past week and was nearly broken down. Do let me hear from you again as soon as you like. With kindest regards to Mrs. L and yourself, I am very sincerely yours, Wm Nephew King.

From Macon, Alvin dashed off a letter on July 21 to his friend John Robin McDaniel, and eight days later, from his office at his company, Hose and Fire, Lynchburg, Virginia, John Robin replied:

Mr Wm Alvin Lloyd, Macon, Geo. Dear Sir, Yours 21 inst to hand, I regret to hear of the delay in your case, and do not understand it. I would with pleasure write to Genl Mercer, if I had any acquaintance with him, but I have not. A letter from me to President Davis could do no good, for if he knows of me at all he knows me as one who never was one of his warmest friends but now no accounts of his policy, or efficiency, and have not been particular in expressing my opinions, because I go for the cause of my country, and not more. I trust however you will be soon released and that your health will be completely restored. Be pleased to present my regards to Mrs. L. Your friend, Jno Robin McDaniel. [280]

Alphabetical Boyd swore that he finally arrived in Washington in late July or the first of August 1862. During his direct examination in 1872, the question was put to him about his visit to Mr. Lincoln: "Where did you come from on that occasion?"

Answer: "From Richmond."

Question: "For what purpose did you visit Mr Lincoln on that occasion?"

Answer: "To carry dispatches and letters from Lloyd to the President."

Question: "What did these dispatches and letters relate to?"

Answer: "They related to the movements of the troops at Richmond, towards Maryland, to the harbor defenses of Savannah, and to the imprisonment of Lloyd, his trials and tribulations."

However, in his 1865 deposition, Boyd had sworn that "he does not know what information was contained" in this package so delivered. So, in 1865 he didn't know what was in the package, but by 1872 he did.

While up in Washington delivering the latest dispatches, Boyd testified that he was offered a contract by Lincoln on July 29, 1862, similar to the one Lloyd had, but at half the salary. This is the wording: "Mr T.H.S. Boyd is employed to go South and return with dispatches or other useful information. He will be allowed one hundred dollars per month. Signed A. Lincoln, July 29 1862." When asked where the contract was, Alphabetical said he'd left it with his (unnamed) lawyer in Baltimore. All this according to Boyd's deposition of July 19, 1865. After the war he was never called upon to show it as evidence. Just as well, as it never existed.

Dr. King, clearly sympathetic to Lloyd's sufferings in Savannah, on August 3, 1862, wrote to "W. Alvin Lloyd" in Macon:

My Dear Sir, Upon my return to the city, I found a letter from you which had been in this office for some days, which will account for the tardiness of my reply. I am indeed glad to hear of your parole, tho' I have not had time to ascertain its source, as I have been up in the Barracks to see Gen Mercer about it and to find out the other questions you desired answered, but he was not in. I will see him to-night or in the morning, and let you know as early as possible. I am sorry to hear your health is no better, but keep your spirits up.

This next passage must have meant the world to an increasingly incapacitated and depressed Lloyd, sure that his right to a fair trial had been denied him and convinced his unendurable punishment would kill him. It seemed Dr. King was determined to save him.

You have seen the darkest day, since your health will, with the invigorating influence of a pure atmosphere, freedom from confinement, and a plenty of exercise, soon return, to cheer both yourself & Mrs. L, poor thing, her sufferings have been almost as much as yours. I am so glad you have found a just & good friend in the kind-hearted & noble soul Col. Brown. Get him motivated [illegible] he will see justice done to you, that which has been shamefully & basely denied by that "Tub of Guts," Col. R. [Rockwell] who, dressed in a little brief authority sits [illegible] "Monarch of all he Surveys." He will have a reckoning [illegible] friends when this war is over. He knew you asked for nothing but your rights due to you at a military tribunal, you furnished the necessary papers to bring an open trial & prove you guilt or innocence, but took them & laid them away, caring little if you lived to see the postponed trial, or whether you ever had a trial or not. Humanity should prompt him to action, if nothing else, but there is not a spark of it in a thousand such hearts. If it is, it is so carefully buried that it will never come to light. I have written you not one letter since you left, not because I did not feel like it but because I did not have a moment to spare. I thank you for your solicitude in regard to my health. I am pretty well run down & have much to do in [illegible] as the summer months are down on us in great earnest. We have [illegible] fevers, and the troops are suffering no little. I shall tell the General about the state of your health. Could you not get the questions in regard to who pays the expenses of paroled persons answered by Col. Brown? before I could write to you again, but I shall do so at as early a date as possible. The Hebrew [jailer Russell] gnashes his teeth when he thinks how I served him. If I had my way, I would make him gnash them open to the gums, & then gum it to the bone. He will get his [illegible] at a future day when the [illegible] Mayor of the city of Savannah [illegible] With kind remembrance to Mrs. L & the boy & good wishes for you and your cause. I am, my dear Lloyd, very sincerely your friend, Wm Nephew King.[281]

The time when Lloyd was brought to his knees, the time of his great suffering, is perhaps coming to an end. But his freedom, what resembles his freedom, is not at all what he'd wished for, wanted, or dreamed.

10

Grave Suspicions

I F LLOYD RELIVED HIS AGONIES, HIS FEARS OF BEING CONVICTED AND hanged, the times when no one could or would save him except a kind doctor who'd taken pity on his plight—and the young wife who'd stayed by his side—had the man he'd been, the man he was now, had he changed at all? And if he wept with relief when the day he'd longed for arrived, there was no fanfare, no music in the terse orders, the few lines on paper that set him free.

> *Order 427, Head Qrs, Dept. Georgia, Savannah. Sept. 14/62. Lt. Col. George R. Hunter, Cmdg at Macon, Georgia, will at once release from confinement and arrest, Mr. Lloyd, a political prisoner, placed there by orders of these Hd. Quarters. By order of Brig Genl Mercer.*[282]

Exactly nine months after he was taken into custody in Savannah, "In obedience to special order from Brig Genl Mercer commanding this military department, Col. R. Hunter, Lt. Col & commandant of post, Mr. W. Alvin Lloyd, a political prisoner detained in custody by his order, is hereby released and honorably discharged from custody and set at liberty." An honorable discharge. It appears there were no caveats and no additional restrictions.[283]

But during a cross-examination in 1872, when Lloyd's estate was trying to collect the remainder of his claim, Alphabetical Boyd was asked this question, "When was Lloyd discharged from prison finally?"

"I don't know that he was ever discharged finally," he answered. "He was discharged with a paper of surveillance with orders to report at Richmond—in the fall of 1862."

"Where was he when he got this paper of surveillance?"

"At Macon, Ga."

"Were you at Macon when he was discharged?"

"Yes, Sir."

That was not possible. On September 1, 1862, at Jaspers, Alabama, T. S. Boyd enlisted as a private in Company B of the 13th Alabama Battalion, an outfit known as the Partisan Rangers. On October 1, Private Boyd deserted, never to be seen again. Might this T. S. Boyd have been a different man? No. There can be no doubt that this is T. H. S. Boyd—our man. The following year Alphabetical was in Richmond, and on April 30, in an unsuccessful job-seeking letter that he wrote to Secretary of the Treasury Christopher Memminger, he included the following in his resume: "Having been in action in the field since the commencement of the war as First Lieut of Read's Artillery, afterwards as Capt of Partisan Rangers in the west, when I contracted a painfull Rheumatism, from exposure, compelling me to resign."[284]

However, as for Alvin's "honorable release" document, there can be no reason to doubt its authenticity. It is extant. Its authenticity was not questioned by the US War Department when their lawyers came to study it in 1865. But was Lloyd on parole, as Dr. King seemed to think, or truly "set at liberty?" Under surveillance, according to Boyd? It is fact that the Confederate authorities had to let Lloyd go for lack of proof. They may have communicated with authorities in Richmond, especially General Winder. But would Alvin stay away from Richmond, from any town where he'd caused a ruckus, been under suspicion, defrauded minstrels, stolen a wife, or bilked a business? Certainly not. He was back, back on the rails. The belching, billowing engines, the whistles, the coal smoke and wood smoke, were his freedom, his *necessary* as he had been locked away, far from the tracks that carried him everywhere.

On September 24, 1862, Alvin, Virginia, and Clarence left Macon together on the Central Railroad. After 111 miles and almost eight hours on the train, they arrived at Millen, Georgia, where they transferred to the Augusta & Savannah Railroad to take them the fifty miles remaining up to Augusta, to Virginia's friends and relations, where Alvin might recuperate. It was the first time in almost a year that Virginia and Clarence, that anyone outside Macon or Savannah, had seen Alvin outside the confines of captivity.[285]

After four days he left his family in Augusta and "arrived at Richmond on Wednesday night, Oct. 1. All the hotels being full, went to a private boarding house on Grace St., near 9th. Remained until Thursday morning. Procured a room at the Exchange Hotel."[286]

But here Boyd, seven years later, must intrude: According to his 1872 testimony, it was in October that Alvin, being still on parole, reported to General Winder in Richmond. Boyd was very sure of this: "Yes, it was in the fall." It had been on March 1, 1862, while Alvin was in prison in Savannah, that General John H. Winder had been appointed Provost Marshal General of Richmond. Now he would surely know Alvin Lloyd was back in town and did not seek to detain him.

But in Alvin's 1865 claim, he says he "remained [in Richmond] 7 days, visiting and taking plans of the fortifications, etc, etc." This, of course, is not true. It is calculated, "proof" to the US War Department that even after his imprisonment, his infirmities, he had been an indefatigable Yankee spy, risking everything.

The truth is far more prosaic: He left Richmond at 6:00 p.m., on Thursday, October 9, in company with Nellie Dooley, his wife's maid. Nellie would say in her 1865 deposition that the Lloyds had not employed her during the nine months of Alvin's imprisonment. Where she was and what she was doing during that period is not stated. However, she was almost certainly in Richmond, Petersburg, or Lynchburg.

"Arrived at Lynchburg Friday morning, October 10th, at 3½ o'clock. No room. I met my true friend Jno. Robin McDaniel, who had loaned me money during my imprisonment at Savannah and Macon," Alvin wrote.

But when Nellie Dooley gave her deposition in 1865, she said October was the month she left Lynchburg for the lines, carrying a letter for personal hand delivery to Abraham Lincoln. She claimed she got as far as Richmond before being turned back by pickets, and had to return the letter—unopened, of course—to her employer in Lynchburg. However, according to Alphabetical Boyd he now took over the dangerous chore, and, with the letter by now expanded to a package, succeeded in getting back across the lines, where he met his brother Charles C. Boyd, then a Union soldier stationed in Washington, DC.

The two of them went to see Mr. Lincoln on October 20, according to Alphabetical's June 3, 1865, deposition. However, Charles Boyd says, in 1872: "It was sometime in November 1862 that I went with my brother to see the President." Charlie was now a willing participant in the fraud. "At the time I went with my brother to the President, the President gave him $250. The President seemed very much pleased at the information." With fictions piled upon fictions, contradictions abounding, there is a sense of being trapped in a circus fun-house mirror of old. That is why truths, microscopic and often mundane, must be extracted.

For example and in truth, Alvin left Lynchburg on October 10, and on Saturday, the eleventh, arrived at Petersburg, leaving there the following day. On Monday, October 13, he "arrived at Augusta with my little boy's nurse Ellen Dooley." He would leave her there with his family.

Four days later, on October 17, Alvin left Augusta, and the following day arrived at Columbia, leaving there on Wednesday the twenty-second, at 5:15 p.m., bound for Charleston. He was on the move again, alone. He arrived in Charleston at 2:30 a.m. on October 23, and, of course, Alvin claims that he spied. He "remained 2 days, visiting defenses, gunboats, etc, etc." He left Charleston at eight-fifteen the night of Saturday, October 25, 1862, and arrived back in Columbia the same day. Alvin "visited Alexanders and Glazes Foundrys & machine shops doing work for the rebels . . . also the camps, etc." Alexander's, and Glaze & Shields, were two separate foundries in Columbia.

At 8:00 a.m., on the twenty-sixth, he left Columbia, and arrived at Charlotte, just across the North Carolina line, at 3:30 p.m. He was out of Charlotte that evening, he claims, but where was he bound? In his concocted testimony he says he went to Goldsboro, North Carolina, arriving there on the twenty-seventh. "Remained two days, visiting usual places." He claims he went on from Goldsboro to Wilmington, on the Carolina coast, arriving there on Friday, October 31, and that he "remained 3 days, visited forts, defenses, etc, etc." Leaving there on November 2, he arrived at Richmond the next day. But this is another fiction so he could assert that he was spying on the Atlantic defenses. The truth is, he never went to

Goldsboro or Wilmington. He left Charlotte heading to Richmond, and was in Richmond by the last day of the month. The next five days he was back and forth the twenty-two miles between the capital and Petersburg.[287]

Under the heading of 1862, in his original diary, he included the following rather odd notations:

Receipts in Petersburg, Va., 1861.

Nov. 1st, Petersburg RR—$100;

Lynch & Callender (Factory)—$50;

Thos. Calligan (Foundry)—$25;

Nov. 5th, 1861—Mechanics Cotton Factory—$12.50;

Nov. 5th, 1861, South Side RR—$100.

Receipts in Richmond, Va.

Nov. 3rd 1861: Crenshaw & Co. (Factory)—$50;

Va. Central RR—$100;

Richmond & Petersburg RR—$50;

Nov. 4th, 1861: Richmond & Danville RR—$100.[288]

At first glance it would seem Lloyd had simply listed his 1861 receipts under the wrong year, or perhaps wrote 1861 when he should have written 1862. An honest mistake, perhaps? But no. It is all part of the lie. This rigorous timekeeper, this schedule-obsessed man, would never have confused early November 1862 with early November 1861, as the latter was precisely when he was busy marrying the actress Annie Taylor three times in Louisiana.

Then the original diary entry continues: "Left Richmond, Va., on Wednesday morning, Nov. 5th/62, at 4.15 o'clock, for Petersburg. Arrived at 6 a.m." However, his redone entry, and he must emphasize how imperiled he is again, reads: "Remained 2 days," and he then claims he left Richmond on the fourth, "and dodged the detectives who were ordered to arrest me. Walked over Mayo's Bridge. Remained in Manchester all night." Next morning, Wednesday, November 5, 1862, he "took the cars going at full speed." He "arrived at Petersburg at 7 a.m. Nov. 5th."

Another original diary entry reports his arrival in Petersburg: "Was placed under arrest & paroled until 'Pannill,' the ProvoMarshall could telegraph to & get a reply from Genl Jno H. Winder at Richmond. The dispatch from Genl Winder came at 12 o'clock, ordering my confinement. I was then put under arrest at 8½ pm, Wednesday, Nov. 5/62."

At Petersburg, for the 1865 claim Alvin said he "was arrested on orders from Genl Winder at Richmond, by the Provost Marshal—Pannill—of Petersburg. My baggage and person searched, but nothing found upon to order me to prison." He continues: "I was set at liberty next day, Nov. 6th 62." He then left for Lynchburg at 5:00 p.m.[289]

This account differs somewhat from the very detailed one given by Virginia, who claimed, "On or about the 5th of November 1862, she received a note from her husband, who was in Manchester, directing her to take the cars for Lynchburg on the next morning [the sixth] in order to avoid the rebel detectives; that she did so, and was joined by him at Burkeville, Va." Burkeville was fifty-three miles down the Richmond & Danville line, and was the junction where one picked up the Southern RR train going to Lynchburg.[290]

On Friday, November 7, 1862, Alvin and his entourage were back in Lynchburg. Or, as Alphabetical Boyd says, under oath in 1872, "Mr Lloyd received from Mr. John Robin McDaniel of Lynchburg, Va., $500 in gold, $1000 Confederate money, and gave as security Mrs. Lloyd's diamonds and furs and jewelry, including watches. Owing to the strict surveillance of the rebel detectives, he gave up the idea of returning North, and went to Richmond."[291]

The resumption of his precious guide was of critical importance to Alvin. It was what he'd done before and knew how to do. It was the only way he could have made money so that even if he did consider fleeing the South, he had nothing left anywhere.

In Lynchburg, Alvin reported that "I was again arrested by the detective sent on my track from Richmond by Genl Winder, who, with the asst Provo Marshal of Lynchburg searched my baggage and person, as well as that of my wife (see Provost Marshal's discharge dated Lynchburg, Nov 9th, 1862). The directors of the Va. and Tenn. Railroad censured Thos. Dodamead for advertising in my Guide, stating that Lloyd was an abolitionist and the road would never patronize Lloyd or any other Yankee."[292]

Of this departure, in 1865, Alvin says, "Left Lynchburg in charge of Winder's detectives, Nov. 8th, 1862," and "arrived in Richmond same day."[293]

Richmond: The Confederate capital was a disturbed and disturbing mix of inhumane prisons bulging with Union captives, roaming bands of thugs, men and women—black and white—arbitrarily jailed for treason, but rarely tried. Alvin "was taken before General Winder." Alvin's 1865 expense sheet reads: "Nov. 1862. $100 amt paid to Genl John H. Winder to discharge me from imprisonment and observation. See Discharge Nov. 11th 1862 (Paid in gold)."[294] The important thing here to note is this: Lloyd was never imprisoned in Richmond, as he later claimed.

The discharge, dated November 11, 1862, reads: "Having had W. Alvin Lloyd under observation and having carefully and thoroughly examined with his case, and having made a thorough examination of his papers, I am unable to discover anything to reflect upon his loyalty to the Southern states, and I therefore discharge him from further observation. John Winder."[295]

Imagine Alvin's relief as he bribed his way out of a potential disaster, surely remembering the fate of Union spy Timothy Webster: exposed, captured, charged, tried, convicted, and hanged. This seems to be the month that Lloyd would later claim was when he paid one hundred dollars in gold to Winder, as well as money for a new suit, groceries, and other bribes. Part of Lloyd's later expense account was for the new custom-tailored dress uniform for Winder. Boyd claims he was present when the general was being measured for it. It is true that Winder's extreme vanity, his puffery and pomp, made him vulnerable to flattery.

Elizabeth Van Lew, the head of "Richmond's Unionist under-ground," boasted of her ability to flatter Winder into allowing her to visit Union prisoners. In the guise of a well-meaning, food-bearing, charitable eccentric, Van Lew would frequently receive critical intelligence from these prisoners that she would encrypt and transmit to her ring of spies. And if she learned that a captive soldier was going to be released or exchanged, she would slip dispatches to them that were meant for Federal authorities. She remained undetected until well after the war. Had Winder learned of her activities, she would have been hanged.[296]

In addition to Winder's vulnerabilities, rumors were rife in the South that he drank excessively, was brutish to all but Marylanders, employed his thuggish detectives to brutalize citizens without due process, and habitually received bribes.

Lloyd charged the US government for expenses incurred while in Winder's keep. His 1865 expense account includes the following two items, their dates of application being suitably vague—1862, 1863, and 1864: "$200—amount paid to Genl John H. Winder in Virginia during the years 1862, 1863, and 1864, to [illegible] him" and "$125—amount paid to Holt Richeson [actually Richardson], etc, Richmond, Va., for suit of clothes for Genl John H. Winder, being $1200 in rebel money, being equal to $125.00."[297]

The Richardson suit affair is puzzling. Alvin, and this is in character for him, didn't pay Mr. Richardson. Of record is a copy of the second half of a mild dunning letter to Alvin from W. Holt Richardson (the first half is not extant, and that's unfortunate, as it would give the date). The fragment begins, "is to be had. So far I have not been able to get a peas [*sic*] that I thought would suit you. We are haveing Stearing times now. So far we have been successful." He continues: "Thinking that you might not be able to get back to Richmond for some time to come, as The Rode is so taken up with troops." Now comes the dun: "As money is very scarce and time very dull, I thought I would ask the favour of you to send by Express the amt you owe us, unless you think you can return soon. Yours truly, W. Holt Richardson & Co." The creditor, in totting up his bill, says, "Genl Winder's bill—$1200, Byds—$420." Making a total of $1,620 due. It is not known who or what "Byds" is.[298]

Ever unfaithful to the truth, Boyd reports what Totten has instructed him to say about Lloyd's clandestine activities in Richmond. "While in Richmond, he visited the various departments, and collected some valuable information as to the coming campaign of the rebel armies in the Gulf states. This was the latter part of November 1862. He gave me the dispatches to deliver to Mr. Lincoln, which I did, coming by way of Southwestern Virginia and Kanawha Valley."[299]

"I met my brother in Washington," continues Boyd, "and in his company delivered the dispatches to Mr. Lincoln. I returned to Richmond."[300]

Apart from these impossibilities, in fact, Alvin embarked on another journey. He was truly and legitimately in the "land of cotton," rocketing though tiny towns with astonishing speed. The cotton and woolen mills of the South, especially those of North Carolina and Georgia, were drafted for the cause, and became almost exclusively workhouses for the production of war supplies and goods no longer obtainable from outside the Confederacy. The thirty-nine cotton mills and nine woolen mills in the Tar Heel State, for example, sent everything they made to Raleigh, and, indeed, that state, especially the Piedmont area, with its many waterways and its cheap labor, was the only one that clothed its own troops—and the state had forty regiments to provide uniforms for. So, the mills of both states were of critical importance.

Alvin knew his factories, and, despite Alphabetical Boyd saying Alvin was spying in Richmond in the latter part of November, he set out from the Confederate capital with Virginia, Clarence, and Nellie on November 15 to make a tour of these establishments, selling ads for his upcoming edition, whenever that would be. As compensation for the uncertainty, and for paying cash up front, his customers would be guaranteed two editions for the price of one. It was a hard sell, but Alvin was a hard salesman, and most of the factories went along with the idea even though his first new edition hadn't even come out yet. In fact, he had no idea when it would come out. As it happened, it was May 1863, from Richmond. That first edition of the "New Series" is not extant, but the one from June is, and as proof, there are ads for most of these people he visited in his whirlwind mill tour of 1862–1863.[301]

With his family in tow accompanying him on yet another arduous journey, his first stop was Columbia, South Carolina. He arrived there at six o'clock at night on Friday, November 21, 1862. Witness a man, perhaps for the first time in his life, perhaps by choice or though misfortune, taking some responsibility for his family. "My little boy Clarence was taken sick. Remained 5 days," he writes. And stops. They left Columbia on Monday, the twenty-fourth, on the South Carolina Rail Road, and the following day arrived at Augusta, Georgia, where Virginia, as usual, would stay for a while.[302]

From December 3, 1862, in rapid order he was in one town and then another, like a machine. He carefully chronicled all these stops throughout his tours, these rapid runs through the heart of Georgia. This tour to obtain revenue is the reason he needed a pass from President Lincoln to go south. And there is no reason to disbelieve this fast-moving money grab, as most of the ads do appear in the extant issues of his guide. Remembering that he was recently incarcerated, his complete recovery from the illness that apparently plagued him is apparent. Here was a man of fierce drive and nearly superhuman energy. Often these factories he visited, these mills, would be out beyond urban limits, because originally, when they were built, it was of paramount importance to have the mill right in the middle of the cotton fields, to expedite flow from the enslaved cotton pickers to the manufacturer.

As 1863 dawned, Alvin sped through Georgia, past hundreds upon hundreds of slaves laboring in the cotton fields—and though the Confederate states would summarily ignore and defy this momentous event, on January 1, 1863, President Lincoln's Emancipation Proclamation was issued, declaring "that all persons held as slaves within the rebellious states are, and henceforward shall be free." Though many slaves fled—or tried to flee and were caught, punished, or killed—the plantation owners, the cotton kings, the entire industry remained, though altered. Moderately.

Finally, on January 3, Alvin was able to place an ad in the *Charleston Courier* for his guide: "Presidents, Superintendents, Officers of Railroads, are requested to send the latest schedules to W. Alvin Lloyd, Richmond, who desires and intends to issue immediately his new issue of the *Southern Steamboat and Railroad Guide*."[303] Now he couldn't, wouldn't stop. Sunday, January 4, found Alvin riding the cars out of Columbus bound for North Carolina.

One of the features in Alvin's *Railroad Guide* about this time was "a list of all the cotton and woolen factories in the Confederacy, with names of proprietors and post office of each factory"—useful information for his readers but never intended to provide intelligence to the Union. These factories and their owners were well known. Alvin Lloyd's entire cotton factory tour was strictly to collect revenue, nothing more.

Lloyd left Alamance on February 1, 1863, bound for Wilmington, North Carolina, where he arrived on the third. Although he doesn't mention this, Alvin was probably taking a week at the beach to rest and care for his ailing little son.[304]

But he must later fictionalize this visit. After all, he must prove to the Federal authorities that he'd never stopped spying. "Visited the forts, camps, etc." is all he says of this week on the coast. He and the family left Wilmington on Sunday, February 8, and "arrived in Richmond Feby 10th. Remained 20 days."[305]

Lloyd slipped from view over this period. Most likely he was resting again. Nearly a month later, he left Richmond on Monday, March 2, 1863, and headed for Petersburg, arriving there the following day. On the fourth he left Petersburg, and on Thursday the fifth of March arrived in Salem, Virginia, near Roanoke. "Remained 7 days."

It was during this time that Boyd claimed, "I next met Lloyd in Salem, Roanoke Co., Va., and accompanied him to Salisbury, N.C. Lloyd then traveled all over North Carolina and Georgia, and visited all the cotton and woolen factories in those states, and made a report of their hands, capacity, and quantity of cloth manufactured. This was in Jan'y, February, March and April of 1863. I was with him a portion of the time, about three weeks."[306]

Lloyd left Salem, Virginia, on Thursday, March 12, 1863, and the next day was in Farmville. "Remained 1 day." He "arrived at Whites & Blacks S.S. RR Station, March 15th." He means Blacks & Whites—today's Blackstone—in Nottaway County, equidistant between the towns of Wellville and Nottaway, and fifty miles southwest of Richmond. The station was on the Southside Railroad. "Remained 6 days." He left Blacks & Whites on Saturday, March 21, and arrived at Petersburg the same day.[307]

On Sunday we find him in Raleigh. "Remained 9 days." Close to midnight on Thursday, April 2, 1863, according to Boyd, the quartet left the state capital going west on the North Carolina Railroad. Here Alphabetical Boyd's time with Lloyd was up, he claimed. As for Boyd's accompanying Lloyd from Salem, Virginia to Salisbury, North Carolina, there is no mention of this in Lloyd's Enclosure 13, nor is there any mention of Salisbury, and nothing about Boyd.[308]

Early in the morning Alvin pulled into Durham Station, twenty-six miles down the track. "Remained 15 days." Durham, like many other towns in North Carolina, had been somewhat divided in its views on secession, and was still that way when Alvin arrived there. Here poor whites and poor free blacks lived cheek by jowl, working their small plots. Here, at Durham, was the old Bennett Place, where General William T. Sherman would accept General Joseph Johnston's surrender on April 26, 1865.[309]

The Lloyd group were back on the North Carolina Railroad on April 18, and 128 miles later, pulled into Concord the following day, Sunday, April 19. "Remained 17 days." Alvin took time out from his family to go and visit the town's steam cotton mill.[310]

On Tuesday, May 5, 1863, Alvin was out of Concord and "arrived at Richmond" the next day. Finally, finally, and after this astonishing dash through the cotton lands, he had the ads and the content for a new publication. *Lloyd's Southern Railroad Guide*, New Series Number 1, Volume 1, came out in early May of 1863, printed in handsome style by Messrs. George P. Evans of the *Whig* building, in Richmond. No more steamboats. The first guide since Old Series Vol. 8 No. 2 that had been issued as far back as February 1861. On May 7, 1863, Alvin Lloyd proudly dropped a copy of his new guide on the desk of the editor of his landlords, the *Richmond Whig*, and the following day left town. It would be eight months before he got back to Richmond, and then under very different circumstances.[311]

On Tuesday the twelfth of May 1863, W. Alvin Lloyd was back in Concord, North Carolina. The next day Virginia, Clarence, and Nellie returned to Augusta, while Alvin left town alone in the other direction, heading for Mobile, where not so long ago he'd wooed and won the young actress Annie Taylor. This mission to Mobile was different. His guide was to be published there. And that guide, his mouthpiece, was the bull's-eye on his back.

11

Shot Down Like a Dog

ON MAY 23RD, 1863, TWO DAYS AFTER ALVIN LLOYD ARRIVED IN MOBILE, he was arrested "by the Provo Marshal's Mr. Parker from Massachusetts upon complaint of Mr Chamberlain, also from Massachusetts, proprietor of the Battle House, Mobile, and was kept in confinement, searched, & papers examined. There was nothing to warrant my detention & Parker discharged me." Discharged. Freed. No proof. It is familiar. And most importantly, though Alvin repeatedly lies to the US authorities about his frequent, long prison terms, he has only been incarcerated twice: Very, very briefly for bigamy in Memphis, nine months in Georgia. Twice. Just twice.

And for the benefit of his claim, he is a Yankee vigilante committee of one. "Mobile is full of Northern men who are the very worst secessionists and fire-eaters."[312]

At this time, much of Dixie was strewn with war dead. From battle campaigns won and lost, and the great prayer that Robert E. Lee's Army of Virginia would crush the Yankees, with Richmond under threat of invasion, with wins and heavy losses on both sides—the internecine bloodletting—the heaving and pitching of a seemingly endless war, Alvin Lloyd had fueled and would fuel again an already raging fire. With words. In his guide. What he wrote and muttered in public hit a nerve. Hit many nerves. This puzzle of a man with an unstoppable compulsion to attack—parrying and thrusting without fear of consequence—would never, couldn't ever, end well.

Now, with the stench of prison trailing him like foxfire, Lloyd came to a city that, though there were Unionists sprinkled among the populace, had by now declared itself pure Confederate, boldly vowing not to be "conquered and held in subjugation by an enemy whom its people have grown up detesting."[313]

The Federal blockade of Mobile Bay led by Union Admiral David Farragut had greatly suppressed trade and decimated the economy. Even though the blockade-runners, the low, fleet ships that slipped frequently undetected though the blockade "maintain[ed] a trickle of trade in and out of Mobile," privations and poverty were perceived as Yankee attacks.[314] The city's vital defenses were on high alert as were most residents. In fact, even those impugned by Alvin for being of northern origins were not the enemy.

And the man Alvin claimed arrested him on a "complaint," Gideon Marsena "G. M." Parker, was the Provost Marshal of Mobile. He was originally from Connecticut, although he had been in Mobile since he was fourteen. After the war, he would become Mobile's mayor. He'd married the sister of Francis Henry Chamberlain, the proprietor of the Battle House Hotel. Hence the connection and this duo's united front against Alvin Lloyd, who had come to town to prepare and publish his guide. And he did. That is the wonder of it. Though it is not known where in the city the guide was printed, here it was, at last. Now it was a cause for celebration after the long delay that was prison, after his tear through cotton country to amass monies to publish. The June 1863 edition of *Lloyd's Southern Railroad Guide* cost fifty cents. "New Series Volume One, Number Two, with one hundred and thirty-eight pages," he announced. This number was "the second issued since July 1861, when we were (as before published) driven from New York by an Abolition mob at midnight. We are not in right trim yet; a month or so hence our Railroad friends and the public may look for a better appearance of the *Guide*. We will shortly have our new map ready [it actually came out on or around October 10, 1863, from Mobile]. We have met with good cheer from every quarter and our *Guide* shall be a correct one or not at all. But it will require a little time to get the railroad men posted as to our whereabouts."[315]

Despite the good cheer, and because Alvin could not resist, he found an opportunity to retaliate against Chamberlain the hotelkeeper. In print.

"The Battle House in Mobile is for rent: address J. Emanuel, President of the Battle House Company, Mobile. We hope some good Southern man will take charge of this house; it will pay. We believe that a majority of the stockholders would prefer a Southern man as a tenant. Rent: $14,000 per annum."[316]

The guide included the railroads of Texas and a map of Charleston Harbor. As there had to be a lot of complimentary ads in this edition, piggybacking on the May edition, he knew he was going to be strapped for cash for a while, so he came up with another moneymaking venture: "I would most respectfully offer my services to my friends in the country, and all other who may need them, to act as an Agent in this City for any Negroes who may have been or are now at work on the Fortifications near Mobile, and will collect any claims due them for such services."[317]

This issue is essentially an advertiser for Mobile, pages eighty-two through the end being taken up with ads from that city, complete with elaborate lithographs; Jarvis Turner's Mobile Marble Works were busy and would get busier as they serviced the dead—"monuments, tombs, Gravestones" and "mantles, grates." Commission merchants, wholesale grocers, slave auctioneers and auction houses, and the "wines, liquors & grocers,"—pages sixty-four to the end are ads. Pages twenty-eight to sixty-three are occupied with railroad schedules copied from Hill & Swayze's 1862 *Confederate States Steamboat & Railroad Guide*, and hopelessly out of date.

"We shall publish our *Guide* in Mobile hereafter," Alvin wrote, full of optimism, as he managed to revivify, strengthen, and like his beloved engines, steam ahead.[318]

And he did, at least for a while. The July edition also came out, from Mobile, prepared in June. And on occasion and much delayed by weeks, mail and newspapers like the *New York Herald* and other northern publications trickled into the city.

Perhaps Alvin Lloyd was sitting in a restaurant in Mobile, and as a former New Yorker himself was reading the *Herald*'s news and came upon the death notices. "On Monday, June 1, Lloyd, Ernest P., only child of Harriet and W. Alvin Lloyd, aged 22 months and 9 days."[319]

This is the child whose birth notice was published in the *Herald* while Alvin was in Canton, Mississippi, celebrating not only his recent freedom from Captain Klinck and the Memphis ordeal but also the Confederate victory at Manassas just as the bigamy stories about him were breaking all over the country. The mother, Harriet, is unknown. Another wife? Another child, a lost child, unknown to Alvin? Another mystery. And as for Alvin's true cause—the Confederacy—news of Lee's crushing defeat as he attempted to invade the north at Gettysburg, the three days of July 1 to 3, had reached all in the south.

On Saturday, July 18, 1863, Alvin left Mobile and arrived in Montgomery later that day. While he was there—and here is the reason for this fast exit—someone in Mobile wrote a letter to the *Memphis Appeal*, explaining Alvin's departure from the city.

Quite a storm in a teapot has been raging in our city the past few days. A.M. [sic] Lloyd, publisher of Lloyd's Railroad Guide, a comparative stranger, I think, in the city, published in the July number of his periodical the names of several prominent citizens who had business connections or families in the North. . . . This wholesale inferences were most unfair. It happened that several gentlemen whose Southern principles and practical patriotism were beyond question, had their families in the North—as indeed Capt. Semmes of the Alabama [Raphael Semmes, captain of the raider ship Alabama did have families in the North until recently]. . . . These gentlemen came out with cards in the daily press, denouncing Lloyd as a "liar," "slanderer," "scoundrel," "imposter," etc., one gentleman warning him to leave the city within twenty-four hours from the date of his card.

Alvin was exposed.

In the meantime, he published a card, stating that he was responsible, etc. Doubtless, in the list published in the railroad guide were names of disloyal men, men who had refused Confederate money, and who are enemies at heart to our cause, but the tried and true men who were denounced with the suspected, defeated whatever patriotic object the writer had, and the traitor can take shelter behind the known loyal men who had been wrongly attacked. Had Lloyd known more of the status of the prominent citizens he might have done good; as it is, he has done harm.[320]

Alvin had in fact done great harm to himself. He had been warned.

And in Richmond, on his own path to ruin, at this very time, Alphabetical Boyd was brought into Judge Halyburton's courtroom. His Honor heard both sides of the argument—that Boyd had deserted as a private back in February 1862, and that as an officer (Boyd claimed he was a Colonel) he couldn't be tried as a private, etc., and threw Boyd back in Castle Thunder Prison to await trial by the military authorities as a deserter.[321]

That day, Friday, July 24, Alvin left Montgomery, arriving in Augusta, Georgia, on the twenty-sixth, for a ten-day stay with his wife and child. On Sunday, August 2, he traveled and arrived at Columbia, South Carolina, the same day. He spent two days in the capital of the state where war began and where Sherman's men would burn the city to the ground at war's end. But now, northern prisoners were beginning to accumulate in the ration-deficient Sorghum Prison as Alvin stayed a week for unknown reasons. Perhaps he was trying to find a new place of publication, but to no avail.

On Saturday, August 8, Lloyd arrived back in Mobile. Whether or not the August and September editions of *Lloyd's Southern Railroad Guide* ever came out is not known, but certainly the October–November one did—from Mobile again. This guide had 158 pages. For one dollar it contained the timetables, stations, connections, distances, and fares on all the railroads throughout the Southern states, with a guide to the principal watering places and summer resorts, and sketches of the different cities and towns in the South. Also a list of the best-kept hotels, with a list of all the cotton and woolen factories in the Confederacy, with names of proprietors and the post office of each factory. Pages 64 to 102 contained ads.[322]

As for Alphabetical Boyd, who would swear at different times that he was anywhere and everywhere, was, in fact, on August 12, 1863, in Richmond, extremely ill. The Confederate army records report "Private T.M. Boyd [*sic*], post office Clarksburg, Md. [which was, indeed, T.H.S. Boyd's home address], of Company I of the Louisiana 1st regiment, was admitted to General Hospital No. 13, in Richmond, suffering from acute diarrhea." The following day, diarrhea or not, he was thrown into Castle Thunder Prison. They fed him "Bennett's Diarrhoea Killer," obtainable at W. Peterson & Co, druggists at 155 Main Street. A few doses were all you needed. Unless it was colic diarrhea, for which Mr. Peterson recommended Extract of Jamaica Ginger. And, if you couldn't get to Mr. Peterson's in time, J. W. Randolph, the stationer at 121 Main, could offer you "Any Quantity of Paper!"[323]

Alvin was not similarly afflicted. But the letter, the tempest of a letter that arrived in Mobile, might well have sickened him.

> *Geo. W. Adams, supt of Central Georgia RR, residing at Savannah, Ga., wrote a letter to [Major L. J.] Fleming, engineer & supt of the M & O RR [Mobile & Ohio], stating to him that he understood that W. Alvin Lloyd was in Mobile, and that Lloyd was a spy, and had been confined in Chatham County Jail in Savannah, and had made his escape from that place and was in the employ of the Yankee Govt—to be on his guard and to inform the citizens of Mobile of the fact Lloyd was a scoundrel and abolitionist. This letter was shown to several citizens of the place, and given to the editor of the* Mobile Register & Advertiser *(John Forsyth) to publish.[324]*

To make matters worse, in his guide, after a long series of cautions, words to the wise, pat phrases of instructions advising his readers to "betray no trust, divulge no secret, condescend to compliance rather than continue an angry dispute," on and on comes blackmail. After this exhausting list of homilies and hymns to righteousness—bulleted in bold print—is a "LIST OF NAMES OF MEN DOING BUSINESS IN MOBILE WITH FAMILIES RESIDING IN THE NORTH." Couched in a plea, but more of a warning, Alvin advises "A.J. Mullaney, Newton St. John, L. Merchant, Dr. Mandeville, J.F. Woodhull and G. Rapalie," as "good friends of the South," to have their "families join you in Mobile."

Remembering the hard fears bubbling near to boiling in Mobile, Alvin has incited violence. In his own words:

> *I was caught by several citizens of the place, who advised me to leave. The Northern men who had endeavored to injure me by asserting I was an abolitionist & spy, I denounced them. They, 30 or 40, attacked*

*me and shot me 8 times, one ball through the lung, one severed the
spine, which paralyzed me. I was confined to my bed (not expected to
live 2 weeks) for 3 months. I am yet paralyzed.*[325]

The historical truth is vastly different: In Mobile, on October 1, 1863,
just as his October issue of the guide was being published, Alvin was
shot down "like a dog" on the street by Andrew J. Mullany. Exactly where
on his body the bullets entered is not known, but the shooting almost
killed him. What actually seems to have happened on that fateful day is
that Mobile resident Andrew Mullany, one of the men accused of Union
sensibilities by Lloyd in his guide, approached him on the street with the
intention of accosting the slander-mongering publisher. Lloyd, ever ready
for attack, "snapped his revolver twice" (cocked the weapon) and pointed
it at the oncoming Mullany. Andrew Mullany shot Lloyd several times. It
may have been nine times, as some papers reported, or eight, as Alvin said,
and the badly wounded man had to be dragged to his residence, where
he lay near death for several weeks. Mullany gave himself up and was
subsequently released on bail. Alvin's life was despaired of, and the press
reported the event, some even saying he was dead.[326]

Although he didn't die, the cost to Alvin was horrendous. That part is
true. Alphabetical Boyd sums up Alvin's terrible state in his 1872 deposition: "When Lloyd went South in July 1861, he was in enjoyment of
good health and had every appearance of a man who would live a long
life. When he came back in June 1865, he used a crutch and cane, and
was constantly under the care of a physician and so until his death. His
lungs were affected, and he also had paralysis of the back and leg, which
was considerably shrunken and shortened. This paralysis occurred in
Mobile—first in Savannah, and afterwards in Mobile." By that is meant
that Alvin definitely and without question suffered in Savannah, perhaps
even to the extent of some form of severe rheumatism or arthritis. But as
for the crutches and the paralysis there is no question that came after the
shooting, and not before.[327]

As if by design, Virginia or Alvin summoned help, real help, from
Virginia's brother, Eugene Higgins, a shipping agent and commission
merchant. Higgins wrote to Jefferson Davis on December 5, 1863, from

Mobile. The letter is a paean to Alvin. It is a defense of Alvin. Higgins wrote:

There is a case, I think, if you had known of it, that would have you to act. It is this. Wm Alvin Lloyd, a true Southern Rights man, who has been treated shamefully by the authorities at Savannah, and here too. He has had the moral courage to publish the names of men speculating in Mobile whose families reside at the North. They are, Sir, enemies to our cause. For publishing these men in Mobile . . . he was attacked by these Yankee traitors, and shot down like a dog on the first of October last. Yes, Sir, for publishing facts against these Yankees, he is a cripple for life. You, Sir, can appreciate the acts of a true man to our cause. Mr Lloyd has lost everything he possessed by these Yankees, and was striving to rid Mobile of the nest of Yankee traitors (and it is full) when he was shot down.

And here is the request:

Now allow me, Sir, an humble citizen, to suggest to Your Excellency, to give Mr Lloyd some position to maintain himself and family. He is advanced in life, and the Provost Marshall here is a young man, and would do better service in camp than here in Mobile, and his assistants are all young men. I in common with nine tenths of Southern men in Mobile, would love to see you appoint Mr Lloyd Provost Marshall of Mobile. Of course, Sir, you act as best suits your taste. Very respectfully, Eugene Higgins. I think, Sir, this is a case where you would do a noble act by appointing this man to some office. He is despairing. Mr Lloyd is the publisher of Lloyd's Southern RR Guide & Map. He is well known throughout the whole Confederacy. Respectfully, Eugene Higgins.

It is as if Lloyd is unknown to Jefferson Davis or Eugene Higgins thinks that to be the case. A peculiarity, to be sure, considering Lloyd's frantic letters to the Confederate president from Savannah. But of course, thousands of people wrote to Jefferson Davis throughout the war.[328]

Alvin says: "Left Mobile for Richmond, Va., Dec. 22nd 1863, sick and wounded." With his powers of resurrection, his will to live on and move on no matter how he incurred the violence he incited, Alvin Lloyd astonishes. This sick and wounded phoenix is somehow back on his feet.

On the way to the Confederate capital, he went to his family in Augusta to repair. Six days later, on December 28, he managed to visit the offices of the local paper, the *Constitutionalist*, handing them a free copy of his latest guide. The paper printed the news of Alvin's shooting the following day. Even an event as insignificant as this might be picked up by newspapers around the country, especially if it involved a notorious scoundrel who had, perhaps, once resided in their town. For example, the *Macon Telegraph* of January 2, 1864, wanted its readers to know that "W. Alvin Lloyd, the *Railroad Guide* man, who was shot in Mobile some time since, and reported dead, was in Augusta, on crutches, a few days ago, slowly recovering from his wound."

On Wednesday, January 6, 1864, Alvin arrived in Richmond.[329]

The *Richmond Daily Dispatch* of January 8, 1864, had this: "Loyd's [*sic*] *Railroad Guide*. Mr. Loyd [*sic*], the proprietor of that most valuable publication, the railroad guide, has commenced the publication of a map in connection with it. The map is accurate and well gotten up. The representations of Charleston Harbor, and the islands around it, is very interesting just at this time. Mr. Loyd, who was shot recently in Mobile, did not die of his wounds, as reported."

The *Richmond Examiner* of the same date, January 8, 1864, says: "Lloyd's Railroad Map. We are indebted to Mr. W. Alvin Lloyd, of Mobile, for a copy of his beautifully executed Railroad Map for 1864. It is said to be the only correct map of the railroads in the Southern Confederacy in existence. We take occasion here to correct the report which we published some time ago, that Mr. Lloyd was dead, having been killed in a street fight in Mobile. The facts are these: A party of Yankees living in Mobile, infuriated by Mr. Lloyd's exposure of them, attacked him in the street and in the affair he received nine pistol wounds some of them very severe, which disabled and confined him to his bed for several weeks. His escape from death was miraculous. He is still in a crippled condition, being upon crutches."

According to Alphabetical Boyd's 1872 deposition, "January, February and March 1864, I saw Lloyd in Richmond. He was getting information in regard to the fortifications, and as to strength and location of Confederate troops around Petersburg and Richmond. He sent this to Mr Lincoln by a blockade runner."[330]

As for Boyd's statement here, Alvin was indeed in Richmond, and so was Boyd, but not as he claimed, recently returned to Richmond after seeing President Lincoln in Washington. As fact, and again, the historical record negates the fictions, on the night of January 28, 1864, Boyd's room on Franklin, between 8th and 9th, was entered in his absence and robbed of a trunk, containing about three thousand dollars worth of valuable clothing. He called the police and offered a large reward. Was it clothing or incriminating papers within the trunk? On June a vest would turn up, sported by Aleck Brace, Ann Newton's slave. Aleck swore he bought it from Fanny Jones's slave Pat, who swore he bought it from another man. The case against Aleck Brace was dismissed.[331]

Actually, what Lloyd and Boyd were doing was putting together the next editions of the *Railroad Guide*. Unmolested, it seems. But in 1864, Alvin's experience in the South—the arrests, desperation, and poverty of 1861, a year culminating in his long term of imprisonment at Savannah, and 1862, most of which was behind bars or under arrest, not to mention the continued poverty and uncertainty about his family—was to change for the better.

By 1864, with the Confederate government facing inevitable defeat, *in extremis*, and far too preoccupied to bother with the likes of him, hobbling on crutches, with his resurgent powers intact, Alvin Lloyd was working again and being paid for his guides by the Confederate government. He was profiting, selling, and clearly not perceived as an enemy of the Confederacy.

Proof lies in several invoices and letters. A requisition dated February 2, 1864, was obtained at the request of US authorities by Francis Lieber, the author of the first laws of conduct in the field and later an archivist tasked with collecting Confederate documents. This requisition of the Secretary of War on the Secretary of the Treasury is "in favor of W.A. Lloyd for the sum of $860 payable out of the appropriation for incidental and contingent expenses of Army," and marked 'Special.'" As well, there is a receipt for ten copies of Lloyd's Southern railroad maps, fifty dollars total, for use in General Winder's office.[332]

On October 3, 1865, in his letter to Stanton outlining the letters he'd found in the Confederate archives regarding Lloyd, Lieber writes, "I would also call attention to the account, heretofore transmitted, of W.A. Lloyd, for ten of his war maps, furnished to the Rebel secretary of war, and the requisition upon the same fund, covering the same." This last refers to a note, dated February 1, 1864: "Hon. Secretary of War. Ten copies of W. Alvin Lloyd's War Map. $50. Richmond." Then it says, "Received payment" and was signed "W. Alvin Lloyd."[333]

There is another note, dated, February 1, 1864, from the Adjutant General's office: "W. Alvin Lloyd sold 100 copies of his 'Southern RR Map' to C.S. Engineers Bureau, for which he received $500. Dated Richd., Va., Feb. 1/64." And yet another from February 1, 1864: "Confederate States of America. 25 copies of Lloyd's RR map. $150." And another, for "40 copies of W. Alvin Lloyd's Southern Railroad maps, at $5 each—total $200, for the Confederate States Nitre & Mining Service." Alvin also received $125 for twenty-five copies of the map for the Ordnance Department, also February 1. And another of that date, for ten copies, at five dollars a copy, from the Navy Department.[334]

And now came a ploy, a dodge, a familiar and typical Lloyd and Boyd dance.

The *Daily Richmond Examiner* of Thursday, March 24, 1864, carried this open letter, written that day from the office of *Lloyd's Southern Railroad Guide*, Richmond, by the publisher himself, William Alvin Lloyd: "The public are cautioned against paying moneys or giving advertisements to Thomas H.S. Boyd, on account of *Lloyd's Southern Railroad Guide*, as he has been discharged from the employ of the undersigned—said Boyd being unworthy of confidence or respect."

On the surface, it looks as if the two had a falling out. But it was not so. This was as might be remembered, an old game the two men played well. As long as the publisher took out an ad disclaiming his agent—in this case, Boyd—then all debts owed by the publisher that had been incurred by the agent were now legally uncollectable. Alvin had been doing this for years, as had all other con men in this field. It seems that Alphabetical had to make himself scarce for a while, so he joined the Confederate army again.

Alphabetical later claimed (in private life when he sought admittance to the Confederate Soldiers' home) that in April 1864 he joined the 47th Battalion of the Virginia Cavalry as a lieutenant colonel, hence his use after the war of the name Colonel T.H.S. Boyd. However, was he actually a lieutenant colonel? Was he ever in the 47th? The 47th was formed in April 1864, yes, but Major William N. Harman was major in command, and major is lower than a lieutenant colonel, so Alphabetical would have shown as the commander, not Harman. In December 1864 the 47th would be merged into the 26th Virginia Cavalry. There was a Lieutenant Colonel Boyd commanding the 14th Veteran Reserves in 1864, but this was Carlysle Boyd, not T.H.S. Boyd.

However, in April 1864, the Confederate Army records do show a Thos. Boyd being enlisted by Captain Stewart in Richmond on April 15, 1864, as a private in Company N of the 2nd Regiment of the Virginia State Reserves, formerly the 19th Regiment of the Virginia State Militia. This man was soon transferred to Captain William A. Jenkins's company, that is Company E of the 2nd Regiment Virginia Reserves. We duly find a Private T.H.S. Boyd in Company E of that regiment. Then, army records of July and August of 1864 show a Private T.H.S. Boyd, actually physically present in Company E, of the 2nd State Reserves, Virginia Militia. "Colonel Boyd" sounds a lot better than "Private Boyd." No matter what the rank, a Confederate soldier is a Confederate soldier and Boyd was certainly that. Not admitted to the Union authorities, of course, but certainly one of the large cracks in the case, among many discoveries in the investigation that helped to prove the Lloyd fraud.

Alvin left Richmond on Wednesday, April 6, 1864, and arrived in Atlanta on the twenty-first, a Thursday. He gives us no clue what he was doing for the two weeks it took him to get to Atlanta, but one has to guess he was in Augusta, that town being Virginia's base for most of the Civil War. "We went to Augusta, Georgia, together, and to Atlanta. This was about April or May, 1864." So says Boyd in his 1872 deposition.

Lloyd does mention Atlanta in April, as we have seen, but not Augusta. Lloyd may have forgotten about Augusta, but it's unlikely. It was a 171-mile trip direct from Augusta to Atlanta on the Georgia Railroad.[335] In regard to this trip, Boyd claimed to be traveling with Lloyd, but at that very moment, he was serving valiantly in the Virginia Cavalry, or as he sometimes noted, in the 2nd State Reserves. It is simply not possible for him to have been in two places at once.

Nonetheless, Alvin and his accomplices use Atlanta for a couple of additional reasons. One is that in 1865 the maid, Nellie Dooley, falsely testified that in or around April 1864, Lloyd gave her a letter to take to Lincoln. She claimed she got as far as the Rappahannock River before being turned back by pickets, and had to return to Atlanta with the letter. The truth is that on June 1, 1864, Alvin's *Southern Steamboat and Railroad Guide* came out, now priced at five dollars, published in Atlanta. Of the 136 pages, the last 90 contained ads.

On Sunday, June 5, 1864, Alvin left Atlanta, and the following day went up to Columbus, Georgia. He was in Columbus six days, leaving on the twelfth, on the Montgomery & West Point Railroad, arriving in Montgomery the same day. He left Montgomery on Monday the thirteenth, and the next day was in Selma, Alabama. That day, Colonel Josiah Gorgas, Chief of the Confederate Ordnance Bureau at Richmond, wrote this note: "This department will take twenty five copies of Lloyd's Rail Road map, to be delivered."[336]

Another bit of historical truth now intrudes. On Wednesday, June 15, 1864, Alvin passed through Jackson, Mississippi. Again, it's quite possible that during Alvin's four-day stay in Selma, Alabama, he managed to pass through Jackson on the fifteenth. It's just that he forgets to mention it, which is odd in that that was the very morning the eastern mails had failed to get through to Jackson, the Montgomery stage road having been rendered impassable due to the recent heavy rains. And his stopover in Jackson was long enough for the press to report it. And Alphabetical Boyd, who swears he was with him throughout this period, never gets a mention in the press like his boss does. Alvin, in his very detailed itinerary, never once mentions Boyd accompanying him. But that's because Alphabetical was, in real life, with his regiment.[337]

Alvin left Selma on Saturday, June 18, 1864, and on the twenty-first arrived back in Mobile, not leaving there until July 11. On Wednesday the thirteenth he arrived at Atlanta, and on that day received fifty dollars in Confederate money from the Navy for two copies of his *Railroad Guide*. He left Atlanta on the fourteenth, getting to Augusta the following day. On the twenty-first he arrived at Columbus, and left there on Monday the twenty-fifth. On the twenty-sixth he arrived in Danville, Virginia, left there on July 28, 1864, and arrived in Richmond that night.[338]

Lloyd amazes. He has overcome. He has profited. Though crippled, he has summoned strength enough to make these numerous dashes about Dixie, as of old. What will await him now as he returns to Richmond? Has he, like most Confederates, been buoyed by the news of General Jubal Early's attack on the defenses of Washington, DC, between July 11 and 12? Is this a harbinger of victory, or a flash, a false hope, a stab at the near impossible? For the Confederate forces are weakening. Lloyd is coming into view now. He is growing stronger, unlike Dixie, the land he roams. For Dixie is dying.

12

By Order of President Jefferson Davis

ALVIN LLOYD WAS IN RICHMOND AND IT WAS THE MORNING OF JULY 29, 1864. On that day, it seemed he may have made his way to the Confederate White House on Main Street to see Jefferson Davis, for things were happening, albeit seven months later, as a result of Virginia's brother Eugene Higgins's letter to the Confederate president. On the very day Lloyd was in town, James A. Seddon, the Confederate secretary of war and surely not a defender of Lloyd's, wrote a letter to Major General Dabney Herndon Maury, the commander of the Department of the Gulf.

Imagine the general, expecting to do battle with invading Union ships at any moment, reading an order from President Davis about William Alvin Lloyd. Yet, here it is:

> General, I send you a paper from which you will see that it is the desire of the President that Mr. W.A. Lloyd should be employed in connection with the business of the Provost Marshall's office in your city. He seems to have a turn for detective duty, and he might be employed as such detective or police agent in the pay of the commander, and receive his compensation out of the Secret Service money. From his information, it would appear that illicit trade is still carried on in cotton & other commodities with the enemy.

As in so much of Lloyd's self-proclaimed insider-status claims, this one begs believability. Seddon, under presidential pressure, it appears, adds this caveat, this doubt:

He [Lloyd] believes it will be in his power to obtain such information as to enable you to break it up. It will be well to give him any reasonable facilities for attaining such result, as he will thus show how far his representations are exaggerated or delusive. Yours respectfully, J.A. Seddon.[339]

However, an order from the president is just that, no matter what the secretary of war implied. But Alvin never became a Mobile detective nor did he go anywhere near Mobile again.

And as for Boyd, he was now back in Castle Thunder prison, one of several drear and overflowing places at this time in the war. There is this item from the *Daily Richmond Examiner* of August 11, 1864: "Gone to the Castle Again. Thomas H. Stockton Boyd, or alphabetical Boyd, an exceeding nice young man, and William H. Shellings, equally nice, and detailed for 'light duty,' have been sent to the Castle, for threatening, with force of arms, to assault Sergeant Hanley of one of the reserve companies." Bill Snellings and Tom Boyd were certainly privates in Company E of the 2nd Virginia State Reserves. This little episode kind of puts a crimp in Alphabetical's career as a colonel, not to mention a bilk he was planning in Richmond.

About the time of Alphabetical's latest misfortune, on August 2, Alvin left Richmond, arriving at Columbia, South Carolina, on Friday the fifth. On that day, back in Mobile, Union Admiral David Glasgow Farragut's squadron steamed into Mobile Bay. The Confederate defenses there included not only warships but also mines, called torpedoes. Farragut's forces assaulted Confederate Admiral Franklin Buchanan's squadron, charged with guarding the three forts at the entrance of the bay. When one of Farragut's men yelled out to the admiral that the bay was heavily mined, allegedly, Farragut shouted back, "Damn the torpedoes, full speed ahead!" Meanwhile, in the Carolinas, Alvin remained in Columbia for nine days, leaving on Sunday, August 14, and on the following day arrived at Wilmington, North Carolina. He left Wilmington on Friday the nineteenth, and the following day was in Charlotte. He left Charlotte on the twenty-eighth, and later that day was in Augusta, selling ads and finding investors for his guide.[340]

In his 1872 deposition, Alphabetical Boyd says of Lloyd, "I left him in Augusta about first September 1864 and returned to Richmond. He was engaged in procuring information in regard to the movement of the Army of [Confederate] Gen'l Jos. E. Johnston, afterwards commanded by [Confederate] General Hood."

Here Alphabetical's fiction implies he must have talked his way out of Castle Thunder and joined Lloyd on the road, arriving with him in Augusta on the twenty-eighth of August 1864. Not so. The Confederate Army records are quite clear that T.H.S. Boyd was physically present for the August 1864 muster roll with his company, as he had been for the July roll.

Later, Boyd was in Richmond on September 16. As the city, the South, reeled at the news that General William Tecumseh Sherman's forces had captured Atlanta on September 2, a death knell was sounding over the Confederacy. The news—grim and grimmer still—the defeats, the dark and rapid bulletins frightened most southerners. But life in the common-criminal demimonde went on. On that day, as the *Richmond Dispatch* reports, Boyd was arrested for bilking Philip Whitlock, owner of a clothing store, and lodged in the lower cage by Officer John W. Davis.[341]

And in the same paper, the *Richmond Dispatch*, on September 19, 1864: "Thomas H.S. Boyd, formerly a captain in the Confederate service, was charged with forging the name of J.W. Allison, of Lynchburg, to a receipt for one year's house rent amounting to $1300, and obtaining $975 from Philip Whitlock under false pretences. The absence of important witnesses induced the Mayor to postpone the matter till this morning."

The *Richmond Examiner* of September 20, 1864, describes Boyd as "a gay young man from Maryland who, for several years, led an adventurous life in Richmond, getting into ugly scrapes periodically, but managing to squirm out of them without detriment to his liberty."

As for Alvin, finally, he found an investor for his guide. James M. Willis was a young man from Georgia, a former druggist and actor who'd served as a hospital steward during the first two years of the war. After becoming ill with typhoid fever, he was on convalescent leave and never returned to his regiment, the 14th Alabama Infantry. But thanks to a fortunate marriage, he was now a banker and broker, with a large amount of money. A lucky break for Alvin. They struck a partnership deal on September 26, 1864, the new firm of Lloyd & Willis to produce, for five years, a publication called *Lloyd's Southern Railroad Guide and Railroad Map*, something they counted on to be of great use to the Confederate government. It was under their banner that the October 1864 edition came out, published in Augusta.[342]

October was the very month Alphabetical Boyd claimed to have joined Lloyd in Atlanta, full of Union troops readying to march with Sherman to the sea. Despite Boyd's claim that he was in fact in the city, for the entire month of October 1864 he had been sent back to jail, the new trial not being until November 25. All Alvin mentions in his itinerary for this time period is Augusta, where he was heavily involved with his new company, Lloyd & Willis; nothing about Boyd.[343]

Alvin left Augusta on Thursday, October 27, 1864, and "Arrived in Richmond October 31st at 3½ a.m." Alphabetical Boyd, in his 1872 deposition, says, of Lloyd, "He joined me in Richmond about October 1864." By "joined me," Boyd must mean "came to see me in jail," because that's where Alphabetical was, languishing on a narrow cot behind bars. Boyd continues, "He had several packets of information. They were sent to the President. I can't think of the name of the person by whom they were sent. The contents related to the number of troops commanded by Jos. E. Johnston, and also number and location of General Lee's Army, then in front of Richmond and Petersburg."[344]

Abraham Lincoln's re-election on November 8 was met with outrage and agitation throughout the tattered Confederacy. There would be no stopping the war now. Amid all this, on November 21, 1864, in the court of Judge Lyons in Richmond, an indictment was found against Thomas H. S. Boyd for larceny. Then this from the *Daily Richmond Examiner* of November 24, 1864: "Criminal Court. Judge William H. Lyons— Wednesday, November 23, 1864—The only case heard in this court today was that of Thomas H.S. Boyd, indicted for grand larceny, in stealing thirteen hundred dollars from Philip Whitlock. The jury convicted, and the judge sentenced him to one year's confinement in the Penitentiary," The jury recommended him to executive clemency by the governor. This was all appealed.[345]

On December 21, 1864, the day Sherman captured Savannah and informed Lincoln that this city was his Christmas present, the *Daily Richmond Examiner* reports this item: "Criminal Court. Judge William H. Lyons. Tuesday, December 20, 1864. Court was occupied this morning with the case of Thomas H.S. Boyd, indicted for obtaining money under false pretences from Philip Whitlock, upon a forged paper. The accused was tried once before upon the same indictment, convicted and sentenced to the Penitentiary for one year. Upon the plea of prisoner's counsel, Colonel Evans, the judge set aside the verdict, and granted a new trial. The jury again convicted, finding him this time guilty of attempting and committing the felony of obtaining money under false pretences. Counsel for prisoner moved in an argument for another new trial, but the Judge overruled the motion, and sentenced Boyd to twelve months confinement in the city jail."

This from the *Daily Richmond Examiner* of December 29, 1864: "Pardon Application. The counsel and friends of Thomas H.S. Boyd, convicted of obtaining money under false pretences and sentenced to the city jail for one year, have made an application to the Governour for his pardon. Boyd was first tried, convicted and sentenced to the Penitentiary for one year, but the Judge granting a new trial and setting aside the verdict, he was again convicted and sentenced to the jail for the time specified."

But in his 1872 deposition, Boyd swore that Lloyd "went to Wilmington, N.C., and Columbia, S.C. This was about December '64 and January '65. He was taking descriptions of batteries, gunboats, and general outlines of the water defenses of the approaches to Wilmington. He came on to Richmond, and sent a report to Mr. Lincoln in the early part of January 1865. He sent it through a prisoner exchanged from Castle Thunder, who was employed by Seward. I gave it to the prisoner, who was named Scully, myself." This Scully mentioned is not necessarily John Scully, one of Pinkerton's detectives who was so involved in the Timothy Webster case of 1862. It was a name Boyd pulled out of thin air. "I read the dispatches," Boyd testified. "They also contained information as to the number and force of the armies around Petersburg and Richmond."[346]

According to Enclosure 13, Alvin left Richmond on January 26, 1865, which means he had spent three straight months in the Confederate capital. There is no record of heartache, no weeping for the sure end of the world as they knew it, from either Boyd or Lloyd. Just travel, more travel, and more falsehoods. On January 28, Alvin arrived in Greensboro, leaving there the following day, a Sunday. On the thirty-first he arrived at Columbia and left on February 4, 1865, and arrived at Richmond on the sixth, leaving there on Thursday the ninth.[347]

This notice was placed in the Richmond *Daily Dispatch* on February 27: "Lost between Dr. E. Powell's office, on Tenth street, and my residence on Ninth and Clay streets, a due bill for twenty-five hundred and eighty dollars, drawn by Colonel W. Alvin Lloyd in my favor. This is to caution the public against trading for the same, as payment has been stopped. L. Bowser."[348]

Lloyd left Columbia on the fifteenth. On Monday, February 28, he arrived in Richmond. Boyd claimed that Lloyd was still sending dispatches to Lincoln. "He made a report in March 1865. It was sent by a blockade runner named Anderson. It contained, among other things, the exact amount of men under General Lee's command, which was 42,000 men, including infantry and artillery, but not cavalry. He got the information from Major Taylor, Assistant Adjutant General on General Lee's staff, from the morning reports. He stayed in Richmond until the news came that General Lee would have to uncover Richmond."[349]

Alphabetical Boyd was "pardoned out" by the governor on March 3, 1865. That's a fact. The *Richmond Dispatch* of March 4 tells us that. That really does seem to imply that Boyd was in jail at the time of the "pardoning out." However, he was not in jail at that time. He was not in Richmond. He was not even in the South. Union records report that on January 20 a rebel deserter crossed the lines into Bermuda Hundred, near Hopewell, Virginia, where the Union Army of the Potomac was camped. His name was Private Thomas Boyd, 2nd Regiment Virginia, and, at Bermuda Hundred, he took the oath of allegiance to the United States. On January 21 he was received and processed by the Provost Marshal of Washington, DC, and on the twenty-fourth sent to that city. His weapons—his Colts—were taken, and transfer was furnished to Norfolk, Virginia. That was the end of the war for Thomas H. S. Boyd, but soon his supporting role as Lloyd's accomplice in the fraud against the US government, would begin.

As for Alvin Lloyd, he would, in a matter of days, be part of another flight, a desperate flight of an entire government.

13

Leaving Dixie

It was April 2, 1865: A day fraught with panic. A night of terror. The Yankees were coming. Frightened residents hastily packed foodstuffs and china, boxes and baggage. Flee. Die at the hands of the invaders. No one knew. Under the cover of darkness trains had left, carrying soldiers, government documents, officials, and their families who'd leapt aboard. Crowds thronged the streets, pressed against the Richmond & Danville Railroad depot doors, desperate to get on a train out. Others crammed into carriages and horse carts, dragging trunks and baggage, possessions, pets, all in a panicked horde, fleeing the city. Some jumped in the James River, trying to swim away. Crowds of slaves prayed that "Father Abraham's" promise of freedom was truly theirs at last.[350]

It was 11:30 p.m. Another half hour and the chimes of midnight would ring. If Jefferson Davis's train didn't get out within the next few minutes, and across the Mayo Bridge into Chesterfield County, the president, the entire Confederate cabinet, dozens of officials, clerks, all the passengers on all the cars would all be stuck in the capital to await the occupying Union forces thundering toward Richmond.

Somewhere in the madness of the night the rebel capital died. William Alvin Lloyd, Virginia, Clarence, and Nellie joined panicked throngs in a crush to seek safety, somewhere . . . anywhere. Perhaps the Lloyd party was obscured by smoke, the dense black smoke that billowed from Engine Number 24 as it waited patiently for the president who had not yet arrived.

Early that morning, General Grant broke Lee's lines at Petersburg, and at 10:40 the awful news arrived at the Confederate war department—the government would have to flee Richmond. Jefferson Davis called an emergency cabinet meeting at noon. An hour later the evacuation of the capital started. As Richmond diarist Sallie Brock tells us, terror penetrated into every house. "Union troops, no longer obstructed, streamed toward Richmond." At 7 o'clock that evening, Richmond received the last in a series of telegrams from Lee, repeating his urgent advice: "I think it absolutely necessary that we abandon our position to-night."[351]

And now, approaching midnight, where was Jefferson Davis? Time, there was no time. Finally, Davis and E. L. Harvie, president of the railroad, came out of the office where they'd been sequestered for the last hour with Secretary of War Breckinridge. Stay or go? Davis was fevered, conflicted, in denial. He'd lingered, praying, hoping for a turn of events that would never come. At last, Davis climbed aboard.

Like many others who would say they were on the car that carried the president away, William Alvin Lloyd claimed that he, Virginia, Clarence, and Nellie were there, though not in the presidential car, but in another car, one of a long line of cars.

And of what was happening in the city, "After nightfall," Sallie Brock wrote, "Richmond was ruled by the mob."[352] Many government documents, the valuable leavings of a government abandoning its capital, were strewn about, pitched from windows or burnt to ash in great pyres. Stores of liquor, ordered destroyed by city officials, were set upon. "Whiskey ran in the gutters ankle deep; and . . . half-drunken women . . . fought to dip up the coveted fluid in tin pans, buckets, or any vessel available," Thomas Cooper DeLeon remembered.[353]

As the Confederate president fled into an uneasy dawn, Richmond was burning. Determined to destroy the warehouse stores before the Yankee invaders came, and "ignoring the possibility that selective fires could not be contained," warehouses and flour mills were set on fire, and soon much of lower Richmond was an inferno. "The roar of the flames was heard above the shouts of people pushing through the black smoke as embers jumped from roof to roof."[354] When the arriving Union troops fought to put out the fires, Brigadier General Edward Hastings Ripley of Vermont wrote, the Confederacy "died like a wounded wolf, gnawing at its own body."[355]

Alphabetical Boyd, who it must be remembered had, by this time, deserted and was now home in Maryland, later claimed in the courts that Alvin Lloyd, amid the frenzy, amid the news of evacuation, "went to see President Davis, Secretary Benjamin, and Quarter Master General Orton." This Orton, to whom Boyd is referring, was actually A. R. Lawton, Alvin's old nemesis from the Savannah days, who, after being wounded at Antietam, had been Confederate quartermaster general since August 1863.[356]

"We went to Danville, Va., on the same train of cars with Davis's staff." That's Boyd again, and he expands upon this many years later, in the admissions ledger in 1895, at the Confederate Soldiers Home in Pikesville, Maryland, which was his last residence on earth: "Left Richmond April 2 1865 in charge of special car, in same train that carried President Davis and his family. Saw the last interview between President Davis, his cabinet and General Lee."[357]

Every Richmond & Danville train out of the capital stopped at the great junction at Manchester. Passing through town, and crossing over the Richmond & Petersburg tracks, the long Davis train was an object of wonder to the people by the side of the road. The silhouette of the fireman, already blackened by the billowing pine smoke and flying sparks, was seen slinging wood from tender to furnace as the train picked up speed and headed out into the clear and calm night, hugging the west bank of the river. Time had run out, had ended for the Lost Cause.[358]

Alvin knew the Richmond & Danville well. He had traveled this line on many an occasion. Through Coalfield to Powhatan, then south to the Junction—Burkeville Junction—that the train reached at dawn.[359]

In Danville every available room was filled with clerks, government workers, and, eventually, Richmond refugees. In the words of one officer traveling with the Davis party: "Every private house in the city was thrown open to all in our train."[360]

In the words of W. Alvin Lloyd in his prepared itinerary, at Danville, he "Stopped at the residence of L.A. Yates." Louis Augustus Yates was a very well off shoemaker, aged forty, born in Culpeper, living with his wife Martha, their two daughters, Martha's mother, and an apprentice.[361]

Robert E. Lee surrendered to Ulysses S. Grant at Appomattox Court House on April 9, thus effectively ending the war. As Boyd wrote, "Soon after, news came of the Armistice [the word "surrender" had originally been written here, but had been replaced] "at Appomattox C.H., and the death of President Lincoln." As for Appomattox Court House, Jefferson Davis received the news at 3:30 on the afternoon of the tenth, when Captain William P. Graves reached Danville after an all-night ride from Appomattox Court House. According to Micajah Clark, the bad news "came with the paralyzing shock of a sudden earthquake," and prompted Davis to go farther south immediately. "We stayed there [Danville] a few days," says Boyd. "Lloyd left his family there, and we [Lloyd and Boyd] went to Greensboro, N.C. [allegedly on the train that left Danville at eleven o'clock on the night of Tuesday, April 10, with Jefferson Davis and his entourage aboard]."[362]

They arrived in Greensboro late the next afternoon. Whereas Danville had been friendly, even welcoming, to Davis and his retinue, Greensboro, which had always been a pro-Union city, was downright hostile, to the point of almost refusing accommodations to the refugees. This meant that most of them had to sleep in the railroad cars. Davis got rooms in the city with Colonel Wood.[363]

Boyd says of Greensboro: "Gained information as to army of J. E. Johnston. Sent it by negro servant to Petersburg, with instructions to give them to the commanding officer at Petersburg." When reporting this, Boyd asserts that Alvin heard this information from General Beauregard, who did arrive in Greensboro not long after the Davis party. In the president's railroad car office, Beauregard was asked by the president to report on General Johnston's progress against the advancing Federal war machine of General Sherman. Beauregard was less than sanguine. In fact, he recommended surrender. Davis ordered him to send for Johnston, who reported to Davis on the morning of Wednesday the twelfth, again in the car at Greensboro. Johnston strongly urged suing for peace with Sherman, but Davis refused to consider such an idea, instructing him to beat Sherman and then take on Grant.[364]

The next day, the thirteenth, John C. Breckinridge, Jefferson Davis, Judah Benjamin, and Generals Johnston and Beauregard met in Davis's car.[365] Incredibly, Boyd testified that this was Alvin's last report to President Lincoln.

On April 27, 1865, General Horatio Wright entered Danville, or, rather Colonel Hyde did. To quote Alvin in Enclosure 13, "The town of Danville was occupied by the Union forces on Thursday, April 27th/65. The Sixth Corps, commanded by Major Genl Wright. The people of Danville, as a general thing, are disloyal." Here is Lloyd making sure the Federal government would see he was, as usual, ready to expose treasonists.

As well, he produced a blizzard of minutiae to convince Federal authorities that he was their man on the ground. In place. In Danville. On the lookout for Rebels.

Mr. Walker [James McKenzie Walker], the mayor who has been re-appointed by General Wright; J.C. Voss, merchant [Colonel James C. Voss]; John Holland, manufacturer of shells, etc, for the Rebel Govt; and the man at whose house the first secession flag was raised—Sutherland [actually William Thomas Sutherlin], was a major and quartermaster for the Rebel Govt, and one of the members of the convention that voted Virginia out of the Union; Capt. W.J. Clark, merchant [Mr. Voss's next-door neighbor, William J. Clark]; Wicker Keen, merchant [this is Wicher Kean, with whom Congressman Bruce had stayed]; Elisha Keen, member of the Rebel Legislature; Moore, who stabbed a negro soldier while passing through Danville.[366]

These and others of the same stamp have taken the oath of allegiance. Mayor Walker said publicly, "that after the Yankees came to Danville he would never accept the position of Mayor of the city if proffered to him." Yet he did accept it, from Genl Wright. Samuel Moore (citizen) who killed the Union soldier (Negro) who was a prisoner of war in July 1864, is doing business at this time in Danville. He cut the Negro's throat—a number of citizens witnessed it. Alva Woodray, blacksmith [this man is an Alvin Lloyd invention], and Robt Cole witnessed it, and will testify to the fact. Robert Harter lives near White Oak Point, 4 miles from Danville, knocked a Union soldier (prisoner) down with a stone. Linc Patterson of Danville witnessed it. Isaac Reeves tried to steal a watch from a Union soldier, who was a prisoner, and in the scuffle, a man by name of Ferguson, resident of Danville, shot the soldier for daring to resist. About 300 prisoners of war (colored soldiers) who were kept in prison at Danville [this was not a true prison—rather six tobacco warehouses], only 25 survived from the cruel treatment of those who had charge of the prisoners, and the 25 that did survive were retained as slaves, and given up to their pretended owners. These facts were given me by Col. Long, adj. of Col. Hyde (at this time stationed at Danville) [Colonel Thomas W. Hyde, commander of the Third Brigade, from Maine, who, it will be seen, had left Danville by the sixteenth], and is [sic] thoroughly reliable.[367]

On Thursday, May 18, 1865, according to Lloyd, "A young man, Captain Chase, called at the house where myself and family were stopping, and informed the proprietor, Mr Yates, that he was entertaining in his house a Yankee spy—by the name of Lloyd." He signs this final document, "Wm Alvin Lloyd, Danville, May 18, 1865." And so this final accusation by Captain Chase left the readers (the Federal authorities) with the words "Yankee spy." It was perfect.

In his June 3, 1865, deposition, Alvin says he was in the insurgent states until May 24, 1865. However, Alphabetical Boyd says: "Lloyd reported to General Wright commanding 6th Corps at Danville, Va., and he furnished Lloyd, his family, and myself, with transportation to Washington about June 1, 1865, a few days after the first, from the 1st to the 5th." This is impossible as Lloyd, Boyd, Virginia, and Nellie were in DC several days before they deposed there for the first time on June 3, 1865, and Lloyd's pass has a May date franked on the back of it.

In fact, the last of Wright's Sixth Corps left Danville on May 16, so Lloyd must have secured transportation from Wright on or before that date—certainly not after it, as Wright was no longer there. It wasn't until the nineteenth that the 12th New Hampshire, acting on Wright's suggestion, entered Danville to protect the town. This means, then, that if Wright did arrange transportation for Lloyd, then Lloyd, like Wright, was out of Danville by May 16. Also in late May 1865, Alvin was pressing his claim for back salary, and by June 1 had hired a lawyer to expedite that ambition—both events occurring in Washington, DC. So sometime during the next week, Alvin, Virginia, Clarence, and Nellie must have taken the Danville Railroad back up to Richmond, and from there made their way to City Point, in Prince George County, Virginia, on the south bank of the Appomattox, where that river comes out into the James, about twenty miles south of Richmond.

Alvin's little group would have made the trip either by steamer down the James River, or by taking the Richmond & Petersburg Railroad down to Petersburg, and then cutting across from there on the City Point Railroad. Whatever their route, they arrived at City Point, where General Grant had been headquartered from 1864–1865. There was a huge supply depot and field hospital on-site.[368]

At City Point, Alvin produced the pass from Abraham Lincoln that he'd received on July 13, 1861. It is not known how he secreted this critical document, kept it safe during the war when his belongings, not necessarily his clothing, were repeatedly searched. There are a few possibilities: Possibly Nellie hid it on her person for a time, as she would later swear that she'd hidden the fictitious contract in her undergarments while with Lloyd in Lynchburg. As there was no contract, it is probable that she was referring to the pass. Or when in Savannah when Lloyd was allowed to send out letters from prison, imagine his fierce need to send the pass away immediately, the pass from the enemy president, stating, "Special business." If that was the case, he would have reclaimed the pass from whomever he'd sent it to. But at City Point, Alvin's pass was produced and franked (stamped and dated).[369]

Once Alvin and his retinue were legally processed through into Federal territory, from City Point they would have taken a steamer down the James, past Newport News, and into Chesapeake Bay before swinging up into the mouth of the Potomac River and proceeding upstream until they got to Washington. Alvin would contact Boyd in Maryland and together they would, in a matter of days, begin to lie their way to a great deal of money.

14

Anatomy of a Fraud

SEE LLOYD RIGHT WHERE WE LEFT HIM, IN ENOCH TOTTEN'S OFFICE ON June 1, 1865. His life—the horrors and highs of that life; the great drama, the music, and the man—errant and outrageous—the telling of the story has ended. The young lawyer must have been riveted. Here Totten was in a city teeming with competition, a fresh face with a fresh shingle, and William Alvin Lloyd stumbled into his office with a claim that has all the necessary elements to make Enoch Totten a substantial legal name in the nation's capital. Better, this man Lloyd, this broth of showman and criminal, is now a sympathetic weary cripple, swearing he has served and suffered for Abraham Lincoln and the Union cause. William Alvin Lloyd was too good to pass up.

Needed now was great speed. If this claim was to go anywhere, speed was of the essence. Claims of various sorts were starting to come in already, from all over the country; Totten knew this, and it wouldn't be long before the War Department got bogged down with paperwork. So Totten would build, create, massage, and mold the anatomy of a fraud.

Here, in more detail, is Totten's plan, his design, as he navigates pitfalls, embellishes, and wends his way through the thicket that is Lloyd's time in the war: First there is the matter of a verbal contract with the president that Lloyd reported to Grant's office, this alleged spying contract that Lincoln had given Lloyd back in 1861. No—and he is firm about this—a verbal contract would not suffice. There has to have been a written contract. A written contract? But Grant's office was told it was verbal. That is a problem. That's on Grant's endorsement, right there in black and white. Verbal. Can a verbal contract be a written contract at one and the same time? How's that possible? It used to be written, but now that it's been lost it's merely verbal. Why was it lost? It was, they decide, destroyed. How about by Nellie the nursemaid, at, say, Lynchburg in 1862, to stop it falling into enemy hands, to save the spy's life? That will do. So, it started out as a written contract. Now it's verbal, that's all. Now what exactly did that contract say? Lloyd and Totten create the wording. This contract is the focal point of the claim. Indeed, it is the only focus of the claim for Lloyd's back pay. Two hundred dollars a month for four years.

That's $9,600. But there can be more. Totten suggests, what about expenses incurred during the war? The contract they are creating doesn't mention expenses. It just says two hundred a month salary. Totten decides he will press for expenses. After examining Lloyd's expense sheet, Totten adds another $2,380, bringing the claim against the US government to $11,980. An even bigger sum. Nothing like settling on a definitive claim, down to the nearest dollar.

And about witnesses who will perjure themselves for Lloyd? Well, the "witnesses" are not only available, they are in Washington at this very moment, ready and willing, primed to say and do whatever was needed. Virginia, Boyd, Nellie, and even young Clarence, if necessary. Perhaps a five-year-old boy wouldn't make a good witness, but the others will do. They will need more, but these will make a good start.

They will all be deposed under oath on June 3, two days away, in front of notary John Callan. All four statements must be close, but not too close, otherwise the authorities might become suspicious. They have two days. They must rehearse—drill—rehearse. And so, on June 3, these four appear before notary John Callan, in Washington, DC.[370]

Because they will be deposed, not interrogated, their statements sworn under oath will—Totten and Lloyd hope—suffice, convince, and prove that William Alvin Lloyd was in fact Abraham Lincoln's most secret of secret agents.

It begins. He begins. Another chapter begins. A very debilitated Lloyd takes a seat before the notary and raises his right hand. By now, because the spying contract had no longer been verbal but in writing, he reproduces the wording of that contract "according to the best of my recollection."

The bearer, Mr W.A. Lloyd, is authorized to proceed South and learn the number of troops stationed in the different points and cities in the insurgent states, procure plans of the fortifications and forts, and gain all other information that might be beneficial to the Government of the United States, and report the facts to me, for which service Mr Lloyd shall be paid two hundred dollars per month. [Signed] A. Lincoln. July 13, 1861.

Lloyd then goes on to describe in detail the events of November 7, 1862, at Lynchburg, when he says the contract was destroyed. Then, "I have no other written evidence of said contract . . . except the pass . . . written and signed at that time by the President." Of course, this last wording is sleight of hand. You see the pass, now you see the contract, because Alvin the prestidigitator tells you to. In reality, the pass, as genuine as it is, is just a pass to go south, one of many Lincoln gave out to people during the war. Possession of a pass is absolutely no proof that there was a contract. Reality is suspended. And notary Callen is merely a paid scribe.

Alvin then claims that he immediately set about his business, on July 13, 1861, went to Tennessee, and finally, after faithfully adhering to the terms of the contract, emerged from the insurgent states on May 24, 1865. He briefly mentions his periods of imprisonment: several weeks in Nashville and in Memphis, nine months in Savannah, three months in Macon, eight months in Richmond, and several weeks in Mobile and Lynchburg, each time as a Yankee spy, a grand total of more than two years behind bars, and that during the greater part of 1863 he was paralyzed as the result of his cruel confinements.[371]

Just to keep the historical record straight—for at times, reality, like a defaced daguerreotype, is blurred, unrecognizable—in fact, and it bears repeating, there were only two times Alvin was imprisoned in the South, for a total of nine months, not the "more than two years" that he claims. But Totten will, in time, summon "ringers," men paid to give false witness, who will testify to Lloyd's various incarcerations.

Alphabetical Boyd, also deposing on June 3, 1865, claimed that on July 13, 1861, he accompanied his employer, Lloyd, into the Southern states "on special business of the United States Government," and that he "continued with him in said states as his assistant in obtaining information concerning the rebel forces for the benefit of the United States Government from that time until the 24th day of May 1865."[372]

So, there they were, as claimed. Lloyd and Boyd, intrepid, fearless Lincoln men working ceaselessly as spies for four years. Alphabetical's "best recollection" of the wording on the contract is identical to that of his employer, with the exception of one letter (the "s" at the end of the word "services"). But then it would be, if he had been with his boss for four long years. If he had been, that is.

Boyd swears that he accompanied Alvin to Memphis in July 1861. In the deposition he further states that it was here that he first saw the contract, and that he often secreted it in times of danger. He then says, foolishly and forgetting, that on October 7, 1862, Nellie Dooley destroyed it, "as he is informed, and verily believes." So, by his own admission, T.H.S. Boyd was not present at the burning of the contract in Lynchburg. That he wasn't there is bolstered by the fact that he gets the date wrong. According to Alvin and Virginia, the date of the burning of the contract was November 7.

Boyd says that in July 1862, at Savannah, Lloyd gave him a package of letters to be delivered to Mr. Lincoln, which Boyd did later that month. In July 1862, Lloyd was certainly in Savannah, had been for the last seven months, but imprisoned in the Chatham County Jail. What possible documentation could he have had that would have been of any use to Lincoln? Boyd claims he did not know the contents of this package. By 1872, when he came to depose again, his memory had improved, as we shall see.

Still with Boyd's deposition of June 3, 1865, he says he performed a similar function in October of 1862, and that on the twentieth of that month he delivered a second package to the president. This time he did know the contents—"fortifications, troop strengths, and the number of troops in Lee's army." He does not say where Lloyd was when he handed him this second package.[373]

Virginia was up next. She claimed she joined her husband at Clarksville, Tennesse, on October 1, 1861, that she was with him at the time of his imprisonment in Savannah, and that she was permitted to visit him a portion of the time, as she was also at Macon, Geogira, and in Richmond. Unfortunately, the Lloyd Papers are missing a section of this deposition, so we don't get to learn how she remembered the wording of the contract.[374]

Ellen R. "Nellie" Dooley is the next deponent. She sets the scene by stating that she has been Virginia's attendant since December 10, 1859, and has remained so to this day (June 3, 1865). She had come south with Mrs. Lloyd, and remained with Mr. and Mrs. Lloyd throughout the duration of the war, with the exception of the nine months that Alvin was in jail at Savannah. It is not revealed where she was during those nine months. She claims that for a long time prior to November 5, 1862, the contract was in her possession. One might well gather from this that before Alvin was jailed in Savannah in December 1861, he gave Nellie the contract, which she secreted in her undergarments, which is how she came to know the contents by heart.[375]

But Totten, and he was in charge, was concerned that these sworn depositions might not convince the federal authorities of the veracity of the claim. He decided more was needed. More detail. For the next week or so, Alvin went through his "journal," the one he had prepared so carefully during his four years in enemy territory, making a copy for presentation to the War Department. This "newly revised" journal gave his every movement from July 13, 1861, to May 24, 1865—where he had been, whom he had seen, monies collected, and, most critically, peppered with fictitious spying episodes. By the middle of June it was finished. The document was fourteen pages long and would as has been noted, eventually become known as Enclosure 13 of the Lloyd Papers.

More detail. More, Totten demanded. On June 13, 1865, T.H.S. Boyd made another deposition, this one to the effect that he had been present when Lincoln gave Lloyd the contract, that he heard Lincoln offer the job to Lloyd, heard the president mention two hundred dollars a month, and saw the great man sign a piece of paper that he gave to Lloyd. Boyd believed it to be the same piece of paper he first saw in Memphis in July 1861.[376]

And now, for further evidence, Totten obtained a medical affidavit from Dr. John Frederick May, a professor of anatomy and physiology, one of the most eminent surgeons of his time. Thus it was a brilliant coup on the part of Totten to bring him in to examine Alvin in Washington, on June 14, 1865. Dr. May's verdict would go a long way—if only it was favorable to the claimant. There are various ways one can make sure of such a verdict from such a high-flying medical witness, especially when a large fee is involved.[377]

Dr. May was fresh from the newspapers as not only the man who had poked his index finger into the hole in Mr. Lincoln's head and declared that there was no hope, but also as one of the identifiers of the dead body of John Wilkes Booth, the very assassin who had created that hole. Curiously, two years before—in 1863—this same Dr. May had operated on a tumor in Booth's neck. That was the only time he had ever seen Lincoln's assassin alive. Now, when confronted with the cadaver before him, May exclaimed, "There is no resemblance in that corpse to Booth, nor can I believe it to be that of Booth." Colonel Lafayette Baker had succeeded Pinkerton as head of the Secret Service. It was Baker who personally escorted Dr. May to Booth's remains that day. Some say it was Baker who persuaded May to change his opinion. May himself, in his bizarre 1887 paper, *The Marked Scalpel*, says that it was the two-year-old scar on the back of the cadaver's neck that convinced him the dead man was Booth.[378]

Dr. May's veracity, if not his competency and motives, speaks for itself: "Washington, June 14, 1865. This is to certify that I have examined Mr. W.A. Lloyd who, I am informed, has been afflicted with partial paralysis (hemiplegia) from long continued confinement in the Libby & other Southern prisons." Alvin was never in Libby Prison, in Richmond. For Dr. May to name this infamous prison based on hearsay is notable and disturbing. Who would have told him this? Lloyd? Totten? Obviously someone did.

Mr. Lloyd's left inferior limb still gives evidence of the above mentioned disease. It is smaller than the other limb, its action is still impeded in locomotion, & its sensibility is considerably affected.

The imperfect use of the member is at once seen in his gait, & its sensibility I have ascertained by pricking it at different points with a sharp pointed instrument. Altho' I have not attended Mr. Lloyd professionally, & therefore am ignorant of the previous history of his case,

I would yet state that paralysis can be induced by long continued hard usage, & sleeping on the ground, or in damp & unventilated apartments, which Mr. Lloyd informs me has been the cause of his disease. Jno. Fredk. May, MD.[379]

With its fresh padding, the Lloyd case moved forward. On June 16, 1865, Major William W. Winthrop was standing in for Judge Advocate General Joseph Holt, who at that time was immersed in the trial of the Lincoln conspirators and deep in the business of paying the duplicitous Sanford Conover, aka Charles Dunham, Holt's original star "witness" at the conspirators' trial. Winthrop had just finished reviewing the Lloyd case as presented thus far, and now wrote a letter to Secretary of War Edwin Stanton, "in the matter of W.A. Lloyd's demand for compensation as Special Agent of the Government." Winthrop then discusses the pass, and says, "This is in the handwriting of the late President, and bears his signature, with the date of July 13, 1865."[380]

Winthrop cites numerous letters and documents provided by Lloyd, and then sums up: "It is the opinion of this Bureau that the evidence submitted by the claimant clearly shows that he was employed as alleged, and that the expenditures reported were not, under the circumstances, unreasonable or improbable." Winthrop also says, "It is believed that the claims of Mr Lloyd should be allowed."[381]

Remember that all Winthrop has read are the rehearsed statements of Lloyd and his accomplices and that he seems to believe them. "But it may be remarked that it is somewhat singular," Winthrop writes, "that he should have engaged in such services, remained absent for four years in the meantime communicating with the Government, without having received any money for salary or expenses before starting, or during the period of his absence. It is therefore recommended that the account of the Contingent Fund in the hands of the Executive during this period be examined in order to ascertain, if possible, whether they contain evidence of any payments to Mr Lloyd. If they fail to show this, it is believed that the account should be allowed and paid."

Totten's clever orchestration, his inventions, his client, and his witnesses are, so far, winning.

Stanton received this letter the same day, and on June 22 he returned it to the Bureau of Military Justice for examination by Judge Holt himself. The busy and beleaguered Holt complied, and on June 26 returned Lloyd's claim papers along with a letter to Stanton. "While they make out a strong prima facie case in support of the claim, there are circumstances surrounding the transaction and the testimony offered which suggest further investigation as necessary before a final determination is arrived at."

He goes on to say, "In the absence of all record evidence of the existence of the contract alleged to have been made with the claimant by the late President, and in the absence, too, of any correspondence with him, and considering the magnitude of the sum demanded, it is believed that the claimant should be turned over to Congress or to the Court of Claims, where his claim, & the proofs adduced in its support can be subjected to tests which the executive branch of the Government has no power to apply."[382]

"No power to apply." Alvin would not, could not air his secrets in a public court. Judge Holt's advice and skepticism sent Totten scurrying.

Two days later, following quickly up on the suggestion made by Major Winthrop that President Lincoln's contingency funds, if they were of record, be examined, Totten wrote to the late president's son, Robert T. Lincoln, then living in Chicago. Totten asked Robert Lincoln if he or the president's widow Mary Todd Lincoln knew anything about William Alvin Lloyd. Robert Lincoln's reply of July 11 forms Enclosure 41 of the Lloyd Papers: "My dear Sir, your letter of June 28th has been forwarded to me. The private papers of my father cannot be examined for several years. For any purpose. Mrs Lincoln does not know of any transaction of the kind to which you refer. If your client has been in the Secret Service of the Govt., there is, without doubt, evidence of it in the war Dept. I regret that it is impossible for me to supply any. Very truly yours."

Undaunted and with a new design, a new, improved plan, beginning on June 30, 1865, Enoch Totten began to file additional affidavits in support of the Lloyd claim. Several men, the "ringers" paid to testify, some of whom existed in real life, and some who used false names, would make these additional depositions.

Marcellus Howser was the first to be deposed, on June 30, in Washington. At that time a deponent was required to supply someone who would vouch for him, for his character, his veracity, and his overall credibility as a trustworthy witness. The same day, Robert G. Beale, warden of the district jail, vouched for Marcellus. Beale had known him for a year or two, had even employed him when, on occasion, he had had to send prisoners to the Albany Penitentiary, in New York. "I selected him as one of my guard, and I found him diligent and reliable, and place the fullest reliance on his integrity & fidelity."[383]

Mr. Howser, born on April 5, 1847, in Frederick County, Maryland, was just eighteen. In this deposition, he claims to have been present, along with Lloyd and Boyd and Lincoln, at the moment the contract was signed on July 13, 1861. It is not explained how a boy of just fourteen came to find himself in such illustrious company at the president's house that day. But Mr. Howser remembered the interview clearly. After all, it's not every day a teenager gets to be in on an interview with the president of the United States. According to Mr. Howser, Lloyd asked Mr. Lincoln if he could be of any service to him while he was in the South, and the president answered in the affirmative. Then came the contract, at two hundred a month, and finally—and this is something new—that if Lloyd should die in the execution of his duties, then the money was to go to Mrs. Lloyd. No one else during the mass of 1865 depositions ever mentions this last clause. Mr. Howser also says he has known T.H.S. Boyd for more than twelve years, and that Boyd had always been a "loyal and true citizen of the United States."[384]

John P. Hamlin vouched for the next witness, Asbury Baker. Mr. Baker claims that he temporarily found himself in Washington, DC, on business, in July 1861, "on or about the 15th thereof." At least, according to the deposition he made in Washington on June 30, 1865, the same day as Marcellus Howser. Baker claims to have been acquainted with Lloyd for the past four years, something rather difficult, surely, as W. Alvin Lloyd had spent those very four years deep in enemy territory. He claims that Alvin showed him the contract on July 13, 1861. He even quotes considerable portions of that contract. Asbury Baker said he had also known Alphabetical Boyd for more than fifteen years. He also claimed that for almost three years he,

Baker, had been a resident of DC, which is difficult to reconcile with the fact that in 1863 he was living in Baltimore, at 7th Street, and working in that city as a clerk for Messrs Johnson & Sutton. Perhaps, though, what Mr. Baker had in mind when he said he had been three years a resident of Washington, was that late in 1864, he and three fellow clerks in Baltimore were caught selling goods to Confederate blockade-runners and thrown into the Old Capitol Prison, in Washington.[385]

On July 15, 1865, Alvin deposed again, a new element being introduced: His life was at risk. That if it should become known through the South that he had been employed as a secret agent of the government during the Rebellion that such notoriety would work great injury to him, and would not only injure his business, but, he believed, would endanger his life; that he thought he ought not to be compelled to go before Congress or any other tribunal to substantiate his claim; that such a course would change his evidence from the secret archives of the War Department to public records of the Court of Claims or Congress, as he was advised and believed. He therefore respectfully asked that he may be allowed the amount of his claim by the Honorable Secretary of War.[386]

Next was Charles T. Moore, of the City of Philadelphia, to depose in front of a Baltimore notary public on July 15, 1865, claiming that he had been with Lloyd in Memphis in July 1861. This particular testimony, Totten knew, was central to an understanding of Lloyd's time in Memphis. The rather mysterious Mr. Moore—i.e., the very mysterious Mr. Moore—had never been heard of or from until the moment he deposed, and would never be heard of or from again.

Charles T. Moore swore he had "known W.A. Lloyd for fifteen years and more" and that he "went in company with Mr. Lloyd from Louisville, Ky., in July 1861, to Memphis, Tenn." It is somewhat odd that, while the *Memphis Appeal* ran an article on Lloyd's arrival, they never mentioned Mr. Moore. What is downright curious is that Alvin Lloyd never mentioned Mr. Moore at all, ever.[387]

Moore claimed he "saw, in Lloyd's possession, a card, signed by the late President," and then went on to recite the wording of the pass, accurately, to the letter. "Also saw and read a paper, signed by the late President," and he then proceeded to quote the fictitious contract.[388]

The man called on to vouch for Charles T. Moore was one Harvey Williams, of Philadelphia City, Pennsylvania, who deposed at the same time, and in the same place, as Mr. Moore. Mr. Williams swore that he had been well acquainted with Mr. Charles T. Moore for the last twelve years, and that he knew him to be a "gentleman of full credit and belief." Harvey Williams seems to have been the only man who ever lived who knew Charles T. Moore, but that may be because Harvey Williams never existed by that name either.[389]

So, who were Charles T. Moore and Harvey Williams, in real life? Of course, without knowing, one can only guess. However, there was a young man named Charles T. Harvey, who would soon make a rather dramatic appearance.

On July 18, 1865, Mr. and Mrs. Lloyd both deposed again in Washington, DC. The thrust of Virginia's deposition was that on September 15, 1861, she was in New York City when she was "informed that her husband was imprisoned as a spy in Memphis." Being a dutiful and faithful wife she immediately began making preparations to go to her husband, and toward the end of the month set out for Dixie, accompanied by more than twelve hundred dollars in gold. What she failed to mention was that she was also in company with her child and nursemaid. When she finally reached Memphis, and found Alvin in prison, she had precisely twelve hundred dollars left, which she promptly handed over to the inmate. That's the end of the story. We don't know what Lloyd did with this extraordinary sum of money, but presumably it was used to bail him out. Virginia did go on to say that from time to time during her long subsequent stay in the South, she was forced to dispose of her diamonds and jewelry for ten thousand dollars Confederate money, which was equivalent to about a thousand in gold.[390]

There are major problems with Virginia's sworn testimony. The most glaring is that Lloyd was not in prison at Memphis, or indeed anywhere, at the time Virginia claims. He had done a night in the Memphis jail back in July 1861, for bigamy, and that case had made the New York papers. Both the *Herald* and the *Tribune* had covered that one in big headlines, so many in New York would have known of Alvin's bigamous crimes.

In her June 3, 1865, deposition, Virginia has herself rendezvousing with her husband at Clarksville, Tennessee, on October 1, 1861. How could that be, if Alvin was in prison in Memphis? Virginia must have meant that by the time she got to Tennessee, Alvin had been let out of jail. That's how he could have met her at Clarksville. But it would have been much better for all concerned if she had made this clear in her deposition. But how could it be clear?

At some stage just prior to July 18, 1865, something terrible was alleged to have happened to Lloyd's original journal, the one from which he had drawn up what is of record, the later concocted summary known as Enclosure 13. The original met with an unfortunate accident. "Partially destroyed," is how Lloyd put it in his deposition of July 18. Alas, all that was left were a few diary pages of his time in the prison at Macon in 1862, and a sprinkling of sundry other pages. First the destruction of the Abraham Lincoln spying contract back in Lynchburg in 1862, and now this.[391]

Stunning, then, that they continue, that Totten has allowed them to continue.

Alphabetical Boyd made a further deposition on July 19, 1865, in Washington, in front of notary public James H. Causten. It will be remembered, from Boyd's June 3, 1865, deposition, that on or around July 15, 1862, he had received a package from Lloyd in Savannah, and had later that month handed it safely to President Lincoln. Now, come July 19, 1865, he has remembered something else about that meeting with Mr. Lincoln, something he had forgotten to mention on June 3, and something he had also failed to remember when he made his June 13 deposition, to wit, Mr. Lincoln had given him, Boyd, his own personal spying contract. Rather significant that "he was employed in the month of July 1862 by President Lincoln to go into the Southern States on special business; that the President wrote the terms of such employment in his presence in the words and figures following, to wit: 'Mr T.H.S. Boyd is employed to go South and return with dispatches or other useful information. He will be allowed one hundred dollars per month. July 29, 1862. A Lincoln,'; that the original in the handwriting of the President of the United States, of which the foregoing is a true copy, is now in the possession of his attorney in the city of Baltimore, Md."

This alleged contract was never produced, of course, nor was there ever an inquiry about such a document. Finally as sworn, it must be assumed that Boyd was regularly and faithfully paid by the Chief Executive, per the terms of the contract. Which is more than can be said for Lloyd, who never got paid at all. If, like Lloyd, Boyd had not been paid, then why didn't he press his own claim through Totten, especially as he swore he had his own, signed contract sitting there safe in his lawyer's office in Baltimore, just ready and waiting to be picked up?[392]

An old acquaintance of Lloyd's now enters the picture. John Roper Branner, president of the East Tennessee & Virginia Railroad, happened to be in Washington on August 4, 1865. Several of his company's bridges had been destroyed during the fighting, and the line was consequently in desperate trouble. The Federal government had to swing into action very soon, or Branner would be ruined. For the action he had in mind, he had in his pocket a couple of distinct points of leverage. His friend, Samuel Milligan, judge of the Supreme Court of Tennessee, was a great friend of Lincoln's successor, President Andrew Johnson, a Knoxvillian like Branner and Milligan. Perhaps most important, though, was that Andrew Johnson owed John Branner a favor due to something that had happened in Knoxville back in 1861, when General Thomas Hindman had been the star of an evening party (Knoxville was his home too, originally). Hindman was a little the worse for wear and his rabid secessionism was showing with increasing vehemence as the drinks wore on, when he learned that that Senator Andrew Johnson was going to be speechifying for the Union the next day at Rogersville. He immediately proposed sending troops to Rogersville to capture Johnson. John Branner, then in charge of the railroad, heard of this, sensed that such a punitive movement would not serve him or his railroad well, and rerouted the trains, thus saving the future president of the United States from certain arrest and probable lynching. John Branner got his bridges rebuilt.[393]

While he was about in the nation's capital, Mr. Branner was induced to write a letter to William Alvin Lloyd, most likely at the urging of Totten, who felt this Branner statement would help Lloyd's case. In fact, it is possible that Totten was handling Branner's claim. The thrust of the letter, Branner's grammar intact, as in the original, recalled "a conversation we

[Lloyd and Branner] had on the cars from Knoxville, Tenn., to Bristol, Tenn. in July 1861, in regard to the rebellion, and you informed me that you was out South to collect debts due you by the Southern railroads, and that I was the only man who had paid you anything at that time."[394]

There are a few problems with Mr. Branner's letter. First, there is no room for such a train trip in July 1861. And Alvin never claimed to be in Knoxville in July 1861, and Bristol is never mentioned in Lloyd's itinerary or in any of his accomplices' statements.

Branner continued: "You also informed me you was a Union man, opposed to the war and the rebellion, and that the South would be compelled to submit to the laws and government of the United States. You also exhibited to me a pass from President Lincoln for you to pass the Federal lines, and gave me to understand that you was acting for him in collecting up all the information you could for the benefit of the United States Government."[395]

Branner never claims to have actually seen the contract and this whole Branner episode must be regarded as falsehood, created and prompted by Enoch Totten.

On August 8, 1865, Samuel Milligan vouched for Branner, and President Andrew Johnson vouched for both Branner and Milligan. That's the way things were done. It goes a long way in a claim if you have the president of the United States vouching for you: "I am directed by the President to state that any statements made by J.R. Branner and Sam Milligan are entitled to the fullest of credit. They are both men of the highest character. W.A. Browning, President's Secretary."[396]

According to W. Alvin Lloyd's initial deposition of June 3, 1865, he spent eight months in prison in Richmond at some stage of his career, although he didn't say when, and he didn't name the institution in which he was so unfortunately lodged. In Virginia's deposition of the same date, she claimed to have visited her husband in prison in Richmond. Again, nothing more specific than that. In his June 14, 1865, report, Dr. May let it slip that he had been informed that Alvin had been in the notorious Libby Prison, in Richmond. As Enclosure 13, presented on July 16, 1865, as part of his additional evidence, Alvin had drawn up the most extraordinarily extensive and detailed itinerary of his life in the Confederacy during the war. On reading and rereading Enclosure 13, it dawned on someone—probably Enoch Totten—that, although Lloyd was in Richmond on a dozen or so brief occasions during the course of the war, nowhere in that document did he mention being in prison there. What was worse was that nowhere could anything remotely like an eight-month incarceration be squeezed into an already busy schedule. They couldn't now redo Enclosure 13—an earlier draft had already gone to the War Department—but they had to do something. The error was too glaring. They had to act quickly, blindingly quickly. Imagine a summer storm caught in a camera's frame. Then next see the remains of a flashflood, a street with ankle-high water, obscuring a cobbled walk. The evidence, the papers that are the evidence lie ruined in the water. Now see new paper and new ink on a desk. Notes, scrawls, new evidence, a new man, a new "ringer." He is Theodore Woodall.[397]

Woodall is forty years old, an illiterate, brutish Maryland policeman living in Baltimore. Totten himself deposed Woodall in Washington on August 11, 1865. In this deposition, Woodall swears he was in Richmond in 1861 and 1862 up to October of the latter year, when he returned north. And that's true. That's where he was. What he was doing all that time in the new Confederate capital is not mentioned, and neither is why he left Richmond in October 1862, or how he got north. But it is known, and it's just as well for the Lloyd claim that Woodall didn't mention it in his deposition.[398]

Woodall claims that during the year 1861, he was "informed by Mr. Samuel MacCubbin, chief of Winder's rebel detectives, that Mr. Wm A. Lloyd had been arrested, and was imprisoned in Savannah, Ga., on a charge of being an agent of the United States Government." Woodall also claims he knew, of his own knowledge, that "Mr. Lloyd was regarded by the Rebel authorities as an agent of the United States, and was constantly watched and followed by the Rebel detectives."[399]

He goes on to say that, during a part of the year 1862 he (Woodall) was "a detective for the United States, in Col. L.C. Baker's force," and that he "returned to Richmond in the month of May 1863, and remained there until July 1864," when he "came North and remained." It is true that, after he got back North in 1862, he worked for Colonel Lafayette

Baker (Allan Pinkerton's replacement as head of the Federal Secret Service) sometime in the last three months of the year.

He claims that, during his stay in Richmond he knew Mr. William A. Lloyd.

Mr. Woodall swears, "There was a great outcry against him [Lloyd] in Richmond, and he was denounced by the people there as a Yankee spy, and was arrested, and thrown into prison ('Libby') [Woodall's parentheses and quotes] by the Rebel authorities for being an agent of the United States Government." Such an outcry would have made the Richmond press. It didn't. Second, Alvin was never in prison in Richmond. No, Theodore Woodall was confusing Alvin with someone else. That someone else was Theodore Woodall.

Woodall had begun his professional life as a house painter, hated that, and so became a cop. Didn't care for that either, and, in turn, because there was nothing else he could really do, just drifted into being a flatfoot on the Baltimore & Ohio Railroad. In 1859 he was badly beaten up by "plug uglies," the infamous and thuggish gangsters. Woodall became a plug himself, and went around brutalizing people. He'd finally found job satisfaction, even though the pay was somewhat irregular. On April 19, 1861, a week into the Civil War, when the 6th Massachusetts Regiment came through Baltimore, a local secessionist mob fired on them, thus initiating the Baltimore Riot, the first blood drawn during the Civil War. One of the plugs who shouldered a musket was Ted Woodall.[400]

In July–August 1861, John H. Winder became inspector general of posts in and around Richmond, and, in order to do his job more effectively, he needed a goon squad. So, he imported from Baltimore a bunch of particularly vicious plugs, led by Samuel MacCubbin, who, soon enough, would become Winder's chief of police. In October 1861, Theodore Woodall joined the squad. That's what he was doing in Richmond—he was one of Winder's detectives, notoriously cruel and violent. However, Woodall proved too enthusiastic in his post, and was indicted for extorting money from a Richmond grocer. Choosing to sacrifice the October wages of $124 he was entitled to as a Winder detective, Woodall fled Richmond via a flag-of-truce ship in October 1862. This "man of evil fame," as the *Richmond Daily Dispatch* would later call him, was jailed for twenty days upon his arrival in the North, and then released on parole. He readily found employment in Washington as a detective on the force of a man as disturbingly corrupt and self-aggrandizing as himself—Colonel Lafayette Baker. In such a capacity, several visitors from the South who recognized him saw Woodall on the streets of Washington. Ten days later he was arrested again and thrown into the Old Capitol Prison until January 1862, when he was paroled to Baltimore.[401]

In Baltimore, Woodall was arrested for disloyalty to the Union, not once, but twice, on March 12, 1863, and again on May 27 of that year. However, he beat the rap by "volunteering" to become a Yankee spy, and a few days later, was back in Richmond, reporting to General Winder. Within a couple of weeks of his arrival back in Richmond, he was arrested by the mayor on the charge of being a suspicious character, and for sending information to the Yankees. Woodall wasn't particularly good at being a Yankee spy. He was thrown in jail to await trial, and, in July, finally found guilty, but released on bail of seven hundred dollars, if he stayed out of trouble. Winder needed thugs like Woodall and took him back on his squad, even made arrangements for Woodall to be paid the money he was owed from the year before. The last evidence of Woodall in Dixie is that, on September 17, 1863, while in Wilmington, he received $235 for one month and seventeen days services as a Winder detective.[402]

Lafayette Baker writes of Woodall being one of the detectives who chased John Wilkes Booth after the Lincoln assassination, and that took place in April 1865. So, by the time Woodall testified in the Lloyd claim in August 1865, the Booth hunt would have been something to brag about indeed. However, in his deposition, taken a mere few months after the assassination, Woodall doesn't even mention it. In fact, nowhere in his deposition does he even say he was with Baker in 1865.

If anything, as much as Totten tried to orchestrate Woodall's testimony, it only clouded the issue, and after 1865, fortunately for Totten and his client, the subject of Lloyd being in prison in Richmond was never raised again.[403]

By order of the secretary of war, the new evidence presented by Totten was referred from the War Department to Judge Advocate General Holt on July 17, 1865, for his remarks. That was the same day Lloyd wrote to Stanton: "I hope and pray that you will order a final decision rendered in regard to my claim, either to pay me what I have worked and suffered for and which is justly mine, or let me know positively that it will not be paid as I am under heavy expenses here, and have been for over 8 weeks [this puts his arrival time in DC at between May 15 and May 22, probably closer to the latter], and if I am to lose my just dues [and here is the alarm], I must not longer waste time. You, Sir, know well that if my case goes before Congress or Court of Claims, it will become public, and although there have been four traitors hanged [he means the Lincoln assassination conspirators—Lewis Payne, Davey Herold, George Atzerodt, and Mary Surratt—on July 7] there are many more lurking about our country who would not hesitate to stab me in the dark if they knew my business for the past four years. Mr. Stanton, I look to you to have my case decided, and give me the 'justice' you said I should have."

By August 16, Judge Holt was writing to Stanton that, "the belief is entertained that its payment would be justified." Holt had done not merely a volte-face on the subject of Lloyd, but a double somersault. Something had changed his mind since June, and it wasn't, as Holt claimed, the additional "evidence" supplied by Lloyd in the interim. This new evidence, when subjected to close examination, was just as starkly implausible as the original evidence, if not more so.

What made Holt do a 180-degree turn? Was it Holt's fierce and faithful attachment to Abraham Lincoln that made him swallow a stew of bogus evidence meant to disorient and confuse? Was Holt moved by Lloyd—Lincoln's self-proclaimed spy—a man who claimed he'd served and suffered for the lost leader? It would be astounding if Holt had not actually met Alvin Lloyd between June and August. Two men talking together, finding out that they were both from Louisville, had both arrived in that town at the same time back in 1830, and, to cap it all, that Holt's second wife was first cousin to Alvin's stepmother. Was that of importance?

Things were now going Lloyd's way, but on August 26, 1865, a dark cloud appeared not on the horizon but right in Alvin Lloyd's face, one that portended a hurricane that might well blow the entire claim train right off the track.

Judge Holt, even as "the fates of Jefferson Davis and his top subordinates remained in limbo," in his dogged pursuit of Jefferson Davis's involvement in the Lincoln assassination, sent chief US Government Archivist Francis Lieber to Richmond to retrieve whatever Confederate documents he could. He hoped that lurking therein might be the damning evidence needed to finally put the noose around the neck of the ex-Confederate president. Lieber never found that evidence but he did find documents on William Alvin Lloyd, a man he knew to be making a claim with the War Department at that very moment.[404]

On August 26, 1865, Lieber wrote a letter to Secretary of War Stanton: "Sir, I have the honor to transmit a Bill presented to the rebel Secretary of War by W. Alvin Lloyd, who, it is understood, is now urging a claim against the United States War Department for alleged Secret Service in the insurgent states performed under direction of the late President."[405]

The bill Lieber had found was dated February 1, 1864: "Hon. Secretary of War. Ten copies of W. Alvin Lloyd's War Map. $50. Richmond." Then it says, "Received payment," and was signed, "W. Alvin Lloyd."[406]

There were several other notes, all from February 1, 1864, which Lieber did not find. One was from the Confederate adjutant general's office: "W. Alvin Lloyd sold 100 copies of his 'Southern RR Map' to C.S. Engineers Bureau, for which he received $500. Dated Richd., Va., Feb. 1/64." Another reads: "Confederate States of America. 25 copies of Lloyd's RR map. $150." Yet another, relating to "40 copies of W. Alvin Lloyd's Southern Railroad maps," at five dollars each—totaling two hundred dollars, for the Confederate States Nitre & Mining Service. Alvin also received $125 for twenty-five copies of the map for the Ordnance Department as well as $50 for ten copies, at five dollars a copy, from the Navy Department, proof that Lloyd was busy selling his wares in the Confederacy.[407]

But the one bill Lieber did find caused a stir within the US War Department. Alvin and Totten were forced to come up with a suitable answer. On September 27 Lloyd wrote personally to Stanton, explaining things, and the following day had the letter notarized by John Callan: "I have the honor to state to you that during my term of service as a Special Agent of the United states, in the so-called Southern Confederacy, I published a 'Rail Road Guide,' giving a plan and maps of the various rail roads in the states then in rebellion against the Government; that the said publication was made sometime in 1863; that I sold about five hundred of the maps, one copy of the maps is herewith submitted for examination, to the rebel government, which were taken by the various departments."

This is clever reasoning, one that Totten and Lloyd hoped would convince Stanton. Lloyd continues:

I was under observation at the time of the said publication in the detective department of the rebel government, and resorted to this business in order to cover up my real designs, and to have some ostensible occupation as a means of support, to account for my presence in the rebel dominions. I had at that time but recently been released from a rebel prison on a charge of being a "Yankee spy," that it was well and widely known through the South that I had been engaged in the publication of "Rail Road Guides" for many years, and I adopted this particular business as being better calculated, on that account, to disarm suspicion and to relieve myself from observation in the said detective department, in order that I might be able more fully to carry out the instructions given to me by President Lincoln; the money obtained from the sale of these "Guides" was used in defraying my expenses; that the rebel government refused for a long time to buy said maps, but on being pressed, on the ground that I had suffered a long and wrongful imprisonment, the various departments consented to, and each of them did, take a few of the maps, amounting in all to five hundred copies, but that they were afterwards cast aside as useless [and useless they indeed were; the one attached to this enclosure is—well—useless]. I am fully of the belief that the publication of these guides was actually necessary to prevent my being confined in a rebel dungeon on suspicion of being a "Yankee spy"; that the said publication did actually relieve me to a great extent from the observation and suspicion of the rebel detective police force, and enabled me to perform my duty as a secret agent in the employ of the Government; that I thus considered it to be my duty to mislead the officers of the so-called Confederacy in this manner, and that I am still of that opinion.[408]

Lieber was still determined to locate Confederate documents that might be damaging to Jefferson Davis, and Stanton advised that Lieber keep an eye out for anything pertaining to this man Lloyd. And Lieber did. And he found more. On October 5, he was able to write to Stanton that "after careful search, the following are the only papers in this office which I have been able to find relating to W. Alvin Lloyd." The documents listed were:

1. The Lloyd letter to Secretary Judah Benjamin, dated Savannah, February 21, 1862.
2. Lloyd letter, same date, to Confederate Adjutant General Samuel Cooper.
3. Second Lloyd letter to Cooper, dated Savannah, February 25, 1862.
4. Second Lloyd Letter to Benjamin, dated Savannah, March 17, 1862.
5. Letter of General Lawton to President Davis, dated March 21, 1862, making a report in the case.
6. Letter of A. R. Lawton, March 29, 1862, addressed to G. W. Randolph, referring to previous report.
7. Virginia Lloyd's brother Eugene Higgins's letter to President Davis, dated December 5, 1863, Mobile.
8. Rockwell's letter to Benjamin, dated Savannah, December 19, 1861.
9. "Requisition of Sec of War on Sec of Treasury in favor of W.A. Lloyd for the sum of eight hundred and sixty dollars [Confederate money]—payable out of the appropriation for Incidental, Contgt Exp of Army," and marked "special." Dated February 2, 1864.[409]

All very damaging.

But time was pressing upon Stanton and all his subordinates in the War Department. Judge Holt and others were all in favor of paying Lloyd, but Stanton still had reservations. The Lieber letters only added to what was a natural lawyerly caution, but something had to be done very soon, to get rid of this Lloyd case and move on to other things. And so came a Totten/Lloyd victory. And with it an incredible glimpse into the world of harried, gullible US officials:

The Secretary of War directs the amount of expenditures reported by the Judge Advocate General ($2380) in gold, or its equivalent, to be paid. He does not feel justified in paying the salary or compensation for services claimed. The case is referred to the Adjutant General to pay the above specified sum out of the fund in his hands, leaving the claimant to pursue his claim elsewhere for the residue. [Signed] Edwin M. Stanton, Secretary of War, Oct. 9, 1865.

But was expediency the only reason Stanton felt obliged to overcome his natural caution in the Lloyd case? He could equally have just said no. Could there have been another reason? Something to do with Judge Holt?

In early May Judge Holt had made a pact with the devil. At that time it was rumored that Jefferson Davis had been involved in the Lincoln assassination. Judge Holt wanted this to be true, and, as we have seen, was taking steps to try to implicate the ex-Confederate president, who was now languishing in Fort Monroe. Judge Holt wanted to hang Jefferson Davis. All he needed was proof. Sanford Conover appeared to him as Mephistopheles appeared to Faust.

Conover claimed to have the proof, and he was prepared to sell it. Judge Holt was prepared to buy. However, by the middle of June 1865 evidence was coming in that Conover was a bilker, and that Holt was being taken. And he was. Throughout July the evidence mounted until any sane man would have admitted he'd been conned. But so irrational had Holt become in his hatred of Jefferson Davis that he circled the wagons, with his pet informant Conover right in the center of the circle.[410]

Assistant Judge Advocate General Edward D. Townsend, of the adjutant general's office, actually paid the money in gold to Alvin on October 10, 1865, $2,380. Stanton had instructed the advocate general's office to pay to Lloyd "in gold, or its equivalent." What Stanton quite clearly meant is, if not gold, then the equivalent of gold, that is, $2,380 in some other form—silver, perhaps. E. D. Townsend was the man to whom the task fell of actually handing Lloyd the money, but he seems to have misread Stanton's instructions, misunderstood them, didn't see the comma in Stanton's sentence, or something, and assumed that he was to pay Lloyd the equivalent of $2,380 in "today's money," October 1865 money. Taking into account inflation, and doing the math, he duly paid Lloyd $3,427.20—over a thousand more than he should have. Although he later admitted this to General Hardie, the mistake was never dwelled on—by anyone—and the official figure went down in the history books as $2,380 paid.[411]

Paid. A big win.

Of all the players in Lloyd's light and shadow show, it is the director, the ringmaster Enoch Totten, who must demand the loudest applause. He must bow first. Then, they all must bow.

15

Lay of the Last Minstrel

PICTURE LLOYD STRUGGLING DOWN THE STEPS OF THE WAR DEPARTMENT. Picture a purse of gold, the spoils of a great gamble. The day Lloyd got the money his victory over the Yankee government was complete. Totten and Lloyd's well-orchestrated fraud, the additional witnesses—the straw men paid to lie—resulted in the fog of deceptions that duped federal officials. Lloyd would, in all probability, justify the imposture. Hadn't some of his own Confederate countrymen repeatedly accused him of being a Yankee spy? Hadn't he been hunted, arrested, and suffered, nearly dying in their keep? So when he came back from his war he would have reasoned that it was right that he should pose as the very thing they'd accused him of: Lincoln's personal secret agent. Now Lloyd was the proud owner of almost $3,500 in gold, not greenbacks, a less stable currency that could only be converted into gold "at a set ratio determined by Wall Street speculation."[412]

When the average Union soldier earned roughly sixteen dollars a month, the two hundred dollars Lloyd claimed President Lincoln promised him monthly for his purported perilous service stood in marked contrast. By 1865 the cost of the war had ballooned from one and a half million dollars a day to over three million obtained by taxing US citizens as early as 1861 with the Revenue Act. The rest was obtained through import tariffs, corporate donations, and other private sources. Now, after four long years, the government coffers were drained. With claims abounding there was little if anything to spare for the man they believed spied for the late, lamented president.

But there Lloyd was, with the starch, though not the strut, for strutting would have been impossible given his infirmity, ironically, newly minted, no longer broke, in the enemy's capital city on a crisp autumn day. Soon he would no doubt find his accomplices and small son. With his former financial state blindingly spare, perhaps he had made his way to one of the boardinghouses that dotted the city—brick and wood-framed humble places—where six dollars a week bought food and board. They had waited for this day. But the spoils of his war wouldn't last very long at all given Lloyd's profligate ways. Worse, he couldn't keep all the gold for himself. He'd have to portion out some of it out. Totten had to have his share and the "witnesses" had to be paid off, though it seems that Lloyd never told Totten he'd gotten over a thousand more than he should have gotten after E. D. Townsend adjusted the amount for inflation. Lloyd would have to pay Boyd. If he didn't, given Boyd's explosive nature, his clerk might expose them all, or worse. He'd have to provide for Virginia and Clarence. He owed them. Mostly, he owed her. Through all the degradation, through his most fearful days, she'd stood by him; lied for him, stayed married to him, and now was likely helping him stand and walk. Little Clarence had seen his father incarcerated, sick, and hopeless. And Nellie Dooley, who'd also lied obediently, he'd have to give her something.[413]

If he and his entourage went off for a celebration, into the streets of the changed and changing city, they couldn't help but see the parade of the First District Colored Regiment, a brass band and drum corps accompanying them with much pomp as they marched "down F. Street from Campbell Hospital" on their way to the Executive Mansion, where they would parade before President Andrew Johnson. Just that day, the *Evening Star* reported Johnson saying, "this was a white man's country and always would be." At the reviewing stand, their commander Colonel John Holman, along with much of the cheering black population of Washington City, heard the president thank the troops of the Colored Regiment for their twenty-six months of service in the field, then warned them not to "lead a life of idleness" now that they were free.[414]

For Lloyd and others like him, there was a new order, new rules, a new country, not his own. Not ever his own again.

Despite Lloyd's victory, Washington City was not a good place for him to remain. It was again in turmoil as Joseph Holt was prosecuting the war-crimes trial of Henry Hartmann Wirz at the Court of Claims room in the Capitol. The keeper of the Andersonville Prison death camp where more than thirteen thousand Union soldiers had perished was "scorned, loathed, despised, hated by all men and women," the *New York Times* and *Boston Advertiser* correspondent reported. It was impossible not to be riveted by hundreds of horrific accounts of suffering and death that permeated the papers as survivors of the camp came forward, some wanting to pronounce a death sentence and "shoot the miserable creature" themselves. The specter of the noose, the sure knowing that Wirz would hang, must have haunted Alvin Lloyd. The horrors of that Savannah prison, the screams of the slaves and the taunts of his jailors—you should hang, Yankee bastard—and the bullets that almost killed him in Mobile were not that far away—the stuff of nightmares.

Word on the street had it that Holt was still seeking more evidence from Charles Dunham, and paying him out of War Department funds in his obsessive drive to bring all Confederate authorities to trial. If Holt or Stanton questioned, found new evidence—or worse—and found Lloyd's claim utterly bogus, he might well be tried for defrauding the government. A treasonable offense. Totten may well have urged Lloyd away. Not all the money was won but Totten had other claims. This crooked lot, this crooked claim might have weighed heavy on him. Or not.

Sometime over the next ten days Lloyd would leave the city.

After casting about for possible locales, he decided on Philadelphia, the second-largest city in the country, an anti-slavery, abolitionist haven that had given more than one hundred thousand men to the war and had lost twenty thousand, whose manic steel and anthracite coal industry built the rails, locomotives, and weaponry that helped sustain the Union. Now it was "a center for veterans' organizations, such as the Loyal Legion and the Grand Army of the Republic," providing "projects, activities, pensions and initiatives for the widows and orphans."[415]

It was there in Philadelphia, on October 31, that William Alvin Lloyd arrived at the grand Girard House Hotel, on Chestnut below 9th Street. During the war the hotel had been commandeered as a uniform factory and hospital. Now it once again catered to a wealthy set. "W.A. Lloyd of Washington, DC," the *Philadelphia Public Ledger* noted, was a guest. He'd come to start up the guide again. It was a success once. Just before and during the war, his readers loved his pro-Southern, accusatory editorials, the beautiful lithographs, and if he couldn't always pay the advertisers, well, he'd find a way this time. Or not. It was a smart little publication once and it would be again, though not as incendiary. Lloyd would find a new voice, new readers. A new audience. He'd use his money to make more money. He'd need new equipment, a new rotary printing press, the finest with six cylinders and good young assistants who'd do the lifting and the fitting, the inking and the type setting, the rolling of the boards on paper. Good, heavy paper. Or he would rent space in a building that housed printers and the equipment would be at the ready. He would sell the ads and glad-hand as before. And as for Boyd, he hadn't rotted in a prison, been threatened with hanging. He deserved a pittance. Or nothing. Perhaps his new city of Philadelphia fortified him, made him less afraid of his former underling's wrath. To hell with Boyd.

Lloyd found a place where he could get a good deal renting space in the Franklin Buildings, a five-story structure in Franklin Square on Sixth Street, near Arch. Printing offices, bookbinders, and all manner of publications were well established there. Here, he would breathe new life into his long defunct guide, now to be called *W. Alvin Lloyd's Rail Road Guide*. No more steamboats. No more catering to and cajoling his southern countrymen. No more incendiary editorials. The country was at peace now; why shouldn't he be as well? On December 23, the *Illustrated New Age* gave a list of hotel arrivals: "Mrs. Colonel [he'd dubbed himself a colonel] Lloyd and fam., NY." They would have Christmas together. And they had money, at last.

Lloyd was between Philadelphia and Baltimore constantly over the next several months, traveling, soliciting ads, and on occasion, as he was wont to do, cheating customers. His brother, J. T., aglow with the prospect of a completely virgin territory, was doing the same thing in England. Alphabetical Boyd was still involved with Alvin, waiting with ever-growing anger and frustration for his long-promised cut, which never came. But somehow, now, in his new high-wire state, Alvin did not seem to fear the wrath of Boyd, or if he did, he banished it, as he was wont to banish all things unpleasant, perilous, or threatening, until something or someone cracked the fragile ice he skated on in those days of reinvention.

Nor did a share of the profits ever come for the young Baltimorean named Charles T. Harvey, who had been hired by Lloyd to sell space in the guide and was owed five hundred dollars in commissions, but it soon became apparent that he wasn't going to get it. And though Alvin ignored the warning signs that his two young associates were plotting against him, they were.

On January 30, 1866, T.H.S. Boyd was arrested in Baltimore, "charged with embezzlement and also with forging a check . . . in the name of Wm. S. [*sic*] Lloyd . . . for fifty dollars on the National Mechanics Bank." After an examination "before Justice Spicer," he was bound over to the Grand Jury. On February 17 he was formally charged with "passing a counterfeit check on the Mechanics Bank," as well as the forgery of Lloyd's name. His bail was set at two thousand dollars.[416]

And as he and his boss were apparently bonded at the bone, and almost unbreakable, with Lloyd's help, Boyd beat the rap. On February 27, he, Alvin, and a mysterious lady named Miss Marston all arrived at the American Hotel, across from the Philadelphia State House.[417]

On March 14, 1866, after Alvin Lloyd left room 4½ at the hotel to go soliciting again, Alphabetical Boyd and Charles Harvey—Alphabetical with his ever-present huge Bowie knife stuck in his belt—took the opportunity to break into Lloyd's trunk, rooting for money. They found two hundred dollars, as well as jewelry and some very compromising papers. The mayor of Philadelphia issued a warrant for their arrest. And so they were. "Two young men formerly clerks in the establishment of William A. Lloyd . . . charged with stealing money, jewelry and valuable papers from the trunk of William A. Lloyd."[418]

Lloyd's papers were later found in Boyd's trunk when he was caught. Locked up in either trunk, these papers were sheer powder kegs and it is a wonder that Lloyd hadn't destroyed them. If they fell into the hands of the Washington City authorities he'd defrauded, he would be exposed. And arrested. The documents likely forged by Boyd were in Alvin's keep—a catalogue of Rebel correspondence and a fake commission as a colonel. The purpose of this double charade was the stuff of recklessness, and within it, the stink of treason. Among the documents was "a letter from Jefferson Davis to 'Colonel' Lloyd relative to the best manner of depreciating the Federal currency, passes from Lloyd to General Winder, letters from prominent rebels, maps, his commission as a colonel in the Rebel army, etc." Would that Lloyd had truly been made a colonel, dashing about the South in a dress uniform studded with epaulets. And his jailors would never have seen his face, or starved him or sickened him. The rank, the lost glory, was a fantasy; forged, stolen, found, and reclaimed. And kept. That was madness.[419]

There were more details reported about the robbery. When "Colonel Lloyd of the government service," as the *Philadelphia North American* wrote, "got back to the American, and found what had happened to his trunk, he was around at the Mayor's office within moments." Alphabetical and Harvey were in jail for a couple of weeks. "One paper found in Mr. Boyd's trunk purporting to bear the signature of 'Colonel Lloyd' was pronounced to be a forgery." Finally, Charles Harvey was discharged, but Boyd was booked for forgery, larceny, and carrying a concealed deadly weapon. (That would be his enormous Bowie knife.) However as a reflection of the bizarre Lloyd-Boyd dance, he was rescued by his employer and given a sum of money to buy his way out of jail.[420]

Charles T. Harvey wasn't so well taken care of; in fact, he wasn't taken care of at all, and on May 15, 1866, he wrote a very damaging letter to Secretary Stanton about his former employer, who had moved out of the American and was now living with his family at the Continental Hotel, one of the country's best, a grand, fine place. Newly and joyously profligate, the Lloyds enjoyed the hotel's grandeur, just as president-elect Abraham Lincoln had on February 23, 1861, on the way to his inaugural. To get to their rooms they would have to climb "a freestanding stairway from the lobby to the second floor, and a one hundred and sixty–foot second-floor promenade that opened to a second-floor balcony," and walk along the inlaid marble floors.[421]

While Alvin was fulfilling his promise of luxury evermore, Stanton received Charles T. Harvey's letter. It was so damaging, and its repercussions were so great, at least for a time.

"Sir, one Wm. A. Lloyd has a claim against the Government for Secret Service, part of which . . . he had already recovered. I understand he is about to make an effort to collect the balance."

And then came the bombshell: "This Wm A. Lloyd is a notorious scoundrel. . . . I have every reason to believe his claim upon the Government to be false and utterly without foundation." Harvey explains how he has come to know this.

"A young man by name Thomas H.S. Boyd who has been confidential clerk for Mr Lloyd for the past six years, informed me that Mr. Lloyd had committed a fraud upon the Government by false representation and forgery of deceased officers' names." Harvey said that Lloyd, Boyd, his wife, and nurse were "his principal actors in the fraud" and that the witnesses Boyd named were paid to swear falsely. "He [Boyd] further informed me that Mr. Lloyd had promised him half of the money produced by the claim, and that he now refused to satisfy his promise. Therefore he intended to make a full confession to you." And if Alvin, dining nightly in splendor at the Continental, had known of Harvey's letter, this betrayal by a lowly clerk would have enraged him, threatened him, likely ruined him. Of course he had not seen Harvey's letter. Had he, the second portion would have relieved him temporarily. Lloyd usually won, no matter the means employed.

Harvey revealed that Lloyd had persuaded Boyd to return to his employ. For money, of course, *and* for the promise of money, he would not expose the Lloyd fraud.

"This leads me to believe that Mr. Lloyd has agreed to his former terms," Harvey writes, "especially as I understand he [Lloyd] is making arrangements to collect balance of his claim." Finally Harvey offered his help to Stanton. "In investigating this affair, I will cheerfully inform your agents of any further particulars in my power, should you desire it. I can give you satisfactory references as to my character. Very respectfully, your obedient servant, Charles T. Harvey, No. 11 South Street."

And there it was: the whole canard. While Harvey's letter made its way across the ranks for proper consideration, Lloyd soldiered on. He would never tell the truth of his supposed service to the Union government. Not then. Not ever.[422]

When *Lloyd's Railroad Guide* (Vol. xiii) finally came out in June 1866, the *Illustrated New Age* called it a "useful and valuable publication, interspersed with fine engravings," crediting Colonel Lloyd with "taking an active part in the trials of the last four years." Was this the beginning of a public revelation on Lloyd's part or a tease, these "trials"? If he dropped a hint or two of his wartime activities to the newspapers as he pressed them to promote and review his *Railroad Guide*, it was just a hint, a nudge and a wink, nothing more.[423]

The *Philadelphia North American and United States Gazette* was even more acclamatory, comparing Lloyd's guide with the "best and fullest published in any city." Admiring the steel plate engravings, the forty pages of ads, and the "number of pages devoted to humorous matter . . . a decided improvement upon the earlier issues," the *Gazette* called the guide a way to "extend the influence of Philadelphia."[424]

Alvin continued to put the guide out on a monthly basis from Philadelphia at 202 South 9th Street. In October, his last edition had come out and he hadn't seen true profits. He'd been too profligate. The hotel bills—the life of a swell he'd longed to lead again and was marvelously leading—broke him. Again. And if the time for a guide like his had passed—and even the popular *Appleton's Guide*, the go-to for travelers, was becoming less essential—he was defeated. He could not compete. As for his brother, J. T., he was roaming the northeast as a mapmaker and well-known bilker and though he would have sympathized with Alvin's plight, he'd problems of his own, as he was always one step ahead of the police.

So again, in his desperation, Alvin huddled with himself. But instead of fading, folding, and dying, he revived.

Was it the memory of applause, the seduction of applause, the din of applause? The old songs that he'd heard when he was still young and whole, and the hot August night in Louisville when the tambo, bones, and banjos, bewitched him. Now he would return to that life, reclaim it and himself. Again. But could he perform? Surely now, unless he were to advertise himself as a lame but game manager, and that would be a freak show, he must summon strength and find his way back to his old ways as the high-stepping showman he once was. He would make it big again or die in the try.

And so it was in January 1867 that W. Alvin Lloyd put together a new mammoth incarnation of his old touring show, despite warnings of a possible countrywide financial crisis, one that would be particularly hard on the entertainment world. The immense cost of the Civil War, the rebuilding and retooling of industry, coupled with independent, unschooled banking firms flooding the marketplace. And after all, wasn't entertainment a luxury? "Managers of traveling troupes are trimming their sails to meet the gale," the *Daily Cleveland Herald* reported. "In the main, the business is on the decline, and but few managers of traveling troupes, however wealthy they may be, have the nerve to face the impending storm."[425]

But an impending storm, whether from warnings in the press or in the dark skies that preceded the fierce gales of his childhood—the devil winds that sent steamboats toppling on the Ohio, and the floods that followed—does not appear to have bothered him. Or he did not let it bother him. Alvin proudly announced his reincarnation. The *Springfield Republican* called him "the popular manager of olden times." Well, the olden times would be new again. He'd see to that. This troupe was to be called Lloyd & Bidaux's Minstrels, named to cash in on the ever-growing fame of Gustave Bidaux, the French baritone who had been with Lloyd's Minstrels just before the Civil War, and who would now be one of the stars of this new enterprise.[426]

As he'd done before, Alvin assembled all the best available talent of the day, both musical and vocal, no expense spared. He promised them all huge salaries and if he doubted he could always pay them, never mind. He was back on top, signing minstrels, instructing the advance men, and picturing the money that would come rolling in. A stellar band they were. Happy Cal Wagner, a southerner from Mobile, was "Tambo." Charley Reynolds was "Bones." Happy Cal and Charley were two of the three celebrated comedians with this troupe. The third was the famous Johnny Booker, the former little Sam Roberts, Alvin's stepbrother, the Louisville boy who'd come to town with his mother. Johnny Booker was now an established minstrel with his very own popular and much sung ditty.

I went down de back ob de fiel'
A black snake cotch me by de heel
I cut my dus', I run my best

Run my head in a hornet's nest
Oh, do, Mr Booker, do!
Oh, do, Johnny Booker, do.[427]

There are variations on this song, of course, and one of them is reputedly heard in *Gone With the Wind*. Way back when, Johnny Booker's mother had married Thomas G., the drunken tailor. But he was still Sam Roberts back then, a little kid, and would spend a lot of time with Alvin at the Marion House, which Mrs. Lloyd ran. From there it was a change of name, and a year or two after Alvin had joined the minstrel world, Johnny Booker followed his stepbrother into the game, becoming one of the early minstrel comedians and managers. In the early days he made famous a few songs that had great vogue, "Meet Johnny Booker at the Bowling Green," and "Johnny Booker, Help Dis Nigger." By early 1852 he was already a celebrated comic star vocalist and over the next fifteen years would play with all the greats in the business, including being a member of Lloyd's new troupe in 1867.[428]

Luminaries like Bill Delehanty and Tom Hengler, the world-renowned clog dancers, had earlier that month played their last event together as a team, freeing them up for Alvin's minstrels. The quartette consisted of M. Ainsley Scott, H. J. Jackson, Ed Seymour, and Monsieur Gustave Bidaux. There were, among others, James Koehl, the "wonderful flageolet [a small flutelike woodwind] soloist," and his brother Jake.

Also along were J. B. Murphy, the famous composer and author, the interlocutor, or master of ceremonies of the show; and Harry Stanwood, the Canadian banjoist. Charley Currier was the business agent, and Charles Wilkinson the advance agent for the troupe. Virginia Lloyd was with her husband as he reclaimed his former status. Imagine this young woman—the war years not that far behind her—with a child and a husband she cared for in spite of all his agonies that came to be her agonies. The very steel of her as she tended to him on the nights when he ached all over and could barely stand, or brought him home after he'd assaulted a man for a perceived insult, for something he thought he heard. In this Lloyd incarnation, Virginia was a fixed star. And Alvin, remarkably, was growing stronger, or at least seemed to be transfused with energy. The survivor, the boy in him, the little Louisville boy who'd cut cloth and become a man of dubious cloth, was made new.[429]

Lloyd & Bidaux's Minstrels opened on Friday evening, February 1, 1867, at the Concert Hall in Danbury, Connecticut. The hall was jammed, and hundreds were turned away at the door. The *New York Clipper* praised Lloyd-the-man and his marvelous troupe: "An entertainment complimentary to that gentleman's tact and business qualifications for organizing the company," noting he was known for his "uniform kindness" to the company during the organization, proclaiming it the "best performance ever given in Danbury." This reclaimed world, this extraordinary passage in the life of W. Alvin Lloyd, the kaleidoscope through which these days gleamed, glory days he'd never dreamed to see again were back, sparkling anew. And on it went. At each stop there was praise, glorious, unending praise.[430]

The next night they played at Franklin Hall in Bridgeport—a small concert and lecture venue—to a "two hundred and seventy five dollar house," where on that very corner, in the church that abutted the hall, when little more than a child, Virginia had married Alvin Lloyd.[431]

To publicize the opening of his show, Alvin had a set of playbills "engraved and printed in colors, a set of bills . . . which for the beauty of execution can hardly be excelled," the *New York Clipper* raved, wishing them "a decided success." All afternoon and evening it poured down with rain in Bridgeport, but, notwithstanding, people were again turned away.[432]

Then on they went to Hartford. "The great troupe of the age . . . the Monarchs of Minstrelsy," the *Springfield Republican* raved. But as in Bridgeport, the hall was too small to hold the numbers who came to see the show. Next up, the townsfolk of Springfield, worked up to a fever pitch by reading the ads, flocked to the new Music Hall in their town.[433]

On to New York, to concert halls packed with cheering audiences, blazing through cities: Albany, Troy, Utica, Syracuse, Oswego, Geneva, with master of ceremonies W. Alvin Lloyd heading the cast list, as usual, the crowd hugely in tune, the papers raving. By March 2, Charlie Wilkinson had been dismissed as advance agent, and Tom Warhurst was brought aboard in that capacity. In an ad, Alvin warned people that as from February 12, no business dealings that anyone had with Wilkinson on behalf of the troupe were valid. This was a typical scam played by a practiced scammer. The advance man would arrange not only the bookings, but the press as well. This meant that Lloyd & Bidaux's Minstrels were not responsible for any debts that Charley might have accrued since that date. Yes, it was legal, as long as you put the ad in the paper, disclaiming your man's actions. That way, you didn't have to pay for any ads after that date. Just like the ad-grabbing scams of old when Alvin was a publisher. In the meantime, Charley Wilkinson was paid off and went on his merry way.[434]

Late March saw them in Sandusky, and then at the Young Men's Hall in Detroit. "Much credit is due to manager Lloyd and his gentlemanly ushers for the manner in which they endeavored to make the audience comfortable, and obtain seats for as many as possible," the *Detroit Free Press* said. "In fact, the manager seems to leave nothing undone to elevate the character of the business in which he is engaged, and no expense is spared to make the entertainment first-class." They loved Gustave Bidaux singing "My Boy, How Can I See You Die," the anguished tale of a mother who'd lost her son to the war, and guffawed when Cal Wagner performed his comic song, "The Wandering Irishman," a parody of a tippling, dancing fellow. The whole performance, according to the paper, contained almost none of the "objectionable features of Negro minstrelsy," meaning that the stereotypes, the plantation ditties that made audiences roar with laughter, were frequently replaced by mournful songs of love and loss, songs redolent of post-war agonies and immeasurable grief. And because blacks were emancipated and slavery was dead, the images of the cheerful or wily Negro outwitting or submitting to the master were fading away. In the North, at least. But for the audiences of the ruined South, still clinging to and denying that the old ways were forever gone, the Jumping Jim Crows and Zip Coon characters were as popular as ever.[435]

On March 26 and 27, Lloyd's troupe played Turner's Opera House in Dayton, Ohio, and on the twenty-eighth opened at the Opera House in Columbus, Ohio, for a two-night run. Large and opulent, the houses hosted the greatest tenors of the day and of course—for rollicking nights of music and mirth—minstrels! The audiences were immense, and the newspapers did nothing but rave. "Artistic genius," waxed the *Daily Ohio Statesman*. "What could be more magnificent," they added, "than the ballads of Bidaux and Jackson, and the bass solo of Ainsley Scott?" On the first night, Mr. Jackson sang "Kathleen Mavourneen," a lament for a lost darling, a mavourneen. "Kathleen, mavourneen, the grey dawn is breaking, The horn of the hunter is heard on the hill. The lark from her light wing the bright dew is shaking, Kathleen, mavourneen, what! Slumbering still?" The following night the demand was so great that Jackson sang it again. Cal Wagner and Charley Reynolds brought the house down in fits of laughter with their "Jimmy, Let's Go Home." On the second night, Tom Hengler was too ill to appear, so his act "Southern Flirtation" had to be substituted with Bill Delehanty, who "gave us as fine a specimen of bone playing as we remember ever to have witnessed." One of the finest afterpieces ever presented before a Columbus audience was the seriocomic operetta, "Old Shady's Visit," arranged by Johnny Booker. "There is no doubt but that Lloyd & Bidaux's are in all particulars, the finest troupe now traveling. They will return here on or about the 10th of April," reported the *Statesman*. The receipts for the two nights amounted to $1,119.20.

On April Fool's Day they arrived in Cincinnati in grand style, for a five-night and two-afternoon engagement with much ballyhoo, a la Barnum. "A chariot, drawn by gaily caparisoned horses, and containing Lloyd's excellent brass band, paraded the streets," informing all they passed that Lloyd & Bidaux's Minstrels would be performing that night at Mozart Hall. The Mozart was crammed with an "appreciative and fashionable audience. Over two thousand tickets were sold, a profitable return to the managers," that is, Mr. Lloyd.[436]

At the Mozart, at least—and even generally speaking—the doors would open at seven-thirty in the evening and the show would begin at eight. Admission was fifty cents if you wanted to be in the parquette dress circle, or thirty-five cents for the gallery. On Wednesday and Saturday there were well-advertised family social matinees, commencing at two in the afternoon. Again, the papers, which would in those days review each performance, raved. A big emphasis was placed on how acceptable the show was for ladies and children. Other minstrel troupes may have been vulgar, but Lloyd's show was clean. And fun. Suitable for the whole family. Perhaps this was a bit of redemption, as Virginia and Clarence were with him and it did not seem that Alvin was straying, jolted by the realization that perhaps for the first time in his adult life he did not or could not stray.[437]

Saturday, April 6, was not only the last night of Lloyd & Bidaux's Minstrels in Cincinnati, it was the last night for Bidaux—period. Lloyd posted notices in the *Cincinnati Daily Enquirer* and the *Cleveland Leader* papers of April 6 through April 19: Among the announcements for his minstrels was this: "Gustave Bidaux has been discharged from my employ, for practices too disgusting to mention, and is no longer in any way connected with my company. W. Alvin Lloyd." Practices too disgusting to mention? What might he have done? Likely it was just the old scam, with a paid-off Bidaux going away. The name of the company was immediately changed to Lloyd's Minstrels.[438]

The minstrels stayed in Cincinnati for a few days, while Alvin and advance man Tom Warhurst went up to Columbus to pave the way for next week's performance. One of Tom's chores was to drop into the offices of the *Daily Ohio Statesman* on April 6 and pitch the editorial staff. That and a display ad went a long way toward favorable press: "Col. Lloyd's management of the auditorium is perfect and complete, and deserves more than a passing notice." The *Statesman* wouldn't be so happy when the troupe failed to pay their advertising bill.

During this time, one of Alvin's excesses would play its part in the demise of the company. Happy Cal had a performance all the way up in Cleveland, and, amid much publicity, Alvin hired a private train for him. However, the $110 had to come from somewhere, and it duly came out of the company's wages budget.[439] That was the day, April 10, that W. A. Lloyd was meant to be in court in Cincinnati for assault and battery. There is no record of whom he assaulted. The case was continued until the following morning, with no resolution apparent. Perhaps Alvin bought his way out of this, too.[440] By then the troupe was in Columbus, with their Monster Brass Band, for "positively one night only" at the Opera House. "No ordinary troupe could have called together so many people on so foul a night," reported the *Statesman* the following day. The paper lamented that the singing was not so good as on their previous visit, and they missed the sweet voice of Jackson, and the deep, sweet tones of

Ainsley Scott, and the cheery face of Johnny Booker. They were touched by "Little Barefoot," the bathetic tale of a poor child driven to beg in the streets. "Mister! Please give me a penny, for I've not got any Pa . . ." But the most popular act of the evening was Cal Wagner in his huge elephant suit and his lumbering dance around the stage. From there, on to bigger turns as a man, not a beast, Cal went to Cleveland, Ohio.[441]

Still in Ohio, Alvin's troupe was on to Zanesville, Newark, Cleveland, and Toledo, and then into Jackson, Michigan. By late April they were back in the northeast, replaying scenes of their earlier triumphs—Buffalo, Syracuse, Utica, Albany, Springfield, New Haven, Hartford. Standing room only, and the papers were still raving—not one black cloud in the press.[442]

But on May 29, 1867, in Newport, they disbanded and rested. Surely Alvin needed to stop, to gain strength and bask in this greatest of great tours. The *New York Herald* of June 2 reports that Colonel Alvin W. Lloyd, the successful proprietor of Lloyd's Minstrels, with Happy Cal Wagner, J.B. Murphy, Major S.B. Filkins, and Lt. W. Preston [i.e., Billy Preston, of the company] were luxuriating at Newport, and that Col. Lloyd was reorganizing his troupe preparatory to inaugurating the coming season.

On June 19 they were due to appear in New Haven, but the performance was canceled due to a "difficulty" between Lloyd and two of his comedians. Six days later, Andrew Johnson, the president of the United States, was in New Haven. Pickpockets abounded. One of the victims was "Col. Lloyd, who had a $690 gold watch stolen." Again, they canceled a scheduled performance, this time at Syracuse on June 29.[443]

They were at Clarendon Hall, Ashtabula, Ohio, on the night of July 6, then in Cleveland again for a two-night run, July 9 and 10, at Brainard Hall. From there it was on to Union Hall, in Jackson, Michigan, on July 18. Then it was Toledo on July 21, and the following day they arrived in Adrian, Michigan. That morning Alvin and Virginia ran off with the money, leaving the company stranded, unable to get out of town. An appeal was published in the local paper to get the unlucky minstrel troupe train fare, and a special benefit was given at the hall. The receipts amounted to twenty-eight dollars. Not much, even in those days.[444]

For the next month or so, the press all over the country had a field day with the runaway Lloyd, the "precious rascal" and "unmitigated scoundrel," who had once "been in the service of the Union." The *Fremont Journal* (Ohio) of August 9 added a new twist: "He was a rebel agent at Washington during the war."[445]

The newspaper in Lockport, New York, reported the story and remarkably came to Alvin's defense, adding, "Col. Lloyd and his troupe are well known in this city, having given several entertainments here, and so far as the swindling of printers is concerned we can say that he paid his bills promptly in Lockport at each visit."[446]

But to make matters worse, one of the creditors found Alvin's trunk at the American Express office in Adrian and had it seized for debt. When Officer Hines opened the trunk, he found the compromising contents that Alphabetical Boyd and Charles Harvey had found earlier in Philadelphia. The papers itemized the contents, branding him "as not only a scoundrel but a sneaking spy and rebel."[447]

As the news storm was raging, Alvin was in St. Louis announcing he was about to come out with yet another issue of the *Railroad Guide*. Bigger, better than ever before. After his six-week tear through the city, he fled, "after receiving several thousand dollars from merchants for advertisements which were to be put in a new railroad guide he professed to be about to publish, but hasn't published yet." And then, the *Syracuse Daily Courier* huffed, "This Lloyd is a scamp if one half is true that is reported of him. Wonder where he thinks he will go, when he shakes off his mortal coil, if he cheats the printer."[448] If the mortal coil, or the dreaded noose, was tightening, Alvin was surely at his final mile. And then he wasn't. He headed back to Baltimore, to the Union Hotel.

There are time lapses and Alvin is obscured until May and June of 1868, when two events happened in Washington. First, Edwin Stanton resigned as secretary of war, and, three weeks later, the Special Claims Commission, which had been set up in 1866 to deal with war claims of all types, changed its name to the Board of Claims, and now fell under the presidency of Major General James Allen Hardie, assistant inspector general. This would have a major impact on the Lloyds.

But was Alvin in these missing months regrouping, exhausted, atoning? Not likely. He was again working with his brother, J. T. It was for Alvin his last stab at a career: A play. A *Foul Play:* a foolish, overdone piece that after much chicanery and shenanigans made Alvin and J. T. Lloyd Broadway producers. As Alvin was then pretty broke, and had five hefty judgments against him remaining unsatisfied within the legal system, it was J. T. who put up the money, or at least the promise of money. He himself had at that very moment in time a whopping sixty-five judgments, as a clerk of court's investigation would shortly discover. Together the two brothers were looking down the barrel at a total of more than twenty-six thousand dollars in court problems. And that was just in New York City.[449] On Monday evening, August 3, 1868, *Foul Play* opened at the New York Theatre. Right from the beginning people stayed away in droves. So, for want of paying customers, the Lloyds tried to fill the house with shills, or "deadheads" as they were known, to occupy the seats. In spite of this, the theater was never more than half-filled, and the brothers continued to paper the house.[450] While all this was happening, on the afternoon of the twenty-first of August, 1868, Alvin was walking up Broadway and had just reached the New York Hotel when he ran into fellow minstrel kings Dan Bryant, Bill Newcomb, and that long drink of water Nelse Seymour. On a good day, Nelse would swing a leg over your head, just to let you know how short you were, but today wasn't one of those days. Friendly immediately turned unfriendly and Dan horsewhipped Alvin up and down Broadway.[451]

The press savored the news of Alvin's whipping. For example, the *Rochester Daily Union* of September 1, 1868, reports this: "Dan Bryant and Colonel Alvin Lloyd of the New York Theatre were the principal actors in a supplementary act of 'Foul Play' near the New York Hotel on Wednesday last. A horsewhip is said to have been the most flourishing attraction in the dramas as here enacted, and the ever popular Dan succeeded, as usual, in walking off with all the honors." The horsewhipping, the shock to the system of an already frail man, likely contributed to Alvin's rapid and final decline.

By September 15, Alvin was admitting in the press that the play was losing money, and "wished it in hell before he had anything to do with it."

He thought *Foul Play* was the "poorest and trashiest piece that was ever put on the stage."[452] After much cheating, fighting, and drear theatrical politics, Alvin and J. T. left the theater world, forever.

J. T. went back to bilking the British, but in person this time rather than through agents. He and Ella and the kids took a ship for Liverpool and returned to New York the day after Christmas, with a new addition to the family—young Florence.[453]

If an announcement caught Alvin's eye, he would have seen his errant clerk had moved far away from him, beyond him. The item was about Professor Allen Ryan, a magnetic lecturer and orator from Ohio. In early 1869, Master Rolla Ryan, "a wonderful boy orator," was traveling in Cincinnati with his father, Professor Allen Ryan, and "T.H.S. Boyd, manager."[454]

Now failure stalked Alvin once again. Weakened, despondent, he went back to Washington City, back to the War Department, where three years before he'd stumbled down the marble steps clutching the bag of gold. This time, surely the last time, for he was so very tired, he begged an audience with the secretary of war. Was he not justly entitled to this money and might the secretary send his request to Major General James A. Hardie, the assistant inspector general, managing a new Board of Claims?

December 8, 1868,

W. Alvin Lloyd verbally requests that his claim for compensation for services rendered as spy or special agent be re-examined. The Secretary of War directs that the claim be re-examined, and reported upon by the Board of claims.[455]

On December 10, 1868, the board referred to the assistant adjutant general for the paper in the case, and other information the department might have, or have heard. This letter was received on December 11, 1868.

That day, E. D. Townsend, of the adjutant general's office in Washington, wrote of the large amount he'd paid Lloyd:

Respectfully returned to Major General Hardie, President Board of claims, together with the previous papers on file in this office in the matter of the claim of W. Alvin Lloyd. On the 10th of October 1865, in accordance with the order of the Secretary of War, I paid out of a special fund in my hands the sum of $3427.20, which was the value on that day of $2380—in Gold, being amount of expenses incurred by Lloyd in the South. It was the opinion of the Secretary of War at the time that this was all the War Department was authorized to award, and that the claimant should, for further relief, be turned over to Congress, or the Court of Claims, where the proofs adduced in support of his claim could be subjected to tests which the Executive branch of the Govt had no power to apply."

Townsend then goes on to quote Stanton's letter of October 9, 1865, directing the amount to be paid. And he has the Charles T. Harvey letter in hand. He is obviously suspicious.

Attention is respectfully called to the accompanying letter from Charles T. Harvey, received since the above amount was paid, which throws discredit upon the claim of Mr. Lloyd, and which it is deemed should be carefully investigated in connection with the claim. Inasmuch as there is no fund under the control of the Department from which a claim of this nature and of such a magnitude could be allowed, it is respectfully submitted to the Secretary of War that no further action should be taken in the matter and that the claimant should present his claim either before Congress or the Court of Claims. E.D. Townsend, Asst. Adjutant General.[456]

On December 21, 1868, Major General James A. Hardie of the Board of Claims sent the incredibly damaging Harvey letter to General Stewart Van Vliet, deputy quartermaster general, in Baltimore, asking him if he would be kind enough to investigate Harvey's character. Van Vliet went to work, and early the following year would report back to Major General Hardie.

It was all too much, the waiting, taking this great chance, and by then, Alvin was too sick to continue this new claim so Virginia had to do it for him. He was near death, or so it seemed, in the apartment he shared with Virginia and Clarence at 202 West 24th Street, New York City, a low-rise building at the corner of Seventh Avenue. As his wife hovered over him, and if he asked for forgiveness, it was for everything: For a life, a selfish life, pocked with lies, betrayals, and more lies. But Virginia would not let him die alone.

While Lloyd lay dying, the investigation of Charles Harvey had begun. "Deputy Quartermaster General's office, Baltimore, Md. Jany. 4, 1869. Stewart Van Vliet, Deputy QM Gen. Brevet Major General, US Army." Van Vliet was writing to General Hardie.

> *General, I have the honor to acknowledge the receipt of your communi-*
> *cation of the 21st ult., in reference to the standing of Chas. T. Harvey*
> *of this city [Baltimore], who has made serious charges against one Wm*
> *A. Lloyd, who has a claim before the Court of Claims. I have seen Mr.*
> *Harvey & have made enquiries about him & my impression is that*
> *he is a person whose statements can be relied on. It appears that Lloyd*
> *was engaged in selling* Rail Road Guide Books *& that Harvey was*
> *employed by Lloyd to sell them & which so employed, he (Lloyd) swin-*
> *dled Harvey, according to the latter's statement, out of $500. Hence*
> *Harvey's hostility. Harvey obtained most of this information concern-*
> *ing Lloyd from one Boyd, who was a private clerk of Lloyd's. A year or*
> *two ago, Lloyd figured quite extensively in the* Police Gazette, *when*
> *his portrait was given to the public, as well as a brief history, which*
> *latter was anything but flattering. I would suggest that Mr. Harvey*
> *be called before the Board of Claims. I return herewith his letter. Very*
> *respectfully, Yr Obt svt, Stewart Van Vliet, Deputy QM Gen.* [457]

Unfortunately, this *Police Gazette* portrait and brief history that Van Vliet describes is a myth, concocted by Harvey. Van Vliet never corroborated it. He couldn't have, as it doesn't exist.

On February 18, 1869, Virginia Lloyd wrote her first letter to General John M. Schofield, the secretary of war. In case Schofield was not aware of the particulars, Virginia filled him in. It seems that Alvin, in his extreme incapacitation, made this intrepid young woman his amanuensis.

New York, Feb. 18th, 1869.

Mrs Lloyd craves the indulgence of the Honorable Secretary of War, and begs to inform him, inasmuch as General Hardee [sic] in his note, written by your instructions, says, "Mr Lloyd's claim has not yet been decided upon by the Board of Claims." She is fearful there has been some mistake made, as it has been before the Board of Claims, and been decided upon by Judge Holt, and about one third of the amount paid by Mr Stanton, then Sec of War.

Virginia stresses that Lloyd's expenses are outstanding and reiterates Holt's decision was that

. . . the full amount should be paid, and it was left with Mr Stanton, who did not like to take the responsibility of paying the whole amount, but did pay Mr. Lloyd the amount he had expended out of his own private means while in prison, and informed him he would take his salary under consideration.

There the affair has rested since 1865.

Now, General, why should the Government pay part of a just claim, and not the whole of it? It must be all right, or all wrong? The claim is in Adjutant Townsend's office. The case has been thoroughly acted upon, and only needs your decision, General, to be paid. Regret exceedingly having to annoy you so very much, but Mr Lloyd's severe illness prevents him attending to business himself. It is but a small matter, and I firmly rely, General, upon your giving the case your immediate attention, and beg you will communicate with me here that I may not be compelled to leave my suffering husband. President Johnson has informed Mr Lloyd he would pay the claim in a moment, if he had the power to do so, but he had no means wherefrom to draw. An early answer, General, will be expected by Yours Most Respectfully, Virginia V Lloyd.[458]

A few weeks later, after being ignored, there came a new, even more desperate plea, "Midnight. New York. March 8th, 1869."

Midnight; as if the darkness, the hour, like a fire bell in the night, might deserve a fast response. Virginia reminds Schofield that it has been a week since she's last written:

I fear his [Schofield's] valuable time has been so engrossed with business of, to him, greater moment, that he has forgotten my petition. Our physician has informed me Mr. Lloyd should be taken South now, while he has a little strength to go, for, sinking as fast as he is with quick consumption, he will, in a very short time, be unable to be moved at all.

Only Schofield can spare her husband, she says.

I would not annoy you, General, but Mr. Lloyd, having been particularly unfortunate in business, and his protracted illness, compels me to ask you for the amount the Government is indebted to him, and I beg of you, as you value the life of one dear to you, do not let my poor husband die, when, by ordering his claim paid, you can, with God's help, prolong his life, for the Doctor says if he gets to Florida, he may live some time. He watches the mail so eagerly each day, and with each disappointment grows perceptibly worse. It is so very hard, General Schofield, to see him suffer so, for that which belongs to him. He asked me a moment since if I thought Genl Schofield would ordered [sic] his money paid, or whether he would have to lay here and die. I try to cheer him, and keep him hopeful, for I feel "God is with the right"—and it is right—all honest debts should be paid, and I beg you by every endearing tie you have on earth, do this deed of justice, for you are invested with the power.

And now Virginia is begging and audaciously composing Schofield's hoped-for reply.

Let me cheer my suffering husband with the announcement "Genl Schofield has ordered your claim paid, and you shall start immediately South," and may God bless and prosper you and yours through life shall be the daily prayer of myself and of one who at best is not very long for this world, my loved and honorable husband. Relying upon, and firmly trusting in, you I am, with Great Respect, Virginia V Lloyd.

Schofield never answered. On March 10, Dr. Sylvanus S. Mulford, a former prominent Union army surgeon during the war, visited Alvin for the last time. And if he were conscious, one of the last faces he would see would be that of a Yankee.

Over the next week, the great game, the great errant dazzle that was the life of William Alvin Lloyd, was sputtering to a close.

A montage: There is an older man on crutches, one leg twisted under him. Next, a shadowed face peers though thick prison bars.

In the background: A calliope pumps and whistles the strains of *My Old Kentucky Home*.

Frozen mid-leap, ragged, bewigged leaping in the air—Jim Crow grins. A minstrel troupe raises their tambos, bones, banjos, and accordions. Toasting, perhaps, saluting Alvin Lloyd, or are they aiming pistols at him?

Women, many women, very young, bejeweled and beribboned, pose together in sunlight.

A boy huddled by a lamppost in the streets of Butchertown, thick smoke from brewery vats obscuring his face.

A pair of small, calloused hands stained with dyes, held up to frame.

Cue a moist summer wind blowing from the Ohio. Cue the darkness.

It was March 17, 1869.

Lloyd's death certificate states the primary cause of his demise was "Phetrisis [*sic*] Pulmonalis," a wasting and deadly lung disease: tuberculosis. The secondary cause was "tuberculous [*sic*] Diarrhea." His bowl was rotting away. An agony.[459]

Virginia buried him two days later, in Woodlawn Cemetery, in the Bronx. It was a two-grave lot—NW1883, Section 16, in the Spring Lake Plot. The lot was owned by Virginia V. Lloyd. However, only one person would ever be buried in it—William Alvin Lloyd.

His fraud remained undetected. The rest of the claim, unpaid. But there was more to come of it. Much more. It was not over. It was not.

16

Post Lloyd Ergo Propter Lloyd

EVEN AFTER HIS DEATH, MERE DAYS AFTER HIS DEATH, WILLIAM ALVIN Lloyd is haunting the government authorities. To some, he is a puzzle, to others, he is "in hell." And there is a new wrinkle. Needing absolute proof of the real Lloyd—imposter or brave, unsung hero-spy—Colonel George Gibson Jr. of the War Department has sent Pinkerton detective Harry W. Davies, superintendent of Pinkerton's National Police Agency in New York, to gather information. The first response to Lloyd's background check—as it has been three years since he walked away with the gold—is in a letter from Harry Davies to General Delos B. Sackett, a close associate of detective Allan Pinkerton and former inspector general under Pinkerton's wartime employer, General George B. McClellan.

"Today one of the operatives was informed by a creditor of Lloyd's 'that Lloyd was in hell,'" Davies wrote, "and we find in the *New York Herald* and *World* of today a notice of the death of Wm Alvin Lloyd, and from what we can learn, I am convinced that he is the same man you are after. Lloyd, within the last two or three years, has been publishing a Railroad Guide, manager of a theatre, and also proprietor of a minstrel troupe. I will forward you any further particulars I may get regarding the antecedents of this man."[460]

If Davies' letter was truly written on March 20, then he couldn't yet have seen the *Herald*'s death notice, as it wouldn't appear until the following morning, Sunday. Either the paper he had been looking at was the *Tribune*, which did carry the notice on the twentieth, or his letter is simply misdated; it should read March 21. Odd for an agency whose eye allegedly never closed, dozed, or sank into deep slumber.

General Sackett was in Philadelphia on April 23, 1869, at the Headquarters of the Military Division of the Atlantic, in the Inspector General's Office, when he sat down to write a letter to Colonel Gibson at the War Department in Washington, DC. "I promised you if I found anything further regarding Wm A. Lloyd to forward it. Since my last letter, I have ascertained from Mr. Allen [*sic*] Pinkerton that there was no person employed on Secret Service by the United States between July 61 & 63 named Wm A. Lloyd. After July '63 Pinkerton cannot say who was employed."[461]

From 1860 Pinkerton served Lincoln as his protector and head of his Secret Service until December of 1862. One would think that very service should have included the name of William Alvin Lloyd, Lincoln's trusted agent in the Confederacy, as Lloyd alleged that Lincoln hired him on July 13, 1861.

While Lloyd was being vetted postmortem, Virginia was determined to press on, determined to extract more money from the bogus claim she'd abetted. She'd descended on a new official, General John Aaron Rawlins, Grant's old right-hand man who had taken over as secretary of war on March 13, 1869, just four days before Alvin died.

In this letter to Rawlins, Virginia wrote from her brother Eugene's house in Providence, Rhode Island, on April 27.

> *Some three months since, I was promised by Major Gibson, under instruction from General Schofield, that my husband, William Alvin Lloyd's claim should be decided in a few days, but the few days have rolled into weeks and months, and there has been no decision yet. In the mean time, General, God has seen fit to take my husband "home." He died on March 17th, and I stand in need of the money owing him. I write to you personally, General, feeling assured you will sympathise [sic] with me in my great trouble, and give me an early reply. If necessary, I will come on to Washington. Please have the case investigated, General, for it is a most just debt, and as it has been thoroughly examined and about one third of it paid, I cannot see why there is such a delay. It only requires your signature, General, and I trust you will not long with hold it. Anxiously awaiting your reply, I am in great bereavement.*[462]

Still, to no avail. But on May 4, 1869, Secretary of War Rawlins, on the recommendation of the inspector general, approved the action to refer the claimant to the US Court of Claims. That day, May 4, General James A. Hardie wrote a summary of the Lloyd case, repeating the "service" Lloyd had performed for President Lincoln. In the same letter he mentioned that Virginia and Clarence were destitute.[463]

Just at the time Alvin's brother, J. T., was in the news again for swindling small-town newspapers, General Rawlins died on September 6, 1869, and General William T. Sherman took over as interim secretary of war. Perhaps the thought of badgering Sherman, the man who effectively killed her beloved Confederacy, was intimidating to Virginia. There is no record of Virginia corresponding with Sherman because there was no correspondence.

Also, on that very day, September 6, 1869, Walter Chisholm's small, exclusive, and pricey school in the Bronx reopened for the new term, with young Clarence Lloyd, son of the late W. Alvin Lloyd, as one of the pupils, as the 1870 New York census indicates.[464]

And though Clarence's father was gone, the players in the Lloyd charade were still afoot. By the end of the year 1869, Alphabetical Boyd, back home with his widowed mother and his two brothers, had begun, with the help of some associates, a monthly publication called *Boyd's Office Directory*, packed full of useful information for the reader, and not to be, but surely intended to be, confused with William H. Boyd's famous long-standing city directory of Washington. Asbury Baker, one of the "witnesses" deposed in 1865, was clerking in a notions store in Baltimore, and Charles T. Harvey, the man who'd told Stanton in 1866 that Lloyd and his accomplices were actors in a great fraud, was still a bookkeeper living with his father in Baltimore.[465]

Virginia, clearly plagued and haunted by the damaging Charles T. Harvey letter that remained in the keep of Federal authorities, had to do something about it, about Harvey. Through Alphabetical Boyd she arranged to meet with Harvey in Baltimore, but they couldn't reach a financial settlement that would make him retract the incriminating charge. The next meeting was at the St. James Hotel, in Washington, in August 1870, with the same players. Apparently Harvey demanded five hundred dollars to keep silent. Virginia refused and offered three hundred. Harvey refused. Now that Charles Harvey wouldn't be bought off as easily as they had thought, the Totten gang had to make every effort to ruin the young man's credibility. Alphabetical's brother, Charlie Boyd, was brought in, as was a ringer—Abner Young Lakenan—to defame Harvey. On September 6, 1870, Virginia pushed the trio into the notary's office in Washington.

Alphabetical swore under oath to have known Harvey for fifteen years, the first three of which he was in business with the man he was about to excoriate. But that was before Harvey became "a disreputable and drunken character . . . an habitual drunkard and a person of low character and evil fame, which he has been now for more than twelve years."

Charlie Boyd swore that he had known Harvey for twelve years and repeated the habitual drunkard slur, adding, ever since he had known him he was "A man of bad repute in the neighborhood." When "Harvey is excited with liquor, he is exceedingly reckless in his statements."

Mr. Abner Lakenan said he had met Harvey only a handful of times since they first ran into each other in July, two months previously. Mr. Lakenan claimed to have been at the meeting at the St. James, and that Harvey said at that meeting that his letter was written out of malice because Lloyd had cheated him. Lakenan added, "He [Harvey] further stated at said meeting that for the consideration aforesaid he was willing to retract the said letter in the most careful manner, and to that end he would swear to anything except that he himself was a liar. He said he would not go to that extent." Despite only a bare working knowledge of Harvey he was now able to describe the man as "very indecent and brutal," and claimed that judging from "Harvey's walk and conversation," he was a "man who was utterly given over to vice, and destitute of moral character."[466]

As if in answer to Virginia's prayers, there was a new war secretary, Major General William Belknap, a lawyer who'd served with valor during Sherman's Atlanta campaign. From Washington, DC, on March 18, 1871, Secretary Belknap wrote to Virginia, who was then residing at John Minnelli's boardinghouse at 56 West 11th Street in New York City. "Madam, I have caused a careful examination to be made of the claim presented by you for compensation for service alleged to have been rendered by your deceased husband as a spy for the United States government during the rebellion, and have to inform you, as the result of that examination, that the claim cannot be allowed."[467]

This was the end of the road with the War Department's Board of Claims, and it should have ended there, but it was not the end for Virginia, not by a long way. Alvin had not left a will, as such, and therefore legally was referred to as an intestate, but he did have an estate to be disposed of, a past estate and a future estate. On May 13, 1871, Enoch Totten became the administrator of William Alvin Lloyd's estate.

So six years after he first designed and orchestrated Lloyd's case in 1865, Totten had returned to his masterwork. On May 22, 1871, Totten reopened the claim for the balance of the money due Alvin for his spying activities, and filed the case with the US Court of Claims. He thus became what is technically termed "the claimant." In his sworn statement, he tells the story in brief of William Alvin Lloyd and how he came to spy for Lincoln. But this is a somewhat new version. After Totten addresses the particulars of Lloyd's alleged services to the President, his additional inventions note that "On or about the 13th day of July, 1861, William A. Lloyd, entered into a contract with Abraham Lincoln, President of the United States acting in behalf of the United States, whereby he agreed to proceed to the states then in insurrection against the Government, to obtain, for the use of the United States, information concerning the number, condition, and situation of the troops of the insurgents, and of the plans and projects of the leaders of the rebellion, and to transmit the same from time to time as he might have opportunity, to the said Abraham Lincoln, for which service the United States agreed to pay said Lloyd, at the rate of two hundred [200] dollars per month, for so long a time as he might continue in said service, together with his reasonable expenses incurred in and about said service. A written memorandum of said contract was drawn and signed by said Abraham Lincoln, and delivered to said Lloyd, but it was subsequently destroyed by said Lloyd, to prevent the same from falling into the hands of the rebel authorities who had arrested said Lloyd on a charge of being a spy or secret agent of the United States."[468]

There are four major areas in which Totten's new version diverges from the original. The first has Lincoln acting in behalf of the United States. Of course, it's certainly true that he was not acting in behalf of, say, the Confederate States of America but, as the US Court of Claims would subsequently demonstrate, Abraham Lincoln had been acting only for himself, not for the country. In the second area, the wording is very different in Totten's claim than it is on the "contract." Surely it would have been better for Totten to have stuck to the "original wording," and not embellish it, as he did. In the third, nowhere until now is Lincoln said to have even hinted at expenses. And the fourth area—and most illuminating—is this part about the memorandum.

Totten's justification, if anyone should call him on it, went something like this: Lloyd's contract with Lincoln had originally been a written contract, yes, but because Lloyd had been forced to destroy that written contract during the war, by the time he got to Grant in 1865 he no longer had a written contract and was forced to use the word "verbal," because that's all he had now. No one called Totten on this issue—at the time, anyway.

Now, six years later, certain persons were finding Totten's explanation rather specious, even downright unsatisfactory. Besides, other points were being raised about this verbal vs. written contract, for example, if there had been a written contract, where was Lincoln's copy? A contract is between two persons, not just one. So, a new, revised solution was needed, and Totten duly came up with it.

Yes, the contract was verbal, Totten wrote, but Lloyd wanted some sort of proof from Lincoln, so the president dashed off a *memo* there and then, in his office, and handed it to Lloyd, asking him if that would "cover the ground."

In effect, then, according to Totten, what Lloyd allegedly was toting around so dangerously throughout the Confederacy in 1861 and 1862 was not a contract, but a written memorandum. However, the effect would have been the same. If it had been found by Rebel detectives Alvin would have been hanged just as expeditiously as if it had been a real contract, or so Totten claimed.

Totten's bill against the US government was $9,753.32, for forty-six months and twenty-three days work performed by W. Alvin Lloyd. This did not include the $2,380 paid by Stanton as Lloyd's expenses, but using Totten's mathematics it took Lloyd's government service up to the date of June 6, 1865, the date of the first deposition. Totten was saying, therefore, that Lloyd's compensation must include the last two months—i.e., since the end of the war—the two months since Abraham Lincoln had been assassinated. The logic behind this is incomprehensible. What would he have been spying on, and for whom?[469]

On June 1, 1871, the Assistant Attorney General George W. Parsons requested a full report of the Lloyd case from the War Department. The War Department's Assistant Judge Advocate General William McKee Dunn then got on the case, but the machine rolled slowly. After a mass of correspondence between various departments, Dunn finally got back to Assistant Attorney General Parsons on November 9, 1871.[470]

At a well-appointed office at 627 Walnut Street, in the city of Philadelphia, a small group of men met on October 14, 1872. Their purpose was to secure a deposition at the request of the claimant [Totten]. This was attorney Totten's first active step in the next stage of the Lloyd claim, the opening gambit in the chess game that was the US Court of Claims. W. Alvin Lloyd was dead, so there was no longer any fear of reprisals from Rebel avengers if the story came out in open court.

Those present at the deposition included Samuel C. Perkins, ex-officio commissioner of the Court of Claims; Charles A. Gray, representing the attorney general of the United States (the United States being the defendant); and James W. Latta, a Pennsylvanian, a Union army captain who'd served in the 119th Pennsylvania Regiment. Latta was also a prolific war diarist, now working for Totten as his stringer in Philadelphia, representing the claimant.

Finally came the star of the show, the deponent himself, Marcellus Howser, now almost recovered from the dangerous wound he had received in Washington City back on March 11, when Frank M. Jones shot him at Mr. Burns's house on 8th near K, for "undue familiarity" with Mrs. Jones.[471]

My name is Marcellus Houser [it was actually Howser]

My occupation is publisher

My age is twenty seven years

My residence the past year has been in Washington, District of Columbia, up to April 3, 1872, and since that date at No. 1139 South 16th Street, Philadelphia.

It was to be a question-and-answer session, with the answers coming from Howser. He was first sworn to tell the truth, the whole truth, and nothing but the truth, and then the answers contained in the deposition were written down by the commissioner in the presence of the witness, and afterwards read over to the witness.

Question: "Did you know William Alvin Lloyd in his lifetime? If so, how long, when, and where?"

Answer: "I did know him. It was in 1858. I first met him in Cincinnati. I knew him in Washington. I knew him in Baltimore. I met him in 1861, in Washington. I knew him up till the time of his death. I parted with him in 1866."

Question: "What was his business?"

Answer: "He was a map publisher. A publisher rather of a railroad guide. I was employed with him."

During the cross-examination, Howser was asked what time in 1861 he saw Lloyd, to which he replied, "In June, I think, after the interview with the President. I left the city, and did not see Lloyd again until 1865."

Howser's would be the first of five question-and-answer depositions made toward the end of 1872 to support the new Lloyd claim. These interrogatories were designed to be used later in court, at the actual trial, if it ever came down to that. These preliminaries were not a trial. Consequently, cross-examining lawyers are not going in for the kill. There was no need for them to do that, not at this stage of the game, anyway. However, that didn't prevent them from asking some very clever questions sometimes—and some very puzzling ones as well.[472]

On October 25, 1872, Enoch Totten sent out requests by mail for three individuals to depose in New York at 10:00 a.m., November 15, 1872, before John J. Latting, Commissioner for the Court of Claims, at his office at 20 Stassen Street. Frank H. Howe would be Totten's man there, and Alexander J. Gray would represent the United States. Those summoned were Virginia V. Lloyd, Marcellus Howser, Ellen Dooley, "and such other witnesses as may be produced."[473]

Why would Totten want Howser to depose in New York when he had just deposed in Philadelphia? That doesn't seem to make much sense, but, in fact, it does. It was only after that deposition on October 14 that lawyer Totten had reluctantly come to the conclusion that Lloyd had acquired the Lincoln contract a little too easily. More was needed, more effort, more color, and much more detail about that meeting with Abraham Lincoln in the White House. That's why Howser was required again. But Howser never showed up for that November 15 deposition. Neither did Nellie Dooley, the maid. Virginia herself came up at the appointed time, of course, in company with a new man, a new face, a new name. Another ringer.

My name is Francis Joseph Bonfanti.

My occupation is professor of languages and interpreter to the courts.

[An advertisement had been appearing regularly in the New York Herald *since May 29, 1872: "French, Italian, Spanish. Private lessons. Thorough instruction. Combined theory and practice. Professor Bonfanti, 241 West Fourteenth Street, or at Translation Bureau, 66 Broadway.* Anglais aux Etrangers.*"]*

My age is forty one. [Actually he was forty-three.]

My residence the past year has been in the city of New York. 241 West 14th Street.[474]

Totten's man Frank Howard Howe was Senator Timothy Otis Howe's son, a literate and literary-minded young man, for whom lawyering was a pragmatic career choice, not a passion. Frank Howe was twenty-two when he was admitted to the bar in Washington, and now he needed a job. Fortunately he didn't have far to stroll, right into the law office of his brother-in-law, Major Enoch Totten. The very first mission Totten gave him was to travel to New York in order to depose Virginia V. Lloyd and J. F. Bonfanti. Frank was inattentive, incompetent, and if the testimonies had been heard at a trial instead of a preliminary interrogatory, Totten's claim on behalf of the Lloyd estate would have collapsed, deemed a fraud then and there.[475]

Bonfanti was never cross-examined. One can only suppose that the counsel for the defense was happy to sit back and watch Bonfanti and Mr. Howe hang themselves.

Frank Howe asked Bonfanti the date he originally met Alvin Lloyd, to which the linguist replied, "End of 1859, or beginning of 1860, while stopping at the Metropolitan Hotel, in Broadway." Bonfanti says, of Lloyd: "He was publishing Railway Guides and directories—*Lloyd's Railway Guide*, I think it was called."[476]

Bonfanti hadn't always been a professor. Not by a long way. F. J. had spent his whole life as a rich adventurer—traveler, mercenary soldier, and writer. He had fought as a major for the Turks in the Crimea and as a general for the Mexicans, and had been an observer of the California Gold Rush. At the outbreak of the Civil War he was a professor at an academy in New Orleans, and on March 22, 1862, enlisted as a private in Greenleaf's Horse, in Louisiana—that is, in the Confederate Army. On June 6 that year he went AWOL from Camp Williamson, at Tupelo, Mississippi. That was one month and six days after General Butler entered New Orleans. On June 14, 1862, Bonfanti was declared deserted. He had found a more interesting occupation—peddling drugs to the Confederate Government—quinine, calomel, and potash. By 1872 he was back in New York, and on November 15 he deposed along with Virginia.[477]

On November 26, 1872, T.H.S. Boyd, Charles C. Boyd, and Theodore Woodall were all invited to be deposed in Washington on November 30, in the presence of Court of Claims commissioner John Cruickshank.

Alexander J. Gray would represent the defendants (i.e., the United States) while Mr. Totten himself would appear as counsel for the claimant. The Boyd brothers accepted the invitation to appear. Mr. Woodall didn't. So, altogether, five persons—Marcellus Howser, Virginia, Bonfanti, Charlie Boyd, and Alphabetical Boyd—all in favor of the claimant, were deposed in late 1872, and interrogated by their own counsel. All except Bonfanti were also interrogated by the counsel for the defense.[478]

These 1872 testimonies shed light on the case, on the five deponents themselves, on Totten and his surrogates, on the defense lawyers, and on the late William Alvin Lloyd. Mostly due to the damaging Harvey letter of 1866, Totten had various issues he wished to present, re-present, or hammer home.

First was the initial trip from New York to Washington, in order for Alvin to get a pass to cross the lines south. We know he left New York with the merchant's daughter, his new paramour, and we know he arrived in Louisville on July 15, 1861, with the girl in tow. We know he left Louisville the following morning, alone, and that he arrived in Memphis on the night of the sixteenth.

It was hard to fix a date for his departure from New York. The only time Alvin himself ever gives a date is in his letter to Jefferson Davis, written from Memphis on July 18, 1861, in which he says he left New York on July 11. As will be seen from the 1872 depositions, it was probably July 10. In his letter to President Davis, Alvin doesn't mention going to Washington, of course, but he did go to Washington, because he got the pass from Lincoln to cross the lines south, and that pass was dated July 13, 1861.

The only time the actual trip from New York to Washington is ever mentioned is in Bonfanti's November 15, 1872, deposition, replying to a pertinent question asked by his own counsel, Frank Howe. "It was during our journey to Washington that Mr. Lloyd mentioned to me that he was personally and intimately acquainted with President Lincoln."[479] So now we have Bonfanti, a wholly new character, in Washington with Lloyd.

According to Bonfanti, Lloyd told him that he intended trying to go south, and that he hoped to get a pass from President Lincoln through the lines, and that his (Lloyd's) main object was to collect money that was due him from several of the railroad companies. "He mentioned also that he intended speculating on his own account, I think in cotton or tobacco." If Frank Howe had been really committed to this case, he would have sensed danger with this reply and stopped the Bonfanti deposition then and there. But he let it go. What followed is a trip into the realm of the ludicrous.

Bonfanti's stated object in wishing to accompany Lloyd to Washington was that he also intended going south on business of his own in New Orleans, where he had been residing before, and where he had some property. Lloyd told him that he would try to get a pass for him at the same time he asked for his own.[480]

Even Virginia, in her November 15, 1872, deposition, doesn't mention the trip from New York to Washington. All she says is that she was in Washington with her husband on July 13, 1861. She makes no reference to the preceding few days, except to imply that the Lloyds were staying in a lodging house in the capital at that time. However, if Virginia was in Washington on July 13, then she came down from New York with Alvin, as well as with the child and the maid. But that can't be, of course, because the last person in the world to accompany Alvin and his new paramour—the merchant's daughter—would have been Virginia. So, in 1872, Virginia is once again lying under oath. She did not go to Washington in July 1861. And neither did her child Clarence, or the maid Nellie. The three of them were ensconced in the cottage in Westchester County, New York.[481]

Alphabetical Boyd maintained in his 1865 depositions, and again in 1872, that he was with Lloyd in Washington in July 1861, even though all the Confederate military records prove that he was in Louisiana. So, according to his testimony, he too came down from New York with his employer. So, to sum up the party line as it was being presented in late 1872, there would have been a sextet making that train trip from New York to Washington on July 10, 1861—Lloyd, Virginia, Clarence, Nellie, Boyd, and Bonfanti. A far cry indeed from Lloyd and the paramour of record in the *Memphis Appeal*.[482]

The idea of William Alvin Lloyd being a good friend of Abraham Lincoln's prior to the July 13, 1861, meeting was only dreamed up in

November 1872. It had to be, for why was it not mentioned back during the 1865 claim? It would have been such a monumental feather in Lloyd's cap that he would probably have made off with ten thousand dollars. But back then, no one had thought of it. Even as late as October 1872 Marcellus Howser fails to mention anything like that at all, and, given his very detailed account of what transpired at that July 1861 meeting, he would certainly have used this ace, if he knew about it. No, it is not until Virginia's 1872 interrogation that this concept is first brought to light. She says, of the contract, that it "bore Mr Lincoln's signature, which I had seen a great many times previous." She knew it was Lincoln's signature because he "was a personal friend of my late husband's, and wrote to him a number of times."[483]

Bonfanti, when asked if he knew anything about Lloyd's previous acquaintance with Mr. Lincoln, replied, "It was during our journey to Washington that Mr. Lloyd mentioned to me that he was personally and intimately acquainted with President Lincoln."

> Question: "Did you ask Mr Lloyd to use his influence with Mr Lincoln to obtain you a pass?"
>
> Answer: "I did."
>
> Question: "Did he promise to introduce you to the President?"
>
> Answer: "He did."

Bonfanti testifies that when Lloyd finally introduced him to the president, Mr. Lincoln "spoke to Lloyd as if they were on terms of intimate acquaintance. He addressed Mr. Lloyd by his last name, calling him familiarly 'Lloyd.'"[484]

It was pushing it hard to get Charlie Boyd in on the act, but they did.

"My name is Charles C. Boyd, 29 years of age, messenger in the Treasury Department, Washington, DC."

In his November 1872 interrogation, Charlie is asked about that day in July 1861, when Lloyd reputedly showed him the contract. He is asked how did he know it was Lincoln's handwriting. He answered, "I know it from the fact that Mr. Lloyd had in his possession before that a note signed by Mr. Lincoln."[485]

But it was up to Alphabetical Boyd to tell the most detailed stories. When asked in November 1872 about his early days with Lloyd—1859 and 1860—he has this to say about the summer and fall of 1860, that he "met Abraham Lincoln, who was afterwards President, in Chicago, sometime before the election. I was present at an interview between William A. Lloyd and Abraham Lincoln at the Sherman House in Chicago, some two or three weeks previous to the election. Understood from the conversation that Lloyd had a previous acquaintance with Mr. Lincoln, and that Lloyd was on terms of intimacy with him. Lloyd stated to me that if Lincoln was elected, he (Lloyd) would have a good place, or words to that effect."

So, suddenly in November 1872, it transpires that Lloyd was an old friend of the president's. The deponents are all maintaining that Lloyd had three interviews with Lincoln—July 11, July 12, and July 13. Boyd says he went to the first one, on July 11, 1861. Leaving his wife, child, and nurse in the boardinghouse, Alvin, accompanied by Alphabetical Boyd, went off to see the chief executive at what was then usually called the President's House. On November 30, 1872, Boyd claimed, "I was present in Washington City with Mr. W.A. Lloyd on or about the 10th of July 1861." Of course, Boyd was serving in the Confederate army at that time. More than that, even, Boyd swears, in the same statement in the same deposition, "Visited the President in company with W.A. Lloyd, and was present at an interview with Abraham Lincoln, then President of the United States." In his cross-examination by the US counsel, Boyd says that this initial interview took place "about the 10th or 11th of July 1861." The US counsel asks him, "Were you present at this interview?" to which Boyd replies, "I was, Sir."

In his cross-examination, in response to the US counsel's question, "What was done or said at the first interview?" Boyd replies, "After the usual salutations which take place between persons who have not met for some time, and compliments by Mr. Lloyd on his election, Mr. Lloyd told Mr. Lincoln he had a favor to ask of him."

Boyd says in his direct examination, all in one breath, it seemed:

Mr. Lloyd wanted a pass, or permission, for himself and <u>myself</u>, to pass to and from, through the lines so as to allow Mr. Lloyd to collect and settle outstanding claims he had against Railroad companies, etc. Mr Lincoln told him that he would do so, but would like to employ him as a secret agent for the Government, to furnish him with information direct, as the Government at that time was without any reliable or responsible agents in the rebellious states, and he was greatly in need of some trustworthy and competent person who had complete and thorough knowledge of the geography and topography of the states in rebellion, and he knew that Lloyd, by having been a publisher of a Railroad and Steamboat Guide, and also of "Disasters on the Western and Southern Waters," with maps giving all steamboat landings on the tributaries of the Mississippi, and also of a "Directory of Steamboat Engineers," etc., plying the Southern waters, would be of great service to him and the country, and wished him to do the service.

[Here is a new detail.] Lloyd did not accept at that time, as it was a hazardous and difficult service, but said he would call in a day or two.

Boyd then says, "He went back the next day. I was not present at the interview." That would make the next day the twelfth. In his cross-examination, Boyd says, "I was present at two interviews, and heard him say he had several others." When Boyd says he was at two interviews, he is referring to those of the eleventh and the thirteenth.[486]

Bonfanti says he was not at the first interview with Lincoln—the one on the eleventh—but according to his (Bonfanti's) November 15, 1872, deposition, Lloyd told him about it two or three days after it happened, told him that "the President wanted him while South, to procure all reliable information he could regarding the Rebel forces, movement of troops, commissariat, etc., and to send to him, the President, all such information whenever he had a chance of so doing. That for this, the President promised to give him a monthly sum of two hundred dollars. That he was to see the President again the next day, I believe in reference to the same subject."

Based on this fiction, why did Alvin take so long to tell Bonfanti? But in fact he must have told him on the very day of that first interview—the eleventh. This has to be the case, because Bonfanti says that Lloyd "was to see the president again the next day, I believe in reference to the same subject."

So, by his own admission, Bonfanti is going along to that second meeting—the one on the twelfth. Either way, Bonfanti was very much against the spying idea. He has become Lloyd's advisor: "I told him that I thought it would be foolish in him to accept any offer of the kind, simply because the compensation offered was far below the value of his services, if good. To this, Mr. Lloyd answered that the getting of a pass from the President would greatly help him in his own private affairs, that the President would grant no pass without receiving something in return for it [this is new material], and that Mr. Lloyd considered the two hundred dollars per month offered not as adequate compensation for the services he was to render, but as a help to him, Lloyd, in the payment of any expenses he might be put to in the forwarding of dispatches and the gathering of information."

So, when Alphabetical Boyd says that Lloyd "went back the next day. I was not present at the interview," that next day was Friday the twelfth. Bonfanti, when asked if he went with Alvin to that particular meeting with Lincoln, replied, "I did."

Back to Bonfanti: "You saw the President on that occasion?" Meaning the second meeting, the one on July 12. Bonfanti said he did. Furthermore, he said he heard the conversation Lloyd had with Lincoln.

This series of concoctions are all the work of Totten, whose witness, Bonfanti, is lost in a thicket: forgetting, remembering, and forgetting.

Then, finally, an open probe, to force Bonfanti to elaborate, "State the substance of it [the conversation with Lincoln]."

Hence the substance of the meeting of the twelfth, as recounted by Bonfanti:

Mr. Lloyd began the conversation by reminding the President that he had called according to appointment. The President appeared to be anxious to secure the services of Mr. Lloyd. Mr. Lloyd having

introduced me, and mentioned that I was going South, asked the Pres-
ident if he would give me a pass also, and I promised that if he did give
me a pass, I would give Lloyd any information that I might pick up
without making it my special business to do so. Whilst the President
and Lloyd were talking the matter over, an official of some kind came
in to say to the President that he was wanted, or something of that
kind, and the interview was broken off, and the President said to call
the next day at twelve.

Question: "Did the President express himself as confident of Lloyd's
ability to perform this service?"

Answer: "He did."[487]

Virginia, deposed on the same day as Bonfanti—November 15, 1872—was asked during direct examination, "Where was Mr. Lloyd in the summer—in the first part of July 1861?"

Answer: "In Washington."

More specific still was the question put to her during the cross-examination in the same deposition: "Where were you on the 13th of July 1861?" which elicited the response, "Washington City," as though she, Lloyd, Clarence, Nellie, Boyd, and Bonfanti were together on that momentous day.

Back to Virginia's direct examination, the question was then asked: "Are you aware of Mr. Lloyd's visiting Mr. Lincoln the President at any time in July 1861?"

Answer: "He left the house to go to see the President," meaning, of course, the Washington boardinghouse.[488]

As they have framed it, at high noon on Saturday, July 13, 1861, in the Executive Office of the President's House in Washington, DC, W. Alvin Lloyd, Alphabetical Boyd, Bonfanti, and the fourteen-year-old boy named Marcellus Howser, met with Mr. Lincoln . . .[489]

The president had already met Boyd, of course—according to Boyd, anyway—once in Chicago in 1860, and again on July 11, only two days before this meeting now about to commence. Bonfanti he had met the previous day, the twelfth. As for Mr. Howser, what a teenager was doing in this company at this very juncture must have been a real mystery to Mr. Lincoln, as it seems to have been, indeed, to Mr. Howser himself.[490]

Bonfanti was asked about that fateful meeting of the thirteenth. His reply, in sum, is that he called at twelve o'clock, in company with Lloyd and Boyd, and that all met with Mr. Lincoln. He does not mention young Howser. Boyd said Lloyd told the president that he had thought over the proposal made the day before, and had decided to accept it, provided that the president would agree to the two hundred dollars per month being paid to Virginia should he be killed, or die, or be kept prisoner, by the Rebels while in this service. "The President, without saying yes or no, wrote a paper and passed it to Lloyd, saying, Will that do? . . . Lloyd read it aloud."

Question: "You heard it?"

Answer: "I did."

Question: "Did you read it yourself?"

Answer: "I cannot swear that I did."

When asked to state the substance of the paper that he'd heard read, Bonfanti gave the outline of the now familiar contract but with the important addition, "the compensation for such service to be fixed at two hundred dollars per month to be paid to Mrs. Lloyd, in case of accident to her husband." There is stress being laid on Virginia here, enormous stress. Marcellus Howser had volunteered this information back in 1865, but on October 14, 1872, when he deposed again, he failed to mention it—another reason Totten had wanted Howser back again on November 15, 1872. But Howser didn't show, so they needed a ringer to rework this information about Virginia as beneficiary—hence Bonfanti.

Question: "This is in substance what you heard read by Mr Lloyd?"

Bonfanti's whole testimony is reluctant. He is stumbling. And why shouldn't he, yanked into this fraud in haste? His answer was: "This is in substance what I heard read, but I cannot say that it was put in that the money was to be paid to Mrs. Lloyd. I recollect the contents of the paper rather from what was said at the time than from actual recollection of what I heard read at the time."

He then goes on to say that Lloyd agreed, that the President signed the paper that Lloyd had read, and gave it to him. Lloyd then asked for three passes, one for himself, one for Boyd, and one for Bonfanti. "The President wrote them on three bits of stiff paper and gave them all three to Mr. Lloyd." Apparently, Lincoln signed them all. All three.

One of the later questions asked was, "What was the date of this last interview?" to which Bonfanti replied, "The 12th or 13th July."[491]

Boyd said: "On the 13th of July 1861 I was in company with Lloyd and Joseph de Bonfanti and had an interview with the President in which the President told Lloyd he would give him a pass and $200 a month and pay his expenses. To which Mr. Lloyd agreed."[492]

Now it is Marcellus Howser's turn, deposed twice over the years, first on June 30, 1865, and again on October 14, 1872. In 1865 he made it quite clear that the one and only meeting he attended was the famous one, on the thirteenth:

> *Mr. Lloyd said to the President that he was going South into the rebellious states; that he had business with the railroad companies, and was extensively acquainted with the railroad men in those states, and asked the President if he could be of any service to him. The President answered that he could, and that he desired that he (Mr. Lloyd) should go to the insurgent states and make observations touching the strength of the enemy and report all things to him that might be of the slightest benefit to the United States Government; and that for such services, Mr. Lloyd should be paid at the rate of $200 per month; that in the event of Mr. Lloyd's death during such services there, he said the money should be paid to Mrs. Lloyd; that he saw the President hand to Mr. Lloyd at the time a paper which Mr. Lloyd afterwards said contained the terms of his contract.*

In the same deposition, Howser claimed T.H.S. Boyd was also at this meeting. Bonfanti is not mentioned.[493]

In 1872 Mr. Howser was asked, during direct examination, if he was present at any conversation between Lloyd and President Lincoln, and if so, when was it, where, and what was that conversation?

Answer: "In July 1861, it was, I think."

Mr. Howser had obviously attended so many presidential occasions that he couldn't recall the exact date of this one. A similar insouciance afflicted most of the Lloyd gang from time to time.

"I was present at the President's House in company with Mr. Lloyd and Mr. Boyd at a conversation which occurred with reference to—" He leaves this sentence unfinished, while he regroups. "What I heard was this. Mr. Lloyd stated to Mr. Lincoln that he was going South, and that as he was well acquainted with the Southern Country, as his business was principally South, publishing a Railroad map and guide of the Southern Country, that, under the circumstances, he thought he could be of some benefit to the Federal cause."

This makes Mr. Howser the only one who recollects this spying business as being Lloyd's idea. Everyone else remembers it as Lincoln's.

Howser continues, "The sum substance of his argument, or proposal, was that, for a certain sum, he would undertake to furnish the Government, from time to time, with such news as would benefit them; that for the same he would receive two hundred dollars in gold per month, for his services. This is the sum and substance of the conversation that I heard."

Marcellus Howser was then asked what, if any, agreement was made for the payment of this sum of money.

Answer: "I understood at the time that Mr Lincoln, for this sum, two hundred dollars per month, in gold, employed Mr. Lloyd."

Question: "How did you understand this? Did Mr. Lincoln say this?"

Answer: "Mr. Lloyd stated to Mr Lincoln that he was going South, and that his business being principally with the South, publishing a *Southern Railroad Map and Guide*, under the circumstances he could afford the Government some service, and the question asked by Mr. Lincoln what remuneration he wished for such services as he proposed to render. Mr. Lloyd named the sum before mentioned, two hundred dollars."

Then Mr. Howser drops a bombshell, "Further I wasn't present [meaning that from that point on in the meeting he wasn't present]. I left the house [the White House] at the time. Afterwards I seen [Howser's grammar] a pass from Mr. Lincoln. The pass was shown to me by Mr.

Lloyd, passing Mr. Lloyd to and fro through the Federal lines South for an unlimited time, with Mr. Lincoln's signature."

Obviously Mr. Howser had an appointment far more pressing, and is thus not a firsthand witness from that point on.[494]

Then the deal was done. As Boyd says, "Mr. Lincoln then wrote a contract on a piece of paper and read it aloud to Lloyd and asked him if that would cover the ground."

Bonfanti remembers it slightly differently: "The President, without saying yes or no, wrote a paper, and passed it to Lloyd, saying, 'Will that do?' Lloyd read it aloud."

In essence, and allowing for discrepancies in memory, the wording of the contract was repeated.

All that remained now was the question of the passes.

Bonfanti says, "Mr. Lloyd then asked for three passes, one for himself, one for Mr. Boyd, and one for me. The president wrote them on three bits of stiff paper and gave them all three to Mr. Lloyd. That is all I recollect of this interview."

Question: "By whom were the passes signed?"

Answer: "By the President alone."[495]

Boyd's recollection of that moment offers a slight variation: "He [the president] delivered the contract and pass for Mr. Lloyd to Mr. Lloyd, and each of the individual passes to Mr. Bonfanti and myself."[496]

They recited the wording of the pass: "Allow the bearer, Mr. William. A. Lloyd to pass our lines south and return on special business." It was signed "A. Lincoln," and dated July 13, 1861.[497]

It must be noted that, while Alvin's pass came up as a subject of discussion during the 1865 depositions, Alphabetical Boyd's did not. It wasn't until 1872 that *his* pass is referred to.

Question: "You say you received a pass from Mr. Lincoln. Have you that pass?"

Answer: "No, Sir, it was stolen from my trunk at Canada West, at the Tecumseh House."[498]

Another topic that had to be addressed fully in 1872 was the genuineness of Lincoln's handwriting on the pass. It was the wording in Harvey's 1866 letter that prompted this: "forgery of deceased officers' names."

What did Harvey have in mind when he made this accusation? He might have meant the contract, but equally he might well have been referring to the forged letters found in Alvin's trunk in Philadelphia, letters from high Confederate officers, including Jefferson Davis. As there was no court-room exhibit of the contract with the president's actual writing on it, this in itself wouldn't have worried Totten. What worried him, by extension, was the pass. In other words, would authorities question Lincoln's hand-writing, its authenticity?

No one had ever doubted the authenticity of this pass, and no one ever would again. But Totten had to tackle the issue head on, just in case someone did ask.[499]

Marcellus Howser was the first deponent to be asked this, on October 14, 1872. He was able to recognize Mr. Lincoln's handwriting on the contract because he had "a book with all the government officials in. I was at one time under Genl Rucker in the Quartermaster's Department, and I have seen the signature very frequently. By those means I became familiar with it."

Virginia, under cross-examination in 1872, was asked, "How did you know it to be a contract executed by Mr Lincoln?" to which she replied, "It bore Mr Lincoln's signature, which I had seen a great many times previous."

Although she said she never actually saw Lincoln in the process of putting pen to paper, she was quite sure she had seen his writing in the past. She knew the writing on the contract was the president's because he "was a personal friend of my late husband's, and wrote to him a number of times." These alleged letters from Lincoln to Lloyd have never been seen, nor did anyone at the time ask to see or verify them. A search through the Lincoln Papers has yielded nothing.[500]

Charlie Boyd, in 1872, was asked by Totten, "Did you see the signature to the contract in Lloyd's possession, and, if so, was the signature genuine, and, if genuine, how do you know it?" To which Charlie replied, "I took it for genuine because he was so glad to have this contract, and, if it had not been genuine, he would not have made such preparation to go. I know Mr. Lincoln's signature, and believe this to have been genuine."

Question: "Did you ever see Mr Lincoln write his signature?"

Answer: "No, Sir."

Question: "Were you employed in the Department in 1861, 62, or 63?"

Answer: "No, Sir. Since the War, I have been employed in the Treasury Department."

Question: "Have you seen original documents in the department, signed by Mr Lincoln during your service?"

Answer: "I have seen a letter that Mr. Lincoln wrote and other papers. I believe—the signature to the contract with Lloyd to have been Mr Lincoln's genuine signature."

He was then cross-examined by Alexander J. Gray, for the United States.

Question: "You state that Mr. Lloyd showed you a paper, to the contents of which you have testified here, which you believed to be signed by Mr. Lincoln. How did you know it was Mr. Lincoln's handwriting?"

Answer: "I know it from the fact that Mr. Lloyd had in his possession before that a note signed by Mr. Lincoln. Since that, I have seen papers signed by Mr. Lincoln. I have every reason to believe it was genuine. I know too that he was going up to see the President every few days."[501]

As if these muddled, contradictory depositions weren't disturbing enough, in November 1872 something disturbing and potentially damaging happened to Enoch Totten.

One of the most important linchpins in the claim had always been that Alvin had been arrested in Memphis in July 1861 for being a Yankee spy. This was the party line in 1865. It was as solid as testimony can be.

Now in November 1872, someone must have slipped an old newspaper clipping in front of lawyer Totten, probably from the July 25, 1865, edition of the *New York Herald*, titled, "Lloyd the Bigamist." Suddenly, things were not looking so good. Totten would have checked with Memphis, and with Louisville. Things were looking worse. "Lloyd the bigamist." It had been all over the papers back in 1861. It was to be hoped that the opposition didn't have this *Herald* clipping.

They didn't use the expression "damage control" back then. Lloyd was dead, as was Captain Klinck, the Memphis jailer, so neither could testify one way or the other. But Totten had to work fast. He could say that Alvin's written itinerary, Enclosure 13, might well have been off by a few weeks, in spite of newspapers placing him there, as might his money accounts that placed him fairly and squarely in Memphis on July 17 and 18, 1861. That mysterious 1865 witness, Charles T. Moore, who claimed to have been with Alvin in Memphis in July of 1861, was now nowhere to be found.

But there was still one player who would be vulnerable, and that was T.H.S. Boyd. Even though Alphabetical, in all his 1865 depositions, had never mentioned the Memphis jail, Totten could imagine the counsel for the United States asking Boyd the reason for Mr. Lloyd's arrest in the said city of Memphis in July 1861. Totten could not allow this to happen. He had to rewrite history, and if anyone brought up the 1865 depositions, he'd simply have to bluff his way out.

As for Lloyd leaving Washington on July 13, 1861, and arriving in Memphis on the seventeenth, Totten decided, the date must be changed.

On July 13, 1861, immediately after getting his pass to cross the lines, Lloyd left Washington on the train for Cincinnati. And of course, he was not alone. He had his "new paramour" with him, as the Louisville paper of July 16, 1861, tells us the day after Lloyd arrived back in his hometown. We also know that on the morning of July 16 he left Louisville without the girl, and arrived late that night in Memphis. That is from the *Memphis Appeal* of July 17. And then came the well-covered bigamy business and a night in jail, and then Alvin headed south. That's all substantiated.

In his June 3, 1865, deposition, Alvin said "on the said 13th day of July 1861 I entered upon the discharge of my duties as said special agent and proceeded to Tennessee."[502]

In her 1865 deposition, Virginia made no mention of herself being in Washington. However, by 1872 she was claiming to have been in Washington in July 1861, when Lloyd got the contract. When asked at what "time Mr. Lloyd crossed the Rebel lines to go South," she replied, "Very soon after the contract was given. It may have been toward the latter part of July 1861."

The departure date of July 13 is now a thing of the past.

Question: "Did you follow soon after?"

Answer: "Yes, Sir."

Question: "Where did you next meet him?"

Answer: "At some little town in Tennessee, but I do not now recollect the name." She had certainly had no problem remembering the name of Clarksville, Tennessee, in her 1865 deposition.

She then says that Alvin "went to Memphis, and to Nashville. I do not recollect which he went to first."[503]

Bonfanti, when asked how long he remained in Washington after the July 13, 1861, Lincoln interview, replied: "Until the morning of the 21st of July."

Question: "Where did you go on the 21st?"

Answer: "I was trying to go South. I left for Nashville that day."

Question: "Was Lloyd with you when you left?"

Answer: "Yes, he was."[504]

Suddenly, as well as Boyd, we have Bonfanti accompanying Lloyd to Tennessee. Totten instructed them to say they left Washington on July 21, not the thirteenth (the day Alvin got the signed Lincoln pass). And Totten told them to say they went to Nashville, rather than Memphis. Stay clear of Memphis, Totten would have demanded. That's the bigamy arrest. That's trouble.

Back in 1865, when everyone was testifying and documents of all sorts and sizes were flying around, and enormous detail of places and persons was being bandied about, the name Bonfanti never, ever came up. How could the dashing and flamboyant Bonfanti have left such little impression upon so many persons?

But on November 15, 1872, Bonfanti swore that he left Washington on July 21, 1861, in company with W. Alvin Lloyd, bound for Nashville.

Then, two weeks later, on November 30, 1872, T.H.S. Boyd was deposed. The first thing he said when Totten got him on the stand was, "Lloyd left Washington for the South on or about the 18th day of July 1861."

The date bears no resemblance to the truth, or to that given by the deponents in 1865, or to that given by Bonfanti only two weeks before. But this is nothing compared to what follows. The counsel for the defense (i.e., the United States) asks Mr. Boyd if he left Washington with Mr. Lloyd at that time. The US counsel has just read over Alphabetical Boyd's

1865 deposition, in which Boyd and Lloyd left for Memphis together, and therefore must have been somewhat startled when the affiant responded, "No, Sir."

Gone are the days when Alphabetical Boyd left Washington with Lloyd on July 13, 1861, bound for Memphis. So, if Alphabetical didn't go to Memphis with Lloyd, what did he do? Obviously, Mr. Boyd was having a problem keeping up with the new lies he was meant to tell. And of course, in July 1861 he was, according to Confederate records, still a private in Louisiana.

When asked, during his December 7, 1872, cross-examination, when he left Washington, Boyd replied: "I left four or five days after the first battle of Bull Run." Bull Run having taken place on the twenty-first, this then places Boyd's departure from Washington on or about July 25. However, a little later in the very same cross-examination, he is asked, by the same US counsel, where he was in the month of July 1861, after the thirteenth, to which Boyd replied: "I remained five or six days in Washington." That then puts his departure from Washington at July 18 or 19.

Boyd then talks about what happened to Alvin Lloyd when he left Washington. Boyd has already said, at the start of his direct examination the week before, that "Lloyd left Washington for the South on or about the 18th day of July 1861." Now, in his cross-examination, he replies to the same question with, "Some four or five days after the President had employed him. About the 17th or 18th of July."

In his cross-examination the following week, Boyd has this to say: "I saw him receive transportation in Washington on his papers from Mr. Lincoln to Cincinnati. I received a letter from him dated Cincinnati, also letters from him dated Nashville, Grand Junction and Memphis." He claimed to have received the first of these letters while he was still in Washington.

So if Alphabetical Boyd said he didn't accompany Alvin to Tennessee, where did he go when he left Washington? To the US counsel, under cross-examination, he replies to this question: "I went by Harpers Ferry, and the Valley of Virginia, Lynchburg and Petersburg, to Norfolk." A little later in the same cross-examination, he is asked that same question again, and this is his answer this time: "I went to Frederick and Harpers Ferry, then to Norfolk by way of Petersburg. I arrived in Petersburg in the latter part of July, and in Norfolk the latter part of July or first of August." Given the route he took from Washington to Norfolk, it can only be said that he moved with astonishing speed.

It was in Norfolk that Boyd claimed to have received the last three of the letters that Alvin had been busily sending him en route through Tennessee.

On November 30, 1872, Totten asked Boyd when he joined Mr. Lloyd after his (Lloyd's) departure from Washington. "In Norfolk, Va., about October or Nov. 1861." A week later he was asked the same question under cross-examination by the US counsel, and replied, "In October, I think it was, of that year, 1861—in Norfolk, Va." A question asked very soon afterwards was how long he remained in Norfolk before Lloyd came, to which he replied, "From sixty to ninety days." As he arrived in Norfolk on or around August 1, 1861, this statement confirms that Alvin showed up in Norfolk sometime in the month of October 1861.

Totten eases Boyd into this with the question: "How long did you stay with Lloyd when you joined him in Norfolk, and where did he go, and where did you go when you left him?" Boyd replied: "I remained in Norfolk with Lloyd about two weeks and was engaged in visiting the different fortifications and batteries on both sides of the Elizabeth and Nansemond Rivers, and the camps and fortifications adjacent to Norfolk and Portsmouth. Drew a map of the harbor and batteries on each side, and the number of troops then under the command of General Huger. The map was taken charge of by Mr. Lloyd and sent to Mr. Lincoln. The map went to Mr. Lincoln by a man who was an engineer on a transport between Norfolk and Craney Island. He went in a boat to Fortress Monroe. Lloyd left Norfolk for Savannah about the latter part of November 1861."

Now Alvin arrived in Norfolk sometime in October. If he stayed only two weeks with Boyd there, then it could not have been the latter part of November that he left for Savannah.[505]

But there can be no doubt that Alvin was in Norfolk around this time. In his own itinerary, in Enclosure 13, he says, "Arrived at Norfolk Sept. 17. Remained 2 days. Visited Crany [*sic*] Island, fortifications, camps, etc etc. Met T.H.S. Boyd at Norfolk. Left Sept. 19." And that was written in

1865. However, September 17 is only forty-eight days after Boyd's arrival there, not sixty or ninety. And two days is not two weeks.[506]

To Totten, Boyd in 1872 said, "I received a letter from Lloyd from Savannah, stating that he was in jail. I showed it to a friend of mine who told me I had better destroy it if I did not want to be in jail myself. So I destroyed it." No letter, of course.

During direct examination by Totten, Boyd continues: "I saw Lloyd next time in Savannah in January or February 1862. He was in jail at Savannah. I saw him in jail. I found out what he was in jail for from the Colonel commanding the post. I can't remember his name. He told me Lloyd had been arrested as a Yankee spy, and showed me an affidavit signed by Miss Jordan, an actress who stated that she had overheard conversations between Lloyd and other parties in which Lloyd was sending information to the United States Government, in regard to the plans of fortifications surrounding Savannah. Lloyd was confined solitarily in Savannah for about six weeks, on account of an intercepted dispatch."

Under cross-examination, Boyd was asked how he gained access to Lloyd in jail in Savannah. "I had a permit from the Colonel commanding the post."[507]

Although Boyd couldn't remember the colonel's name, Colonel Rockwell certainly remembered Boyd's. There can be no doubt at all that Colonel Rockwell had heard of Boyd, heard from Annie Taylor Lloyd that a man named Boyd had brought secret messages for Alvin in his boot from Salmon Chase. Lloyd probably mentioned the name of Boyd to Annie at some point. As for the courier fiction, Annie's determination to condemn Lloyd to endless imprisonment is likely the real story. And it is equally certain that Rockwell had no idea of Boyd's first name. And there can be no question that Rockwell, being alerted to this courier Boyd, would, if he had ever met Boyd even once, have thrown him in jail with Alvin. No, far from giving Boyd a permit to visit Lloyd, Rockwell would have swarmed all over Alphabetical Boyd, arrested him on the spot. And even if Boyd wanted anyone to believe this story, his visit to Lloyd in Savannah had to take place before February 20, 1862, because on that date he, Boyd, went AWOL from his camp and headed for Richmond to wangle an officer's commission from Governor Letcher.[508]

In his November 15, 1872, deposition, Bonfanti swears that when he left Lloyd in Nashville, and they went their separate ways, he next met Lloyd in Memphis several months later. The time after that was in New Orleans "about two weeks before General Butler came in. I don't recall when exactly that was." What he means is that he couldn't recall the date. In fact Union General Benjamin Butler came into New Orleans on May 1, 1862. Two weeks before that date would be April 16, give or take a day or two. "I mentioned to Mr. Lloyd that I thought that the Yankees would soon be in town, that I intended going North as soon as possible. Mr. Lloyd said that he was very glad I should do so, as he intended giving me some important papers to take through with me, but that he would first have to go to Chattanooga to get some information of a spy that was in his pay at that place, and that he would return in the course of a very few days. Lloyd left for Chattanooga, and some five days afterwards the city was taken possession of by General Butler."[509]

Bonfanti is extraordinarily time specific. He has been coached to be. A serious embarrassment to Bonfanti's story in that from December 14, 1861, until July 15, 1862, Lloyd was languishing in jail in Savannah. That is a historical fact. He was ailing, in confinement, so a quick escape and dash to New Orleans to meet Bonfanti would be impossible. And then Lloyd would have had to dash back up to Chattanooga, then dash back to Savannah, and break back into the Chatham County Jail without anyone seeing.

There is a whiff of comic opera here.

Bonfanti is not the only one in 1872 who has Alvin Lloyd being in two places at once ten years before. Alphabetical Boyd tells us that Alvin "visited the defenses of Richmond. This was in June 1862. He got information as to strength and location of batteries and number of troops around Richmond."

Question: "What did he do with this information?"

Answer: "He made a report in writing, which he gave to me for Mr. Lincoln, which I delivered in the latter part of July or first of August, to Mr Lincoln in person."[510]

The story of Alvin's arrest and search in Lynchburg on November 7, 1862—including the searching of his wife—is told in his detailed itinerary presented on July 16, 1865 (Enclosure 13). That particular account sounds reasonable, given that there are documents to back it up. What is not mentioned in Enclosure 13 is the contract and especially the destruction of that contract. That's because there was no contract to destroy.

On June 1, 1865, when Alvin came to Totten's office for the first time looking for a lawyer to handle his case, he was stating that his spying contract with Lincoln had been verbal. That's what he had told Grant's office. Totten changed all that and made it written. But because it was said to have been a written contract, that contract had to have been destroyed somewhere, sometime, during the war. November 7, 1862, in Lynchburg, seemed as good a time as any, and they settled on that.

That part of the story, the actual destruction of the contract, is told at only two specific points in time. The first was June 3, 1865, in the original depositions made by Alvin, Virginia, T.H.S. Boyd, and Nellie the maid. Alvin claims that the contract "was destroyed by my family attendant, while the said detectives were searching the persons of myself and wife and the other papers and baggage."

The attendant herself, Nellie the maid, deposed that "the said paper of instructions" was at that time in her possession, and sewed up in her clothing; that she was afraid of being searched by the said detectives, and that the said paper would be found, and she "destroyed the said paper of instructions while the detectives were searching the persons of Mr. and Mrs. Lloyd, by tearing it into small pieces, and scattering the pieces about."[511]

Alphabetical Boyd deposed that the contract was destroyed by Ellen R. Dooley, "as he is informed and verily believes."[512]

Unfortunately, as previously noted, although Virginia talked about this episode, the relevant sheet in the Lloyd Papers has been lost.

That, then, was the sum of testimony provided on June 3, 1865, on the subject of the destruction of the contract at Lynchburg. By 1872, Totten, for some reason, felt that it wasn't enough, that more detail was needed. By now, of course, Alvin was long dead, and therefore could contribute nothing new, which is why Totten wanted Nellie the maid to depose again. But Nellie never came, which just left Virginia among the original adult participants. Obviously they needed to bring in a ringer. The last person in the world a sane lawyer would have allowed in would have been

Alphabetical Boyd, simply because, by his own written and sworn admission of 1865, he had not even been in Lynchburg in 1862. Yet Alphabetical Boyd was the ringer Totten brought in. In addition, Totten brought in half a ringer, Charlie Boyd, Alphabetical's younger brother. Charlie Boyd was there to provide hearsay.

First, the actual date of the Lynchburg episode. In 1865 Alvin claimed it was November 7, 1862. Virginia, although not absolutely specific, seems to agree with that date. Alphabetical Boyd says October 7, rather than November, but then, by his own admission, he wasn't there. Nellie thinks it was November 5.

By November 1872, because more than seven years had gone by since she last deposed, Virginia could do no better than "In 1862. Sometime in November." Like his brother Alphabetical, Charlie Boyd had only heard about the episode, and, wisely, didn't attempt to date it. On the other hand, in his 1872 interrogation, Alphabetical Boyd still maintains it was October, but this time he was there, in Lynchburg, taking a big hand in the destruction of the contract.

As for what happened that day in Lynchburg, whenever exactly that day was, everyone agreed that the Rebel detectives burst in on the Lloyd party with the intention of searching baggage and persons, in the hopes of finding evidence that would incriminate Alvin as a Yankee spy.

Alvin and Virginia both said, in their 1865 depositions, that they were physically searched. They mention no one else undergoing this indignity. Indeed, Nellie the maid, in her own 1865 deposition claimed that she was "afraid of being searched." The question thus presents itself—if Alvin and Virginia were searched, then why wasn't Nellie?[513]

By 1872 Virginia was swearing under interrogation that Alvin was searched. She made no mention of herself being searched. In fact, on the contrary, as shall soon be seen. And Alphabetical Boyd was saying that "all persons" were searched, including himself.[514]

Who was in possession of the damning contract when the detectives broke in? In 1865 Alvin seemed to believe it was Nellie the maid: "it was destroyed by my family attendant, while the said detectives were searching the persons of myself and wife." Nellie was, evidently, in another room, otherwise the detectives would have immediately stopped her.[515]

In 1865, Nellie said, "the said paper of instructions was at that time" in her possession, and sewed up in her clothing. Owing to the lost page in the Lloyd Papers, Virginia must remain forever and frustratingly silent on this issue, at least as she was recalling it on June 3, 1865.[516]

But did Nellie really have the contract sewed up in her clothing? Under 1872 interrogation, Virginia was asked, "Did Mr. Lloyd have the contract . . . on his person there?" She replied, "No. I had it on mine." Was it Virginia or Nellie? Fictions within fictions. Unfortunately, with no 1872 help forthcoming from Alvin or Nellie on this point, and with Charlie Boyd not touching this issue because all he had to rely on was hearsay, we are left with Alphabetical Boyd, who, by now has decided that he was there after all. However, he too remained silent on this.[517]

What happened next was that the contract had to be destroyed, to prevent it falling into the detectives' hands. Alvin said, " it was destroyed by my family attendant." Also in 1865, Alphabetical Boyd claimed that the contract was "destroyed by Ellen R. Dooley (who was the female attendant in the family of the said Lloyd)." But then Boyd wasn't there, as is abundantly borne out by his own words, "as he is informed and verily believes."[518]

Nellie herself, in her own 1865 deposition, said that she "destroyed the said paper of instructions while the detectives were searching the persons of Mr. and Mrs. Lloyd, by tearing it into small pieces, and scattering the pieces about." One can only hope that they were very small pieces, and that the detectives, upon finding them, which they surely would have done, were too unwitting to put two and two together and conclude that the maid's action might be proof of Alvin's guilt.

It will be remembered that, come 1872, Virginia had the contract on her person—in other words, it was no longer sewed up in Nellie's clothing. When asked what she did with the contract, Virginia replies, "I gave it to my nurse, with instructions to destroy it, which she did." Presumably this maneuver was carried out just as the detectives were breaking down the door, rather than, say, as the detectives were searching her.

In her 1872 cross-examination by the counsel for the defense (i.e., the United States), Virginia was asked if she saw the contract destroyed. She replied, "I did not."

Question: "Do you know of your own knowledge that it was destroyed?"

Answer: "I believe it was. I know it."

Then, Virginia was again examined by her own counsel.

Question: "Did your nurse tell you she had destroyed the contract?"

Answer: "She not only told me so. But I was present at the destroying of it, but do not remember of seeing it actually destroyed."

Question: "Do you know in what manner it was destroyed? Whether by tearing or burning?"

Answer: "It was burnt."

Question: "Did you see it burnt?"

Answer: "I don't remember of seeing it destroyed. I was in the same room—but in the confusion I cannot say that I actually saw it burnt."[519]

Still in 1872, Charlie Boyd, who wasn't in Lynchburg in 1862, says: "Mrs. Lloyd said the contract was destroyed by Nelly the nurse. Nelly told me she destroyed it. Mrs. Lloyd told me that because it was destroyed, they got only part of the claim paid. I heard Mr. Lloyd say the same."[520]

Bonfanti wasn't in Lynchburg either, but Totten manages to insert him, albeit obliquely. In his November 15, 1872, deposition, Bonfanti relates a curious tale about meeting Alvin Lloyd in Richmond in either September or October of 1863, one of the two. According to Bonfanti, he had just returned from England by running the blockade, a mission he had been on for Mr. Lincoln, who had asked him to take that route to see how that blockade was run, and to figure out what steps could be taken to stop it. "Mr. Lloyd stated that he had made some maps of the Southern Confederacy. He wanted to send them to Washington. Would I take them? I agreed to do so."

Bonfanti made no mention of Alvin being in jail at this time. "He also said he wished me to get him another pass from the President because he had been taken prisoner, and had lost or destroyed all his papers." He was referring here to the Lynchburg episode and the burning of the contract. "Also if I could get another agreement from the President like the one that had been given him when we came South, because he had been obliged to have that destroyed, and he wished to get another, and have it given to his wife."

Question: "Did he furnish you with these papers? These maps?"

Answer: "He did. There was one map on tissue paper."

Question: "With what directions?"

Answer: "That if I should get to Washington, I should give them to the President with the package of papers that accompanied it. I was to have started the next day."

Question: "Did you leave Richmond?"

Answer: "Yes."

Question: "After this, when did you next see Mr Lloyd?"

Answer: "I have never seen Mr Lloyd since."[521]

This meeting with Lloyd couldn't have been in September or October of 1863, as Bonfanti claims. W. Alvin Lloyd arrived in Mobile on August 8, 1863, and was still there on October 1 when he got shot to pieces. He spent the rest of the month on the verge of death and recuperating there, and didn't leave Mobile until December 22.

We have to dismiss Bonfanti's dates, then, as bogus, and along with them his story. You can't jettison one without the other. But a lying Bonfanti is nothing new. In fact, it is to be expected. But that's not the point here. The point is why did Totten have him say this about the replacement pass? It couldn't just have been to have yet another deponent add weight to the destruction of the contract, even as hearsay, at least not when such a statement appears so ludicrous . . . on the surface. Lloyd came through the lines in 1865 with a July 13, 1861, pass, he presented this pass as evidence in 1865, and this pass is still in existence, in a vault at the National Archives. More to the point, it was very much in existence in 1872, and still dated July 13, 1861, for anyone to see. Why would Totten have Bonfanti say Lloyd had lost it? This makes no sense, at least on the surface.

Totten must have had a reason. But there was the actual physical pass. Why say that Lloyd had lost it? He found it again? Then why have Bonfanti tell this tale in the first place? It's very damaging to the Lloyd claim.

The most detailed description of the destruction of the contract comes from T.H.S. Boyd, who was not there. But by the time of his 1872 deposition, he said he *was* there. "Lloyd told me to go to his room and destroy the contract and papers which might implicate or compromise him. I delivered the message to Mrs. Lloyd, and the nurse and we together destroyed everything that was likely to be dangerous, including the contract. I assisted the servant, and saw the contract torn up and burned."[522]

In 1865, Nellie never mentions a fire. She merely says she tore the contract up and scattered the pieces. Unlike Boyd, she does not mention any other documents, which presumably did not include the pass that, as we know, survives to this day. And she never mentioned Boyd being there.

During his 1872 cross-examination, Alphabetical was again asked about the contract. "It was torn up and burnt—with a number of other papers." And then, in answer to the question, "Did you see it torn up and burnt? And who tore it up and burnt it?" he replied, "I saw it torn up and burnt by Helen Dooley, or rather, she tore it up, and I picked up some of the scattered fragments and threw them in the fire." Totten has now resolved the scattered fragments problem.[523]

The final issue that Totten wished to drive home was how Lloyd had suffered for his country. This is what Boyd had to say in 1872 about his former employer: "His health was much reduced while he was in Savannah. He suffered considerably from paralysis. One leg was considerably shrunken." And then, in response to Totten's question, "What was the condition of Lloyd's health when he went South, and what was its condition when he came back in June 1865?" Boyd replied: "When Lloyd went South in July 1861, he was in enjoyment of good health and had every appearance of a man who would live a long life. When he came back in June 1865 he used a crutch and cane, and was constantly under the care of a physician, and so until his death. His lungs were affected, and he also had paralysis of the back and leg, which was considerably shrunken and shortened. This paralysis occurred in Mobile—first in Savannah, and afterwards in Mobile." The shooting is never mentioned, of course.[524]

On December 10, 1873, John Goforth, assistant attorney general of the United States, drew up his brief for the defense. His comments are sometimes amusing, usually acerbic, and it is quite clear he regards the whole claim as preposterous—"a very likely story," he writes.[525]

But John Goforth was a lone voice in the wilderness. On February 9, 1874, the Court of Claims reached a decision. To a man, they believed the claim, and found in favor of it. However, they were evenly split on whether a president has the right to enter into such an agreement with a spy, and so "the court, upon due consideration of the premises, find in favor of the defendants, and do order, judge, and decree that the said claimant's [Totten's] petition be discharged."[526]

Not accepting this defeat, Enoch Totten then appealed to the US Supreme Court. He drew up his case, and US Solicitor General Benjamin Bristow, representing the United States, drew up his own brief. The solicitor general based his defense on a number of arguments. The first was that the US Court of Claims case had been filed by Totten on May 22, 1871, but that the six-year statute of limitations on such a case had run out eight days before that date, missed it by a week. If only for that reason, the solicitor general argued, the present Supreme Court case should be barred. The solicitor general admitted that the US Court of Claims had somehow overlooked this small but important point.

The defense brief then expounded upon the monthly payments of two hundred dollars as they related to the said statute of limitations. According to the terms of the purported contract, Lloyd was to have received two hundred dollars per month. Each two hundred dollars was therefore a separate accounts item, and was subject to the same term of six years. So, as an example, if the first ever Lloyd payment, the one covering July 13 to August 13, 1861, was not claimed within six years, then it didn't make the statute of limitations. This is false reasoning, because Lloyd did, indeed, make such a claim within six years—he made it on June 3, 1865. In short, the solicitor general did not make a good case for his first point.

But he did raise the all-important point: "Lloyd was a loyal man, engaged in the public service of the United States within the Confederate lines. There was no reason to prevent his being paid by President Lincoln at any time during the war that his accounts were presented. Whilst transmitting 'information,' he had power as well to transmit an order for whatever was due him. The presence of such a man within rebel territory imposed no disabilty because of vicinage upon him." In other words, why didn't Alvin communicate with the president, asking for his contracted monthly fee?

The second argument raised by the solicitor general was "whether transactions of the sort under consideration give to the employees therein a right of suit against the United States." He submitted that the president had arranged to make the Lloyd payments from a "secret service fund" which had been voted to the president by Congress, and therefore, failure of that fund to provide for Lloyd meant that Totten should now have to apply to Congress for payment.

In the October session of 1875, the US Supreme Court issued their verdict. Associate Justice Stephen J. Field delivered the unanimous opinion. The eight other justices were: Chief Justice Morrison Waite, associate Justices Nathan Clifford, Noah H. Swayne, Samuel F. Miller, David Davis, William Strong, Ward Hunt, and Joseph P. Bradley. This court was composed of mainly Lincoln and Grant appointees.

In an almost mirror image of the Court of Claims proceedings, each and every Supreme Court justice believed the Lloyd story, yet at the same time found against the claimants, but for a different reason, one that would have far-reaching consequences. "We have no difficulty as to the authority of the President in the matter," the finding stated. "He [Lincoln] was undoubtedly authorized during the war, as commander in chief of the armies of the United States, to employ secret agents [Lloyd] to enter the rebel lines and obtain information regarding the strength, resources and movements of the enemy; and contracts to compensate such agents are so far binding upon the government as to render lawful for the President to direct payment of the amount stipulated out of the contingent fund under his control."

This critically important finding stood—and stands—prohibiting a public hearing "where a disclosure of the secret service might compromise or embarrass our government in its public duties, or endanger the person or injure the character of the agent." Further, the court found that "the whole service in any case, and the manner of its discharge, with the details of dealings with individuals and officers, might be exposed, to the serious detriment of the public. A secret service, with liability to publicity in this way, would be impossible. . . . The final statement, may be stated as a general principle, that public policy forbids the maintenance of any suit in a court of justice, the trial of which would inevitably lead to the disclosure of matters which the law regards as confidential, and respecting which it will not allow the confidence to be violated. On this principle, suits cannot be maintained."[527]

The Supreme Court justices having established the precedent ruling, but excluding a finding on the recovery of monies, then referred the case to Congress, with a strong suggestion that Totten be paid.

In other words, the Lloyd claim passed out of the legal into the moral, with the pressure now on the legislature.[528]

And so William Alvin Lloyd's claim, the chicanery, shadows, and outright lies, was never challenged. As for Lloyd's widow, Virginia, she had clearly moved on. Or so it seemed.

"Wednesday evening, Nov. 17, at the residence of the bride. D. Williamson Lee and Mrs. Virginia Van Rensselaer Lloyd." The New York newspapers of November 20, 1875, carried paid notices of the marriage. Mr. Lee moved in with Virginia, at 265 Lexington Avenue.[529]

As 1876 rolled around, T.H.S. Boyd was publishing a railroad guide from 915 Chestnut Street, Philadelphia, and Alvin's brother, J. T. Lloyd, and his wife, Ella, were producing maps from the same city.[530]

Incredibly, Enoch Totten was unable or unwilling to let the Lloyd claim go. Just two months later on April 27, 1876, Representative William B. Spencer of Louisiana introduced the Lloyd case to the House of Representatives. Totten was now pressing for $9,153.32, plus interest accrued since June 5, 1865. On May 15, a bill for the relief (payment) of the claimant (Totten) was introduced in the Senate, where it was referred to the committee of claims. The committee examined the case, believed it to a man, adjusted the amount a little, and Senator George Grover Wright, of Iowa, reported favorably on the claim, writing, "On an examination of the contract, however, as set out in evidence, we do not find that there was any provision therein for the repayment to Mr. Lloyd of his expenses."

And then, astonishingly, the finding: "We therefore consider that he should be allowed compensation from July 13, 1861 to April 27, 1865, at $200 per month, amounting to $9093.33, from which is to be deducted the amount allowed and paid him by the War Department as expenses, to wit $2380, leaving, as now due his estate, the sum of $6713.33. We do not think that interest on this amount should be allowed claimant. Your committee therefore report herewith a bill authorizing and requiring the Secretary of the Treasury to pay to Enoch Totten, as administrator of the estate of William A. Lloyd, deceased, the sum of $6713.33, in full, for the personal services of said William A. Lloyd, rendered in pursuance of a contract made with Abraham Lincoln, President of the United States, and recommended that said bill do pass." It then went back to the House, where it was not acted upon.[531]

The memory of Lloyd-as-spy, the claim of Lloyd-as-spy, is gone. Vanished. But again, Totten was not giving up on his dogged pursuit of the money. With the disclosure of a spying contract and any suit by, or on behalf of, an agent so engaged prohibited by the Supreme Court precedent, Totten changed the nature of Lloyd's work for president Lincoln to "legal services." Lloyd, Totten claimed, had been in the South on Lincoln's personal legal business, but never elaborated as to the nature of that business.

On October 31, 1877, Senator Angus Cameron of Wisconsin introduced a brand new bill in the Senate, asking the Secretary of the Treasury to pay $6,713.33. On December 7 the Senate passed the bill without amendment, and it was sent to the House on December 12, 1877. It died there, never acted upon again.[532]

But in spite of Enoch Totten's last legal deception, his last grasp at the remainder of the Lloyd claim, the decision the claim inspired was now indisputably a fixed law, a precedent bearing his name. Known variously as the Totten Doctrine, the Totten Bar, or the Totten Decision, the law was upheld again in 1895. It seemed that William Alvin Lloyd's claim against the US government for services rendered in the Confederacy while a Union spy was not the first of its kind presented to the War Department. On January 6, 1862, one Charles de Arnaud did just that, claimed to have been spying for Generals John C. Fremont and Ulysses S. Grant out west in the early days of the war, even had letters from those generals to prove it. President Lincoln endorsed the claim. Simon Cameron, then secretary of war, balked at the proposed payment of $3,600 and de Arnaud cut his losses, settled for $2,000, and disappeared. He resurfaced in 1891, in the US Court of Claims, but the court cited the Lloyd precedent. On April 24, 1895, Colonel H. C. Ainsworth, United States, summarizing the De Arnaud case in a letter to the secretary of war, used expressions that are shockingly redolent of Lloyd's claim: "It is apparent from an examination of the mass of papers . . . that de Arnaud has succeeded in convincing many persons, including high executive officers of the government and members of important Congressional committees, persons of the highest integrity and the best of judgment, that he actually was . . ." etc. He goes on: "As one studies this case for the first time, with all the facts before him, it will seem more and more astonishing that anyone could have been misled or imposed upon for a moment by such a transparent and baseless fabrication as this portion of de Arnaud's altogether incredible story now appears to be." The case was dismissed, citing *Totten vs. the US*.

It is worth a brief review of the Totten Doctrine, because as will be seen, eighty-seven years later, it was conflated with the very controversial State Secrets Privilege, a rule that bars evidence, or portions of evidence, that impinge on national security from being litigated in a court of law. "While the Courts may examine such evidence closely, in practice they generally defer to the Executive Branch, at which time if the evidence warrants the state secrets privilege, the plaintiff cannot continue the suit without privileged information and drops the case." In fact, the State Secrets Privilege has been described as "Totten's Poisoned Progeny," by Sean C. Flynn, Associate General Counsel and Chief Compliance Officer at Abiomed, and has become to some in the legal community "a major hindrance to litigation that seeks to challenge abuses of executive power in the context of the War on Terror," wrote Professor of Law, D. A. Jeremy Telman."[533]

But in spite of the conflation of the State Secrets Privilege and the Totten Doctrine, there are differences. "In Totten, wrote attorney Frederick G. Jauss, IV, in his abstract of an article by attorney Daniel L. Pines, "the Supreme Court took issue, not with the ability of the President to enter into secret contracts, but with claims brought on the basis of secret contracts. Judicial review of secret contracts for secret services would needlessly endanger national security."

However, wrote Telman, the Totten Doctrine is sometimes invoked when the "government seeks dismissal of tort claims through the State Secrets Privilege."[534] And, eventually the Totten Doctrine "was expanded to all contracts with the government when at the time of its creation, the contract was secret or covert," wrote lawyers Douglas Kash and Matthew Indrisano.[535]

In fact, the second time the Totten Doctrine stood as the reason for dismissing a case was when in 1973, a clerk-typist named John Doe, working in a Communist embassy in the United States, made approaches to the CIA. He wanted to defect. His wife, too. The CIA persuaded the couple to remain in place, but as spies, and Mr. Doe worked his way up to electronics technician, providing good service to his covert handlers, secure in the knowledge that the US government, as part of the deal, would relocate him and his wife when the time came, and look after them for life. However, in January 1982, Mr. Doe informed the CIA that he was a homosexual, and that was the end of his career, and his financial security. The 1947 National Security Act gave the director of the CIA the power to fire an employee if it was considered that that employee was a threat to the state. In 1985, the Does sued the CIA, and, eventually, the case made its way to the Supreme Court in 2005, as *Tenet vs. Doe* (George Tenet being the recently departed director of the CIA at that time). "The respondents' suit was barred by the Totten rule, the finding read, with Justice William Rehnquist "delivering the opinion for the unanimous court."[536]

Long after the death of William Alvin Lloyd, his claim—the tissue of lies, sculpted by Enoch Totten and delivered by him to the highest court in the land—remains. As for the doctrine that bears Totten's name, and its often-conflated progeny, the State Secrets Privilege, both continue to bar the rights of operatives and assets employed by the CIA and other government clandestine organizations to have their day in court. To this day.

EPILOGUE

IF VIRGINIA LLOYD AND ENOCH TOTTEN COULD HAVE PEERED THROUGH a scrim into the future, they would see Lloyd's postmortem influence on the claim, on the falsehood they'd abetted. As for Totten, whose creation bears his name for all time and who had discarded the truth with great zeal, would he be proud? With the ignominious burial of the case at the end of 1877, aside from the initial expenses granted by Secretary of War Stanton way back in 1865, had it all been for nothing—all that effort, the lies, the greed?

But although Virginia may have been unhappy with the outcome of the claim, after such a long and desperate haul through the courts, she was finally free of it. And she'd not been caught, exposed, shamed. Ever the survivor, she and her new husband, David Williamson Lee, along with eighteen-year-old Clarence Alvin Lloyd, packed their bags, rented out the house in New York, and moved to South Orange, New Jersey. But if stability, happiness, a better life for Virginia and her son seemed possible, it was not.

Her husband, David Lee, was dying of liver and kidney ailments. On January 18, 1886, rather than continue to suffer, D. W. Lee shot himself in the head. Virginia came home to find him. Lee's family made sure Virginia got nothing from his estate. Two years later, in Brooklyn, on September 27, 1888, Virginia married the wealthy James Monroe Jacques.[537]

In Newark, on June 8, 1881, Clarence Alvin Lloyd married the widow Mamie Remington Walthour of Thomasville, Georgia. Due to the privations he had suffered as a child, Clarence was frail and sickly and would remain so. At the stroke of midnight, on September 21, 1889, Clarence died of a lingering illness in Thomasville. He left two daughters. Their descendants are alive today, but none of them knew, until recently, that their great-great-grandfather was William Alvin Lloyd, Lincoln's secret spy.

Virginia's brother, Eugene Higgins—who wrote the letter to Jefferson Davis suggesting Lloyd for the job of Provost Marshal of Mobile—was admitted to the Mount Hope Retreat Insane Asylum, run by the Catholic Sisters of Charity, and in the summer of 1880, in Norfolk, he overdosed on laudanum.[538]

Virginia Van Rensselaer Higgins Lloyd Lee Jacques died of apoplexy after a lingering illness in Baltimore at five o'clock in the afternoon on August 11, 1911, at her apartment in the Marlboro. The funeral took place at 3:00 p.m., the following Monday, at Druid Ridge Cemetery.[539]

In 1879 a book came out called *The History of Montgomery County*. Later that year, it went into a second edition, and has since become the classic history of the county. In it can be found this truth: "Among the officers in the Confederate service, none were more distinguished for capacity, efficiency and valor, than . . . Col. T.H.S. Boyd." The author of this work was Thomas Hewlings Stockton Boyd.

Charles Boyd, Alphabetical's brother, resided in Baltimore with his wife, Cecelia, but that wouldn't last, and by the end of the following year he and Alphabetical went back to living with their widowed mother in Clarksburg.[540]

Alphabetical Boyd spent the last dozen years of his life at the Maryland Line Confederate Soldiers' Home, near Pikesville. His death came sometime in 1907, although, in typical Boyd fashion, nobody seems to know precisely when. His tombstone says December 12, the Maryland death records have December 11, and the newspapers reported that it was December 9.[541]

Ellen Robinson "Nellie" Dooley fell out with her employers after the Lloyd caper, and pursued a career in nursing for a while in Rhode Island. In 1880 she married a Massachusetts jeweler named Alfred Acly, and they moved back to Providence, where she died on April 13, 1916.[542]

After deposing for Virginia, F. J. Bonfanti left for Cuba in March 1873, and subsequently for England. In early 1876 he was in Manchester visiting his brother, Harry, who was, at that moment, putting together Bonfanti's Circus. F. J. Bonfanti never lived to see opening night.[543]

Marcellus Howser continued to reside in Washington. In 1873 he got married, and had two daughters, but by 1881 had joined the US Marine Corps, serving four years as a private. An inordinate quantity of his service career was spent in a hospital bed, being treated for gonorrhea and syphilis, which he had picked up while posted in the Far East with the Asiatic Squadron. After a spell as a grocer and clerk, he lost his wife in 1890, and immediately pressed for a Marine pension, but was turned down, and again in 1898. Even as late as 1906, when he was living in Ridgely, Maryland, he was still pushing his Congressman for that pension. He finally got it in 1908. He was sixty.[544]

In the little community of Royal Oak, in Talbot County, Maryland, on December 2, 1880, Charles T. Harvey, who'd written the damaging letter exposing the Lloyd fraud, died at the age of forty-two. He was buried three days later.[545]

Theodore Woodall, the detective, became a railroad ticket agent and later a saloonkeeper in Baltimore, and died on April 1, 1881.[546]

On August 11, 1889, at Johns Hopkins Hospital, in Baltimore, Asbury Baker, one of several false witnesses in the Lloyd claim, died at the age of fifty.[547]

John P. Hamlin, who had vouched for Asbury Baker as a veracious witness in 1865, remained in the restaurant business in Washington, and, in 1881, for a brief while, found himself exposed in the glare of the national spotlight as the foreman of the jury that hanged Guiteau, President Garfield's assassin. Hamlin died on June 8, 1914.[548]

While William Alvin Lloyd had dreamed up the idea to defraud the US government, the man who turned the dream into a reality was lawyer Enoch Totten. With a Supreme Court case that became a precedent ruling bearing his name, Mr. Totten became a prominent, wealthy, highly respected and busy attorney in Washington. He died, much mourned and eulogized by his colleagues, on November 11, 1898. He was sixty-two.[549]

Totten's brother-in-law, Frank Howe, who had done such an inferior job with his first legal mission as Totten's representative at the Court of Claims, got out of the law business, married, moved to New York, and became a writer. He died at forty-nine.[550]

John Robin McDaniel, Alvin's steadfast friend in Lynchburg, was so devastated by the Civil War that he could never recover. From once being one of the leading citizens of Lynchburg, he moved to Washington at the beginning of 1878 and opened up a boardinghouse. On May 14 of that year, he passed away.[551]

E. D. Frost, the Canton, Mississippi, railroad superintendent who had vouched for his friend Alvin Lloyd, died on April 3, 1892.[552]

Confederate President Jefferson Davis was captured just outside Irwinville, Georgia, "on the gray dawn of May 10th, 1865, . . . one month after Lee's surrender." Hard as he tried, Joseph Holt was never able to prove that Davis played a part in or abetted the Lincoln assassination. Jefferson Davis was never brought to trial and served two years in prison at Fortress Monroe, "regarded by a majority of Northerners as the living embodiment of treason." He died on December 6, 1889.[553]

Colonel Jack Brown, Alvin's friendly jailer at Macon, left for Richmond with his regiment, the 59th Georgia Infantry, at about the same time Alvin was released. Jack was wounded at Gettysburg, a ball in each thigh, and captured. He was exchanged from Point Lookout in 1864, and was wounded again later that year—in the right popliteal. After the war he moved between Georgia and Washington, DC, and died on April 2, 1891.[554]

Alvin's friend, railroad executive John Roper Branner, died in 1869 of apoplexy at the age of forty-seven.[555]

Hayne Irby Klinck, the police chief in Memphis who arrested Alvin Lloyd for bigamy in July 1861, lost everything he had when the Federals occupied his city. Broke and desperate, he tried hard for a job as captain in the Confederate Secret Service, only to fall at the battle of Franklin in 1864.[556]

Colonel William S. Rockwell, in large part responsible for Alvin's harsh durance in Savannah, died on January 23, 1870, and was taken back to Milledgeville, while Waring Russell, Alvin's keeper at the Savannah jail, remained in that post for quite a while, finally becoming city treasurer. He died in 1914.[557]

Dr. John Frederick May, the famous surgeon who'd cursorily examined Alvin at the behest of Enoch Totten, died in Washington in 1891.[558]

By early August 1867, Happy Cal Wagner, the former Lloyd's Minstrel, was back in Cleveland, playing with La Rue's Carnival Minstrels. Later that year he came down with yellow fever in New Orleans. Dan Bryant, the minstrel king who horsewhipped W. Alvin Lloyd up and down Broadway, and had been a friend of John Wilkes Booth, died in New York City, in 1875. Gustave Bidaux, whom Lloyd fired in 1867 for the grossest and most unspeakable behavior, died in 1886, and Dave Wambold, the minstrel who had threatened to kick Alvin's head in before the war, died in 1889. Cool White hadn't quite reached seventy when he drew his last breath in Chicago on April 23, 1891.[559]

Johnny Booker, Alvin's stepbrother, continued in the minstrel game for a while, and was then arrested for bigamy in Indianapolis in 1874. He only managed to avoid incarceration by disappearing to the East Indies for a few years. He later became a cobbler in Dayton, Ohio, which is where he died, on October 25, 1898.[560]

Elizabeth Ann "Lizzie" Lloyd, Alvin's very first wife, never remarried, and died in Louisville in 1907, worn away by rheumatism at the age of eighty-four. She is buried in Louisville's Eastern Cemetery. Alvin and Elizabeth Lloyd's daughter, Belle, married J. D. Johnson. He predeceased Belle, who died in 1881. She is buried alongside her mother in the Eastern Cemetery.[561] Alvin's son, Charles William Lloyd, died in Louisville at the age of thirty-four, of stomach cancer. He is buried in Cave Hill Cemetery. He never married.[562]

Thomas G. Lloyd outlived his son Alvin, dying of diabetes in the Louisville City Hospital on November 9, 1870. He was seventy-three years old.[563]

Finally there is Alvin's brother, J. T. Lloyd. By the 1880s, J. T. was fifty, portly, and with a full gray beard and the dark complexion of his Welsh forebears. But his ferocious energy remained undiminished as he embarked on a fresh bilking rampage all over the country, followed by an almost equally determined press campaign to stop him. For the "Great Map Man," as he described himself, the crooked path had, give or take a few serious bumps in the road, been a good one, paved with gold. He was now training his sons in the bilking business, as the press reported, but, somehow, even though the offspring would constantly be in the news, they were never able to acquire the boldness, the panache, of their father, or of their uncle Alvin. As 1890 rolled around, J. T. started a new map company in Baltimore, and it was there, on February 2, 1891, that he died of heart failure.[564]

Another montage? It cannot be. There is no one left in the frame, in the theater, on the stage. The show is over. Only shadows remain.

ACKNOWLEDGMENTS

As we journeyed through the thicket of Lloyd's life and lies, his lawyer's concoctions, the falsified testimonies, and the shadows Lloyd cast at his changing whims, we were ably assisted by fine scholars, document examiners, diligent archivists, various special collections librarians, cemetery historians, and members of the legal community. So, our thanks to National Archives archivist Jane Fitzgerald (Archives 1 Reference Section, Research Services, Washington, DC); the wise and ever-helpful Dr. Lynda Lasswell Crist, editor and project manager of the *Papers of Jefferson Davis*, Rice University, Houston, Texas; Professor Elizabeth Leonard at Colby College, Waterford, Maine; Laurie Verge, director, Surratt House Museum, Clinton, Maryland; Lew Napier at the Cave Hill Cemetery, Louisville, Kentucky; at Eastern Cemetery in Louisville—a valuable historical site that is being lovingly restored but can always use ready, helping hands—Bobby Hunt; Dann Penn and archaeologist Dr. Philip DiBlasi; Jana Meyer at the Filson Historical Society in Louisville, Kentucky; Lance J. Hale of the Kentucky Archives Center; Derek Gray at the DC Public Library: Washingtonian Division; James Blankenship and Chris Boyce at the Petersburg National Battlefield; Tom Neel at the Ohio Genealogical Society; C. Danny Wofford at the Atlanta Masonic Library and Museum; and Elisabeth A. Engel, director of collections and exhibits at the Waukesha County Museum.

For lively conversation and valuable consultation about the Lincoln pass, many thanks to Dr. James M. Cornelius, curator, Lincoln Collection, Abraham Lincoln Presidential Library & Museum (Springfield, Illinois); Dr. Daniel Stowell, director and editor of the papers of Abraham Lincoln (Springfield, Illinois); forensic document analyst Kirsten Singer; handwriting analyst Ellen Schuetzner; autograph dealer Edward N. Bomsey; and Daniel Weinburg, proprietor of the Abraham Lincoln Bookshop in Chicago. To Zack Mazur, who three years ago at the start of this project spent many hours in the New York Public Library retrieving the John

Bakeless Papers. And to Charles Richter at George Washington University, who ably combed through the Joseph Holt Papers at the Library of Congress.

Author Jane Singer's important conversations with Professor Steven Schwinn and Professor Robert M. Chesney added greatly to our understanding of the continuing impact of the Totten Doctrine, the state secrets privilege, and the differences between them. At the start of this project Professor D. A. Jeremy Telman's assertion that our discovery of the Lloyd fraud would "rock the legal community" was an inspiration and an added impetus to forge ahead.

And many thanks to Ryan Martz, who instantly, cheerfully, and diligently helped, big-time.

For his guidance, input, sage advice, and ongoing support as we journeyed together, we thank our agent, William Callahan at Inkwell Management.

To Keith Wallman, Editorial Director at Lyons Press, thank you for continuing to believe in this work as you toiled so mightily on your own. And to production editor Lauren Brancato and copy editor Jessie Shiers, thanks for everything.

To Chuck Eckstein, Jessica Eve Masser, Caspy, and Buster, every day, every moment you have been there.

Notes

1 *Daily National Intelligencer* (Washington, DC), May 24, 1865.

2 Ibid.

3 Walt Whitman. "Return of the Heroes," *The Patriotic Poems of Walt Whitman* (New York: Doubleday, Page & Company, 1918).

4 Ulysses S. Grant. *Personal Memoirs of US Grant* (New York: Charles L. Webster & Company, 1885–86), Volume Two, Chapter LXX.

5 National Archives and Record Administration (NARA), Record Group (RG) 94, M619, Letters Received by the Office of the Adjutant General, Main Series, 1861–1870. The scans of the pass, both front and back, as well as the envelope that contained it, were obtained from the National Archives and are located in a vault reserved for primary source documents deemed authentic. For the particulars of the pass and its final authentication, see the appendix.

6 Quote attributed to President Andrew Johnson when he refused to accept the clemency petition that would have spared the life of Mary Surratt.

7 Herman Melville. *The Martyr*, from *Battle-Pieces and Aspects of the War* (New York: Harper & Brothers, 1866).

8 Edward Steers Jr. *Blood on the Moon: The Assassination of Abraham Lincoln* (Lexington: University Press of Kentucky, 2001), p. 214.

9 NARA, Letters to the Adj. General: Ulysses S. Grant to Secretary Edwin Stanton. May 27, 1865. Lloyd Papers: Enclosure 16.

10 Elizabeth D. Leonard. *Lincoln's Avengers: Justice, Revenge and Reunion after the Civil War* (New York, London: W.W. Norton & Company, 2004). p. 79.

11 A. A. Hosmer to Secretary Stanton, May 30, 1865, Lloyd Papers, Enclosure 39.

12 *Milwaukee Daily Sentinel,* February 22, 24, 25; March 4, 7, 14; June 10, 1865.

13 Caleb Atwater. *Writings of Caleb Atwater* (Columbus: published by the author, 1833), p. 18.

14 John E. Kleber, ed. *The Encyclopedia of Louisville.* (Lexington: University Press of Kentucky, 2001), p. 584.

15 *Louisville Council Minutes,* July 16, 1832.

16 Atwater, p. 186.

17 *Louisville Public Advertiser,* May 21, 1830.

18 Edward Le Roy Rice, *Monarchs of Minstrelsy, from "Daddy" Rice to Date* (New York City, NY, 1911), p. 8.

19 Rice, p. 24.

20 Rice, p. 7.

21 Kleber, p. 640. See also Eric Lott, *Love and Theft: Blackface Minstrelsy and the American Working Class* (Oxford University Press, 1995), p. 22. Dale Cockrell, *Demons of Disorder, Early Blackface Minstrels and Their World* (Cambridge University Press, July 28, 1997), p. 93.

22 *Louisville Public Advertiser,* December 31, 1830.

23 NARA: Confederate Papers Relating to Citizens or Business Firms (Confederate Citizens File), 1861–1865. Record Group (RG) 109—Lloyd, William Alvin. Letter from Colonel William S. Rockwell to W. H. Taylor, February 17, 1862.

24 "The Maroon Book," p. 1, Bullitt County History website. Bullitt County Genealogical Society, Mt. Washington, October 14, 1838.

25 The Proceedings of the Old Bailey, London's Central Criminal Court, 1674 to 1913. John Lloyd, 1727.

26 *History of Men's Clothing* (Geneva, New York: Geneva Historical Society, 2013).

27 Atwater, p. 109.

28 Bullitt letter.

29 Benjamin Cassaday. *The History of Louisville From its Earliest Settlement to the Year 1852* (Louisville: Hull & Brothers, 1852), p. 65.

30 Ibid.

31 *Louisville Daily Advertiser,* March 5, 1841.

32 Cassaday, p. 185.

33 Louisville City Directory, 1832.

34 Filson Historical Society: Louisville. *Protestant Episcopal Orphan Asylum Records, 1835–1924.*

35 *Louisville Journal,* August 23, 1846.

36 William L. Slout, ed. *Burnt Cork and Tambourines : A Source Book of Negro Minstrelsy* (San Bernardino, California: The Borgo Press, 1995), p. 166. T. Allston Brown. "Early History of Negro Minstrelsy: Its Rise and Progress in the United States" (*New York Clipper*), Jan. 11, 1913, p. 1.

37 Thomas Allston Brown, 1836–1918, was dubbed "Colonel" by the press. He liked the sound of it, and kept it. Alvin Lloyd told people that he too, was a colonel, and the press—at least some of them—believed him. See also Slout, *Burnt Cork and Tambourines,* p. 166.

38 William J. Mahar, *Behind the Burnt Cork Mask* (Champaign: University of Illinois Press, 1998), p. 363. *New York Herald,* March 21, 1845, and June 19, 1845; *Mississippi Free Trader & Natchez Gazette,* January 17, 1846; *New York Clipper,* April 13, 1912.

39 *Weekly Nashville Union,* April 30, 1845, and May 7, 1845; *New York Herald,* May 24, 1845, June 14, 1845, and June 19, 1845; *Weekly Nashville Union,* December 3, 1845; *Mississippi Free Trader & Natchez Gazette,* January 3, 1846, January 13, 1846, and January 17, 1846; *Weekly Nashville Union,* October 21, 1846; *The Mississippian,* December 8, 1846; *New Orleans Times-Picayune,* December 18 and 19, 1846; *Nashville Union,* February 17, 1847.

40 *New Orleans Times-Picayune,* December 24 and 25, 1846.

41 *Trenton State Gazette* (New Jersey), February 25, 1847, citing the *St. Louis Reveille* of unknown date; *Weekly Nashville Union,* February 17 and 24, 1847.

42 William Osborne. *Music in Ohio* (Kent, Ohio: Kent State University Press, 2004), p. 411; Jasen and Jones, *Spreadin' Rhythm Around: Black Popular Songwriters, 1880–1930* (New York: Routledge Press, 2005), p. 4. Ken Emerson, *Doo-Dah! Stephen Foster and the Rise of American Popular Culture* (Da Capo Press paperback edition, 1997), p.127.

43 *New Orleans Times-Picayune*, April 11, 15, 22, and 27, 1847; May 2, 1847; and June 4, 5, 9, 13, 19, 20, 1847. *Cleveland Herald*, September 23 and 25, 1847. *Cleveland Plain Dealer*, September 25, 1847.

44 *Mississippi Free Trader & Natchez Gazette*, January 22, 1848.

45 *The Zoist: A Journal of Cerebral Physiology & Mesmerism, and Their Applications to Human Welfare*. Vol. VII, March 1849 to January 1850. (London: Hippolyte Bailliere Publisher, 1850), p. 148; John Stewart, *Confederate Spies at Large* (Jefferson, N.C.: McFarland & Company, Inc., 2007), pp. 143, 144, 146.

46 Walter Barlow Stevens. *St. Louis, The Fourth City* (St. Louis: S. J. Clarke Publishing, 1911), p. 120.

47 William Hyde and Howard L. Conard. *Encyclopedia of the History of St. Louis* (New York, Louisville: The Southern History Company, 1899), p. 1742.

48 *New Orleans Times-Picayune*, October 21, 1849.

49 *New Orleans Times-Picayune*, October 22, 1849.

50 *New Orleans Times-Picayune*, October 23, 1849.

51 *New Orleans Times-Picayune*, October 26, 27, 28, 1849.

52 *New Orleans Times-Picayune*, October 30, 1849.

53 *New Orleans Times-Picayune*, November 2, 5, 12, 13, 15, 19, 23, 1849.

54 *New York Clipper*, January 11, 1913, p. 1.

55 1850 census, St. Louis, September 14 and October 7.

56 1850 census, St. Louis. *Daily Democratic State Journal* (Sacramento), July 3, 1855; *Sacramento Daily Union*, July 6, 1855, in sequence until October 5, 1855.

57 *The Mississippian*, December 20, 1850; *Mississippi Free Trader & Natchez Gazette*, December 27 and 28, 1850.

58 The *Wheeling Daily Intelligencer*, November 15, 1852, p. 3. The article tells the story of Dick running off with another man's wife. For his false pretenses morning up before Alderman Lewis in Pittsburgh, see the same paper, October 6, 1858, p. 3. There are several other stories of Dick's transgressions—bilking printers in St. Louis, and so on. Sliter's last performance was with Alvin Lloyd's stepbrother, Johnny Booker, and he died in Jackson, Mississippi, in May 1861.

59 *Nashville Union & American*, October 30, 1857.

60 Cool White's real name was John Hodges. Colonel T. Allston Brown wrote that he was known as the "renowned Shakespearian jester."

61 *New Orleans Times-Picayune*, January 2, 5 and 7, 1851.

62 *New York Clipper*, August 1, 1891.

63 Brown, "Early History of Negro Minstrelsy," *New York Clipper*, January 11, 1913, p. 1.

64 *Kentucky Tribune*, January 2, 1852, p. 3.

65 Confederate Citizens File.

66 Robert C. Reinders, *End of an Era: New Orleans, 1850–1860* (Gretna, Louisiana: Pelican Publishing Company, 1994), p. 228.

67 This blurb, and the first ad in the new series, appeared in the *Louisville Daily Democrat* of February 25, 1852.

68 A reference to the character of Modus, a shy, bookish, Latin scholar in the popular play *The Hunchback* by James Sheridan Knowles.

69 *New Orleans Times-Picayune*, November 20, 1853, p. 2; *New Orleans Daily Crescent*, November 21, 1853, p. 1.

70 *Kentucky Tribune*, November 11, 1853.

71 *New Orleans Daily Crescent*, May 13, 1853, p. 2, and November 21, 1853, p. 3; *Richmond Daily Dispatch*, November 29, 1853, p. 1.

72 *New Orleans Daily Crescent*, November 21, 1853, p. 3.

73 *New Orleans Times-Picayune*, November 20, 1853; *New Orleans Daily Crescent*, November 21, 1853, p. 3.

74 *Richmond Daily Dispatch*, June 29, 1853, describing the fare aboard the steamer *Robert J. Ward*, at about this time.

75 *New Orleans Daily Crescent*, November 23, 1853, p. 4.

76 *New Orleans Daily Crescent*, November 21, 1853, p. 3; *New Orleans Times-Picayune*, November 23, 1853, p. 2.

77 *New Orleans Daily Crescent*, November 25 and December 22, 1853.

78 *New Orleans Times-Picayune*, January 12, 1854, p. 3.

79 *New Orleans Daily Crescent*, January 12, 1854, p. 1.

80 *New Orleans Daily Crescent*, January 20, 1854, p. 3.

81 *New York Daily Times*, June 30, 1854. By 1856, Alvin would be renting a room in the Madison House across the river in Covington, Kentucky. Where he was actually residing in 1854 is not known.

82 Cincinnati city directories.

83 *Philadelphia Inquirer*, February 18, 1857. Charles Rhodes was then thirty-five, a Rhode Island native long in Philadelphia, well known as a publisher, printer, and broker; Lambert A. Wilmer, *Our Press Gang or, a Complete Exposition of the Corruptions and Crimes of the American Newspapers* (Philadelphia: J. T. Lloyd, 1860). Author and journalist Wilmer's defense of J. T. Lloyd's alleged "persecutions" and numerous, unwarranted arrests makes for great, colorful reading, offering a peek though the window at fisticuff journalism. Even though Lloyd was Lambert's publisher, Lambert claims no prejudice. See "The Case of James T. Lloyd" in Lambert's book, pp. 282–99.

84 *New York Daily Times*, June 30, 1854.

85 Ibid.

86 Ibid.

87 *Cincinnati Gazette*, October 31, 1854, reproduced in the *Washington Evening Star* of November 3, 1854, p. 2.

88 *Daily Nashville True Whig*, July 11 1855, p. 4.

89 *Philadelphia Inquirer*, May 21 and June 4, 1855; *New Albany Daily Ledger*, June 14, 1855.

90 *New Albany Daily Ledger*, February 13, 1856; *Boston Herald*, October 14, 1856.

91 For the episode with Potter, see the *New York Clipper*, January 11, 1913, p. 1. For the information on the *Steamboat and Railroad Directory*, see the *New Orleans Times-Picayune* and the *New Orleans Daily Crescent*, January 9, 1857, and various editions until February 25.

92 *New Orleans Times-Picayune*, February 27, 1858. It does not appear that Alvin served time for this attempted killing of Mackey.

93 *North American & United States Gazette*, June 1, 2, and 4, 1858; *New Orleans Times-Picayune*, June 12, 1858.

94 *Louisville Daily Democrat*, July 7, 1858. *New York Evening Express*, November 17, 1858: "Bridgeport, Ct., 12 instant, Mr. Wm A. Lloyd to Miss Virginia Higgins, of Brooklyn."

95 *Louisville Daily Courier*, June 8 and July 14, 1859.

96 *Louisville Daily Courier*, July 14, 1859; *Louisville Daily Democrat*, July 16, 1859.

97 1860 and 1870 censuses. Union Soldiers' Service Records: Shaw, George T., Kentucky marriages and deaths.

98 *New York Herald*, October 4, 1859, births.

99 Ibid.

100 British Library online.

101 *Encyclopaedia Britannica*.

102 NARA, Lloyd Papers, Enclosure 13, testimony of T.H.S. Boyd, June 3, 1865. This quote comes from Lloyd documents in the National Archives that comprise Enclosure 13, vital records that will evidence the many contradictions in time, place, and circumstances throughout the Civil War. During the course of the war, Alvin kept a diary, or so he said. In June 1865, midway through his claim against the US government, this diary was accidentally destroyed, or so Alvin said. But there were some pages left from this purported diary, and these will be seen throughout the course of this book. Due to the destruction of this diary, Enoch Totten the lawyer asked Lloyd to compile a detailed reconstruction of his movements during the Civil War. The reconstruction was presented to the War Department in July 1865, and forms Enclosure 13 in the Lloyd Papers. Often, as will be seen, the information in Enclosure 13 differs from that to be found in the saved pages of the original diary. So henceforth, when relevant, we will reference Enclosure 13.

103 NARA, Lloyd Papers, Boyd testimony, June 3, 1865. Censuses for 1850, 1860, 1870, 1880, and 1900.

104 NARA, Lloyd Papers: testimony of Nellie Dooley, June 3, 1865.

105 Heaton Norris, Cheshire, baptisms, marriages, and burials. St. Michael, Ashton-under-Lyne, Lancaster marriages. 1850 and 1860 censuses for Fall River, Bristol Co., Massachusetts. 1870 and 1900 censuses for Providence, Rhode Island. Records of the Training School for Nurses, Orange Memorial Hospital, New Jersey. Attleboro, Massachusetts, marriage records, 1880. Providence city directories, 1902–1916. Providence death records, 1916.

106 Abraham Lincoln's inaugural speech, March 4, 1861.

107 *Home Journal* article, reproduced in the *Daily Scioto Gazette* (Chillicothe, Ohio), August 3, 1852; *Milwaukee Daily Sentinel*, August 18, 1852; *Boston Daily Atlas*, August 25, 1852.

108 *Memphis Appeal*, April 27, 1860.

109 *Louisville Daily Courier*, December 17, 1860.

110 *Cleveland Morning Leader*, December 28, 1860, p. 2.

111 *W. Alvin Lloyd's Southern Steamboat and Railroad Guide*, December 1860, January and February 1861; *New York Herald*, December 10, 1860.

112 Ibid.

113 NARA: Lloyd Papers: Enclosures 53–66: Railroad passes. David L. Bright's Confederate Railroads website: csa-railroads.com.

114 *New York Herald*, February 19 and 20, 1861. 1860 census. Rice, *Monarchs of Minstrelsy*, p. 141.

115 *New York Herald*, March 4, 1861.

116 For opening night at Niblo's, see the *New York Herald*, March 27, 28, 29, and 30, and April 1, 1861. For selected but typical reviews, see the same paper, April 2, 4, 8, and 18, 1861. For Jerry Bryant's funeral, see the *New York Clipper* article on Lloyd, January 11, 1913.

117 *New York Clipper*, May 1861, and Brown, "Early History of Negro Minstrelsy," *New York Clipper*, January 11, 1913.

118 Slout, p. 83.

119 *New York Clipper*, January 11, 1913.

120 *New York Herald*, July 6, 1861, p. 5.

121 Confederate Citizens File. Letter from William Alvin Lloyd to Robert E. Lee, November 15, 1862; NARA, M619, Record Group (RG) 94. Letters Received by the Office of the Adjutant General (Lloyd Papers), William Alvin Lloyd to Adjutant General Samuel Cooper, February 21, 1862, Enclosure 6.

122 *New York Herald*, July 6, 1861, p. 5.

123 *New York Herald*, July 4, 1861, p. 5.

124 New York City Census, 1860.

125 Slout, p. 83.

126 *Daily National Intelligencer*, July 2, 1861, p. 3.

127 NARA, William A. Lloyd to Jefferson Davis, January 9, 1862. RG 109, Letters Received by the Secretary of War, 9519-1862.

128 *Sun* (Baltimore), February 27, 1861.

129 James Mackay. *Allan Pinkerton: The Eye Who Never Slept* (Edinburgh and London: Mainstream Publishing, 1996), pp. 102–5.

130 Morgan Dix. *Memoirs of John Adams Dix: Compiled by his Son* (New York: Harper & Brothers, 1883), Vol. 11, p. 19.

131 George Templeton Strong. *The Diary of George Templeton Strong,* Allan Nevins and Milton Halsey Thomas, eds. (New York: The Macmillan Company, 1952), vol. 3, Diary entry, July 15, 1861, p. 164.

132 *Strong Diary*, July 8, 1861 entry.

133 Marguerite Spalding Geery, ed. *Through Five Administrations, Reminiscences of Colonel William H. Crook* (New York & London: Harper & Brothers 1883), p. 16.

134 *Seward at Washington as Senator and Secretary of State: A Memoir of His Life, with selections from his letters, 1861–1872* (New York: Derby and Miller, 149 Church Street, 1891), p. 530.

135 Helen Nicolay. *John Nicolay, Lincoln's Secretary* (New York: Longmans, Green & Company, 1949), p. 84; Stoddard, "White House Sketches, No. II," *New York Citizen*, August 25, 1866. See also, *Dispatches from Lincoln's White House, The Anonymous Civil War Journalism of Presidential Secretary William O. Stoddard*, Michael

Burlingame, ed. (Lincoln and London: University of Nebraska Press, 2002), p. xi
(author's intro), p. 14.

136 Noah Brooks. *Lincoln Observed: Civil War Dispatches of Noah Brooks* (Baltimore:
Johns Hopkins University Press, 1998), p. 84.

137 Ibid. Lloyd Papers, Enclosure 20. See Appendix for Lincoln pass particulars.

138 *Louisville Daily Courier*, July 15, 1861, p. 4, and July 16, 1861, p. 3.; boatnerd.com/
swayze/shipwreck/m.htm.

139 *Louisville Daily Journal*, July 20, 1861, p. 2.

140 *Louisville Daily Democrat*, July 16, 1861, p. 2; *Louisville Daily Courier*, July 15, 1861,
p. 4.

141 *Louisville Daily Journal*, July 15, 1861, p. 2.

142 *Daily Louisville Democrat*, July 16, 1861, p. 2.

143 *Daily Louisville Democrat*, July 15, 1861, p. 4.

144 *Daily Louisville Democrat*, July 16, 1861, p. 2.

145 *Louisville Daily Journal*, July 16, 1861, p. 3.

146 Elizabeth D. Leonard, *Lincoln's Forgotten Ally: Judge Advocate Joseph Holt of Kentucky*
(Chapel Hill: University of North Carolina Press, 2011), p. 146.

147 Charles Dickens. *The Works of Charles Dickens* (New York: Harper & Brothers,
Franklin Square, 1877), Vol. 8, p. 351.

148 Lloyd Papers, Enclosure 13.

149 Ibid.

150 Ibid.

151 Ibid.

152 NARA, RG 109, Letters Received by the Secretary of War, L-369, William Alvin
Lloyd to Jefferson Davis, July 18, 1861.

153 Lloyd Papers, Charles T. Moore deposition, June 30, 1865.

154 Ibid.

155 Death of Ernest P. Lloyd, *New York Herald*, June 2, 1863.

156 Lloyd Papers, Enclosure 13: "Left July 23." Which railroad line it was, the precise
time of leaving Canton, how long the trip was, and which stops were made en route
are from the train schedules published at that time in the newspapers.

157 W. C. Corsan. *Two Months in the Confederate States*, Benjamin H. Trask, ed. (Baton
Rouge: Louisiana State University Press, 1996). This book gives an evocative
description of the Mississippi countryside in the area Alvin was passing through.

158 Lloyd Papers, Enclosure 13. Brookhaven today is the county seat of Lincoln
County, but when Alvin traveled through it was part of Lawrence County. Lincoln
County was not formed until 1870.

159 1860 New Orleans Census.

160 Lloyd Papers, Enclosures 53–66.

161 Lloyd Papers, Enclosure 13.

162 The biographical material on the Browners is from New York censuses and from
the Lloyd Papers, Enclosure 13.

163 David Bright, *Confederate Railroads*.

164 Lloyd Papers, Enclosure 13.

165 Ibid.

166 Ibid.
167 David Bright, *Confederate Railroads.*
168 Ibid.
169 Lloyd Papers, Enclosure 13.
170 Lloyd Papers, Enclosure 34.
171 Lloyd Papers, Enclosure 13.
172 Records of the United States Court of Claims (selected documents from General Jurisdiction Case N. 6329, William A. Lloyd Case). Statement of T.H.S. Boyd, November 30, 1872. Hereafter referred to as the Court of Claims Papers.
173 Lloyd Papers, Enclosure 13.
174 Ibid.
175 Lloyd Papers, Enclosure 44.
176 Lloyd Papers, Enclosures 47–52.
177 Lloyd Papers, Enclosure 13.
178 Corey Recko. *A Spy for the Union: The Life and Execution of Timothy Webster* (Jefferson, North Carolina, and London: McFarland & Company, Inc., 2013), p. 110.
179 Arch Frederic Blakey, *General John H. Winder, C.S.A.*, p. 201.
180 Lloyd Papers, Enclosure 44.
181 Lloyd Papers, Enclosure 13.
182 Ibid.
183 Lloyd Papers, Statement of Virginia V. Lloyd, July 18, 1865.
184 Ibid.
185 Ibid.
186 Ibid.
187 US Court of Claims Papers, 1872, Statement of Virginia Lloyd, November 15, 1872.
188 *Clarksville Chronicle,* September 6, 1861.
189 Lloyd Papers, Enclosure 13.
190 Ibid.
191 Ibid.
192 Library of Congress, Confederate States Army Records (Pickett Papers), vol. 46, frames 13982-84.
193 Library of Congress, Confederate States Army Records (Pickett Papers), vol. 46, frames 13979-80.
194 US Court of Claims Papers, Statement of T.H.S. Boyd, November 30 and December 7, 1872.
195 Lloyd Papers, Enclosure 11.
196 Confederate Soldier Service Records: Boyd, T.H.S.
197 Lloyd Papers, Enclosure 13.
198 Lloyd Papers, Enclosure 42.
199 Lloyd Papers, Enclosure 13. David Bright, *Confederate Railroads.*
200 Lloyd Papers, Enclosure 13.
201 *Daily Nashville Patriot,* October 3, 1861.
202 *Daily Nashville Patriot,* September 27 and 28, 1861.

203 Lloyd Papers, Enclosure 13. *Daily Nashville Patriot*, October 4, 5, 7, 8, 9, and 10, 1861.

204 *Daily Nashville Patriot*, October 9, 1861.

205 Lloyd Papers, Letters Received by the Secretary of War, 9519-1862. Letter from W. Alvin Lloyd to Jefferson Davis, January 9, 1862.

206 *Daily Nashville Patriot*, October 15, 1861.

207 Lloyd Papers, Enclosure 13. US Court of Claims Papers, testimony of Virginia V. Lloyd, November 15, 1872.

208 Lloyd Papers, Enclosure 13.

209 Lloyd Papers, Enclosure 13. David Bright, *Confederate Railroads. Daily Register* (Raleigh), November 2, 1861.

210 Lloyd Papers, Enclosure 13.

211 Ibid.

212 Confederate Citizens File, Col. W. S. Rockwell to Capt. W. H. Taylor, February 17, 1862.

213 Mississippi Marriages Index, 1800-1911. Lloyd Papers, Enclosure 13.

214 Lloyd Papers, Enclosure 13.

215 Ibid.

216 Orleans Parish, Louisiana, Justice of the Peace, Marriage Licenses, 1846–1880. Vol. 11, July 16, 1861–October 26, 1861.

217 Lloyd Papers, Enclosure 13.

218 Ibid.

219 Lloyd Papers, Enclosures 13 and 44.

220 Ibid.

221 Ibid.

222 Ibid.

223 Lloyd Papers, Enclosure 13. Dave Bright, *Confederate Railroads*.

224 Lloyd Papers, Enclosure 13. *Memphis Daily Appeal*, December 8, 1861.

225 Lloyd Papers, Enclosure 13.

226 *Today in Civil War History*: Michael Wilkins. Examiner.com.

227 Jacqueline Jones. *Saving Savannah, The City and the Civil War* (New York: Alfred A. Knopf, 2008), pp. 137–38.

228 *Daily Morning News* (Savannah), December 11, 1861; Jones, *Saving Savannah*, p. 132.

229 *Daily Morning News* (Savannah), December 2, 1861.

230 *Charleston Mercury*, December 14, 1861. *Macon Telegraph*, December 13 and 14, 1861. *Daily Constitutionalist* (Augusta, Ga.), December 13, 1861.

231 *Daily Morning News*, Savannah, and reproduced in all the Southern papers at precisely this time.

232 Lloyd Papers, Lloyd diary, Enclosure 44.

233 Lloyd Papers, Enclosure 13.

234 Mrs. Elizabeth Morse and her husband, Lorenzo B. Morse, along with his brother, Horace, had bought the Gibbons House the year before; *Daily Morning News* (Savannah), January 3, 1861.

235 1860 Census. Joseph Gaston Baillie Bulloch. *A History and Genealogy of the Haber-sham Family* (Columbia, South Carolina: The R.L. Bryan Co, 1901), p. 38. Proceedings of the Grand Lodge, 1871, p. 78.

236 Lloyd Papers, diary pages, Enclosures 45–52.

237 Lloyd Papers, Enclosure 13.

238 Adelaide Wilson. *Historic and Picturesque Savannah.* Illustrations by Georgia Weymouth. "Published for Subscribers by the Boston Photogravure Company," 1887.

239 John S. Billings, Assistant Surgeon United States Army. *Report on the Barracks and Hospitals of the United States Army,* Surgeon General's Office, Washington, DC, December 1, 1870, p. 142.

240 Lloyd Papers, Enclosure 13. Waring Russell had been appointed keeper in 1859. See *Daily Morning News* (Savannah), October 15, 1859.

241 *Documents of the Assembly of the State of New York,* p. 409; Charles Olmstead, "Savannah in the '40s." *Georgia Historical Quarterly,* September 1917; Wilson, *Historic and Picturesque Savannah,* p. 169.

242 Expense sheets for Chatham County Jail, which give the names of prisoners, dates of in and out, an explanation of Waring Russell, and how jailer Russell and others billed the government. Confederate Citizen's File. RG 109, NARA. See: Waring Russell, expenses, March 1862.

243 Much of the following was described to author Jane Singer in an interview with Hugh Golson.

244 Golson. Confederate Citizens File, Waring Russell Expenses.

245 Golson.

246 Francis Lieber letter #8, Lloyd Papers, Enclosure 11.

247 Ibid. Winder didn't seem to know about Alvin Lloyd's guide, or if he did, he chose not to address this. Knowing Winder was prone to jailing many people for perceived disloyalties, though mistaken about Alvin's activities, his suspicions about him must have been regarded with utmost seriousness.

248 NARA, RG 109. Bledsoe to Rockwell, December 30, 1861.

249 Lloyd Papers, Enclosure 13.

250 NARA, RG 109, Letters Received by the Secretary of War, 9519-1862.

251 Lloyd Papers, Enclosure 22. McDaniel letter, January 11, 1862.

252 Lloyd Papers, Enclosure 22. Frost affidavit, January 11, 1862. The photos (ambrotypes) taken of Lloyd have not to date been located, if they still are in existence. Therefore there appear to be no extant likenesses of Lloyd.

253 Lloyd Papers, Enclosure 13.

254 Lloyd Papers, Enclosure 21. McDaniel letter, January 28, 1862.

255 Ibid.

256 Lloyd Papers, Enclosure 38, Frost letter.

257 Confederate Citizens File, Benjamin to Lawton, February 10, 1862.

258 Court of Claims Papers, 1872. Boyd statements, November 30 and December 7, 1872. Confederate Army Records. For the governor's commission and some details about Boyd's desertion from the 1st Louisiana, see the *Richmond Daily Dispatch,* July 25, 1863.

259 Ibid. Boyd statements, November 30 and December 7, 1872.
260 Confederate Citizens File, Rockwell's report of February 17, 1862.
261 Court of Claims Papers, Boyd statement, 1872.
262 Robert E. Lee timeline, WGBH, Boston.
263 Confederate Citizens File, Lloyd to Robert E. Lee, February 15, 1862.
264 Confederate Citizens File, Lloyd to Robert E. Lee, February 17, 1862.
265 Confederate Citizens File, Rockwell to Captain W. H. Taylor, February 17, 1862.
266 Confederate Citizens File, Wayne to Lee, February 19, 1862.
267 Confederate Citizens File, Lloyd to Lee, February 20, 1862.
268 Lieber letters #1 and #2, Lloyd Papers, Enclosure 6.
269 Confederate Citizens File, Lloyd to Lee, February 25, 1862.
270 Lieber letter #3, Lloyd Papers, Enclosure 6.
271 Lloyd to Benjamin, March 17, 1862, Lieber letter #4, Lloyd Papers, Enclosure 6.
272 Lawton's letter to Davis, Enclosure 19 of the Lloyd Papers and also Lieber letter #5. This is the "Lawton report."
273 Ibid.
274 National Archives, RG 109, Letters received by the Secretary of War, L-369.
275 Lloyd Papers, Enclosure 28, King to Lloyd, July 14, 1862.
276 Lloyd Papers, Enclosure 30, King to Lloyd, July 15, 1862.
277 Court of Claims Papers, Statement of Virginia Lloyd, November 15, 1872.
278 Lloyd Papers, Enclosure 13.
279 Ibid.
280 Lloyd Papers, Enclosure 21, McDaniel to Lloyd.
281 This letter is in Enclosure 31 of the Lloyd Papers and contains the envelope it came in addressed to "Mr W. Alvin Lloyd, Esq., Macon, Georgia, Care Col. Brown." It forms Enclosure 26.
282 Lloyd Papers, Enclosure 40.
283 Lloyd Papers, Enclosure 36.
284 NARA, Confederate Army Soldier Service Records, Boyd, T. S.
285 David Bright, *Confederate Railroads*.
286 Lloyd Papers, Enclosure 13.
287 Ibid.
288 Lloyd Papers, Enclosures 44–52.
289 Ibid.
290 Ibid.
291 Court of Claims Papers, T.H.S. Boyd statement, November 30 and December 7, 1872.
292 Lloyd Papers, Enclosure 13.
293 Ibid.
294 Ibid.
295 Lloyd Papers, Enclosure 32, Winder release paper. November 11, 1862.
296 Edwin C. Fishel. *The Secret War for the Union: The Untold Story of Military Intelligence in the Civil War* (Boston, New York: Houghton Mifflin Company, 1996), pp. 551–53.
297 Lloyd Papers, Enclosure 44.

298 Lloyd Papers, Enclosure 23.

299 Court of Claims Papers, T.H.S. Boyd, Deposition, November 30, 1872.

300 Ibid.

301 Mitchell, *The Rise of Cotton Mills in the South*, p. 97. Barrett, *The Civil War in North Carolina*, p. 28. Lloyd Papers, Enclosure 13.

302 Lloyd Papers, Enclosure 13. Virginia's base during the war was at Augusta, Georgia.

303 *Charleston Courier*, January 3, 1863.

304 Lloyd Papers, Enclosure 13.

305 Ibid.

306 Ibid.

307 Ibid.

308 Ibid.

309 Ibid.

310 Lloyd Papers, Enclosure 13. Helen Arthur-Cornett, *Remembering Concord, Articles from the Look Back Collection*. (History Press, 2005), p. 139.

311 Lloyd Papers, Enclosure 13.

312 Ibid.

313 *Mobile Register and Advertiser*, May 10, 1863, p. 1.

314 Wikipedia.

315 *W. Alvin Lloyd's Southern Railroad Guide*, June 1863.

316 Ibid.

317 Ibid.

318 Ibid.

319 *New York Herald*, June 2, 1863.

320 *Memphis Daily Appeal,* July 23, 1863.

321 *Richmond Daily Dispatch*, July 25, 1863.

322 Lloyd Papers, Enclosure 13. *W. Alvin Lloyd's Southern Railroad Guide*, October–November 1863. See illustrations.

323 *Daily Richmond Examiner*, September 7, 1861.

324 Lloyd Papers, Enclosure 13.

325 Ibid.

326 Lloyd Papers, Enclosure 6, is a bill by Mobile doctor E. Eustice, for $1,600 Confederate money, dated November 12, 1863. 1860 census. *Memphis Daily Appeal*, October 5, 1863. *Richmond Daily Dispatch*, October 7, 1863. *Daily Morning News* (Savannah), October 7, 1863. *Raleigh Weekly Standard*, October 14, 1863. *Camden Confederate*, October 16, 1863. *Baltimore Sun*, October 21, 1863. *Daily National Republican* (Washington, DC), October 22, 1863. Columbus, Georgia, *Enquirer*, October 7, 1863.

327 Court of Claims Papers, T.H.S. Boyd deposition, November 30 and December 7, 1872.

328 Lloyd Papers, Lieber letter #7, Enclosure 6.

329 Lloyd Papers, Enclosure 13.

330 Court of Claims Papers, T.H.S. Boyd deposition, November 30, 1872.

331 *Richmond Daily Dispatch*, January 30, 1864. *Richmond Daily Examiner*, June 6, 1864.

332 Lloyd Papers, Enclosure 6.

333 Ibid.

334 Ibid.

335 Lloyd Papers, Enclosure 13. Court of Claims Papers, Boyd deposition, December 7, 1872.

336 Lloyd Papers, Enclosure 44. Dave Bright, *Confederate Railroads*.

337 *Daily Mississippian*, June 16, 1864. Lloyd favored the newspaper with a copy of his June 1864 guide, which had been published in Atlanta at a retail price of $5.00. Confederate money. On that very day in Jackson, frying chickens were commanding $2.50 each at the market.

338 Lloyd Papers, Enclosure 44.

339 Confederate Citizens File, James A. Seddon to General D. H. Maury, July 29, 1864.

340 Lloyd Papers, Enclosure 13.

341 Court of Claims Papers, Boyd testimony, December 30, 1872.

342 *The Daily Intelligencer*, Atlanta, July 22, 1865. Confederate Army Records, J. M. Willis. Mary Walker Hubner. *Charles W. Hubner, Poet Laureate of the South* (Marietta, Georgia: Cherokee Publishing Company, 1976), p. 5.

343 *Daily Richmond Examiner*, November 22 and 24, 1864.

344 Lloyd Papers, Enclosure 13. Court of Claims Papers, Boyd testimony, 1872.

345 *Richmond Daily Dispatch*, November 25, 1864.

346 US Court of Claims Papers, Boyd Testimony, December 7, 1872.

347 Lloyd Papers, Enclosure 13.

348 This ad ran in the *Dispatch* on February 27 and 28, and again on March 1, 1865.

349 Lloyd Papers, Enclosure 13. Court of Claims Papers, Boyd testimony, December 7, 1872.

350 Robert E. Lee's 7:00 p.m. telegram to Jefferson Davis, April 2, 1865. Robert Edward Lee Papers, Virginia State Library, Richmond, Virginia. Sallie A. Brock. *Richmond During the War* (New York: G.W. Carleton & Company, 1867), p. 364.

351 Ibid. Robert E. Lee's 7:00 p.m. telegram to Jefferson Davis, April, 2, 1865. Robert Edward Lee Papers, Virginia State Library, Richmond, Virginia.

352 Brock, *Richmond*, p. 364.

353 DeLeon, Thomas C. *Four Years in Rebel Capitals* (The Gossip Printing Company, 1892). See A. A. Hoehling, and Mary Hoehling, *The Day Richmond Died* (A. S. Barnes, San Diego, California, 1981), p. 104.

354 Jane Singer. *The Confederate Dirty War: Arson, Bombings, Assassination and Plots for Chemical and Germ Attacks on the Union* (Jefferson, North Carolina: McFarland & Company, Inc., 2005), p. 119.

355 Brigadier General Edward Hastings Ripley, "Final Scenes at the Capture and Occupation of Richmond" (New York: Military Order of the Loyal Legion of the United States (MOLLUS), Vol. 111, December 5, 1906), pp. 472–502.

356 Court of Claims Papers, Boyd testimony, December 7, 1872.

357 Ibid.

358 John Stewart. *Jefferson Davis's Flight from Richmond* (Jefferson, NC: McFarland & Company, 2015).

359 Ibid.

360 C.E.L. Stuart, *New York Herald*, July 4, 1865. Stewart, *Jefferson Davis's Flight from Richmond*.

361 Lloyd Papers, Enclosure 13. 1860 Richmond, Virginia, census.

362 Stewart, *Jefferson Davis's Flight from Richmond*. Court of Claims Papers, Boyd testimony, December 7, 1872.

363 Stewart, *Jefferson Davis's Flight from Richmond*.

364 Court of Claims Papers, Boyd testimony, 1872; Stewart, *Jefferson Davis's Flight from Richmond*.

365 Ibid.

366 Edward I. Carter, a plantation owner near Danville, did indeed, while in a drunken rage, stab one of his former slaves to death, but that incident did not take place until after May 19. Carter was arrested and bound over for trial.

367 Lloyd Papers, Enclosure 13.

368 Ron Field, *Petersburg 1864–65: The Longest Siege* (Oxford, England: Osprey Publishing, 2009), pp. 22–23.

369 See Appendix for details of the pass.

370 Lloyd Papers, testimonies of W. Alvin Lloyd, T.H.S. Boyd, Virginia V. Lloyd, Ellen "Nellie" Dooley, June 3, 1865.

371 Lloyd Papers, statement of William Alvin Lloyd, June 3, 1865.

372 Lloyd Papers, testimony of T.H.S. Boyd, June 3, 1865.

373 Ibid.

374 Lloyd Papers, testimony of Virginia V. Lloyd, June 3, 1865.

375 Lloyd Papers, testimony of Ellen "Nellie" Dooley, June 3, 1865.

376 Lloyd Papers, Boyd testimony, June 13, 1865.

377 Lloyd Papers, Enclosure 35.

378 Edward Steers Jr., *Blood on the Moon: The Assassination of Abraham Lincoln* (Lexington: University Press of Kentucky, 2001), pp. 250, 260, 261.

379 Lloyd Papers, John F. May statement, Enclosure 35.

380 Lloyd Papers, Enclosure 15.

381 Ibid.

382 Lloyd Papers, Enclosure 15.

383 Lloyd Papers, Howser and Beale depositions, June 30, 1865.

384 Ibid.

385 Lloyd Papers, Hamlin and Baker statements, June 30, 1865. The *Daily National Intelligencer*, November 18, 1864.

386 Lloyd Papers, Lloyd testimony, July 15, 1865.

387 Lloyd Papers, W. A. Lloyd and Charles T. Moore testimonies, July 15, 1865.

388 Lloyd Papers, Charles T. Moore testimony, July 15, 1865.

389 Lloyd Papers, Harvey Williams testimony, July 15, 1865. There is no record anywhere at that time of a Harvey Williams.

390 Lloyd Papers, Virginia Lloyd and William Alvin Lloyd testimonies, July 18, 1865.

391 Lloyd Papers, Enclosure 17.

392 Lloyd Papers, testimony of T.H.S. Boyd, July 19, 1865.

393 Oliver Perry Temple. *Notable Men of Tennessee* (New York: The Cosmopolitan Press, 1912). See also John R. Branner's letter to Lloyd, Enclosure 42.

394 Lloyd Papers, Enclosure 42.

395 Ibid.

396 Lloyd Papers, Enclosure 42.

397 Lloyd Papers, Enclosure 14.

398 Lloyd Papers, Enclosure 14. 1850 and 1860 censuses. Confederate Citizens File, Woodall, Theodore.

399 Lloyd Papers, Enclosure 14.

400 1850 Census, Baltimore. *Baltimore Sun*, February 24, 1851. *New York Herald*, November 4, 1859, *New York Herald*, November 3, 1859.

401 *Richmond Dispatch*, March 6, 1862. *Richmond Examiner*, November 17, 1862. Confederate Citizens File, Woodall. To get an idea of what kind of man Lafayette Baker was, see the *Washington Herald* article, April 28, 1915.

402 *Baltimore Sun*, March 13, 1863, and May 29, 1863; *Richmond Examiner*, June 15, 1863; *Richmond Enquirer*, July 13, 1863.

403 Other details about Theodore Woodall can be found in Civil War Subversion Investigations, Union Citizens File (NARA) and Confederate Citizens File.

404 Leonard, *Lincoln's Forgotten Ally*, p. 224.

405 Lloyd Papers, Enclosure 10.

406 Ibid.

407 Confederate Citizen's File.

408 Lloyd Papers, Enclosure 9.

409 Ibid.

410 *Boston Daily Advertiser*, June 17 and 26, 1865. *Daily Cleveland Herald*, July 1, 1865. See also, Leonard, *Lincoln's Forgotten Ally* for a full and comprehensive analysis of the Conover/Holt association. As well see Carman Cumming, *Devil's Game: The Civil War Intrigues of Charles A. Dunham* (Urbana and Chicago: University of Illinois Press, 2004).

411 Lloyd Papers. Court of Claims Papers, 1872.

412 "The High Cost of Civil War," Barrons.com: John Steele Gordon.

413 How is it that Totten didn't know how much Alvin actually received in October 1865? When Totten reopened the case in 1871, it is evident from his accounting that he didn't know. What's ironic is that the War Department didn't know either. It was just one of those things that fell through the cracks. Lloyd even cheated his own lawyer.

414 *Evening Union* (Washington, DC), October 10, 1865.

415 Anthony Waskie. *Philadelphia and the Civil War: Arsenal of the Union* (Charleston: The History Press, 2011). *Civil War News*, 2007.

416 *Baltimore Sun*, February 1 and February 17, 1866.

417 *Illustrated New Age*, February 27, 1866.

418 *North American and United States Gazette* (Philadelphia), March 20 and April 3, 1866. *Public Ledger* (Philadelphia), March 20, 1866.

419 *Jackson Citizen and Patriot* (Michigan), July 25, 1867.

420 *North American and United States Gazette* (Philadelphia), April 3, 1866. *Public Ledger*, April 3, 1866, *Philadelphia Inquirer*, April 3, 1866, *Daily Evening Telegraph*, Philadelphia, April 3, 1866.

421 Bradley R. Hoch, "Looking for Lincoln's Philadelphia: A Personal Journey from Washington Square to Independence Hall," *Journal of the Abraham Lincoln Association*, Vol. 25, Issue 2, Summer, 2004.

422 Confederate Citizens File. Charles T. Harvey to E. M. Stanton, May 15, 1866.

423 *Illustrated New Age* (Philadelphia), June 13, 1866.

424 *North American and United States Gazette* (Philadelphia), June 14, 1866.

425 *Daily Cleveland Herald,* February 5, 1867.

426 *Springfield Republican* (Springfield, Massachusetts), February 4, 1867.

427 *Springfield Republican,* February 2, 1867. Rice, *Monarchs of Minstrelsy.* Slout, *Burnt Cork and Tambourines.*

428 1850 Louisville census. Rice, *Monarchs of Minstrelsy.* Slout, *Burnt Cork and Tambourines.*

429 It is of record that Virginia was traveling with Alvin because there was a letter waiting for her advertised in the *Jackson Citizen Patriot* of July 17, 1867. The newspapers of the time would have letters waiting if someone had forwarded the information that they would be arriving in that city.

430 *Springfield Republican,* February 2, 4, 6, 7, and 8, 1867.

431 Ibid.

432 Ibid.

433 Ibid.

434 *Albany Evening Journal,* February 8 and 9, 1867. *Oswego Palladium,* February 22, 1867.

435 *Sandusky Register,* March 18 and 23, 1867.

436 *Cincinnati Daily Gazette,* April 1, 2, 3, 4, 5, and 6, 1867; *Cincinnati Daily Enquirer,* April 2, 5, and 6, 1867.

437 Ibid.

438 *Cincinnati Daily Enquirer,* April 6 and 10, 1867; *Cincinnati Daily Gazette,* April 6 and 10, 1867; *Cleveland Leader,* April 19, 1867.

439 *Cincinnati Daily Enquirer,* April 11, 1867.

440 Ibid.

441 Ibid.

442 *Zanesville Signal* review, reproduced in the *Cleveland Plain Dealer* of April 15, 1867. *Newark Advocate,* April 12, 1867. For their performance in Cleveland, see the *Daily Cleveland Herald,* April 12 and 15, 1867. *Cleveland Plain Dealer,* April 12 and 15, 1867. *Buffalo Courier & Republic,* April 25 and 26, 1867. *Syracuse Courier & Union,* May 8, 1867. *Albany Express,* May 11, 1867. *Albany Knickerbocker,* May 11, 1867. *New York Clipper,* May 1867. *Springfield Republican,* May 11, 13, 14, and 15, 1867. *Daily Hartford Courant,* May 17, 1867.

443 *New York Clipper,* June 19, 1867. *Syracuse Courier & Union,* June 29, 1867. *Springfield Republican,* July 1, 1867. *Albany Evening Journal,* July 5, 1867.

444 *Daily Cleveland Herald,* July 8, 9, and 10, 1867. *Jackson Citizen Patriot,* July 16, 17, 18, 19, and 24, 1867.

445 *Jackson Citizen Patriot,* July 25, 1867. *Albany Evening Journal,* July 29, 1867. *Cincinnati Daily Enquirer,* July 29, 1867. *Toledo Commercial* article, reproduced in the *Fort Wayne Daily Gazette* of August 12, 1867.

446 *Lockport Daily Journal,* August 2, 1867.

447 *Jackson Citizen Patriot,* July 25, 1867, *Cincinnati Daily Enquirer,* July 30, 1867.

448 *Louisville Daily Democrat,* October 23, 1867. *Syracuse Daily Courier,* October 24, 1867.

449 Ibid.

450 Ibid.

451 Rice, *Monarchs of Minstrelsy.* Slout, *Burnt Cork and Tambourines.*

452 *New York Evening Post,* September 15, 1868.

453 New York immigration records, December 26, 1868, passenger manifest of the ship *Australasian.*

454 *Cincinnati Daily Gazette,* January 6 and 7, 1869.

455 Lloyd Papers, Cameron to Hardie, December 8, 1868.

456 Lloyd Papers, E. D. Townsend to Hardie, December 11, 1865.

457 Ibid.

458 Lloyd Papers, Virginia Lloyd to Secretary Schofield, February 18, 1867.

459 William Alvin Lloyd, Certificate of Death #4861: New York Department of Records and Information Services, Municipal Archives, 31 Chambers Street, New York City.

460 Lloyd Papers, Davies to Sackett, March 20, 1869.

461 Lloyd Papers, Sackett letter to Gibson, April 22, 1869.

462 Lloyd Papers, Virginia Lloyd to Gen. Rawlins, April 27, 1869.

463 Lloyd Papers, James A. Hardie summary, May 4, 1869.

464 *Albany Evening Journal,* June 9, 1869.

465 1870 census. 1869 and 1870 Baltimore city directories.

466 Lloyd Papers, depositions of Abner Y. Lakenan, Virginia Lloyd, C. C. Boyd, September 6, 1870.

467 Lloyd Papers, Secretary Belknap to Virginia Lloyd, March 18, 1871. 1870 census.

468 Lloyd Papers, *Enoch Totten, Administrator of the Estate of William A. Lloyd, deceased vs. The United States.* May 22, 1871. No. 6329.

469 Lloyd Papers, Totten statement.

470 Lloyd Papers, Dunn to Parsons, November 9, 1871.

471 *Critic-Record* (Washington, DC), March 13, 1872.

472 Court of Claims Papers, testimony of Marcellus Howser, October 14, 1872.

473 Court of Claims Papers, Totten request, October 25, 1872.

474 Court of Claims Papers, testimony of Joseph Bonfanti, November 15, 1872.

475 *The Michigan Alumnus,* Fall IV, 1897–98 (Ann Arbor, Michigan: Michigan Alumnus Publishing Association, November 1897), p. 177.

476 New York City Census, 1860. F. J. Bonfanti.

477 Court of Claims Papers, 1872. Bonfanti's deposition, November 15, 1872. New York Immigration records. US passport applications, Bonfanti. *Newark Daily Advertiser,* January 24, 1849. *New Orleans Times-Picayune,* July 24, 1849. *Boston Herald,* September 5, 1849. *Weekly Herald* (New York), December 1, 1849. *Liverpool Mercury,* December 14, 1849. *Morning Chronicle* (London), March 17, 1854. *New Orleans Times-Picayune,* May 10, 1854, and May 26 to August 6, 1861. Confederate Army Service Records, Bonfanti. Confederate Citizens File, Bonfanti.

478 Court of Claims Papers, 1872.

479 Ibid.

480 Ibid.

481 Ibid.

482 Confederate Army Records, T.H.S. Boyd. Lloyd Papers. US Court of Claims, 1872.

483 Court of Claims Papers, November 15, 1872.

484 Ibid.

485 Ibid.

486 Ibid.

487 Ibid.

488 Ibid.

489 Ibid.

490 Ibid.

491 Ibid.

492 Ibid.

493 Lloyd Papers, Howser testimony, June 30, 1865.

494 Court of Claims Papers, Howser testimony, October 14, 1872.

495 Court of Claims Papers, November 15, 1872.

496 Ibid.

497 Lloyd Papers, Enclosure 20.

498 Court of Claims Papers, T.H.S. Boyd's deposition, November 30 and December 7, 1872.

499 See Appendix for an analysis of the pass and the proof of its authenticity.

500 Court of Claims Papers, Testimony of Virginia Lloyd, November 15, 1872.

501 Court of Claims Papers, Charles Boyd statement, November 30, 1872.

502 Lloyd Papers, W. Alvin Lloyd testimony, June 3, 1865.

503 Lloyd Papers. Court of Claims Papers, testimony of Virginia Lloyd, November 15, 1872.

504 Court of Claims Papers, Bonfanti testimony, November 15, 1872.

505 Ibid.

506 Lloyd Papers, Enclosure 13.

507 Court of Claims Papers, 1872.

508 *Richmond Daily Dispatch*, July 25, 1863.

509 Court of Claims Papers, Bonfanti testimony. November 15, 1872.

510 Court of Claims Papers, Boyd testimony.

511 Court of Claims Papers. When asked why Nellie Dooley did not appear at the deposition, Virginia said she thought Nellie was dead.

512 Court of Claims Papers, Boyd testimony, December 7, 1872.

513 Lloyd Papers, Nellie Dooley testimony, June 3, 1865.

514 Lloyd Papers, Boyd testimony, June 3, 1865.

515 Lloyd Papers, W. Alvin Lloyd testimony, July 16, 1865.

516 Ibid.

517 Court of Claims Papers, Boyd testimony, November 30, 1872.

518 Lloyd Papers, Boyd testimony, June 3, 1865.

519 Court of Claims Papers, Virginia Lloyd testimony, November 15, 1872.

520 Court of Claims Papers, Charles Boyd testimony, November 30, 1872.

521 Court of Claims Papers, Bonfanti testimony, November 15, 1872.

522 Court of Claims Papers, Boyd testimony, December 7, 1872.

523 Ibid.

524 Ibid.

525 Court of Claims Papers, John Goforth, Brief for the Defendants.

526 Court of Claims Papers, Totten Petition, 1873 and 1874.

527 *Totten v. US*, 92 US 105 (1875).

528 At the time, the Totten ruling was barely mentioned in the press, but two papers that reported it were the *National Republican* (Washington, DC), March 16, 1876, and the *New Orleans Times-Picayune* of May 26, 1876.

529 New York City directories, 1876, 1877, 1878.

530 Philadelphia city directories, 1876 and 1877.

531 *Critic-Record* (Washington, DC), October 31, 1877.

532 *Critic-Record*, December 7 and 12, 1877.

533 Wikipedia; Sean C. Flynn, "The Totten Doctrine and its Poisoned Progeny," *Vermont Law Review*, 2001; D. A. Jeremy Telman, Valparaiso University Law School, December 19, 2012. Valparasio University Legal Studies Research Paper NP. 12–18. "On the Conflation of the State Secrets Privilege and the Totten Doctrine."

534 D. A. Jeremy Telman, Valparaiso University Law School, December 19, 2012. Valparasio University Legal Studies Research. "On the Conflation of the State Secrets Privilege and the Totten Doctrine."

535 Douglas Kash and Matthew Indrisano. "In the Service of Secrets: The US Supreme Court Revisits Totten," *John Marshall Law Review*, Vol. 39, Issue 2, 2006; See also, *Tenet et al, v. Doe et ux.*, No. 03-1395. "Argued January 11, 2005–Decided March 2, 2005." http://caselaw.lp.findlaw.com; Frederick G. Jauss, IV, Abstract of article by Daniel L. Pines, "The Continuing Viability of the 1875 Supreme Court Case of *Totten v. United States*," 53 *Admin. Law. Rev.* 1273.

536 Whitebread, *Recent Decisions*, p. 210. Johnson, *Handbook of Intelligence Studies*, p. 337. *Tenet v. Doe*: http://Law.cornell.edu/supet/cert/03-1395. On January 22, 2008, Senators Edward M. Kennedy, Patrick Leahy, and Arlen Specter introduced a bill (S.2533) called The State Secrets Protection Act. It was not passed. On February 11, 2009, "granting the courts of appeal jurisdiction of an appeal from a decision or order of a district court determining that the state secrets privilege is not validly asserted," was offered as a bill to the Committee on the Judiciary in an attempt to limit the over-reaching use of the state secrets privilege. See H.R. 984, State Secret Protection Act of 2009, govtrack.us/blog/2014/5/12/govtracks-winter-updates. On January 27, 2014, another version was introduced and referred to the "Subcommittee on Crime, Terrorism, Homeland Security, and Investigations." There it rests.

537 *New York Herald*, April 16, 1878, November 5, 1885, January 19 and 20, 1886; *South Orange Bulletin*, January 23, 1886; *New Haven Register*, September 14, 1887. New York marriages, 1888. *Baltimore Sun*, August 12 and 13, 1911. Baltimore Wills, Liber H.W.J., No. 111, Folio 5.

538 1880 census for Mount Hope, Baltimore. *Brooklyn Daily Eagle*, July 10, 1880.

539 New Jersey marriage records, Newark. *Macon Telegraph*, May 29, 1883. *New York Herald*, August 1, 1883. *New York Daily Tribune*, October 2, 1889. *Times-Enterprise* (Thomasville, Ga.), September 24, 1889.

540 Baltimore City Directory, 1879. 1880 census.

541 The Maryland Line Confederate Soldiers' Home records. 1900 census. *Baltimore Sun*, December 13, 1907.

542 Court of Claims Papers, Virginia Lloyd's depositions, 1872, 1900, and 1910 censuses. Providence city directories, 1880–1917. Providence death records.

543 New York immigration records. British birth, marriage, and death records, 1876.

544 1880 census. US Marine Corps records.

545 *Baltimore Sun*, December 4, 1880.

546 1870 and 1880 censuses. Baltimore death records.

547 Baltimore death records: Baker, Asbury.

548 1870 and 1880 censuses. *San Diego Union*, November 15, 1881. *Baltimore Sun*, June 9, 1914.

549 *Milwaukee Journal*, November 12 and 15, 1878.

550 *The Michigan Alumunus,* Volume 1v, 1886–1898, Ann Arbor, Michigan: Michigan Alumunus Pub Assoc., November 1897, p. 177.

551 *Evening Star* (Washington, DC), May 15, 1878. *Galveston Daily News,* May 23, 1878, *Frank Leslie's Illustrated Newspaper*, June 8, 1878.

552 *The Clarion* (Jackson, Mississippi), June 14, 1887.

553 A. J. Hanna, *Flight Into Oblivion* (Richmond: Johnson Publishing Company, 1938; second edition: Baton Rouge: Louisiana State University Press, 1999), pp. 100, 102.

554 *Roanoake Times*, April 3, 1891. *The Sun* (New York), April 3, 1891.

555 *Memphis Daily Appeal*, February 15, 1869.

556 Klinck, Confederate Citizens File.

557 *New York Tribune*, January 24, 1870, *Augusta Chronicle,* August 28, 1914. *Macon Telegraph*, August 28, 1914.

558 *Critic-Record* (Washington, DC), May 2, 1891.

559 *Daily Cleveland Herald*, August 6, 1867. *Cleveland Plain Dealer*, September 18, 1867. *Inter-Ocean* (Chicago), April 15, 1875. *Daily Inter-Ocean,* (Chicago), November 11, 1889. *St. Paul Daily News*, April 25, 1891. Rice, *Monarchs of Minstrelsy*, p. 76.

560 *Indianapolis Sentinel*, April 22, 23, and 24, 1874. Rice, *Monarchs of Minstrelsy*, p. 74.

561 Eastern Cemetery, Dailey Lot, Record book, No. 99: 155.

562 Louisville death records. Clark County, Indiana, marriage records, October 25, 1868.

563 Louisville death records. Cave Hill Cemetery (Louisville).

564 *Syracuse Daily Standard*, March 14, 1887. *Boston Daily Advertiser*, July 27, 1889. *Baltimore Sun*, February 5, 1891.

Sources

National Archives, Washington, DC (NARA)

The Lloyd Papers relating to the claim Lloyd and his heirs made against the US War Department between 1865 and 1871, before the case was referred to the US Court of Claims, are invaluable primary sources. These papers consist of evidence from 1865 and comprise sixty-six enclosures as well as post-1865 letters and documents. There are two parts to the Lloyd Papers. The first is the 1865 claim and the second are those documents relating to the claim made by Virginia Lloyd after her husband's death in 1869. File 640-L-1865. (National Archives Microfilm Publication M619 Record Group 94. "Letters Received by the Office of the Adjutant General," Main Series, 1861–1870, during and after the Civil War period. M619, Roll 375); Letters Received (Main Series); Record Group 94, Records of the Adjutant General's Office. 1870s–1917; National Archives Building, Washington, DC.

In addition to the Lloyd Papers, "The Confederate Citizens File: Papers Relating to Citizens or Businesses Firms, 1861–1870, Record Group (RG) 94," is an important resource consisting of letters to and from Lloyd to prominent individuals, prison correspondence, bills of sale, etc.

As well we have quoted extensively from the "Records of the United States Court of Claims, Selected Documents From General Jurisdiction Case NO. 6329, Record Group (RG) 123. William A. Lloyd Case. 1871–1873."

Supreme Court

The Supreme Court Cases, *Totten vs. the US*, 92, US 105 (1875), and *Tenet et al. v. Doe et ux.* (2005), are critical to the understanding of the fate of Lloyd's claim and its continuing impact on the rights of clandestine operatives.

Bibliography: Part One

Lloyd and his claim appear in various books and articles. All are derivative of the original myth of Lloyd-as-Lincoln's spy. They are as follows, arranged chronologically:

1957. Francis E. Rourke, "Secrecy in American Bureaucracy," *Political Science Quarterly*, vol. 72: Academy of Political Science. Rourke writes that *Totten* was engaged by Lincoln to spy for him.

1963. Allen W. Dulles, *The Craft of Intelligence* (New York: Evanston & London: Harper & Row, Publishers, 1963). In 1965, Globe Pequot Press reprinted/reissued *The Craft of Intelligence*. In this work, Dulles revisits the history of the claim, Lloyd's duties as Lincoln's spy, and the Supreme Court case as he understood it, but never questioned the veracity of the actual claim. Reprint of Allen W. Dulles: *The Craft of Intelligence: America's Legendary Spy Master on the Fundamentals of Intelligence Gathering for a Free World.* (Guilford, Connecticut, Lyons Press; 1st edition paperback.) (April 1, 2006) Paperback reprint.

1974. The *Civil War Times Illustrated*, vol. 13, 1974, advertised an upcoming article, or possibly book, by John Bakeless, called "Lincoln's Conspicuous Spy."

1975. John Bakeless's article, "Lincoln's Private Eye" came out in the *Civil War Times Illustrated*, vol. 14. Until now (2014), this has been the seminal work on Lloyd.

1989. Nathan Miller, *Spying for America: The Hidden History of US Intelligence* (St. Paul, Minnesota, Paragon House, 1989). This work does not offer any new insights and there is nothing about Lloyd himself.

1991. Patricia L. Faust, *Historical Times Illustrated Encyclopedia of the Civil War* (New York: Harper Perennial, 1991). (First published by Harper & Row, 1966.) There is only one sentence on Lloyd and author Faust mentions "Thomas Boyd" in that same sentence.

1992. Alan Axelrod, *The War between the Spies: A History of Espionage During the Civil War* (New York: The Atlantic Monthly Press, 1992). Chapter two is called "The Reluctant Spy," and deals with William Alvin Lloyd. Clearly inspired by John Bakeless's 1975 article, "Lincoln's Private Eye," at least the parts that concern Lloyd. It appears that Axelrod went nowhere else but to the Bakeless article for his information. The first words of the article are, "He was a perfectly ordinary man." Then come eight pages of non-Lloyd material, in a chapter that is eighteen pages long. Mr. Axelrod reintroduces Lloyd with "he was a highly respected businessman." He then goes on to say, "His was a perfectly ordinary business." In contrast to Axelrod's assertion that "none of Lloyd's documents or notes survives," in fact, they have been retrieved, analyzed, and are published in *Lincoln's Secret Spy*.

1996. Christopher Andrew. *For the President's Eyes Only: Secret Intelligence and the American Presidency from Washington to Bush* (New York, Toronto, and Sydney: Harper Perennial, 1996). This book about presidential intelligence portrays Lloyd as a bumbling agent, who did little to help the Union effort. Donald E. Markle portrays him more positively, saying that "despite Lloyd's habit of getting arrested, he managed to provide a few useful reports. Lincoln paid Lloyd's expenses, but never his $9753 salary. After Lincoln was assassinated and Lloyd died, Enoch Totten, the head of the spy's estate, sued the federal government to claim the salary."

1996. Stephen F. Knott. *Secret and Sanctioned: Covert Operations and the American Presidency* (USA: Oxford University Press, 1996).

1998. C. Brian Kelly. *Best Little Stories from the Civil War* (Nashville, Tennessee: Cumberland House, 2nd ed., 1998).

2000. Donald E. Markle. *Spies and Spymasters of the Civil War*. (New York: Hippocrene Books, 2000).

2000. John J. Carter. *Covert Operations as a Tool of Presidential Foreign Policy in American History from 1800 to 1920* (Lampeter (Wales), London, and Lewiston, NY: Edwin Mellen Press, 2000).

2000. Gail Stewart. *Weapons of War* (Farmington Hills, Michigan, Lucent Books, 2000). A mere mention of Lloyd, but nothing new.

2001. David D. Ryan, ed. *Yankee Spy in Richmond* (Mechanicsburg, Pennsylvania: Stackpole Books, 2001). This book purports to be the Civil War diary of Elizabeth Van Lew. In the preface Mr. Ryan has quoted John Blakeless [*sic*] on William Alvan Lloyd [*sic*] as an example of a "quote" Union Spy in the South. p. 2.

April 22, 2001. Gene Johnson, the *Columbian* (Vancouver, Washington), wrote an article on John Doe, the diplomat, and cited the Lloyd case.

June 29, 2004. Walter Pincus, in an article in the *Washington Post*, refers to the Lloyd case but again, repeats that Lloyd was Lincoln's spy.

January 10, 2005. William Adair wrote in the *St. Petersburg Times* (Florida), about John Doe, the contemporaneous diplomat. "President Lincoln secretly enlisted William A. Lloyd to spy on the Confederacy. Lloyd had the makings of a great secret agent. He had a good cover story—he wrote guidebooks about railroads—and had to travel through the South to conduct his research. Lincoln promised him $200 a month plus expenses, according to *Spies and Spymasters of the Civil War*, by Donald E. Markle. In his contract, Lloyd agreed to report on Confederate troops and any plans for 'forts and other battle structures' [a quote invented by Mr. Markle, rather than one from the nineteenth century]. He was to report only to Lincoln. Lloyd apparently was not very good at espionage. He was imprisoned at least twice because of suspicions he was a spy, and, at one point, carried his secret contract in his hat [an anecdote from C. Brian Kelly's book]."

January 12, 2005. Alan Freeman mentioned the Lloyd case in the *Globe and Mail* (Toronto).

March 3, 2005. David Stout (of the *New York Times* News Service) had an article in the *Deseret News* (Salt Lake City) that mentioned the Lloyd case.

2005. Loch K. Johnson. *Handbook of Intelligence Studies* (e-book). By the following year Routledge Press (Abingdon, Oxford, UK, 2006), published a trade edition. This book mentions the Lloyd case while talking about the 2005 John Doe case, and the writer remains justly skeptical.

2005. Kenneth J. McCulloch and James O. Castagnera. *Termination of Employment: Employer and Employee Rights* (West Group, 2005, and Prentice Hall, 2007). "*Totten vs United States*, 92 US 105 (1875) is an 1875 decision in which the Supreme Court said that a Civil War spy named William A. Lloyd could not pursue his claim that President Abraham Lincoln had contracted with him to spy behind the Confederate lines for $200 a month. Lloyd's estate sued the federal government, claiming that only the spy's expenses had ever been covered. The Totten Doctrine holds that those who spy for America cannot later sue over broken promises, because (in the words of the Ninth Circuit dissenters) 'that would require exposure of matters that must be kept secret in the interest of effective,' etc, etc."

2007. *Symposium.* James E. Beasley School of Law.

2007. P. J. Huff and J. G. Lewin. *How to Tell a Secret: Tips, Tricks, and Techniques for Breaking Codes* (Harper Paperback, 2005).

2007. James E. Baker. *In the Common Defense* (New York: Cambridge University Press, 2007).

2009. Floyd Paseman. *A Spy's Journey: A CIA Memoir* (Minneapolis, Minnesota: Zenith Press, 2009). Paperback reissue edition of 2005 and November 8, 2009.

2011. Glenn P. Hastedt, ed. *Spies, Wiretaps, and Secret Operations* (Westport, Connecticut: Greenwood Publishing Group, 2011).

2013. Howard Brinkley, *Spy* (Create Space Independent Publisher, 2013).

BIBLIOGRAPHY: PART TWO

American Jewish History, vol. 91, issues 3-4. Baltimore: Johns Hopkins University Press for the American Jewish Historical Society, 2005.

Arthur-Cornett, Helen. *Remembering Concord. Articles from the* Look Back *Collection.* Charleston, South Carolina: The History Press, 2005.

Atwater, Caleb. *Writings of Caleb Atwater.* Columbus, Ohio (published by the author, 1833), and Bedford, Massachusetts: Applewood Books, (reprint), 2007.

Barrett, John G. *The Civil War in North Carolina.* Chapel Hill: University of North Carolina Press, 1963.

Billings, John Shaw. "A Report on Barracks and Hospitals: With Descriptions of Military Posts." Washington, DC: Government Printing Office, 1870.

The Biographical Dictionary and Portrait Gallery of Representative Men of Chicago, Milwaukee and the World's Columbian Exposition. Chicago and New York: American Biographical Publishing Company, 1892.

Blakey, Arch Frederic. *General John H. Winder, C.S.A.* Gainesville: University of Florida Press, 1990.

Brock, Sallie A., *Richmond During the War.* New York: Carleton & Company, 1867.

Brown, T. Allston. "Early History of Negro Minstrelsy: Its Rise and Progress in the United States." This was a long-running series in the *New York Clipper*, beginning on February 24, 1912, and running through to the end of 1913. A general background on Alvin Lloyd is in the January 11, 1913, issue, on page 1, while another version of the 1867 incarnation of Lloyd's Minstrels is in the December 6, 1913, issue, page 15.

Brown, T. Allston *History of the New York Stage.* Vol. 1, New York: Dodd, Mead & Co. 1903.

Bulloch, Joseph Gaston Baillie. *A History and Genealogy of the Habersham Family*. Columbia, South Carolina: The R.L. Bryan Co., 1901.

Burlingame, Michael, ed., *Dispatches from the Lincoln White House: The Anonymous Civil War Journalism of Presidential Secretary William O. Stoddard*. Lincoln: University of Nebraska Press, 2002.

Christensen, Lawrence O., Foley, William E., Kremer, Gary R., and Winn, Kenneth H. *Dictionary of Missouri Biography*. Columbia: University of Missouri, 1999.

Cumming, Carman. *Devil's Game: The Civil War Intrigues of Charles A. Dunham*. Urbana and Chicago: University of Illinois Press, 2004.

DeLeon, Thomas C. *Four Years in Rebel Capitals*. The Gossip Printing Company, 1892.

Dickens, Charles, *The Works of Charles Dickens*. Harper and Brothers Publishing, 1877.

Dix, Morgan. *Memoirs of John Adams Dix: Compiled by his Son,* vol. 11. New York: Harper & Brothers, 1883.

Documents of the Assembly of the State of New York. Eighty-Ninth Session, 1866. Vol. 4. Nos. 61-85. Albany, New York: G. Wendell, Legislative Printer, 1866.

Emerson, Ken. *Doo-dah! Stephen Foster and the Rise of American Popular Culture*. New York: Simon & Schuster, 1997.

Field, Ron. *Petersburg 1864–65: The Longest Siege*. Oxford, England: Osprey Publishing, 2009.

Fishel, Edwin C. *The Secret War for the Union: The Untold Story of Military Intelligence in the Civil War*. Boston: Houghton Mifflin Company, 1996.

Fraser, Walter, Jr. *Savannah in the Old South*. Athens: University of Georgia Press, 2003.

Gagnon, Michael J. *Transition to an Industrial South; Athens, Georgia, 1830–1870*. Baton Rouge: Louisiana State University Press, 1992.

Grant, Ulysses S. *Personal Memoirs of US Grant*, Volume Two, Chapter LXX. New York: Charles L. Webster & Company, 1885–86.

Hanna, A. J. *Flight Into Oblivion*. Richmond, VA: Johnson Publishing Company, 1938, and Baton Rouge: Louisiana State University Press, 1999.

Hartley, Chris J. *Stoneman's Raid, 1865*. Winston Salem, NC: John F. Blair, Publisher, 2010.

Hoehling, A. A. and Hoehling, Mary. *The Day Richmond Died*. San Diego, CA: A. S. Barnes, 1981.

Hyde, William and Conard, Howard L. *Encyclopedia of the History of St. Louis,* vol. 3. New York, Louisville, St. Louis: The Southern History Company, 1899.

Jasen, David A. and Jones, Gene. *Spreadin' Rhythm Around: Black Popular Songwriters, 1880–1930*. New York: Routledge, Taylor and Francis, 2004.

Johnson, Loch K. (ed.). *Handbook of Intelligence Studies*. Abingdon (Oxfordshire) and New York, 2007.

Johnson, Susan B. *Savannah's Little Crooked Houses: If These Walls Could Talk*. Charleston, South Carolina: The History Press, 2007.

Jones, Jacqueline. *Saving Savannah: The City and the Civil War*. New York: Alfred A. Knopf, 2008.

Keever, Homer M. *Iredell, Piedmont County*. Iredell County Bicentennial Commission, 1976.

Kleber, John, editor. *The Encyclopedia of Louisville*. Lexington: The University Press of Kentucky, 2001.

Kolin, Philip C. *Shakespeare in the South: Essays on Performance*. Jackson: University Press of Mississippi, 1983.

Konkle, Burton Alva. *John Motley Morehead and the Development of North Carolina, 1796–1866*. Philadelphia: William J. Campbell, 1922.

Leonard, Elizabeth D. *Lincoln's Avengers: Justice, Revenge and Reunion after the Civil War*. New York, London: W.W. Norton & Company, 2004.

Leonard, Elizabeth D. *Lincoln's Forgotten Ally: Judge Joseph Holt of Kentucky*. Chapel Hill: The University of North Carolina Press, 2011.

Mackay, James. *Allan Pinkerton: The Eye Who Never Slept*. Edinburgh & London: Mainstream Publishing, 1996.

Martin, Samuel J. *General Braxton Bragg, C.S.A.* Jefferson, North Carolina: McFarland & Company, Inc., 2011.

Mahar, William J. *Behind the Burnt Cork Mask: Early Blackface Minstrelsy and Antebellum American Popular Culture*. Champaign: University of Illinois Press, 1999.

McFeely, William S. *Grant, A Biography*. New York, London: W.W. Norton & Company, 1982.

McKenzie, Robert Tracy. *Lincolnites and Rebels: A Divided Town in the American Civil War*. Oxford University Press, 2006.

McTyre, Joe and Paden, Rebecca Nash. *Historic Roswell, Georgia*. Charleston, South Carolina: Arcadia Publishing, 2001.

Miller, Nathan. *Spying For America*. St. Paul, Minnesota: Paragon House, 1989.

Mitchell, Broadus. *The Rise of Cotton Mills in the South*. Baltimore: Johns Hopkins Press, 1921.

Olmstead, Charles H. "Savannah in the '40s." *Georgia Historical Quarterly*, vol. 1, March 1917. Savannah, Georgia.

Osborne, William. *Music in Ohio*. Kent, Ohio: Kent State University Press, 2005.

Powell, William S., ed. *Dictionary of North Carolina Biography*. Chapel Hill: University of North Carolina Press, 1991.

Proceedings of the Grand Lodge of Free and Accepted Masons of the District of Columbia for the Year 1871. Washington, DC: Republican Job Office Print, 1872.

Recko, Corey. *A Spy For The Union: The Life and Execution of Timothy Webster*. Jefferson, North Carolina, and London: McFarland & Company, Inc., 2013.

Reinders, Robert. *End of an Era: New Orleans, 1850–1860*. Gretna, Louisiana: Pelican Publishing Company, 1994.

Rice, Edward Le Roy. *Monarchs of Minstrelsy, From Daddy Rice to Date*. New York: Kenny Publishing Company, 1911.

Ripley, Edward Hastings. *Final Scenes at the Capture and Occupation of Richmond*. New York: Military Order of the Loyal Legion of the United States (MOLLUS), vol.3, December 5, 1906, pp. 472–502. See also, *Vermont General: The Unusual War Experiences of General Edward Hastings Ripley*, ed. Otto Eisenschiml: Devon Adair Press, 1904.

Scharf, J. Thomas. *History of Western Maryland*. Philadelphia: Louis H. Everts, 1882.

Seward, Frederick William. *Seward at Washington as Senator and Secretary of State: A Memoir of His Life, with selections from his letters, 1861–1872.* New York: Derby and Miller, 149 Church Street, 1891.

Singer, Jane. *The Confederate Dirty War: Arson, Bombings, Assassination and Plots for Chemical and Germ Attacks on the Union.* Jefferson, North Carolina, and London: McFarland & Company, Inc., 2005.

Slout, William L. *Burnt Cork and Tambourines: A Source Book of Negro Minstrelsy.* San Bernardino, California: Borgo Press, 1995.

Steers, Edward, Jr. *Blood on the Moon: The Assassination of Abraham Lincoln.* Lexington: University Press of Kentucky, 2001.

Stevens, Walter Barlow. *St. Louis, the Fourth City, 1764-1909.* vol. 1. St. Louis/Chicago: The S. J. Clark Publishing Company, 1911.

Stewart, John. *Jefferson Davis's Flight From Richmond.* Jefferson, North Carolina: McFarland & Company, Inc., 2015.

Strong, George Templeton. *The Diary of George Templeton Strong (The Civil War 1860–1865).* New York: The Macmillan Company, 1952.

Temple, Oliver Perry. *Notable Men of Tennessee, from 1833 to 1875.* New York: Cosmopolitan Press, 1912.

Thomas, Frances Taliaferro. *A Portrait of Historic Athens & Clarke County.* Athens: University of Georgia Press, 1992.

Walker, Mary Hubner. *Charles W. Hubner: Poet Laureate of the South.* Atlanta, Georgia: Cherokee Publishing Company, 1976.

Whitebread, Charles H., ed. "Recent Decisions, United States Supreme Court." American Academy of Judicial Education, 2004.

Wilmer, Lambert. *Our Press Gang, or a Complete Exposition of the Corruptions and Crimes of the American Newspapers.* "The Case of James T. Lloyd." Philadelphia: J. T. Lloyd. London: Sampson Low, Son & Co., 1859.

Wilson, Adelaide. *Historic and Picturesque Savannah.* Boston, Massachusetts: Boston Photogravure Co., 1889.

NEWSPAPERS

Our study of Lloyd and those associated with him was enhanced immeasurably by the following newspapers:

Alabama
Mobile Register

Arkansas
Daily Arkansas Gazette

California
Daily Alta

Daily Democratic State Journal
Los Angeles Herald
Sacramento Daily Union
San Diego Union
San Francisco Abend-Post
San Francisco Bulletin
San Francisco Chronicle

Colorado
Rocky Mountain News

Connecticut
Daily Hartford Courant
New Haven Daily Palladium
New Haven Register

District of Columbia
Critic-Record
Daily Evening Star
Daily Globe
Daily National Intelligencer
Daily National Republican
Daily Union
Evening Times
Morning Times
Washington Post

Florida
St. Petersburg Times

Georgia
Augusta Chronicle
Atlanta Daily Intelligencer
Augusta Daily Constitutionalist
Macon Telegraph
Savannah Daily Morning News
Savannah Daily News and Herald
Savannah Daily Register
Thomasville Times-Enterprise

Idaho
Owhyee Avalanche

Illinois
Chicago Tribune
Daily Inter Ocean
Rockford Weekly Gazette

Indiana
Fort Wayne Daily Gazette
Indianapolis Sentinel
New Albany Daily Ledger

Kansas
Freedom's Champion

Kentucky
Kentucky Tribune
Louisville Daily Courier
Louisville Daily Democrat
Louisville Daily Journal
Maysville Tri-Weekly Eagle
Weekly Courier

Louisiana
New Orleans Daily Crescent
New Orleans Daily True Delta
New Orleans Sunday Delta
New Orleans Times-Picayune

Maryland
Baltimore Sun
Easton Gazette

Massachusetts
Boston Daily Advertiser
Boston Daily Atlas
Boston Herald
Boston Investigator
Boston Journal
The Congregationalist
The Liberator
Springfield Republican

Michigan
Detroit Free Press
Jackson Citizen and Patriot

Minnesota
St. Paul Daily Globe

Mississippi
The Clarion
Jackson Daily News
Mississippi Free Trader and Natchez Gazette
The Mississippian
Natchez Courier

Missouri
Daily Missouri Republican
St. Louis Democrat
St. Louis Globe-Democrat
St. Louis Herald
St. Louis Republic
St. Louis Reveille
Tri-Weekly Missouri Republican

Nebraska
Omaha Bee

New Hampshire
New Hampshire Patriot and State Gazette

New Jersey
South Orange Bulletin
Trenton State Gazette

New York
Albany Evening Journal
Albany Express
Albany Knickerbocker
Brooklyn Daily Eagle
Buffalo Courier and Republic
Frank Leslie's Illustrated Newspaper
Geneva Advertiser
Harper's Weekly
Lockport Daily Journal
New York Clipper
New York Daily Times
New York Daily Tribune
New York Dramatic Mirror
New York Evening Express
New York Evening Post
New York Evening Telegram
New York Herald
New York Police Gazette
New York Sun
New York Times
New York World
Nunda News
Oswego Palladium
Rochester Daily Union

Rochester Democrat and Chronicle
Syracuse Courier and Union
Syracuse Daily Courier
Syracuse Daily Standard
Syracuse Herald
Weekly Herald

North Carolina
Fayetteville Observer
Raleigh Daily Register
Raleigh News and Observer
Raleigh Semi-Weekly Standard
Raleigh Weekly Standard
Weekly Raleigh Advertiser

Ohio
Cincinnati Commercial Tribune
Cincinnati Daily Commercial
Cincinnati Daily Enquirer
Cincinnati Daily Gazette
Cincinnati Daily Press
Cincinnati Sun
Cleveland Plain Dealer
Cleveland Morning Leader
Daily Cleveland Herald
Daily Ohio Statesman
Daily Scioto Gazette
Fremont Journal
Highland Weekly News
Newark Advocate
Penny Press
Sandusky Register
Toledo Commercial
Zanesville Signal

Pennsylvania
North American and United States Gazette
Philadelphia Daily Evening Telegraph
Philadelphia Illustrated New Age
Philadelphia Inquirer
Philadelphia Public Ledger

Rhode Island
Pawtucket Times

South Carolina
Camden Confederate
Charleston Courier
Charleston Mercury

Tennessee
Clarksville Chronicle
Daily Nashville Patriot
Daily Nashville True Whig
Memphis Daily Appeal
Nashville Banner
Nashville Union and American
Weekly Nashville Union

Texas
Dallas Morning News
Dallas Weekly Herald
Galveston Daily News

Utah
Deseret News
Salt Lake Herald

Vermont
Vermont Chronicle

Virginia
Daily Richmond Examiner
Richmond Daily Dispatch
Richmond Enquirer
Wheeling Daily Intelligencer
Richmond Whig
Roanoke Times

Washington
The Columbian

Wisconsin
Milwaukee Daily Sentinel
Milwaukee Journal

Canada
Globe and Mail (Toronto)

United Kingdom
Aberdeen Journal
Belfast News-Letter
Berrow's Worcester Journal
Blackburn Standard
Bradford Observer
Bristol Mercury
Cheshire Observer
Derby Mercury
The Era (London)
Exeter Flying Post
Freeman's Journal (Dublin)
Hampshire Advertiser
Hampshire Telegraph
Hull Packet
Ipswich Journal
Isle of Wight Observer
The Lady's Newspaper (London)
Lancaster Gazette
Liverpool Mercury
Manchester Times
Morning Chronicle (London)
Newcastle Courant
Nottinghamshire Guardian
Preston Guardian
Reynolds' Newspaper (London)
Royal Cornwall Gazette
Sheffield and Rotherham Independent
Times (London)
Wrexham Advertiser
York Herald

LAW BIBLIOGRAPHY

Professor Robert M. Chesney, Associate Dean for Academic Affairs: Charles I. Francis Professor in Law, University of Texas at Austin, Director-Designate of the Robert S. Strauss Center for International Security and Law. Lawfareblog.com, utexas.edu/law/faculty/rmc2289.

"State Secrets and the Limits of National Security Litigation," George Washington Law Review, 2007. Wake Forest University Legal Studies Paper No. 946676.

In 2007, Chesney wrote, "The state secrets privilege has played a central role in the Justice Department's response to civil litigation arising out of post-9/11 policies, culminating in a controversial decision by Judge T.S. Ellis concerning a lawsuit brought by a German citizen—Khaled El-Masri—whom the US allegedly had rendered (by mistake) from Macedonia to Afghanistan for interrogation. Reasoning that the entire aim of the suit is to prove the existence of state secrets, Judge Ellis held that the complaint had to be dismissed in light of the privilege. The government also has interposed the privilege in connection with litigation arising out of the NSA's warrantless surveillance program, albeit with mixed success so far."

Unlike some other legal scholars, Professor Chesney does not feel there has been an actual conflation of the Totten Doctrine and the State Secrets Privilege as they have been interpreted over time.

Professor Laura Donohue (Georgetown University Law Center). "The Shadow of State Secrets," *University of Pennsylvania Law Review*, Vol. 159, 2010; Georgetown Public Law Research Paper No. 10-10, March 8, 2010.

Sean C. Flynn. "The Totten Doctrine and its Poisoned Progeny," *Vermont Law Review*, Spring 2001.

Douglas Kash and Matthew Indrisano. "In the Service of Secrets: The US Supreme Court Revisits Totten," *The John Marshall Law Review*, Volume 39, Issue 2, 2006.

Daniel L. Pines. "The Continuing Viability of the 1875 Supreme Court Case of Totten v. United States," *53 Admin. L. Rev.* 1273, 1300, 2001.

Professor Steven Schwinn (John Marshall Law School). "The State Secrets Privilege in the Post-9/11 Era," *Pace Law Review*, January 2010, Vol. 30, Issue 2, Winter 2010, Article 23. Schwinn discusses the confusion/conflation between the Totten Doctrine and the State Secrets Privilege. In 2010 Professor Schwinn wrote, "The state secrets privilege started as a common law evidentiary privilege that protected evidence if there was a "reasonable danger that compulsion of the evidence [would] expose military matters which, in the interest of national security should not be divulged. In the cases involving secret executive programs developed in the wake of the 9/11 attacks, however, the Government has repeatedly pressed to turn the privilege into something more like a justiciability doctrine—a claim that would foreclose all litigation on a matter when the very subject of litigation is a state secret."

D. A. Jeremy Telman, Valparaiso University, Valpo Scholar, Law Faculty Presentations and Publications. "Intolerable Abuses: Rendition for Torture and the State Secrets Privilege," 2012. valpo.edu/law/about-us/full-time-faculty/d-a-jeremy-telman.

D. A. Jeremy Telman. "A Corollary to the Totten Doctrine: Wilson v. CIA," November 13, 2009. Professor Telman wrote, "The *Totten* doctrine requires dismissal of a case when 'the very subject-matter' of the case is a state secret. Today's *New York Times* wrote that the Second Circuit has dismissed Valerie Wilson's suit against the Central Intelligence Agency, in which she claimed that the Agency violated her free-speech rights when it required redaction of her 2007 book, *Fair Game*. As reported in the *Times*, the Second Circuit's reasoning is based on a contractual override of Wilson's 1st Amendment rights: 'When Ms. Wilson elected to serve with the C.I.A., she accepted a life-long restriction on her ability to disclose classified and classifiable information.' The problem is that at least some of the information in question had already been leaked to the public *by the government* and in any case was made public and widely reported on. No matter, says the court. The information is still classified, and she is still bound, even if governmental breaches 'may warrant investigation.'"

Appendix

The Lincoln Pass

When William Alvin Lloyd arrived in Washington, DC, to claim he had been President Lincoln's spy throughout the Civil War, among the papers he presented to General Grant's War Department office was a pass to cross the lines. To an untrained eye, the pass looked as if Lincoln wrote it.

But did he?

Though there are specific handwriting flourishes that when compared to authentic examples of Lincoln's signature appear to be the same, the very nature of the Lloyd fraud made us suspicious. Was the pass a forgery, part of the welter of documents Lloyd and his accomplices presented after Lincoln's assassination? T.H.S. Boyd was certainly a forger, a convicted one at that. So was the pass his handiwork? While we possessed a microfilm image of the pass, we were not at all satisfied with its clarity and consulted with experts in the field.

Curiously, during the times Lloyd's belongings were searched throughout the war, there is never a mention of the pass being discovered. So was the item forged after Lloyd and his accomplices learned of Lincoln's assassination?

Jane Fitzgerald, NARA Archivist, Archives 1 Reference Section Research Services, Washington, DC, examined the Lloyd Pass and communicated the following to author Jane Singer:

Dear Ms. Singer: I have just viewed the pass and envelope (front and back of both) in the vault. The envelope is an actual envelope—not a copy. On the front of the envelope appear the following handwritten sentences/notations: The words "Headquarters Armies of the United States, Official Business," are pre-printed on the upper right hand corner. On the front of the envelope appear the following handwritten sentences/notations: 1) Pass signed by Prst.(?) Lincoln. Appears to be

written in black ink. 2) 20 640. L (a.g.o) 1865. Written in red ink.
3) Certified copy of written "Pass" furnished Secy. of War (for Ct. of
Claims) with return of 1859. ago.1872. May 6 ' 7? (cannot make
out number after 7). [This is the date a copy of the pass was sent to the
Court of Claims.] The letters, E.B. 10. All written in red ink. On back
of envelope, handwritten in red ink, is possibly (very hard to read):
In C. 38 E.B. H.? The envelope measures 5 7/16" across and 3 1/16"
up & down. The pass does not appear to be a copy. It measures 3 1/4"
across and 1 3/4" up & down. It is a bit lighter in weight than card-
board—very similar to the weight of a present day business card. Pass
has brownish tint—may be due to grime or aging. On the back of the
pass appears the following: 1) 20 640. L. a.g.o. 1865; Handwritten in
red. 2) round black ink stamp (very faded)—can only read a portion
and I believe it is "Dept. City Point, Va." 3) black ink stamp that reads
"The National Archives of the United States."

The high-resolution digital scans of the Lincoln pass have been
viewed by Lincoln experts Dr. James M. Cornelius, curator, Lincoln Collection, Abraham Lincoln Presidential Library & Museum (Springfield,
Illinois); Dr. Daniel Stowell, director and editor of the papers of Abraham Lincoln (Springfield, Illinois); handwriting analysts Kirsten Singer
and Ellen Schuetzner; Edward N. Bomsey; and Lincoln autograph expert
Daniel Weinburg, proprietor of the Abraham Lincoln Bookshop in Chicago. All have seen the scans of the pass and have said Lincoln's handwriting appears authentic, but any concerns they had could only be put
to rest if they were able to see the original. As such, their opinions were
qualified.

After receiving the scans of the front and back of the pass, it was the
partial City Point frank (stamp) that allowed authors Singer and Stewart
to conclude that the pass was authentic. Here is why: The City Point frank
proved that Lloyd had crossed into Federal territory through City Point,
Virginia. It would have been impossible to forge the frank at the point of
entry. The pass had to be presented to an official who would have stamped
it. After examining the scan, the letters M A Y (the month) are legible
on the back of the pass, but the rest of the date is not. When comparing

the positioning of the month to other scans of authentic passes held in private collections, the size of the letters as well as their positioning corresponded to the Lloyd pass.

After Lloyd had been in Washington for a while, he indicated in a letter to Secretary of War Stanton that he had arrived on or around May 24, 1865. This is believable as the pass was delivered to Grant's office on that day, or on May 25, at the latest. In addition, upon further examination, the pass was folded several times. The folds were not pre-creased and are visible. They were clearly done after the pass was issued as the creases nearly caused the pass to tear. Thus folded, the pass was approximately the size of a quarter and easily concealed. Our inescapable conclusions rest: Unlike William Alvin Lloyd, the man who defrauded the US government and got away with it, the pass he concealed throughout the war is not, as he was, a brazen fake.

INDEX